What the press said to us about

ADVANCED WINDOWS PROGRAMMING

This is the first book on Windows programming I've seen that's truly grounded in the experience of Windows development, and not simply SDK documentation. Once you've wrestled the SDK to the mat, Heller's the man to read before you begin putting your first real application together.

> — Jeff Duntemann
> *PC Techniques*

Deft exposition—not syntactic smoke and mirrors—has an authority you can't mistake. Heller's work . . . is serene in its understanding of whom it's for and why.

> — Hugh Kenner
> *BYTE*

The real computer book of the month is Martin Heller's *Advanced Windows Programming*. The subject of this book is quite over my head; but Martin Heller has always been good at explaining complex concepts in simple language, and this is no exception. If you do advanced Windows programming, you need this; if you don't but you are thinking of trying it, you definitely need it.

> — Jerry Pournelle
> *BYTE*

Martin Heller's *Advanced Windows Programming* stands out, even on my short list.

> — Jim Kyle
> *Windows Technical Journal*

Gets down on paper all those techniques that experienced programmers pass on to each other, and which seldom get coverage in most Windows books. This book is a must.

> — Colin Smith
> Windows Association of
> Shareware People
> *WASP Book Reviews*

Wisdom is the principal thing; therefore get wisdom: and with all thy getting get understanding.

— Proverbs 4:7

The Bible:

I never had any doubt about it being of divine origin ... point out to me any similar collection of writings that has lasted for as many thousands of years and is still a best-seller, world-wide. It had to be of divine origin.

— Ronald Reagan (b. 1911), American president

Advanced Win32™ Programming

Programming

Martin Heller

with Foreword

by

Paul Maritz, Microsoft Corporation

John Wiley & Sons, Inc.

New York   Chichester   Brisbane   Toronto   Singapore

For Eden

Library of Congress Cataloging-in-Publication Data

Heller, Martin
    Advanced Win32 Programming / Martin Heller.
        p.   cm.
    Includes index.
    ISBN 0-471-59245-5 (book/disk set)
    1. Application software.   2. Microsoft Win32 API. I. Title.
    QA76.76.A65H45 1993
    005.4'3—dc20   93-550
                                           CIP

Printed in the United States of America

10 9 8 7 6 5 4 3 2 1

About the Author

Martin Heller develops software, writes, and consults in Andover, MA. You can contact him on BIX and MCI Mail as **mheller**, on CompuServe as **74000,2447**, and by mail care of John Wiley & Sons. Dr. Heller is the author of *Advanced Windows Programming*, also published by Wiley, as well as *Advanced Win32 Programming.*

Martin is a senior contributing editor and regular columnist for *WINDOWS* Magazine and the author of half a dozen PC software packages. He has been programming for Windows since early in the Windows 1.0 alpha test period. He has baccalaureate degrees in physics and music from Haverford College as well as Sc.M. and Ph.D. degrees in experimental high-energy physics from Brown University.

Dr. Heller has worked as an accelerator physicist, an energy systems analyst, a computer systems architect, a company division manager, and a consultant. Throughout his career he has used computers as a means to an end, much as a cabinet maker uses hand and power tools.

Martin wrote his first program for a drum-based computer in machine language in the early 1960s. (No, not assembly language, machine language.) The following year he taught himself Fortran II, and wrote mathematical programs in that language throughout high school.

In graduate school Martin wrote hundreds of programs in MACRO-9 assembler for a DEC PDP-9 computer, and hundreds more Fortran IV, APL, and PL/1 programs for an IBM 360/67. For his Ph.D. thesis he analyzed 500,000 frames of bubble chamber film taken at Argonne National Laboratory and helped take other data at Fermi National Accelerator Laboratory.

At New England Nuclear Corporation (currently a DuPont subsidiary) Dr. Heller developed an automatic computer data-acquisition and control system for an isotope-production cyclotron using Fortran IV+ and MACRO-11 on a PDP-11, with additional embedded 6802-based controllers. When the company acquired a VAX, Martin wrote one of the earliest smart terminal programs, in assembly language for the PDP-11 running RSX-11M.

At Physical Sciences Inc. (PSI) Martin developed a steady-state model of an experimental fuel cell power plant (under contract to the U.S. Department of Energy) in BASIC on a TRS-80 Model 3, and designed more advanced plants in BASIC on an early IBM PC. He developed a DOT-compliant crash sled data analysis program and a brake-testing data-acquisition, control, and analysis system in compiled BASIC for General Motors; he also developed the suite of programs that allowed General Motors to successfully defend itself against a government action over X-car braking systems.

Martin designed and developed MetalSelector, a materials selection and materials properties database program, under contract to the American Society for Metals (currently called ASM International), still in compiled BASIC. He designed EnPlot for the Society's graphing needs, intending the program for Windows 1.0, and put together a team of programmers to write it in C. When Windows 1.0 started slipping its schedule, Dr. Heller and his team implemented EnPlot for DOS instead of Windows.

Martin responded to the ongoing needs of the materials properties community by designing and implementing MetSel2 (at PSI) and later MatDB, in C for DOS, and EnPlot 2.0 for Windows (in both cases as an independent consultant). EnPlot is currently at revision 3.0 (and counting), and runs under Windows 3.0 and above.

While still at PSI, Martin designed two statistical subroutine libraries in Fortran for John Wiley & Sons. Statlib.tsf was a time-series and forecasting library, and Statlib.gl was a device-independent graphing library built on the GKS graphics standard. Both packages are now out of print.

As a consultant, Martin has worked for companies of all sizes to develop, design, improve, and/or debug Windows applications, and has performed strategic business consulting for large multinational corporations. His latest solely developed program is Room Planner, a meeting and conference layout system for the hospitality industry.

Contents

. . . .

to some 30 symmetric multiprocessing systems—and on more than 2,600 computers and peripherals.

- Users need your 32-bit applications to run in the most reliable environment possible. Reliability and security have been "designed" into Windows NT, not added on as a layer afterwards. Features including uninterruptible power supply support and the new Windows NT file system (NTFS), minimize the chance of hardware failure and help ensure fast recovery from any exceptional failures that do occur. Windows NT provides comprehensive security and is government-certifiable at the C2 level of security to guard against inadvertent or malicious tampering. That enables Windows NT—and your Win32 applications—to penetrate new markets.

- Openness is another strategic criterion for a 32-bit operating system. The Windows NT operating system has built-in support for multiprotocol networking, including TCP/IP, NetBEUI, IPX/SPX, and DLC. It supports most networks, including SNA, LAN Manager, NetWare, NFS, Banyan® VINES, and AppleTalk. Windows NT supports distributed computing standards, including Windows Sockets, Named Pipes, and OSF DCE–compatible Remote Procedure Calls (RPC). This combined support makes Win32 an excellent choice for your distributed client-server applications—they can seamlessly access information on different hosts and databases throughout a network.

Understandably, industry participants share our enthusiasm for Windows NT. By the time Windows NT was introduced in mid-1993, more than 73,000 of them had already purchased the Windows NT software development kit, making it one of the best-selling operating systems software development kits ever. Independent software vendors have more than 2,000 32-bit applications for Windows NT under active development. Corporate users are developing another 3,800 applications for in-house use. More than 25 percent are native ports from UNIX®, VMS®, OS/400, and other high-end systems.

Welcome to the world of Win32 and Windows NT—and best wishes for success as you discover the benefits of 32-bit Windows application development for yourself.

Paul Maritz
Senior Vice President
Systems Division
Microsoft Corporation

- Windows NT, a 32-bit operating system for powerful PCs, workstations, and large organizational networks requiring a great client-server solution

For developers, the key to accessing these Windows solutions is the Win32 Application Programming Interface, a from-the-ground-up 32-bit programming interface for application development. Whether you're developing an entirely new application, or porting existing software to Windows from another system, such as UNIX or OS/2, Win32 allows you to write 32-bit applications that are compatible across the family of Windows solutions. Best of all, Win32 allows you to leverage the full advantage of Windows NT—the most powerful, reliable, and open platform for client-server computing. As corporate users increasingly turn to client-server computing for mission-critical and line-of-business solutions, developers will succeed based on their ability to harness Windows NT through Win32 application development.

How can you leverage Win32 to develop powerful, 32-bit applications for Windows NT and the Windows family? With *Advanced Win32 Programming*, you've already taken an important step. Martin Heller has done a masterful job of providing an all-in-one resource to Win32 development. In the pages that follow, you'll find a grand tour of Win32, including clear, abundant, and eminently practical step-by-step instructions and examples. Heller articulates the distinct issues you'll face, whether you're coming to Win32 from 16-bit development, porting from another 32-bit system, or creating an entirely new application.

Heller shows you how to make the transition from the C programming language to C++; how to optimize your Win32 application for Windows NT; how to run a Win32 application on Windows 3.1 using Win32s; even how to support multimedia and pen computing. With Heller at your side, you'll master networking, interprocess communications, and related mechanisms for distributed client-server solutions. You'll even discover how to use Unicode to create international versions of your application. With your Win32-based applications, you'll be able to fully leverage the power, reliability, and openness of Windows NT. Here's a closer look at these advantages:

- Windows NT delivers its power through the same Windows interface and technology already familiar to millions of Windows users. Win32 builds on that advantage by making advanced operating system capabilities available to applications through features such as multithreaded processes, synchronization, security, I/O, and object management. Your users can run more applications, and more powerful ones, at once. Because Windows NT is platform independent and scalable, users will be able to run your Win32 applications on processors ranging from Intel® X86 chips and RISC chips from MIPS and Digital

Our strategy for Windows is to develop a single coherent operating system family that is completely scalable. It spans computers from across pen devices, notebooks, desktop machines, high-end workstations, and even servers and multiprocessor machines. A single consistent operating system family with a common user interface, applications, and programming model brings real benefits to both software developers and their customers:

- Software developers gain a larger market and can save time and money that they might otherwise spend rewriting applications for each new platform and then supporting each platform-specific product. They can come to market faster and at lower cost, while minimizing their concern about investing in a platform with limited market acceptance. Vendors of all types can gain greater freedom to choose their business partners, because everyone speaks a common operating system language. They can also leverage their operating system knowledge to reduce costs.

- MIS managers, administrators, and other support personnel benefit because training, not hardware, is the largest cost in most computer system installations. A single operating system family can reduce training and administration costs for years to come; it simplifies and improves administration, leverages mini- and mainframe legacy systems, and eliminates the costs and headaches of changing over to new systems and platforms.

- End-users benefit, too. They can use an application on one platform (for example, their desktop), and know it will operate the same way on another platform (such as a pen-based sub-notebook). Once they have mastered one application, they will know how to work with completely different ones, because their various applications will work according to a consistent set of principles set by a single operating system. For end-users, this can save time and money; it can also boost productivity and effectiveness.

That is the strategy behind the expanding family of Windows operating system products. We are implementing this strategy through a scalable range of solutions, including:

- A Windows-compatible operating system for Microsoft At Work handhelds and small mobile devices

- Windows 3.1 for midrange and standalone PCs

- Windows™ for Workgroups for networked workgroup computing

Foreword

· ·

It seems a software developer's work is never done. Develop an application for one desktop operating system and—you hope—users will want to run it on other systems, too. Port that application to another system and—if you're lucky—users will want to run it not just on the desktop, but also on the increasingly diverse range of micro-processor-based consumer electronics products and computers, including office equip-ment, handheld devices, portable computers, and very powerful server machines that are mainframes in all but name. Since this growing class of devices can address the computing needs of a widening set of applications, users will be looking to developers to supply not only personal productivity products, but also line-of-business or mission-critical applications.

How many different programming interfaces, operating systems, and form factors will developers have to address as computing options proliferate—and what will be the costs of doing so? The most useful approach for developers is one that lets them preserve and leverage their existing investments of time, money, and code as they address these broad choices. Given the very large base of investment in the industry in and around the Microsoft™ Windows™ operating system and Windows-based products, it makes sense for Windows to offer a cost-effective approach to development, helping to ensure that developers and users of the Windows operating system can easily gain access to new devices and address new applications by building on their existing investment and support structures.

But that's easier said than done. It is very difficult to address today's multiple devel-opment opportunities with a single underlying implementation of an operating system. The techniques and approaches one uses in a portable device, where low memory and power usage is paramount, are very different from the techniques and approaches that one needs in a high-end workstation or server, where security, capacity, and reliability are paramount. These challenges need to be overcome in order to gain the significant benefits of preserving a common user interface and common programming interfaces.

To address this challenge, Microsoft has been expanding Windows from its origin as a single product into a family of products where each family member has a specialized internal implementation but complements the others.

Preface

. . . .

Advanced Win32 Programming is, in a sense, a travel guide or road map. It maps the territory we software developers need to travel from the familiar 16-bit world of Windows to the 32-bit frontier, programming for Windows NT and Win32s.

Why do we have to leave our familiar haunts? The advantages of moving to 32-bit programming from 16-bit programming per se are compelling: many computations speed up automatically, the confining 64 KB segment size becomes a roomier 4 GB linear memory space, and most of the annoying overflow problems having to do with integer ranges disappear. In specific cases, the speedup is dramatic: for instance, when you turn computations that use "huge" 16-bit segment:offset pointers (like the 24-bit color adjustment implemented in the IMAGE2 example in my previous book, *Advanced Windows Programming*) into computations that use "near" 32-bit pointers, you get roughly a factor of five speedup.

Besides the inherent advantages of a 32-bit system, Windows NT has a number of new features that make it attractive. Windows NT supports high-end hardware like MIPS R4000 boxes, DEC Alpha AXP PCs, and symmetric multiprocessing machines. It has an enhanced graphical device interface that includes Bézier curves (a useful family of smooth curves similar to splines), paths (a generalized mechanism for creating and filling complex figures), world transforms (which allow the displayed graphics page to be rotated, scaled, reflected, and/or sheared from the drawing coordinate system), and masking (which allows regions to be excluded from display of a bitmap). It supports multiple threads of execution (a lightweight form of multitasking), several interprocess communication mechanisms, and C2-level security. And, not least, Windows NT comes with substantial networking support.

Win32, the API for Windows NT, is largely compatible with the 16-bit Windows 3.1 API. The basic differences: existing APIs have been widened to 32 bits; new APIs support threads, multitasking, security, Bézier curves, and other advanced features of Windows NT; and, finally, irrelevant 16-bit APIs, such as segment manipulation, have been dropped.

Win32s, a set of DLLs and VxDs that can help you increase the market for your Win32 programs by letting them run on Windows 3.1, is useful and convenient but not a panacea. The new APIs in the Win32 set that support advanced features of Windows NT appear in Win32s (the "s" stands for "subset") only as stubs that return FALSE. You can, for instance, write a Win32s program that tries to create a thread—but you must write the program to work even if the thread creation fails, as it will when running on Windows 3.1.

Win32s is not a completely general solution for building 32-bit Windows applications, either. One major limitation is that it has no provision for directly calling functions in 16-bit DLLs other than supported system functions. Win32 does, however, support several ways to call 16-bit DLL functions indirectly.

Future versions of Windows—starting with "Chicago"—will include much of the new functionality that is in Windows NT. A Win32s program, written to take advantage of advanced functions when they are present, will automatically work better and faster on newer versions of Windows than it does on Windows 3.1. If you want to prepare for "Chicago" learn Win32 now.

I decided to write *Advanced Win32 Programming* for selfish reasons: I wanted to force myself to use the new functionality in Windows NT, and to force myself to migrate from C programming to C++ programming. I've tried to keep a good enough log of my journey for it to be useful as a map for others attempting similar journeys.

I hope you'll find *Advanced Win32 Programming* useful as a guide, whether you're porting existing code from 16-bit to 32-bit Windows, writing new code compatible with both, or jumping into 32-bit Windows programming with both feet. Whether you're new to all this or an old hand, I hope you'll find some ideas and snippets of code here that you can use in your own work. If you haven't already done so I hope you'll also read my previous volume, *Advanced Windows Programming*, which takes you from familiarity with the Windows SDK to the point where you can write substantial, multimodule Windows programs.

To actually use the material in *Advanced Win32 Programming* you should have access to a computer running Windows NT, to copies of the Win32 documentation, to 32-bit C and C++ compilers for Windows NT, to a computer running Windows 3.1, and to copies of the Win32s libraries.

In Chapter 1, "Crossing the Great Divide," we learn to make the transition from 16-bit programming to 32-bit Windows programming. In Chapter 2, "Any Port in A Storm," we move the Image2 example developed in *Advanced Windows Programming* to Win32 as quickly as possible. Then in Chapter 3, "Upping the Ante," we learn to make the transition from C programming to the C++ programming language, encapsulating as we go.

We clean up our ported code, and think about reorganizing it as C++ with classes, in Chapter 4, "A Higher Standard." Then we learn to use some of the advanced features of Win32 in Chapter 5, "Total Immersion."

We take a step back and learn to trade off between the advanced features of Windows NT and compatibility with Windows 3.1, using Win32s, in Chapter 6, "With a Shoehorn." In Chapter 7, "A Little Song, A Little Dance," we begin to apply some multimedia programming; in Chapter 8, "The Pen Is Mightier," we learn to support Pens, Ink, and Tablets.

We learn to use Unicode and do internationalization in Chapter 9, "Lingua Franca," and in Chapter 10, "OLÉ Again," we investigate OLE 2 and perhaps even OLE 3. In Chapter 11, "Citizen of the Galaxy," we examine interprocess communication and distributed computing, and finally in Chapter 12, "The Far Horizon," we look into the future. In addition, for those of you looking for tools, we describe some resources and tools for Win32 Development in the Appendix, "Cornucopia."

That's a lot of material. Never fear: we'll start slowly, and there will be plenty of examples.

It's next to impossible to write a book of this kind without help. First and foremost, I'd like to thank my editor, Diane Cerra, for pushing—and pushing, and pushing—me to actually write the book. Like all writers, I prefer having written. It's okay, Diane: you can put away the bullet with my name on it until the next book.

I'd also like to thank my reviewers: Ed Adams, Roger Grossman, Timothy Larson, Chris Marriott, John Ruley, William vanRyper, and Bjarne Stroustrup. These gentlemen spent a lot of time telling me I was all wet and making me do better, and I appreciate their efforts— now that I have rewritten, and rewritten, and rewritten.

The clean design and layout of this book is the work of Claire Stone Spellman of Desktop Studios, aided and abetted by Frank Grazioli and his production team at Wiley. I did my writing in Microsoft Word for Windows and saved the figures as TIFF files; Claire took the files on diskettes and laid them out in PageMaker for the Macintosh. We'll get the bugs worked out of that process one of these days; meanwhile, Claire worked around a few of them with simple but time-consuming methods like recreating sections from scratch.

Finally, I'd like to thank my wife Claudia and my daughters Tirzah and Moriah for putting up with me as I muddled through another book. It's not easy living with a writer, and my family made sure I didn't ever forget it. Claudia in particular had plenty to put up with, but she won the race: our third child was born after I finished writing the body of the book, but before this book came off the press. It is to that child that I dedicate this book.

Crossing the Great Divide

· ·

There are many ways to get from the east coast of the United States to the west coast. Today, most people fly, but some drive, using one of several possible interstate highways. A hundred fifty years ago, small parties of hardy (or foolhardy) pioneers set out in horse-drawn wagons. They hoped to cross the deserts as quickly as possible, hoped to cross the mountains before the winter snows, hoped to avoid hostile natives.

Not everyone survived the trip. Without good directions, you could get lost in the desert without water, miss the mountain passes. A party whose wealthiest family was named Donner found out the value of good directions the hard way.

Follow me: I've been there and back. I'll get you through safely.

This first chapter is a sort of hazard map: it doesn't show you the best route, but it shows you where the mountains and deserts lie. Later on, we'll find out how to avoid most of the hazards.

Our first obstacle is the very change in word size that induced us to make the trip in the first place. It's a small obstacle; some might say even a trivial obstacle. But it has tripped up many a pioneer.

Word Size Annoyances

The influence of word size on programming is often both over- and underestimated. It is overestimated by people who believe that a larger word size *automatically* makes programs run faster and more accurately, and underestimated by people who ignore the capacity, range, and exception-handling issues that are important when the word size is too small for the problem at hand.

A 16-bit signed integer has a range of -32,768 to 32,767 (32K-1); a 16-bit unsigned integer has a range of 0 to 65535 (64K - 1). A 32-bit signed integer has a range of -2,147,483,648 to 2,147,483,647 (2G-1) and a 32-bit unsigned integer has a range of 0 to 4,294,967,295 (4G - 1).

Limits of 32K and 64K arise frequently in 16-bit Windows programming, sometimes directly because of the size of an integer, and sometimes indirectly because of the maximum size of a memory segment. Sometimes, the limit is a minor annoyance that can be avoided with careful coding; other times, the limit causes a major slow-down in the program. Some examples are in order.

First, a minor annoyance. You might want to find the centroid of a cluster of points in your display space. If the display space is 640 by 480 (the VGA screen) the following code will work correctly for 16-bit integers:

```
#define n 10
int x[n],y[n],xmid=0,ymid=0;

for(i=0;i<n;i++) {
        xmid += x[i];
        ymid += y[i];
        }
xmid /= n;
ymid /= n;
```

The code continues to work on a 1024 by 768 Super-VGA screen. But what happens when you go to print on a 300-dot-per-inch laser printer? The 8.5-inch by 11-inch page would have dot coordinates of 2,550 by 3,300. Once in a while—not often—ten coordinates will add up to more than 32,767, the sum will overflow, and you'll wind up drawing the centroid at the wrong end of the page (or even off the page) since the result will be a large *negative* number. Obviously, if **n** were bigger than 10 the error would occur more frequently.

In the case of the centroid, we can rewrite the code to be more reliable, albeit less efficient and less accurate, without resorting to **long** variables:

```
#define n 10
int x[n],y[n],xmid=0,ymid=0;

for(i=0;i<n;i++) {
        xmid += (x[i] / n);
        ymid += (y[i] / n);
        }
```

Another alternative for this particular problem would be to make **xmid** and **ymid** into **long** variables—that is, use 32 bits just for the working variables. In a 16-bit architecture, that means that the compiler has to generate code to extend the value of **x[i]** and **y[i]** from 16 bits to 32 bits, and has to generate or call code to add two 32-bit numbers using 16-bit registers. That's a poor substitute for the **add** instructions generated by the addition code in the original loop.[1]

What about a more serious case? Consider this code from the PROCESS module of IMAGE2, the final example program in *Advanced Windows Programming*:

```
int dr,dg,db;
double r,g,b,dh,ds,dv,dl,h,s,v,l;
LPBITMAPINFOHEADER lpbi;
RGBQUAD FAR *pRgb;
unsigned char huge *pixels;
unsigned char huge *pb;
unsigned char huge *pb1;
unsigned char huge *pb2;
int colors,i;
DWORD il;
//NOTE: BOUND is a macro that limits the first variable
//  to the range of the second and third variables

lpbi=(VOID far *)GlobalLock(hdibCurrent);
pixels = (unsigned char huge *)(lpbi + lpbi->biSize);
switch(ColorModel) {
    case IDD_RGB:
        for(il=0;il<lpbi->biSizeImage;il+=3) {
            pb=pixels+il;
            pb1=pixels+il+1;
            pb2=pixels+il+2;
            *pb  = (BYTE)BOUND(*pb +db,0,255);
            *pb1 = (BYTE)BOUND(*pb1+dg,0,255);
            *pb2 = (BYTE)BOUND(*pb2+dr,0,255);
            }
        break;
...
```

There are a couple of things to notice in this particular example, which is supposed to alter the colors in a 24-bit image. First of all, the logic is incorrect and the routine fails for some images: instead of looping over the pixels in the entire image linearly, the code should loop over pixels within scan-lines. Why? Because the ends of the scan-lines can be padded out so that the next line will fall on a double word boundary, which throws off the counting by threes. That would be bad enough, but there's worse to come: Windows doesn't necessarily even have memory assigned to the null bytes at the ends of scan-lines. If you found and fixed this bug yourself,

---

[1] Consider the code generated by **c = a*b**, where all the variables are declared **long**. The 16-bit Microsoft compiler will generate a call to a subroutine that does roughly 5 multiplications and 2 additions. Almost any 32-bit compiler will generate inline code for this line that does one multiplication. (Thanks to Chris Marriott for pointing this out.)

congratulations; if you encountered the bug and never understood what was wrong, my apologies. If you never noticed the problem (or haven't worked through *Advanced Windows Programming*), don't feel too bad: for a long time I incorrectly attributed the bug to a rare 24-bit device driver problem, and only understood that the error was mine after the book was in print.

The second and most important thing to notice about the color-correction code is that the pointer variables **pixels**, **pb**, **pb1**, and **pb2** are all **huge**, and that the index variable **il** is a **DWORD**. What that means is that the computation of the secondary pointers **pb**, **pb1**, and **pb2** within the loop is horribly inefficient: it has to recalculate the selector and offset every time so that the offset never exceeds 64K.

Remember that in a 16-bit Microsoft compiler a **near** pointer accesses the default data segment through the preloaded **DS** register. A **far** pointer accesses a specified data segment through the **ES** register loaded from a stored selector immediately prior to the use of the pointer. Arithmetic on **far** pointers assumes that the offset will never exceed 64K, so the selector is never involved in the computation. A **huge** pointer can refer to location greater than 64K from the base of a memory block; it accesses this large memory through a bank of selectors. Arithmetic on **huge** pointers has to constantly calculate the correct selector from the bank and normalize the offset to that selector.

What you're seeing is the 64K segmented memory limit at its very worst. If we compare this code using **huge** 16-bit segmented pointers to the same code using **near** 32-bit pointers and time both, we find the 32-bit version roughly five times faster. That's a compelling speed difference—but one we will notice only with 24-bit images.[2] As it happens, 24-bit images and 24-bit displays are becoming more and more common; therefore, speeding up this kind of code is becoming more and more important. In fact, the miserable performance of this routine (or even a carefully corrected and tuned version thereof) was one of my original motivations for investigating 32-bit Windows technology.

For this sort of code, the flat memory model has a clear advantage over segmented memory models. For debugging, however, the flat memory model can be frustrating: the hardware won't trap index errors for you as effectively as it will when using protected segments. Load a bad pointer or run off the end of an array in segmented protected mode on an 80x86, and you cause a Trap D right at the instruction in error. Do the same thing in flat memory, and you might never find the problem—unless you're either lucky or careful in your coding techniques.[3]

Obviously, we want the improved speed we'll get from 32-bit programming, and

---

[2] This might not be obvious. Surely, any manipulation of a large block of memory will be speeded up by the use of **near** 32-bit pointers versus **far** 16-bit pointers. However, 256 color device-independent bitmaps (DIBs) use a palette, which is small and compact so that color-manipulation code doesn't have to work directly with the much larger image data. 24-bit DIBs have no palette—each pixel in the image contains 3 bytes of color information.

we'll also want the portability to other platforms that comes along with moving to Windows NT. Less obviously, we'll have to be more careful when coding than we might have been in 16-bit Windows, since we've lost the segment-level hardware protection that caught so many types of errors. What can we do about it? We can arrange things so that more of our mistakes are caught at compile time, and fewer are left to give us indigestion later.

Guidelines for Porting from Windows to Win32

With that in mind, let's go over the Microsoft guidelines for porting code from Windows 3.x to Win32. You'll find further information on this subject in the *Programming Techniques* volume of the Microsoft Win32 SDK for Windows NT.

Microsoft suggests using a top–down approach to porting from 16-bit Windows to Win32, rather than a bottom–up approach. What's the difference? The bottom–up approach is careful and incremental: first you move from your current Windows memory model to large model; then you recode all your assembly language functions in C; then you go over your code with a fine-tooth comb; and finally you gingerly recompile for Win32.

The top–down approach is quick and dirty: you dive right in and compile your code for Win32. You fix the code that won't compile as it comes up; when you find code that might be difficult or time-consuming to fix, you stub it out. Once you can compile and link, you test the program and fix any functional problems you find. The advantage is that in the top–down approach you get lots of visual feedback.

The decision about adopting the top–down or the bottom–up approach to porting is really a matter of your own comfort and experience. Do you feel better always having the whole program working (try bottom–up), or would you rather minimize your total time for the port (try top–down)? Have you done many cross-platform ports (try top–down), or is this your first (consider bottom–up)? If you want, you can even mix the two methods—but no matter how you go about it, you will still have to face the same basic hurdles.

What sort of porting problems can you expect? You'll need to change many of your function prototypes, to change the types of some of your variables, and perhaps to switch some old system function calls to newer, more portable equivalents. You might eventually want to update your code to avoid some unsafe programming practices—such as the Windows 3.x convention of using generic variable types for message parameters.

---

[3] Protection in systems like Windows NT is normally at the page level, which in most implementations means that you have 4K granularity. If you really mess up your pointer arithmetic, the hardware will catch the problem, but if you are only off by one you might never notice. On the other hand, each process has its own address space, so you don't have to worry about being overwritten by other programs. W. van Ryper points out that array size errors are more likely to be caught in flat memory implementations if you are careful to initialize your variables.

Nothing involved in such a port is in the least challenging. Much of it isn't even really specific to Windows NT—it's just good programming hygiene. However, it does have to be done to make the port to Windows NT work properly.

In the Beginning Was the WORD

Windows 3.x code often abounds with variables with uninformative types: **WORD**, **DWORD**, **HANDLE**, and so on. The **wParam** parameter to all window procedures is normally of type **WORD**.

As Windows programmers with 16-bit architectural assumptions imprinted in our reptilian hindbrains (you UNIX types are excused—you have imprinted 32-bit architectural assumptions instead), we immediately recognize **WORD** as a 16-bit integer, which corresponds to an **unsigned short** both on 16-bit and 32-bit architectures. Remember, the size of an **int** varies between 16-bit and 32-bit C compilers, but a **short** is always 16 bits and a **long** is always 32 bits.

The **wParam** parameter to window procedures is 16 bits in Windows 3.x and 32 bits in Win32. That means that the intuitive and deeply ingrained **WORD** is not an appropriate type for **wParam** (even despite **wParam**'s Hungarian prefix **w**, which mnemonically signals a **WORD** variable), since an **unsigned short** doesn't vary with the compiler's target implementation. We need another type, one that will vary with the target: an **unsigned int**, defined as **UINT**. We'll use **UINT** for the **message** parameter to window procedures as well, even though it doesn't really represent a change from the Windows 3.x **unsigned** type declaration.

The **UINT** type varies properly with the compiler target, but it isn't safe. What do we mean by safe? It doesn't carry any information about its contents beyond its size and lack of sign. If we want the compiler to catch errors caused by, say, using a window handle as a position, or a global memory handle as a local memory handle, we have to tell the compiler more about the object held in the variable.

How? Create additional types. Fortunately, Microsoft has done that for us already. We don't even have to use the Win32 tools: *most* of the good stuff is already in the Windows 3.1 SDK, although you have to make a small effort to use it: you should **#define STRICT** before you **#include <windows.h>**, and you should also **#include <windowsx.h>**. The following is an extract from the Windows 3.1 WINDOWS.H file edited to show some of the definitions in force when **STRICT** is defined:

```
typedef const void NEAR*    HANDLE;
#define DECLARE_HANDLE(name) struct name##__ {int unused;};\
          typedef const struct name##__ NEAR* name
#define DECLARE_HANDLE32(name) struct name##__ {int unused;}; \
          typedef const struct name##__ FAR* name
```

```
typedef HANDLE*          PHANDLE;
typedef HANDLE NEAR*  SPHANDLE;
typedef HANDLE FAR*   LPHANDLE;

typedef HANDLE           HGLOBAL;
typedef HANDLE           HLOCAL;

typedef HANDLE           GLOBALHANDLE;
typedef HANDLE           LOCALHANDLE;

typedef UINT             ATOM;

typedef void (CALLBACK*   FARPROC)(void);
typedef void (NEAR PASCAL*  NEARPROC)(void);

DECLARE_HANDLE(HSTR);
DECLARE_HANDLE(HINSTANCE);
typedef HINSTANCE HMODULE;

int PASCAL WinMain(HINSTANCE, HINSTANCE, LPSTR, int);
```

If you don't define **STRICT**, you don't get the safety advantage of the new types. (That was a hint.) But even defining **STRICT** doesn't give you all the type safety you really need. The next step—to **#include <windows.h>**—gives you access to an interesting collection of macros to access the system, including *message crackers*. To understand message cracking and forwarding, we'll have to look once again at the parameters to a window procedure.

The Packed Parameter Pickle

In the Windows 3.1 version of WINDOWS.H quoted above, we saw the **HANDLE** type defined as **const void NEAR***. We already know that **NEAR** and **FAR** have no real meaning in Windows NT. How are **HANDLE** and **DECLARE_HANDLE** defined in the Win32 include files? Let's look. It isn't in WINDOWS.H, but one of its many nested H files, WINNT.H:

```
typedef const void *HANDLE;
#define DECLARE_HANDLE(name) struct name##__ { int unused; };
  typedef const struct name##__ *name
```

Again, we've picked the **STRICT** definitions. A pointer in Win32 uses 32 bits, therefore from the definition a handle uses 32 bits. But some window messages in Windows 3.x pack a handle and something else into a **long**. It seems we have a problem.

Let's consider the **WM_COMMAND** message. In Windows 3.x **WM_COMMAND** passes a notification code in **wParam**, and the window handle and command number packed in **lParam**. In Win32, that won't work: instead **WM_COMMAND** dedicates

lParam to the window handle and packs the notification code and command into **wParam**, since each can live in 16 bits.

Obviously, we could sum up our knowledge of **WM_COMMAND** parameter packing with some conditional code, for instance:

```
switch(message) {
//    ... intervening code here ...
  case WM_COMMAND:
#ifdef WIN32
      switch(LOWORD(wParam)) {        //portable (could be common)
        hwndCtrl=(HWND)(UINT)lParam;//portable (could be common)
        notification=HIWORD(wParam);//can't be portable
#else
      switch(wParam) {                //not portable
        hwndCtrl=LOWORD(lParam);      //not portable
        notification=HIWORD(lParam);//can't be portable
#endif
      }
//    ... intervening code here ...
  }
```

This code works. Nevertheless, it is ugly, confusing, and unsafe: there has to be a way to unpack message parameters without conditional code. After all, that's only one message. Just about every Windows message uses its parameters differently. Are we going to have to write conditional code for each one? And how are we going to make sure the final unpacked parameter values are coerced into the proper types?

Now we understand the reason for message crackers. Let's look at the Windows 3.1 cracker and forwarder for **WM_COMMAND**:

```
/* void Cls_OnCommand (HWND hwnd, int id, HWND hwndCtl,
                       UINT codeNotify); */
#define HANDLE_WM_COMMAND (hwnd, wParam, lParam, fn) \
    ((fn)((hwnd), (int)(wParam), (HWND)LOWORD(lParam), \
    (UINT)HIWORD(lParam)), 0L)
#define FORWARD_WM_COMMAND (hwnd, id, hwndCtl, codeNotify, fn)\
    (void)(fn)((hwnd), WM_COMMAND, (WPARAM)(int)(id), \
    MAKELPARAM((UINT)(hwndCtl), (codeNotify)))
```

The cracker macro **HANDLE_WM_COMMAND** generates code to call the function whose pointer is passed in **fn**, with **hwnd** passed through to **hwnd**, **wParam** cast to an **int** and passed through to **id**, the low word of **lParam** cast to an **HWND** and passed through to **hwndCtl**, the high word of **lParam** case to **UINT** and passed through to **codeNotify**, and finally—for some reason that escapes me—a long zero for an undeclared fifth parameter.

Sure enough, that compares nicely with the 16-bit Windows leg of our conditional code. The forwarder **FORWARD_WM_COMMAND** repacks the parameters, neatly undoing the work of **HANDLE_WM_COMMAND**. Now let's look at the Win32 version:

```
/* void Cls_OnCommand(HWND hwnd, int id, HWND hwndCtl,
                       UINT codeNotify); */
#define HANDLE_WM_COMMAND(hwnd, wParam, lParam, fn) \
    ((fn)((hwnd), (int)(LOWORD(wParam)), (HWND)(lParam), \
    (UINT)HIWORD(wParam)), 0L)
#define FORWARD_WM_COMMAND(hwnd, id, hwndCtl, codeNotify, fn)\
    (void)(fn)((hwnd),WM_COMMAND,         \
    MAKEWPARAM((UINT)(id),(UINT)(codeNotify)), \
    (LPARAM)(HWND)(hwndCtl))
```

Are you at all surprised to see that the Windows NT versions of **HANDLE_ WM_-COMMAND** and **FORWARD_WM_COMMAND** correspond almost exactly to the code we wrote for Win32? I thought not.

I certainly don't want to have to reinvent the work that went into writing all those message crackers and forwarders. For simple programs, certainly, we can write conditional code. But for programs of any size we'll get cleaner code for less work by rewriting our message handling using message cracker macros, message forwarder macros, and message handling functions.

Despite our intention to use message crackers, it would be worthwhile to have all the differences in Windows 3.x and Win32 message parameters in one place. In that vein we offer Table 1-1.

In addition to message crackers, WINDOWSX.H contains a number of macros that access system resources in more convenient or safer ways than using the standard system functions directly. Macros like **GlobalAllocPtr** fall into the convenience category. **GlobalAllocPtr** does a **GlobalAlloc** and a **GlobalLock**; **Global-FreePtr** gets a global handle from the pointer, unlocks the pointer, and frees the memory block.[4] These functions weren't built into Windows originally because real mode required you to constantly unlock and lock memory blocks so that Windows would function smoothly. They are possible in Windows 3.1 since real mode is no longer supported; and of course Windows NT has nothing like real mode.

Macros like **DeletePen** protect us from the heavily overloaded GDI object functions. **DeletePen(hpen)** is defined as **DeleteObject((HGDIOBJ)(HPEN)(hpen))**—all that casting tells the compiler enough that we should get a compile-time error if we try to delete a brush when we meant to delete a pen. We probably wouldn't bother with the casting ourselves, at least if we were writing C, since the compiler wouldn't complain about **DeleteObject(hpen)**. If we were writing C++, it would be another story—the C++ compiler is *very* fussy about casting.

---

[4] I am obliged to point out that the macro implementation **GlobalAllocPtr** does not protect **GlobalLock** from seeing a **NULL** pointer in the case when **GlobalAlloc** fails. The only case I know of where this actually causes a problem is under the debugging kernels of Windows 3.x. C. Marriott suggests redefining **GlobalAllocPtr** as a function that calls **GlobalLock** only when **GlobalAlloc** returns a valid pointer. I myself suspect that **GlobalAllocPtr** might move into the Windows or Win32 kernel at some point in the future, since locking memory blocks is becoming archaic.

Table 1-1   Windows 3.x and Win32 Message Parameter Packing

Message wParam	Win 3.x lParam	Windows 3.x wParam	Win32 lParam	Win32
WM_ACTIVATE	state	fMinimized, hWnd fMinimized	state,	hWnd
WM_CHARTOITEM	char	pos, hWnd	char, pos	hWnd
WM_COMMAND	id	hWnd, cmd	id, cmd	hWnd
WM_CTLCOLOR	hDC	hWnd, type	N/A *	N/A
WM_CTLCOLORBTN, WM_CTLCOLORDLG, WM_CTLCOLORLIST- BOX,WM_CTLCOLOR- MSGBOX,WM_CTLCO- LORSCROLLBAR,WM_- CTLCOLORSTATIC, WM_CTLCOLOREDIT	N/A	N/A	hDC	hWnd
WM_MENUSELECT	cmd	flags, hMenu	cmd, flags	hMenu
WM_MDIACTIVATE	fActivate	hWndDeactivate, hWndActivate	hWndActivate	hWndDeactivate
WM_MDISETMENU	0	hMenuFrame, hMenuWindow	hMenuFrame	hMenuWindow
WM_MENUCHAR	char	hMenu, fMenu	char, fMenu	hMenu
WM_PARENTNOTIFY (CASE 1)	msg	id, hWndChild	msg, id	hWndChild
WM_PARENTNOTIFY (CASE 2)	msg	x, y	msg	x, y
WM_VKEYTOITEM	code	item, hWnd	code, item	hWnd
EM_GETSEL	NULL	NULL	lpdwStart or NULL	lpdwEnd or NULL
EM_LINESCROLL	0 nLinesHorz	nLinesVert,	nLinesHorz	nLinesVert
EM_SETSEL	0	wStart, wEnd	wStart	wEnd
WM_HSCROLL, WM_VSCROLL	code	pos, hWnd	code, pos	hWnd

* The Windows 3.x message **WM_CTLCOLOR** contains two handles and a control class type, which would require an extra parameter in Win32. It was therefore necessary to replace the **WM_CTLCOLOR** message with individual messages for the different control types.

But we digress: we were talking about porting to Win32. As we've seen, there's plenty of opportunity to rewrite old code to be safer, if we have the time. We won't always have the time.

When we go to port existing 16-bit Windows code, **LOWORD** and **HIWORD** will be red flags to warn us that the code needs examination, as will **switch** statements, window procedures, dialog procedures, **WORD** types, and generic **HANDLE** types. We'll even have to examine all **struct** definitions: in 16-bit Windows, structures are normally compiled with **-Zp**, which means to pack the structures on byte boundaries, but in Win32 structures are normally compiled with **DWORD** alignment, since some computer architectures require it.

Homonyms and Synonyms

Besides all of these problems, we'll have to look out for Windows system functions with changed parameters and Windows system functions with changed names. For purposes of brevity, we'll call pairs of 16-bit and 32-bit Windows functions that have the same name but changed parameters or functionality *homonyms*, since the names sound alike but the meaning is different. We'll dub pairs with different names but similar actions *synonyms*.

Win32 and Windows 3.x Homonyms and Synonyms

The Win32 and Windows 3.x API sets hold a number of homonyms. Most function pairs are homonyms with one difference that you can safely ignore: the function parameters have different sizes depending on the system integer size. A few functions have differences you'll actually care about.

Most message pairs are homonyms with changed parameter packing. In one case there is a set of message synonyms: the Windows 3.x **WM_CTLCOLOR** message has seven synonyms in Win32, each distinguished by a suffix denoting the type of control whose color is to be set.

One major synonym pattern stems from the use of a **DWORD** return value containing packed *x* and *y* values in several Windows 3.x GDI functions. Since graphics coordinates in Win32 use 32 bits, we find ourselves with another packed parameter pickle. Microsoft's solution was to introduce a new set of compatible APIs in Windows 3.1 and Win32 that return coordinates in a **POINT** structure whose pointer is passed as an additional parameter to the function. The synonyms are almost all named by adding the suffix **Ex** to the original function name.

In many cases, checking the returned **POINT** structure is, well, pointless. Do you really care about the return value from **MoveTo**? Have you ever written code that looks at the *x* and *y* values returned by **MoveTo** to see if they agree with the values passed?

Nevertheless, you have to change your code. Microsoft suggests mechanically changing **MoveTo(hDC,x,y)** to **MoveToEx(hDC,x,y,NULL)** so as to conform to

Table 1-2 Windows 3.x GDI Calls with Windows 3.1/Win32 Synonyms

Windows 3.x function	Windows 3.1/Win32 function
MoveTo (hDC, x, y)	MoveToEx (hDC, x, y, lpPoint)
OffsetViewportOrg (hDC, nXOffset, nYOffset)	OffsetViewportOrgEx (hDC, nX, nY, lpPoint)
OffsetWindowOrg (hDC, nXOffset, nYOffset)	OffsetWindowOrgEx (hDC, nX, nY, lpPoint)
ScaleViewportExt (hDC, nXnum, nXdenom, nYnum, nYdenom)	ScaleViewportExtEx (hDC, nXnum, nXdenom, nYnum, nYdenom, lpSize)
ScaleWindowExt (hDC, nXnum, nXdenom, nYnum, nYdenom)	ScaleWindowExtEx (hDC, nXnum, nXdenom, nYnum, nYdenom, lpSize)
SetBitmapDimension (hbmp, nWidth, nHeight)	SetBitmapDimensionEx (hbmp, nW, nH, lpSize)
SetMetaFileBits (hMetaFile)	SetMetaFileBitsEx (nSize, lpData)
SetViewportExt (hDC, nXext, nYext)	SetViewportExtEx (hDC, nXext, nYext, lpSize)
SetViewportOrg (hDC, nXOrg, nYOrg)	SetViewportOrgEx (hDC, nX, nY, lpPoint)
SetWindowExt (hDC, nXext, nYext)	SetWindowExtEx (hDC, nXext, nYext, lpSize)

Win32. If you're in a hurry and want to minimize the amount of editing you need to do, you can instead define a macro to handle the difference, such as:

```
#ifdef WIN32
#define MoveTo(hDC,x,y)    MoveToEx(hDC,x,y,NULL)
#endif
```

You aren't likely to care about the return value from **MoveTo**, but you'll certainly care about the return value from **GetTextExtent**. There was a **GetTextExtentEx** function in a beta version of Windows 3.1 that was apparently dropped in the production version of Windows 3.1, but that was enough to keep the Win32 designers from using the name. You can consider **GetTextExtent** an irregular verb: the Win32 synonyms are formed by adding the syllable **Point**, as in **GetTextExtentPoint** and **GetTextExtentExPoint**. Both functions return the extent in a **SIZE** structure, which is essentially the upper half of a **RECT** structure.

For reference, Table 1-2 lists Windows 3.x GDI calls that need conversion to their Win32 equivalents.

One pair of Windows 3.x functions falls slightly outside the make-room-for-widened-parameters pattern. The **DlgDirSelect** and **DlgDirSelectComboBox** functions lack a way to limit the amount of information returned. The Win32 and Windows 3.1 equivalents add a buffer size parameter—but they *don't* add it at the end.

DlgDirSelect(hwndDlg, lpszPath, idListBox) should be replaced by **DlgDirSelectEx (hwndDlg, lpszPath, cbPath, idListBox)**, and **Dlg-**

Table 1-2   continued

Windows 3.x function	Windows 3.1/Win32 function
SetWindowOrg (hDC, nXOrg, nYOrg)	SetWindowOrgEx (hDC, nX, nY, lpPoint)
GetAspectRatioFilter (hDC)	GetAspectRatioFilterEx (hDC, lpAspectRatio)
GetBitmapDimension (hBitmap)	GetBitmapDimensionEx (hbm, lpDimension)
GetBrushOrg (hDC)	GetBrushOrgEx (hDC, lpPoint)
GetCurrentPosition (hDC)	GetCurrentPositionEx (hDC, lpPoint)
GetTextExtent (hDC, lpsz, cblen)	GetTextExtentPoint (hDC, lpsz, cblen, lpSize)
GetTextExtentEx(hDC, lpsz, cblen, nMaxExtent, lpnFit, alpDx)	GetTextExtentExPoint (hDC, lpsz, cblen, nMaxExtent, lpnFit, alpDx, lpSize)
GetViewportExt (hDC)	GetViewportExtEx (hDC, lpSize)
GetViewportOrg (hDC)	GetViewportOrgEx (hDC, lpPoint)
GetWindowExt (hDC)	GetWindowExtEx (hDC, lpSize)
GetWindowOrg (hDC)	GetWindowOrgEx (hDC, lpPoint)

`DirSelectComboBox(hwndDlg, lpszPath, idComboBox)` should be replaced by `DlgDirSelectComboBoxEx(hwndDlg, lpszPath, cbPath, idComboBox)`.

If you have code that uses extra window words for handle storage or code that accesses window properties, you'll probably have to modify it, since most of the window word message names have become window long message names in Win32. For instance, `GetClassWord(hWnd, GCW_HCURSOR)` becomes `GetClassLong(hWnd, GCL_HCURSOR)`. Other, more portable functions sometimes exist: rather than use `GetWindowWord(hWnd, GWW_HWNDPARENT)` (Windows 3.x) or `GetWindowLong(hWnd, GWL_HWNDPARENT)` (Win32), you can use the portable function `GetParent(hWnd)`.

Win32 and DOS Int21H Synonyms

As you probably realize, you can't use DOS Int 21H or DOS3Call functions from Win32 programs. There are, however, Win32 functions to support almost all the major DOS services, which we list in Table 1-3. In a later chapter we'll look at an example of how to use the Win32 file I/O functions; for now I should just point out that Win32 system file handles are *not* usable as C runtime library file handles— you can't easily mix the two kinds of file I/O.

What's missing from Table 1-3? There's no direct Win32 function to format a diskette from a program. There is a way to do it, though: you need to call `DevIOCtl` to access the format routine in the floppy disk driver, but that requires knowing

Table 1-3   DOS Int 21H Functions and Their Win32 Equivalents

Int 21H Service	Win32 Function
0Eh	SetCurrentDirectory (lpszCurrentDirectory)
19h	GetCurrentDirectory (cbuffsize, lpszCurrentDirectory)
2Ah	GetSystemTime (lpSystemTime)
2Bh	SetSystemTime (lpSystemTime)
2Ch	GetSystemTime (lpSystemTime)
2Dh	SetSystemTime (lpSystemTime)
36h	GetDiskFreeSpace (lpszRootPathName, lpSectorsPerCluster, lpBytes PerSector, lpFreeClusters, lpClusters)
39h	CreateDirectory (lpszPath, lpSecurityAttributes)
3Ah	RemoveDirectory (lpszPath)
3Bh	SetCurrentDirectory (lpszCurrentDirectory)
3Ch	CreateFile (lpszName, fdwAccess, fdwShareMode, lpsa, fdwCreate, fdw-AttrsAndFlags, hTemplateFile)
3Dh	CreateFile (lpszName, fdwAccess, fdwShareMode, lpsa, fdwCreate, fdw-AttrsAndFlags, hTemplateFile)
3Eh	CloseHandle (hObject)
3Fh	ReadFile (hFile, lpBuffer, nNumberOfBytesToRead, lpNumberOfBytes Read, lpOverlapped)
40h	WriteFile (hFile, lpBuffer, nNumberOfBytesToWrite, lpNumberOfBytes Written, lpOverlapped)

the control codes in the floppy disk driver. You could also open **a:** or **b:** with the **CreateFile** function and treat the floppy as a file—but we're getting ahead of ourselves.

If fact, we're now getting deep into the realm of miscellaneous pains in the nether parts. If you have no C code to port from Windows, and if you are planning to write in C++, you can safely skip to Chapter 3. Otherwise, hang in there: you might need this stuff.

Win32 and Windows 3.x DLL Entry and Exit Synonyms

Win32 DLLs (dynamic link libraries) have somewhat different initialization and termination functions from Windows 3.x DLLs. Fortunately, initialization and termination functions in Windows DLLs are generally very short and simple, especially compared to the rest of the functions in the DLL—which probably won't require much reworking unless you want to support NT-specific features.

Table 1-3   continued

Int 21H Service	Win32 Function
41h	DeleteFile (lpszFileName)
42h	SetFilePointer (hFile, lDistanceToMove, plDistanceToMoveHigh, dwMoveMethod)
43h	GetFileAttributes (lpszFileName)
43h	SetFileAttributes (lpszFileName, dwFileAttributes)
47h	GetCurrentDirectory (cbuffsize, lpszCurrentDirectory)
4Eh	FindFirstFile (lpszFileName, lpFileFoundData)
4Fh	FindNextFile (lpszFileName, lpFileFoundData)
56h	MoveFile (lpszCurrentName, lpszNewName)
57h	GetFileTime (hFile, lpftCreation, lpftLastAccess, lpftLastWrite)
57h	SetFileTime (hFile, lpftCreation, lpftLastAccess, lpftLastWrite)
59h	GetLastError (void)
5Ah	GetTempFileName (lpszPath, lpszPrefix, uUnique, lpszTempFile)
5Bh	CreateFile (lpszName, fdwAccess, fdwShareMode, lpsa, fdwCreate, fdwAttrsAndFlags, hTemplateFile)
5Ch	LockFile (hFile, dwFileOffsetLow, dwFileOffsetHigh, cbLockLow, cbLockHigh)
5Ch	UnlockFile (hFile, dwFileOffsetLow, dwFileOffsetHigh, cbUnlockLow, cbUnlockHigh)
67h	SetHandleCount (nHandlesNeeded) *(no effect under Windows NT)*

In Windows 3.x, you must have **LibEntry** and **LibMain** functions for initialization that are called only when the DLL is loaded. You must also have a **WEP** function for termination.[5]

In Win32, a DLL has a single *optional* initialization and cleanup function documented as:

```
BOOL DllEntryPoint(hDll, dwReason, lpReserved)
HANDLE hDll;
DWORD dwReason;
LPVOID lpReserved;
```

The **dwReason** parameter can be **DLL_PROCESS_ATTACH**, **DLL_THREAD_AT-**

---

[5] Note that in Windows 3.0 the **WEP** function couldn't do much because of a system bug. If you need to write code that is backward-compatible with Windows 3.0, use an explicitly called function to perform cleanup rather than relying on the **WEP**.

TACH, `DLL_PROCESS_DETACH`, or `DLL_THREAD_DETACH`. `DllEntrypoint` is not the actual name of the function: you use your own name and flag the DLL entry with the `-entry` option to the linker.

Win32 DLLs have the option of creating and using thread local storage, using the functions `TlsAlloc`, `TlsSetValue`, `TlsGetValue`, and `TlsFree`. Windows 3.x has no equivalent mechanism for per-thread variables in a DLL. Note that because processes in Win32 have their own address spaces, you can't use a DLL's local data segment to share variables among instances of a process or among different processes. More about separate address spaces shortly.

Why would you use thread local storage? Suppose you have a massively parallel computation to do—say a heat-transfer simulation done by finite differences or finite elements. Each node in the computation has a current temperature, which is updated at each time step based on the temperatures of its neighbors. Conceptually, one of the simplest ways of implementing such a calculation is to devote a thread to each node; each thread only has to perform one relatively simple calculation at each time step. Intermediate results can go on the thread's stack, but each thread needs to publish its current temperature for its neighbors.

Where could you put the temperatures? In thread local storage. The DLL could then copy the nearest-neighbor temperatures among nodes. On a machine with multiple processors, the resulting calculation would be much faster than it would be with a conventional single-threaded iteration.

Windows 3.x DLLs require you to have at least one assembly language module, `LibEntry`. On the other hand, you should attempt to minimize your use of assembly language in Win32 programs and DLLs, since Win32 code should ideally be independent of the host processor. If you want to write DLLs portable between Windows 3.x and Win32 at the source code level, you shouldn't do any customization of `LibEntry`.

More Porting Issues

DLL initialization isn't exactly the only detail changed from Windows 3.x to Windows NT. One major difference—a major improvement—is that message queues in Windows NT are desynchronized.

The Desynchronized Message Queue

In Windows 3.x an application can hang the system by failing to return from a message, although in enhanced mode you can kill the offending application with a Ctrl-Alt-Del to the virtual machine manager. In Windows NT you don't see hourglass cursors for very long—each application has its own message queue, so no application has to wait for another application to return from a message. This can get you into trouble, though, in the rare case of code that truly depends on having complete con-

trol of Windows for the duration of a message, code that can't deal with a **NULL** return from **GetFocus**, or code that depends too much on the global message order in Windows.

I should point out that desynchronizing the message queues means that no single application can hang the desktop—it's just as important as preemptive multitasking. If you try running an application that goes into a tight loop before returning from a message in Windows NT, nothing much will happen. By contrast, both Windows 3.x (with a single system message queue and no preemption) and the OS/2 Presentation Manager (which has preemptive multitasking but is limited by a single system message queue) will freeze up solid if you try the same experiment.

In most cases you won't get into trouble with synchronization unless you add threads to your application—the input queue won't really matter. Once you do add threads, you'll also need to protect critical resources with a Critical Section object, a semaphore, or some other synchronization technique.

Separate Address Spaces

Another somewhat more telling issue has to do with address spaces. All the programs running on the Windows 3.1 desktop, at least in enhanced mode, run in a single virtual machine with a shared address space. Win32 programs running on Windows NT have separate address spaces, which means that they can't easily share memory. The **GMEM_SHARE** and **GMEM_DDESHARE** memory attributes don't do anything in Windows NT: applications that need to share memory should probably create named shared virtual memory blocks using **MapViewOfFile**.

Instance initialization is also affected by separate memory spaces. Every Win32 application instance gets a **NULL** instance handle when **WinMain** is called, whether or not it's the first copy of the application to run. In most cases it doesn't matter, because in Win32 every instance has to register its window classes: the usual code will work properly. In rare cases you really don't want to have more than one instance of an application running—for instance, you might have an application that uses a database without any kind of record or file locking. Until you add the multiuser locking support, you won't want to allow more than one instance of the application to run at a time. You can determine whether there are previous running instances by broadcasting a unique message, creating a unique named pipe, creating and testing for a named semaphore, or by calling **FindWindow**.

We're almost through the "gotchas." If you've hung in this long, you might as well finish.

Extended Filenames

If you have Windows programs that assume that filenames will conform to the 8.3 format limit of the DOS FAT file system, they might have trouble handling NTFS

(New Technology File System) and HPFS (High Performance File System) filenames.[6] NTFS and HPFS filenames can be up to 254 characters long, and can contain multiple periods, mixed case, and embedded blanks. NTFS also supports Unicode filenames. In a worst case, an NTFS filename could be meaningful only in Kanji, which is one of the many national language sets included in Unicode. Don't wire any file naming rules into your programs.

Using the C Runtime Library

Yet another set of issues involves the use of the C runtime library. Some developers use model-independent functions like **_fstrcpy**, from the C runtime library, rather than functions like **lstrcpy**, which is a Windows system function. Because Windows NT has no need for model-independent functions, the 32-bit Microsoft C compiler drops the entire family. What can you do? If your existing code uses **lstrcpy**, it will work correctly as is in Win32. If it instead uses **_fstrcpy**, you'll need to change it to use **strcpy** or **lstrcpy** instead. The easiest way to take care of such problems is (surprise!) simply to include WINDOWSX.H, since it contains the porting macros listed in Table 1-4.

You'll notice that **malloc** and **free** are listed in the right-hand column of Table 1-4. Should you use malloc for dynamic memory allocation? Would it be better to use **GlobalAlloc** or **LocalAlloc** ?

In Win32, it doesn't really matter. Use whichever you want—they each return 32-bit NEAR pointers. In Windows 3.x, it does matter which you use, so if you're writing code that is to be compatible between 16-bit and 32-bit Windows, you can let your 16-bit implementation drive the decision.

If your Windows 3.x code uses large model, your best bet is to use **malloc**, since in the large model of Microsoft C/C++ 7.0 and above, and in Borland C++ 3.0 and above, **malloc** implements an efficient suballocation scheme similar to the technique described as *multiple local heaps* on pages 24–26 of *Advanced Windows Programming*. If, on the other hand, your Windows 3.x code uses medium or small model, you should use **GlobalAlloc** (or the **GlobalAllocPtr** macro) for large objects and **LocalAlloc** (or the **LocalAllocPtr** macro) for small, frequently used, and shortlived objects.

Tools for Porting from Windows to Win32

While you could port all your code from Windows to Win32 manually by either the top–down or bottom–up methods discussed earlier in this chapter, you'd likely find the process both frustrating and boring. Fortunately, Microsoft has provided a tool

---

[6] NTFS is based on HPFS, but adds recoverability and security features. HPFS was, of course, introduced in OS/2.

Table 1-4 WINDOWSX.H C Library Porting Definitions

#define	as
_fmemcpy(x,y,z)	memcpy(x,y,z)
_fmemcmp(x,y,z)	memcmp(x,y,z)
_fmemset(x,y,z)	memset(x,y,z)
_fmemicmp(x,y,z)	memicmp(x,y,z)
_fmemmove(x,y,z)	memmove(x,y,z)
_fstrcpy(x,y)	strcpy(x,y)
_fstrcmp(x,y)	strcmp(x,y)
_fstrcat(x,y)	strcat(x,y)
_fstrlen(x)	strlen(x)
_fstricmp(x,y)	stricmp(x,y)
_fstrstr(x,y)	strstr(x,y)
_fstrncpy(x,y,z)	strncpy(x,y,z)
_fstrncmp(x,y,z)	strncmp(x,y,z)
_fstrupr(x)	strupr(x)
_fstrlwr(x)	strlwr(x)
_fstrchr(x,y)	strchr(x,y)
_fstrrchr(x,y)	strrchr(x,y)
_fstrnicmp(x,y,z)	strnicmp(x,y,z)
_fstrpbrk(x,y)	strpbrk(x,y
_nfree(x)	free(x)
_nmalloc(x)	malloc(x)

specifically to help automate the process, PORTTOOL. In addition, you'll find the STRICT definitions, the macros in WINDOWSX.H, and the compiler diagnostics you get with /W3 all helpful in the porting process.

You'll find PORTTOOL in your Win32 Software Development Kit program group, assuming you've installed the Microsoft Win32 SDK. The program itself is fairly simple. To use it, you open a source file (with FILE / OPEN) and start PORTTOOL scanning for problems in your code (with PORT / INTERACTIVE or PORT / BACK-GROUND). When the program encounters a possible problem, it highlights the source code and suggests a rewrite (Figure 1-1). You are free to change the source with the built-in editor or continue scanning.

I found that PORTTOOL is fairly dumb—it will, for example, complain about keywords it finds in comment blocks—but it is still useful. Once you know how to

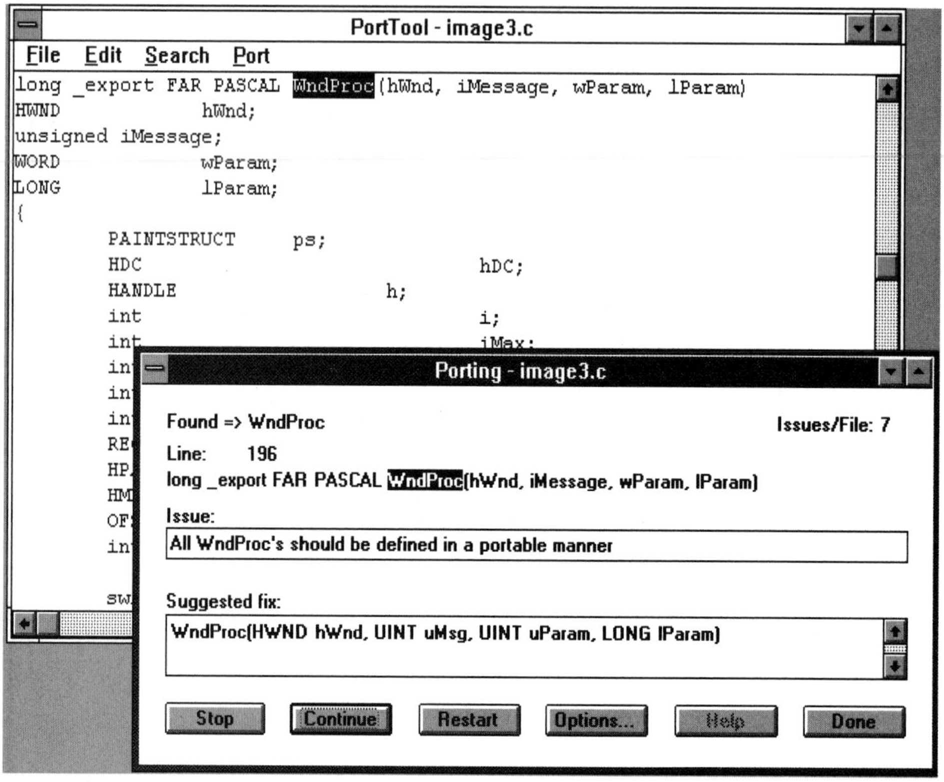

Figure 1-1   PORTTOOL complaining about old-style WndProc definitions.

fix the code flagged by the important PORTTOOL messages and by the compiler, and know what messages you can ignore, you can port an application from Windows to Windows NT in a day or two.

One warning: I'd advise you to always use "Save As..." rather than "Save" from the PORTTOOL file menu. Why? At least in some circumstances "Save" doesn't actually write out the file. In addition, creating an extra file gives you the opportunity to **diff** the two versions so that you can document the changes you made with PORTTOOL.

And Steer Right Onward

In an ideal world, we'd write software once and reuse it for all time. In the real world, circumstances change and we must adapt the software to new situations.

Adapting Windows 3.x software written in C to the 32-bit world of Windows NT can be done without a major rewrite, as we'll show in Chapter 2. On the other hand, we've already seen some of the problems we're likely to encounter. So, in Chapter 3 we'll learn a little bit about the C++ language and formulate a plan for converting our C code to C++, and in Chapter 4 we'll actually attempt the conversion.

Why C++? We'll develop the answer to that question in some detail in Chapter 3. But the short answer is that we want to use C++ to encapsulate implementation details—the differences between Intel and MIPS architectures, between 16-bit Windows and Win32, and the differences between Win32 programs running on Windows NT and Win32 programs running on Windows 3.1 with Win32s. Rather than have the differences constantly in our faces, we'd like them pushed well down, only to be seen when absolutely needed.

Let's return to the wagon train expedition for a minute. We've spread out the maps; we've identified the deserts, the mountains, and the deep rivers. What we'll do next is listen to the stories of parties that tried different routes, so that we can then make an informed judgment about what route to take ourselves.

We move the Image2 example developed in *Advanced Windows Programming* to Win32 as quickly as possible.

Any Port in a Storm

• •

It's about time for a good, old-fashioned concrete example. Let's take the Image2 program developed in *Advanced Windows Programming* and move it to Win32, still in C—we'll save the port to C++ for a later chapter.

As you might expect, not all of the code will change. You'll find full code on the companion disks in the Image3 subdirectory: we'll restrict the printed listings to changes of interest.

In an ideal world, if you were maintaining your own production C code for Win16 and Win32, you probably would want to have a single set of sources with **#ifdefs** for the parts that change between environments, rather than having to maintain two separate sets of sources. In the interest of brevity, clarity, and readability we won't necessarily make every change in this chapter in a way that preserves compatibility with Win16. Don't worry too much about it: we can always merge our sources later, with any one of a number of code maintenance utilities.

The porting exercise we are about to undertake won't be a lot of fun. If you don't have existing Windows code written in C, you can safely skip this chapter. If, however, you do have code to port, you should find this chapter illuminating: the discussion in Chapter 1 of what needs to change from 16-bit to 32-bit Windows will make a lot more sense when you've looked at the required changes to specific pieces of code. Consider Chapter 1 the lecture, and this chapter the lab. Or, if you like the wagon train metaphor, consider this a survivors' story.

Porting IMAGE3.C

It makes sense to start the port of IMAGE3 with its main file. But because IMAGE3 traces its lineage back to the Microsoft SHOWDIB example, and because the SHOWDIB example has already been ported to Windows NT, we can take advantage of some of the work that has already been done. That includes some parameter unpacking macros that I've copied from SHOWDIB.H to IMAGE3.H. I have followed my own advice and defined STRICT in all the C files, but I chose not to use the full-blown message-cracking mechanism of WINDOWSX.H, at least for now.

Selected from IMAGE3.H

```
//this section was swiped from the Win32 version of SHOWDIB.H
typedef POINTS MPOINT;              //for Mouse messages
#ifdef WIN32
//Unpack the WNDPROC parameters we need
#define GET_WM_ACTIVATE_STATE (wp, lp)   LOWORD(wp)
#define GET_WM_VSCROLL_CODE (wp, lp)     LOWORD(wp)
#define GET_WM_VSCROLL_POS (wp, lp)      HIWORD(wp)
#define GET_WM_HSCROLL_CODE (wp, lp)     LOWORD(wp)
#define GET_WM_HSCROLL_POS (wp, lp)      HIWORD(wp)
#define GET_EM_SETSEL_MPS(iStart,iEnd(UINT)(iStart),(LONG)(iEnd)
#define GET_WM_COMMAND_CMD (wp, lp)      HIWORD(wp)
//MAKEMPOINT replaces the Windows-16 MAKEPOINT macro
#define MAKEMPOINT (1)                   (*((MPOINT *)&(1)))
//HUGE is meaningless in Win32
#define HUGE_T
#else
//Backwards compatibility for 16-bit Windows
#define GET_WM_ACTIVATE_STATE(wp, lp)   (wp)
#define GET_WM_HSCROLL_CODE(wp, lp)     (wp)
#define GET_WM_HSCROLL_POS(wp, lp)      LOWORD(lp)
#define GET_WM_VSCROLL_CODE(wp, lp)     (wp)
#define GET_WM_VSCROLL_POS(wp, lp)      LOWORD(lp)
#define GET_EM_SETSEL_MPS(iStart,iEnd)  0, MAKELONG(iStart, iEnd)
#define GET_WM_COMMAND_CMD(wp, lp)      HIWORD(lp)
#define MAKEMPOINT(1)                   (*((MPOINT FAR *)&(1)))
#define HUGE_T                          huge
#endif
...
/* OLD:
void  TrackMouse (HWND hwnd, POINT pt);
— NEW: */
VOID  TrackMouse (HWND hwnd, MPOINT pt);
```

Once we know about these macros, we know how to respond to many of the warnings from PORTTOOL and from the C compiler. Let's bear them in mind as we go through IMAGE3.C.

Our first problem crops up in **WinMain:** we were using a Windows 3.1 system call to find out our memory mode and using that in turn to decide whether or not to use memory DIBs:

```
bMemoryDIB = GetWinFlags () & WF_PMODE;
```

However, **GetWinFlags** and **WF_PFMODE** have been dropped from Win32 on the grounds that they are x86-specific. Microsoft recommends changing **GetWinFlags** calls to:

```
VOID GetSystemInfo (lpSystemInfo)
```

In this particular case, we needn't bother, as a 32-bit system has to have virtual memory available: we can just wire **bMemoryDIB** to always be **TRUE**. Note also that we don't really have to convert the declaration of **WinMain** to an ANSI prototype: the ANSI prototype is declared for us in WINBASE.H and automatically applies. It would, however, be better form to rewrite the declaration, at least to avoid the compiler warnings we'd get when STRICT is defined and to avoid future errors when converting to C++:

From IMAGE3.C

```
int WINAPI WinMain (HINSTANCE hInstance,HINSTANCE hPrevInstance,
                    LPSTR lpszCmdLine,int nCmdShow)
{
        HWND            hWnd;
        WNDCLASS        wndclass;
        MSG             msg;
        short           xScreen, yScreen;
        char            ach[40];

        hInst = hInstance;

        bMemoryDIB = TRUE;   //was dependent on mode in Windows 3.1
```

Next we encounter a compiler warning. Why should the compiler burp on this line?

```
wndclass.lpfnWndProc = WndProc;
```

It seems that **WndProc** is merely a function pointer. The **lpfnWndProc** element of the Win32 **WNDCLASS** structure is typed **WNDPROC**. What do we need to do? Just tell the compiler it's OK, by adding an explicit cast:

```
if (!hPrevInstance) {
    wndclass.style = CS_DBLCLKS;
    wndclass.lpfnWndProc = (WNDPROC) WndProc;
```

Similarly, we need to add a cast for our floating picture window procedure declaration:

```
wndclass.lpfnWndProc = (WNDPROC)FloatPicWndProc;
```

Naturally, we should upgrade the definition of **WndProc** (PORTTOOL catches this, but the compiler might not):

```
/*— OLD:
long _export FAR PASCAL WndProc (hWnd, iMessage, wParam, lParam)
HWND         hWnd;
unsigned iMessage;
WORD         wParam;
LONG         lParam;
—   NEW: */
LONG APIENTRY WndProc(
    HWND hWnd,
    UINT iMessage,
    UINT wParam,
    LONG lParam)
{
```

Note that **_export** and **FAR** are meaningless in Win32. **PASCAL** might well have some meaning (it declares the function's calling convention), but it is possible that the calling convention will change in new implementations of Windows NT. The **APIENTRY** calling-convention definition protects us against such changes.

Next we have a **(WORD)** cast. The third parameter to **OpenFile** is now typed **UINT:**

```
fh = OpenFile(achFileName, &of,
    (UINT) OF_EXIST | OF_MUSTEXIST | OF_NOOPTIONS);
```

We might want to consider changing from the Windows **OpenFile** function to another function for opening a file, perhaps the Win32 function **CreateFile,** the C library stream function **fopen,** or the low-level C library function **_open.** As it is, IMAGE3 has a poisonous mix of file-handling functions that might not work in Windows NT. We'll detoxify the mix once we've identified its parts. Onward:

```
/* — OLD:
if (wParam != hWnd && bNoUgly) {
—— NEW: */
if (wParam != (UINT)(hWnd && bNoUgly)) {
```

Why do we need the **(UINT)** cast here? Because **hWnd** is typed **HWND** and **wParam** is typed **UINT**. The compiler wants our assurance that it's OK to convert between types.

The next change takes advantage of the **GET_WM_ACTIVATE_STATE** macro we defined earlier:

```
case WM_ACTIVATE:
/* — OLD:
 if (!wParam)
—— NEW: */
 if (!GET_WM_ACTIVATE_STATE(wParam, lParam))
 /* app. is being de-activated */
     break;
// deliberately falls through to next message
```

We could, of course, have used an **OnActivate** function declared with a **HANDLE_WM_ACTIVATE** message cracker instead, which would also pave the way for us to use the Microsoft Foundation Classes and C++. Again, this is a minimal port; using message crackers would require a bit more up-front work than the simple macros we've chosen to use.

Another type issue: the **WM_PALETTECHANGED** message needs to look to see if the window handle passed in **wParam** is from another application. Here we properly want to cast **wParam** to **HWND** rather than casting **hWnd** to **UINT**, although in practice there is probably no difference:

```
case WM_PALETTECHANGED:
        if ((HWND)wParam != hWnd) { //cast added for Windows NT
```

Next we have a somewhat more interesting case: we handle the parameter packing in **WM_VSCROLL** and **WM_HSCROLL** messages with macros:

```
case WM_VSCROLL:
        /* Calculate new vertical scroll position */
        GetScrollRange(hWnd, SB_VERT, &iMin, &iMax);
        iPos = GetScrollPos(hWnd, SB_VERT);
        GetClientRect(hWnd, &rc);
/* OLD:
        switch (wParam) {
   NEW: */
     switch (GET_WM_VSCROLL_CODE(wParam, lParam)) {
...
        case SB_THUMBTRACK:
        case SB_THUMBPOSITION:
/* OLD:
             dn = LOWORD(lParam) - iPos;
   NEW: */
             dn = GET_WM_VSCROLL_POS(wParam, lParam)-iPos;
             break;
...
     } //switch
break;
```

```
case WM_HSCROLL:
     /* Calculate new horizontal scroll position */
     GetScrollRange(hWnd, SB_HORZ, &iMin, &iMax);
     iPos = GetScrollPos(hWnd, SB_HORZ);
     GetClientRect(hWnd, &rc);
/* OLD:
     switch (wParam) {
  NEW: */
   switch (GET_WM_HSCROLL_CODE(wParam, lParam)) {
...
     case SB_THUMBTRACK:
     case SB_THUMBPOSITION:
/* OLD:
          dn = LOWORD (lParam) - iPos;
  NEW: */
          dn = GET_WM_HSCROLL_POS(wParam, lParam)-iPos;
          break;
...
     } //switch
break;
```

Only a few more issues remain in this file, as far as we can tell from PORTTOOL and the compiler diagnostics. One issue is to correctly convert **lParam** to something our **TrackMouse** can use in response to a **WM_LBUTTONDOWN** message:

```
TrackMouse(hWnd, MAKEMPOINT (lParam)); //new macro
```

The final issue is that the first parameter to **EnableMenuItem** needs to be a real menu handle, not a generic **UINT**:

```
EnableMenuItem((HMENU)wParam, IDM_PASTEDIB,
  IsClipboardFormatAvailable(CF_DIB) ? MF_ENABLED : MF_GRAYED);
```

There are a string of such **EnableMenuItem** statements, which are all changed by the addition of identical casts. And that wraps it up for IMAGE3.C. The other functions in IMAGE3 shouldn't be quite so difficult to port—not that what we've done so far is difficult.

Porting DIB.C

DIB.C is particularly easy: it was originally taken from the SHOWDIB sample. I started over with the Win32 version of DIB.C and made only two alterations (besides defining STRICT): I changed the **#include** of showdib.h to image3.h, and added some fixup code to the **DibFromBitmap** function to handle 3-bit and 16-bit color drivers.

from DIB.C

```
#include "image3.h" //mh
```

```
...
HANDLE DibFromBitmap (
    HBITMAP      hbm,
    DWORD        biStyle,
    WORD         biBits,
    HPALETTE     hpal)
{
...
//If we have a 3-bit or 16-bit driver, fix things up — mh 6/91

    if(biBits==3)
            biBits=4;
    else if(biBits==16)
            biBits=24;
```

To make the new DIB.C compile I also had to copy a few lines from SHOW-DIB.H to IMAGE3.H:

from IMAGE3.H

```
/*******************************************************/
/* make new sizeof structs to cover dword alignment   */
/*******************************************************/

#define SIZEOF_BITMAPFILEHEADER_PACKED  (    \
    sizeof(WORD) +        /* bfType      */   \
    sizeof(DWORD) +       /* bfSize      */   \
    sizeof(WORD) +        /* bfReserved1 */   \
    sizeof(WORD) +        /* bfReserved2 */   \
    sizeof(DWORD))        /* bfOffBits   */

VOID   ReadBitMapFileHeaderandConvertToDwordAlign(HFILE fh,
        LPBITMAPFILEHEADER pbf, LPDWORD lpdwoff);
VOID   WriteMapFileHeaderandConvertFromDwordAlignToPacked(
        HFILE fh, LPBITMAPFILEHEADER pbf);
```

ReadBitMapFileHeaderandConvertToDwordAlign? Do I have to explain this? Remember that in Windows 3.x, system structures are normally packed, while in Windows NT, system structures are normally aligned. The code for these two functions is enlightening:

```
VOID ReadBitMapFileHeaderandConvertToDwordAlign(HFILE fh,
     LPBITMAPFILEHEADER pbf, LPDWORD lpdwoff)
{
     DWORD off;

     off = _llseek(fh, 0L, (UINT) SEEK_CUR);
     *lpdwoff = off;
/*           BITMAPFILEHEADER STRUCUTURE is as follows
 *           BITMAPFILEHEADER
 *           WORD   bfType
 >           ....             <    add WORD if packed here!
```

```
 *                  DWORD   bfSize
 *                  WORD    bfReserved1
 *                  WORD    bfReserved2
 *                  DWORD   bfOffBits
 * This is the packed format, unpacked adds a WORD after bfType
 */

        /* read in bfType*/
        _lread(fh, (LPSTR) &pbf->bfType, sizeof(WORD));
        /* read in last 3 dwords*/
        _lread(fh, (LPSTR) &pbf->bfSize, sizeof(DWORD) * 3);

}


VOID WriteMapFileHeaderandConvertFromDwordAlignToPacked (
        HFILE fh, LPBITMAPFILEHEADER pbf)
{

        /* write bfType*/
      _lwrite(fh, (LPSTR)&pbf->bfType, (UINT)sizeof (WORD));
        /* now pass over extra word, and only write next 3 DWORDS!*/
        _lwrite(fh, (LPSTR)&pbf->bfSize, sizeof(DWORD) * 3);
}
```

Porting DLGOPEN.C

DLGOPEN.C is another file where we can benefit from work already done at Microsoft. I copied the new version of DLGOPEN.C from the Win32 SHOWDIB example, changed the **#include**, added the definition of **STRICT**, and compiled. The compiler diagnostics reminded me that I had to copy the new function prototypes to IMAGE3.H; I also had to add one simple cast to remove the last compiler warning: the strict prototype for the **DialogBox** function requires a **DLGPROC** rather than a **FARPROC** for the fourth parameter.

```
FARPROC   lpProc;
...
fh=DialogBox(hInstance,"DlgOpenBox",hwndParent,(DLGPROC)lpProc);
```

What problems did Microsoft already correct? I took the precaution of running **diff** (from the Hamilton C Shell[1]) on the old and new DLGOPEN.C files before overwriting the old file.

First, the old version relied on an assembly language function, **chdir**. That is replaced by the Win32 **SetCurrentDirectory** function. Then we have improved prototypes for the exported functions:

---

[1] Hamilton Laboratories, 13 Old Farm Road, Wayland MA 01778. Tel: (508)358-5715.

```
HFILE APIENTRY DlgOpenFile (
    HWND         hwndParent,
    CHAR         *szTitleIn,
    DWORD        flagsIn,
    CHAR         *szExtIn,
    CHAR         *szFileNameIn,
    WORD         *pfOpt);
LONG APIENTRY DlgfnOpen (
    HWND hwnd,
    UINT msg,
    UINT wParam,
    LONG lParam);
```

Of course, we encounter some of the usual pain-in-the-neck API changes. For instance,

```
hInstance = GetWindowWord(hwndParent, GWW_HINSTANCE);
```

changes to

```
hInstance = (HINSTANCE)GetWindowLong (hwndParent, GWL_HINSTANCE);
```

and

```
SendDlgItemMessage(hwnd, DLGOPEN_EDIT, EM_SETSEL, 0, 0x7FFF0000L);
```

becomes

```
SendMessage((HWND)GetDlgItem(hwnd, DLGOPEN_EDIT), EM_SETSEL,
      GET_EM_SETSEL_MPS(0, 0x7fff));
```

The change from **SendDlgItemMessage** to **SendMessage** above does not seem to be significant; both functions are supported in Win32.

More pains in the neck:

```
w = wParam;
```

turns into

```
w = LOWORD(wParam);
```

and along the same lines,

```
switch (GET_WM_COMMAND_CMD(wParam, lParam)) {
/* Single click case */
  case LBN_SELCHANGE:
```

replaces

```
switch (HIWORD(lParam)) {
/* Single click case */
  case 1:
```

and

```
DlgDirSelectEx(hwnd, szFileName, 128, LOWORD(wParam));
```

updates

```
DlgDirSelect(hwnd, szFileName, wParam);
```

You perhaps recall that **GET_EM_SETSEL_MPS** and **GET_WM_COMMAND_CMD** are macros defined in IMAGE3.H to accommodate the changes in parameter packing between 16-bit and 32-bit Windows. You should certainly remember that **DlgDirSelectEx** has improved safety compared with **DlgDir-Select**, that **wParam** can be used portably if you take its low word, and that **GWW_HIN-STANCE** in Win16 became **GWL_HINSTANCE** in Win32.

Porting DRAWDIB.C

So, what's next? DRAWDIB.C is another file that Microsoft has already fixed; however, I made some revisions to that file's original **AppAbout** function in IMAGE2. Those revisions were highly system-dependent—they retrieved the free system resources for Windows 3.0 or Windows 3.1—and might not translate to Windows NT too easily. Following our guiding principle for quick and dirty ports—"When in doubt, leave it out"—we will revert to the simple About box implemented in the new file. Perhaps in a later chapter we'll reimplement the About box to be like the Windows NT Program Manager About box, which reports total and free system memory.

As before, I changed the **#include** from **"showdib.h"** to **"image3.h"** and added **#define STRICT**. Also as before, I copied the new improved function prototypes to IMAGE3.H, replacing the old prototypes, and ran **diff** on the two C files. There were a lot of changes that don't really matter—rewriting **int** as **INT** and **void** as **VOID**—and a few that do matter.

The variable **ptSize** has become type **MPOINT**, as defined in IMAGE3.H, and the **TrackMouse** function has an **MPOINT** rather than a **POINT** as its second parameter.

Every place **wsprintf** was used it has been replaced with **sprintf**. I suspect that this was done to avoid thinking about the changes to **wsprintf** made to support Unicode, but I can't be sure. I *am* sure of the reason that

```
dw = GetTextExtent(hdc, sz, len);
dx = LOWORD (dw);
dy = HIWORD (dw);
```

was changed to

```
{SIZE size;
(VOID)GetTextExtentPoint(hdc, sz, len, &size);
 dx = size.cx; dy = size.cy;
 }
```

After all, **GetTextExtent** was dropped from the Win32 API set: there was no real alternative for the programmer doing the port but to recode as **GetTextExtentPoint**. Pushing on: one interesting usage in DRAWDIB.C is

```
UNREFERENCED_PARAMETER(fDraw);
```

What is this UNREFERENCED_PARAMETER construction? Actually, it's a macro defined in WINNT.H that merely adds a benign reference to a parameter to avoid compiler warnings. Interestingly enough, the macro definition also includes directives that appear to be for Gimpel Software's PC-LINT:

from MSTOOLS\H\WINNT.H

```
//
// Macros used to eliminate compiler warning generated when formal
// parameters or local variables are not declared.
//
// Use DBG_UNREFERENCED_PARAMETER() when a parameter is not yet
// referenced but will be once the module is completely developed.
//
// Use DBG_UNREFERENCED_LOCAL_VARIABLE() when a local variable is
// not yet referenced but will be once the module is completely
// developed.
//
// Use UNREFERENCED_PARAMETER() if a parameter will never be
// referenced.
//
// DBG_UNREFERENCED_PARAMETER and DBG_UNREFERENCED_LOCAL_VARIABLE
// will eventually be made into a null macro to help determine
// whether there is unfinished work.
//

#if ! (defined(lint) || defined(_lint))
#define UNREFERENCED_PARAMETER(P)          (P)
#define DBG_UNREFERENCED_PARAMETER(P)      (P)
#define DBG_UNREFERENCED_LOCAL_VARIABLE(V) (V)

#else // lint or _lint

// Note: lint -e530 says don't complain about uninitialized
// variables for this.  line +e530 turns that checking back on.
// Error 527 has to do with unreachable code.

#define UNREFERENCED_PARAMETER(P)            \
    /*lint -e527 -e530 */ \
```

```
    { \
        (P) = (P); \
    } \
    /*lint +e527 +e530 */
#define DBG_UNREFERENCED_PARAMETER(P)          \
    /*lint -e527 -e530 */ \
    { \
        (P) = (P); \
    } \
    /*lint +e527 +e530 */
#define DBG_UNREFERENCED_LOCAL_VARIABLE(V) \
    /*lint -e527 -e530 */ \
    { \
        (V) = (V); \
    } \
    /*lint +e527 +e530 */
#endif // lint or _lint
```

The remaining changes in the file will look familiar from earlier discussions:

```
SetWindowOrg(hdc, ptOrigin.x, ptOrigin.y);
```

becomes

```
(VOID)SetWindowOrgEx(hdc, ptOrigin.x, ptOrigin.y, NULL);
```

since **SetWindowOrg** was dropped from Win32.

```
fh = OpenFile(achFileName, (LPOFSTRUCT) &of, OF_READ);
```

becomes

```
fh = OpenFile(achFileName, (LPOFSTRUCT)&of, (UINT)OF_READ);
```

to accommodate the changed flags, as likewise

```
_llseek(fh, dwOffset, SEEK_SET);
```

becomes

```
_llseek(fh, dwOffset, (UINT)SEEK_SET);
```

Finally, we find that **huge** pointers have been replaced by the **HUGE_T** pointers, where **HUGE_T** is a macro defined in IMAGE3.H as **huge** for 16-bit Windows and nothing for Win32. For example, the **CopyHandle** function contains

```
BYTE HUGE_T *lp;
...
lp = (BYTE HUGE_T *)GlobalLock (h);
```

Porting PRINT.C

The last file we can steal from SHOWDIB is PRINT.C. I went through the usual drill. There wasn't much to do, nor are there many changes to write about. The exported prototypes didn't even change, although two callback functions got new prototypes using the APIENTRY calling sequence:

```
BOOL APIENTRY AbortProc (HDC, SHORT);
BOOL APIENTRY PrintDlgProc (HWND, WORD, UINT, DWORD);
```

Notice in the following that the **MakeProcInstance** calls have been removed for Win32 with an **#ifdef WIN16** clause. I wonder why? Technically, they are harmless: **MakeProcInstance** exists in Win32 strictly as a do-nothing for backward compatibility with 16-bit Windows code. On the other hand, removing them this way reminds us that they do nothing, so that we don't go looking for missing or incorrect **MakeProcInstance** calls when we go to debug our Win32 application. (Remember, missing **MakeProcInstance** calls are a common cause of program errors in 16-bit Windows.) Let's consider the consequences of removing the **MakeProcInstance** calls as we read the code:

```
FARPROC  lpfnAbortProc        = NULL;
FARPROC  lpfnPrintDlgProc = NULL;
...
BOOL PASCAL InitPrinting(HDC hDC, HWND hWnd, HINSTANCE hInst,
                         LPSTR msg)
{
    bError     = FALSE;      /* no errors yet */
    bUserAbort = FALSE;      /* user hasn't aborted */
    hWndParent = hWnd;          /* save for Enable at Term time */
#ifdef WIN16
    lpfnPrintDlgProc = MakeProcInstance (PrintDlgProc, hInst);
    lpfnAbortProc    = MakeProcInstance (AbortProc, hInst);
#endif
    hDlgPrint = CreateDialog (hInst, "PRTDLG", hWndParent,
                   (DLGPROC)lpfnPrintDlgProc);
    if (!hDlgPrint)
      return FALSE;
    SetWindowText (hDlgPrint, msg);
    EnableWindow (hWndParent, FALSE);            /* disable parent */
    if ((Escape (hDC, SETABORTPROC, 0,
            (LPSTR)lpfnAbortProc, NULL) > 0) &&
      (Escape (hDC, STARTDOC, lstrlen(msg), msg, NULL) > 0))
      bError = FALSE;
    else
      bError = TRUE;
    /* might want to call the abort proc here to allow the user to
```

```
         * abort just before printing begins */
        return TRUE;
}
...
VOID PASCAL TermPrinting(HDC hDC)
{
    if (!bError)
        Escape(hDC, ENDDOC, 0, NULL, NULL);
    if (bUserAbort)
        Escape (hDC, ABORTDOC, 0, NULL, NULL) ;
    else {
        EnableWindow(hWndParent, TRUE);
        DestroyWindow(hDlgPrint);
    }
    FreeProcInstance(lpfnAbortProc);
    FreeProcInstance(lpfnPrintDlgProc);
}
```

Notice also that I've added a cast to **DLGPROC** for **lpfnPrintDlgProc** in the **CreateDialog** call, and that the **FreeProcInstance** calls have *not* been removed. Well, technically **FreeProcInstance** should be another do-nothing in Win32, but I'm a little concerned about what will happen if **FreeProcInstance** is called with a **NULL** argument.

Do I sense a bug? If WIN16 is undefined, then **lpfnPrintDlgProc** will be **NULL**; not only will **FreeProcInstance** possibly do something undefined, **Create-Dialog** will certainly fail. What we have here is somebody at Microsoft caught in the middle of drawing diagrams.[2] For clarity, let's remove the partially drawn diagrams, and properly cast the return values from the **MakeProcInstance** calls while we're at it:

```
BOOL PASCAL InitPrinting(HDC hDC, HWND hWnd, HINSTANCE hInst,
                LPSTR msg)
{
    bError      = FALSE;      /* no errors yet */
    bUserAbort = FALSE;       /* user hasn't aborted */
    hWndParent = hWnd;            /* save for Enable at Term time */
    lpfnPrintDlgProc =
            (FARPROC)MakeProcInstance (PrintDlgProc, hInst);
    lpfnAbortProc    =
```

---

[2] In his or her defense, I should point out that I am working from a beta SDK. By the way, I use the term "drawing diagrams" somewhat idiosyncratically, to mean a tentative effort. My usage is based on a true story.

A good friend of mine was, as an advanced medical student, doing his first appendectomy. The patient happened to be obese, and my friend was not sure that he had found the correct location for the incision. So he made the incision gingerly, barely penetrating the fatty layer.

The supervising surgeon: "Drawing diagrams, Doctor?"

```
            (FARPROC)MakeProcInstance (AbortProc, hInst);
   hDlgPrint = CreateDialog (hInst, "PRTDLG", hWndParent,
            (DLGPROC)lpfnPrintDlgProc);
```

Overall, that was fairly easy. But now we've got to fix up our own functions without the benefit of Microsoft's scrutiny.

Porting Our Own Functions Using a Top–Down Approach

The files GIF.C, PCX.C, TGA.C, VICAR.C, and RAW.C all have similar structures: they each contain at least the high-level code to open a bitmapped graphics file, read the contents, and convert the image to a DIB (device-independent bitmap).

All of these files use **far** (or even **_far**) and **huge** keywords, which we can change to **FAR** and **HUGE_T** macros so that they will go away when compiled for Win32. **FAR** is defined as **far**, which is in turn defined as a blank string, in WINDEF.H; **HUGE_T** is defined as a blank string for Win32 and **huge** otherwise in IMAGE3.H. The **_far** and **huge** keywords are not defined anywhere if we compile for Win32—they will cause compiler errors.

Most of these files also use the **_fmemcpy** C library function; as you recall from Chapter 1, that function doesn't exist in the 32-bit C runtime, but is defined as **memcpy** in WINDOWSX.H. So we start our port of each of these files by editing the beginning of the file to read:

```
#define STRICT
#include <windows.h>
#include <windowsx.h>
#include "image3.h"
```

Then we globally change all **_far** and **far** keywords to **FAR**, and all **huge** keywords to **HUGE_T**. Additionally, we change all dialog function prototypes to use the **APIENTRY** calling convention.

Then we compile, and add casts whenever we get warnings about incompatible types. Finally, we test and debug the application.

To test and debug, however, we need to get all source files to at least compile— whether with their full functionality enabled or with difficult parts commented out.

So let's continue with the TIFF functions. You may recall that our TIFF reader was based on some public-domain Unix code from Berkeley. You may also recall that it generated reams of compiler warnings and didn't work particularly well—at least partially because it was originally 32-bit code.

We could do almost the same editing on the TIFF functions as we did on the other file-reading functions. But there is no need to add STRICT and WINDOWSX.H to every

TIFF function, or even to change **_fmemcpy** calls: all the TIFF modules include
TIFFIO.H. So we can make at least some of the changes in a common place:

from TIFFIO.H

```
#define BSDTYPES                      1
#define USE_PROTOTYPES                1
#define USE_VARARGS                   0
//#define __STDC__                    1
#define _WINDOWS                      1
#ifndef MSDOS
#define MSDOS                         1
#endif
#ifndef M_I86
#define M_I86                         1
#endif

#include "tiffcomp.h"
#include "tiff.h"

#ifdef _WINDOWS
 #ifndef FAR
  #define STRICT                      //added for checking
  #undef NULL
  #undef TRUE
  #undef FALSE
  #include <windows.h>
 #endif //ifndef FAR
 #include <assert.h>
 #define exit(X) assert(1)
 #include <windowsx.h>               //added for definitions
 #ifdef WIN32                        //is 32-bit
  #include <malloc.h>
  #include <string.h>
 #else                              //not WIN32: use far fns.
  #undef malloc
  #undef free
  #undef strcpy
  #undef strlen
  #undef realloc
  #define malloc(a) _fmalloc(a)
  #define realloc(a,b) _frealloc(a,b)
  #define free(a) _ffree(a)
  #define strcpy(a,b) lstrcpy(a,b)
  #define strlen(a) lstrlen(a)
 #endif //WIN32 else clause
#else                              //not _WINDOWS
 #define FAR
#endif //_WINDOWS
#define PTIFF TIFF FAR *
```

This done, IMAGE3 compiles and links. It even runs, after a fashion—but some
functions don't work properly, and others cause the program to terminate.

Proof of the Pudding

As you might expect, debugging IMAGE3 under Windows NT was relatively straight-forward. I built the modules I thought relevant to the problem at hand for debugging, and brought the program up under WINDBG. Usually I set a breakpoint at the code that handles the menu item in question, and stepped through from there.

I found a number of problems, but no major surprises. One category of problem was simple oversight: I knew perfectly well that all **int** types in structures that reflect the organization of files on disk needed to be changed to **short int**, but I forgot to look for such instances. I also knew that structures from disk needed to be packed in memory—the default in Windows, but not in Win32—but forgot to add the necessary **#pragma** statements. The PCX structures needed both sorts of changes:

PCX.H

```
#pragma pack(1)                     //added for Win32
typedef struct pcxhdr {
      BYTE manu;     //10=ZSoft
      BYTE ver;
      /*      0=PaintBrush 2.5
              2= 2.8 w/palette,
              3= 2.8 w/o palette
              4= PC Paintbrush for Windows
              5= Version 3.0 + of PC Paintbrush, PC
                    Paintbrush +, and     Publisher's Paintbrush */
      BYTE encod;            // 1= PCX RLE
      BYTE bpp;              // Bits per pixel - 1, 2, 4, or 8
      short int Xmin;        //Window dimensions (short int for Win32)
      short int Ymin;
      short int Xmax;
      short int Ymax;
      short int Hdpi;        //Horizontal resolution
      short int Vdpi;        //Vertical resolution
      RGBTRIPLE pal1[16];  //palette
      BYTE junk;
      BYTE planes;           //number of color planes
      short int BytesPerLine;
             //number of bytes to allocate for a scanline plane
      short int paltype;
             //1=Color/BW, 2=Grayscale (ignored in PB IV, IV+)
      short int Hscrsize;          //horizontal screen size (PB IV)
      short int Vscrsize;          //vertical screen size (PB IV)
      BYTE filler[54];
      } PCXHDR;
/* Note: If ver=5 there may be a VGA 256 color palette at the end of
the file. Check for it at the end of file less 769 bytes: the value
will be 12 if there is a 256-color palette */
typedef struct pcxpal256 {
      BYTE flag;     //12= 256-color palette present
      RGBTRIPLE pal2[256];
```

```
        } PCXPAL256;
#pragma pack()              //restore default struct packing
```

Another class of problem came from mixing file handles. For TIFF files, the cure was to stick to the C library:

from TIFFCOMP.H

```
//the following conditionals were changed for Win32 to avoid
// mixing file handle types
#ifndef ReadOK
#if defined(_WINDOWS) && !defined(WIN32)
#define ReadOK(fd, buf, size)  \
  (_lread(fd, (char FAR *)buf,  (UINT)size) == (UINT)size)
#else
#define ReadOK(fd, buf, size)  \
  (read(fd, (char *)buf, size) == size)
#endif
#endif
#ifndef SeekOK
#if defined(_WINDOWS) && !defined(WIN32)
#define SeekOK(fd, off) \
      (_llseek(fd, (long)off, L_SET) == (long)off)
#else
#define SeekOK(fd, off) \
      (lseek(fd, (long)off, L_SET) == (long)off)
#endif
#endif
#ifndef WriteOK
#if defined(_WINDOWS) && !defined(WIN32)
#define WriteOK(fd, buf, size)  \
      (_lwrite(fd, (char FAR *)buf, (UINT)size) == (UINT)size)
#else
#define WriteOK(fd, buf, size)  \
      (write(fd, (char *)buf, size) == size)
#endif
#endif
```

The same strategy worked for VICAR files:

from FILEIO.C

```
#define STRICT
#include <windows.h>
#include <windowsx.h>
#include "image3.h"
#include "vicar.h"
#include <sys\types.h>
#include <sys\stat.h>
#include <fcntl.h>
```

```
#include <io.h>
#include <stdio.h>
#include <ctype.h>
#include <string.h>
#include <dos.h>

#define MaxOpenFiles  10    /* Maximum number of open files at one
time */
     /* Magnetic disk I/O using MS-DOS */

struct FCBtype
     {
     char filename[80];
     int handle;
     } FCB[MaxOpenFiles];

int OpenDisk(filename, unit, IOmode, p_blocksize, status)

/* OpenDisk opens a MS-DOS file using standard I/O.*/

char filename[], IOmode[], status[];
int unit, *p_blocksize;
{
     char accessmode;
     int filehandle;

     strcpy(status, "");
     *p_blocksize = 128;
     strcpy(FCB[unit].filename, filename);
     accessmode = toupper(IOmode[0]);
     if (accessmode != 'W')
          accessmode = 'R';
     if (accessmode == 'W')
          filehandle = open(filename,
            O_CREAT | O_TRUNC | O_WRONLY | O_BINARY, S_IREAD
            | S_IWRITE);
     else
          filehandle = open(filename, O_RDONLY | O_BINARY);
     if (filehandle == -1) {
          strcpy(status, "Error opening file : ");
          strcat(status, FCB[unit].filename);
          }
     FCB[unit].handle = filehandle;
     return(0);
}

int ReadDisk(unit, buffer, startblock, numblocks,
     p_blocksread, status)
/* ReadDisk reads blocks from MS-DOS file to buffer. */
int unit, numblocks, *p_blocksread;
long startblock;
unsigned char far *buffer;
char status[];
```

```
{
    long pos;
    int i, bytesread;

    strcpy(status, "");
    pos = lseek(FCB[unit].handle, 128 * startblock, SEEK_SET);
    if (pos == -1) {
            strcpy(status, "Error reading from file : ");
            strcat(status, FCB[unit].filename);
            return 0;
            }
//The following line dies in Win32 under WinDbg and otherwise fails
// Why? The integer file handle from the C runtime open is not the
// same as an HFILE
/* OLD
    bytesread = _lread(FCB[unit].handle, (LPSTR) buffer,
                  128 * numblocks);
*/
//Revert to C lib reading instead of using _lread:
    bytesread = _read(FCB[unit].handle, (LPSTR) buffer,
                  128 * numblocks);
/* patch for quick look tiles with filler bytes - mdm 12-15-88 */
    if (strnicmp(FCB[unit].filename +
            (strlen(FCB[unit].filename) - 4),
            ".QLK", 4) == 0 && buffer[1892] == 94) {
            for (i = 0;  i < bytesread / 2048;  i++)
                    _fmemmove(buffer + (i * 2048) + 1892 - i * 156,
                            buffer + (i * 2048) + 2048 - i * 156,
                            bytesread - (i + 1) * 2048);
/* OLD:
            _lread(FCB[unit].handle,
            (LPSTR) (buffer + 28380), 1892);
   NEW: */
            _read(FCB[unit].handle,
            (LPSTR) (buffer + 28380), 1892);
            }
    if (bytesread == 0) {
            strcpy(status, "Seek beyond end of file : ");
            strcat(status, FCB[unit].filename);
            return 0;
            }
    if (bytesread == -1) {
            strcpy(status, "Error reading from file : ");
            strcat(status, FCB[unit].filename);
            }
    *p_blocksread = (bytesread - 1) / 128 + 1;
}
```

A different sort of problem cropped up in some of Microsoft's code. When IMAGE3 undoes an edit, the title of the image doesn't quite fit the expectations of code that expects a legitimate FAT filename:

from DRAWDIB.C

```
VOID SizeWindow (HWND hWnd)
{
    CHAR  *pstr;
    CHAR  Name[60];
    RECT  Rectangle;
    RECT  rectClient;
//  INT   dx,dy;
//  MPOINT pt;
    BITMAPINFOHEADER bi;

    /* Get information about current DIB */
    DibInfo(hbiCurrent,&bi);

    /* Extract the filename from the full pathname */
    pstr = achFileName + lstrlen(achFileName) - 1;
    while ((*pstr != '\\') && (*pstr != ':') &&
           (pstr > achFileName))
        pstr--;
```

The code above would die ignominiously in the **while** loop. Why? The pointer would run off the beginning of the string and cause a memory protection trap. Changing the order of evaluation of the clauses fixed the problem:

```
    /* Extract the filename from the full pathname */
    pstr = achFileName + lstrlen(achFileName) - 1;
    while ((pstr >= achFileName) && (*pstr != '\\') &&
           (*pstr != ':'))
        pstr--;
```

And, of course, I needed to fix the code that does gray-scaling and color correction for 24-bit color images:

from PROCESS.C

```
//Otherwise, change the colors
else {
 lpbi=(VOID FAR *)GlobalLock(hdibCurrent);
 pixels = (unsigned char HUGE_T *)(lpbi + lpbi->biSize);
 linebytes = WIDTHBYTES(lpbi->biWidth * lpbi->biBitCount);
 linewidth = ALIGNULONG(linebytes);
 switch(ColorModel) {
     case IDD_RGB:
     //loop over scan lines
     for(i=0;i<lpbi->biHeight;i++) {
             il= i * linewidth;
             //loop over pixels within the scan line
```

Figure 2-1 BAREFOOT.BMP after gray-scaling and lightening by IMAGE3.

```
for(j=0;j<linebytes;j+=3) {
      pb=pixels+il+j;
      pb1=pb+1;
      pb2=pb+2;
      *pb  = (BYTE)BOUND(*pb +db,0,255);
      *pb1 = (BYTE)BOUND(*pb1+dg,0,255);
      *pb2 = (BYTE)BOUND(*pb2+dr,0,255);
      }

   }
break;
```

As you can see, the code above corrects the loop structure from the code shown in Chapter 1. Remember, DIB scan-lines are double-word aligned and may have padding at the end of the line if the width in bytes is not a multiple of 4. The variable **linebytes** contains the actual number of bytes in each scan-line, and the variable **linewidth** contains the scan-line length including padding. The other color models and the three gray-scaling algorithms all have the same loop structure.

And there we have it: IMAGE3 works better and faster than IMAGE2 ever did, with only a few days' porting effort. Figure 2-1 shows the result of using IMAGE3 to gray-scale and lighten one of the color photographs from *Advanced Windows Programming.*

I think it's obvious at this point that porting from 16-bit Windows to 32-bit Windows isn't difficult, although it can be a pain in the neck. On the other hand, in an ideal world we shouldn't have to go through all that: moving from Windows 3.1 to Win32 should be a simple matter of recompiling and relinking.

That, in a nutshell, is the promise of C++ and the Microsoft Foundation Classes: that we can maintain one set of sources that will work for 16-bit and 32-bit versions of Windows, on any hardware supported by Windows. With that in mind, let's learn a little bit about C++.

In which we learn to make the transition from the C programming language to the C++ programming language, encapsulating as we go.

Upping the Ante

. . . .

One way to hide the differences between programming for Windows 3.1 using 16-bit words and Windows NT using 32-bit words is to write class libraries using C++. The implementation details will be held inside the classes—our applications will use the classes but will not see or depend on the details.

I'm not going to try to teach you C++ from scratch. There are a number of good books that will teach you C++ better than I ever could, some of which are listed in the Recommended Readings at the end of this book. And I'm the last person who should teach C++, as I've fought it, kicking and screaming, for years.[1]

On the other hand, we don't want to jump into the deep cold waters of a new language without preparation. So what I will do is to tell you a little about the differences between C and C++, to solidify my case that C++ will help us produce readable source code that is compatible with both 16-bit and 32-bit Windows. Along the way, I'll expose you to most of the new concepts you'll need to read the code in the rest of the book.

---

[1] What I've fought, really, is having to learn C++ and object-oriented design myself in the face of continual pressure to get software out the door. As you'll see while reading this chapter, I've since resigned myself to the inevitable. Despite my choice of C++ here for reasons spelled out in the text, part of me still wants to write carefully optimized, totally nonportable, assembly language.

If you are already an experienced C++ programmer, by all means skip most of this chapter: you'll be bored with most of my exposition of C++ fundamentals, although you might enjoy the last few sections. If you haven't already become intimately familiar with C++, please read on, but do plan on picking up some additional references, as I have space only for the merest introduction to the language.

Bjarne Stroustrup, the designer of C++, tells us: [2]

> *The C++ programming language is designed to*
> - *be a better C*
> - *support data abstraction*
> - *support object-oriented programming*

The question, of course, arises as to what these statements mean. Stroustrup speaks of C++ as "a better C" in the context of its support for traditional procedural and modular programming. He cites classes and user-defined types as the C++ features that support data abstraction. And he considers derived classes and virtual functions the facilities that support object-oriented programming.

"Be a Better C"

Most good C code is also C++ code. It might not be elegant C++ code, but it should compile and run properly without much porting effort.

The key word here is "good." Bad C code often isn't legal C++ at all. If you want to see the sort of bad C code I mean, have a look at the results of the annual Obfuscated C Code Contest (which you can find collected in Don Libes' book *Obfuscated C and Other Mysteries*, Wiley, 1992). If you're not familiar with the Obfuscated C contest and wonder why it matters, you might consider the origins of the contest. Landon Noll, the contest's founder, writes:

> *The contest was motivated by reading the UNIX source code to the Bourne shell (/bin/sh). I was shocked at how much simple algorithms could be made cryptic, and therefore useless, by a poor choice of code style. I asked myself, "Could someone be proud of this code?"*

The most-abused and least-safe parts of C are probably the preprocessor, pointers, unions, and the **printf** and **scanf** function families. Additional areas of danger and confusion in C are function parameter mismatches, incorrect type conversions (both implicit conversions and explicit conversions with casts), dynamic memory

---

[2] Stroustrup, B. *The C++ Programming Language*, Second Edition, Reading, MA, Addison-Wesley, 1992, p. 13.

management, and error handling. Let's look at if and how C++ addresses each of these deficiencies.

Avoid the Preprocessor

There are reasonable uses of the preprocessor, such as:

```
#define PI          3.14159f
#define TABSIZE     3
#define WINAPI      _far _pascal
#define CALLBACK    _far _pascal
#define FALSE       0
#define TRUE        1
#include <windows.h>
```

and there are unreasonable uses of the preprocessor, for instance this entry by Lennart Augustsson from the 1985 Obfuscated C Code Contest:

august.c

```
#define p struct c
#define q struct b
#define h a->a
#define i a->b
#define e i->c
#define o a=(*b->a)(b->b,b->c)
#define s return a;}q*
#define n (d,b)p*b;{q*a;p*c;
#define z(t)(t*)malloc(sizeof(t))
q{int a;p{q*(*a)();int b;p*c;}*b;};q*u n a=z(q);h=d;i=z(p);
i->a=u;i->b=d+1;s
v n c=b;do o,b=i;while(!(h%d));i=c;i->a=v;i->b=d;e=b;s
w n o;c=i;i=b;i->a=w;e=z(p);e->a=v;e->b=h;e->c=c;s
t n for(;;)o,main(-h),b=i;}
main(b){p*a;if(b>0)a=z(p),h=w,a->c=z(p),a->c->a=u,
a->c->b=2,t(0,a);putchar(b?main(b/2),-b%2+'0':10);}
```

How does C++ help us with this kind of stuff? First, it often refuses to compile this sort of abuse of the preprocessor. And second, it offers us alternatives to **#define**. This particular code does compile as C, but not as C++, using MSC, and it even runs for a while: it prints a table of the primes in binary until it runs out of stack.

I don't want to imply that C++ is a cure-all for bad style and bad code: it isn't. You can write spaghetti FORTRAN in any language, if you're sufficiently perverse. But C++ at least offers you some viable alternatives to tying the preprocessor in knots. Actually, the C++ design philosophy was "to allow you to express more things conveniently and efficiently" more than it was to "prevent you from writing 'bad' code the way paternalistic languages such as Pascal and Ada" do.[3]

---

[3] Bjarne Stroustrup, private communication.

To understand how we can benefit from an alternative to **#define**, let's return to a simple, reasonable example:

```
#define PI 3.14159f
```

This is good C style, because pretty much anyone reading **PI** in the body of a program will correctly guess its meaning and usage. But the compiler proper will never even see **PI**—it will only see the substitution **3.14159f** emitted by the preprocessor. That means that **PI** never gets into the compiler's symbol table, that **PI** will never appear in an error message (the numeric substitution will appear instead), and that **PI** will not be viewable from a debugger.[4]

What does C++ offer as an alternative? Try this:

```
const float PI = 3.14159f;
```

Using this definition, **PI** is an authentic compiler symbol, it is properly typed **float**, and your code can't change it since **PI** is declared **const**. Note that the **#define** form, while inferior to **const**, is still legal: C++ doesn't forbid it, it just allows you to write something better.

Another hazard of **#define** is in the declaration of macros that look like functions, but which have unintentional side effects. For instance, it is common to see something like

```
#define SQR(x) (x) * (x)
```

written for efficiency. What happens when we take **SQR(y++)**? Reading the expression as a function you'd expect it to return the original value of **y**, squared, and leave **y** incremented by one. What it will actually do is return **y*(y+1)** and leave **y** incremented by two.

What C++ offers us instead of a macro, as an efficient alternative to a full-blown function call, is an **inline** function. For the simple case of **SQR(x)** we can define:

```
inline int SQR(int x) { return x*x; }
inline double SQR(double x) { return x*x; }
```

If the compiler is willing, each call to an **inline** function will be turned into some time-efficient code in the linear instructions stream rather than into a less time-efficient call to an external function body. If the compiler isn't willing to inline a given function (for whatever reason), it will generate a normal call to a function body.

You'll note that I've made two strongly typed **inline** definitions of **SQR**, one for integers and one for doubles. In C, this would be an error because of the name

---

[4] The gist of this discussion was suggested by the section *Use **const** and **inline** instead of **#define*** in *Effective C++* by Scott Meyers.

conflict. In C++, each function name is *dressed* or *mangled* to include information about its argument and return types, to allow just this kind of *overloading*.

The compiler decides which declaration to use for a given instance by applying a set of pattern-matching and promotion rules to the arguments. Writing **SQR('c')** would cause the compiler to promote **'c'** from **char** to **int** and then to generate inline code using the **int** version of **SQR**.

Writing **SQR(3.14f)** does not, as you might expect, cause the compiler to promote **f** from **float** to **double** and then to generate inline code using the **double** version of **SQR**. The compiler doesn't know whether to increase the precision from **float** to **double** or decrease it to **int**, so it generates an error message. If you wanted to be lazy and use the **double** form of **SQR** for a **float** variable, you could add an explicit cast; but it would be much better to go ahead and add the **float** version of **SQR**.

In an ideal world, I would only have to write one version of **SQR**—there would be a compiler facility to help generate all the variations. In fact there is, on paper if not in every implementation: C++ offers the *template* facility to help you avoid writing lots of identical functions with different argument types. Templates also provide data abstraction in the original sense of the term: you write one piece of code for an abstract data type, which is instantiated for several actual data types.

One more comment on overloading is in order here. Overloaded functions are good in that they supply a consistent and type-safe interface. At the same time, they can be confusing to people trying to read or reuse your code, because they hide their type information. C++ allows you to write better code than you could in C—but it also allows you to write an obfuscated mess.

Pointers and References

In C, a function can't modify its arguments: the function works with a copy of the argument, which is *passed by value*. Of course, the function can return a value as well. That's all well and good if you are working with one-word types, but can involve massive overhead if you pass structures.

To allow a C function to modify a value, you have to pass a pointer to the value. That works, and the generated code is efficient, but the source code is ugly and often difficult to read. The quest for efficient parameter passing in C leads to code that abounds in indirection, full of constructions like ***p**, **p->member**, **p[i]**, **&array[0]**, and worse.

C++ adds the FORTRAN-ish mechanism of calling by reference, which combines the efficiency of pointers with more readable code. Consider:

```
typedef struct tagWINDEBUGINFO
{
    UINT     flags;
    DWORD    dwOptions;
    DWORD    dwFilter;
```

```
      char      achAllocModule[8];
      DWORD     dwAllocBreak;
      DWORD     dwAllocCount;
} WINDEBUGINFO;

typedef WINDEBUGINFO WDI;

WDI SetDebugOptions(DWORD dw,WDI w1,WDI *w2, WDI& w3)
{
      w1.dwOptions  = dw; //w1 passed by value
      w2->dwOptions = dw; //w2 passed as pointer
      w3.dwOptions  = dw; //w3 passed by reference
      return w1;    //return w1 by value
}
```

What's happening here? The code involving **w1** causes the entire structure to be copied twice: once to pass the value of **w1**, and once to return the new value. The code involving **w2** is much more efficient: the pointer is copied, and the options are updated in place. We accept the shorthand **w2->dwOptions** as an abbreviation for **(*w2).dwOptions** through long experience with C, and we put up wearily with reading more complicated pointer expressions for lack of a better alternative.

Now, what about the code involving **w3**? In the function body, it looks just like the code involving **w1**. However, the construction **WDI& w3** in the argument list tells the C++ compiler that **w3** is passed by reference; consequently, the code generated for handling **w3** is nearly identical to the code generated for handling **w2**.

You might be thinking to yourself "Oh, pointers aren't so bad. I'm used to them." But I'll bet you can think of many times you've been faced with a pointer expression you couldn't read, and many times you've had to write a pointer expression several times before you got it right. It can be especially challenging reading Windows pointer code.

Try reading these rather basic functions, which allocate and free a matrix on the Windows global heap:

```
#include <windows.h>
typedef double FAR * LPDOUBLE;
typedef LPFLOAT FAR * LPLPFLOAT;
typedef LPDOUBLE FAR * LPLPDOUBLE;
extern double far * far * dmatrix(int nrl,int nrh,int ncl,
      int nch,unsigned short *ph);
extern void free_dmatrix(double far * far * m,int nrl,
      int nrh,unsigned short h);
int NUMERICAL_ERROR=0;

void nrerror(char error_text[])
{
  NUMERICAL_ERROR++;
  MessageBox(NULL,
```

```
        (LPSTR)error_text,
        (LPSTR)"CAUTION: Numerical Error",
        (WORD)MB_OK|MB_ICONEXCLAMATION);
  return;
}

LPLPDOUBLE dmatrix(int nrl, int nrh, int ncl, int nch, PHANDLE
ph)
{
 int i;
 LPLPDOUBLE m;
 LPHANDLE pH1;

        if((*ph=GlobalAlloc(GMEM_MOVEABLE,(DWORD)(nrh-nrl+1)
                *(sizeof(LPDOUBLE)+sizeof(HANDLE))))==NULL)
                nrerror("allocation failure 1 in dmatrix()");
        else
                m=(LPLPDOUBLE)GlobalLock(*ph);
        m -= nrl;
        pH1=(LPHANDLE)(&m[nrh+1]);

        for(i=nrl;i<=nrh;i++) {
                if((*pH1=GlobalAlloc(GMEM_MOVEABLE,
                        (DWORD)(nch-ncl+1)*sizeof(double)))==NULL)
                        nrerror("allocation failure 2 in dmatrix()");
                else
                        m[i]=(LPDOUBLE)GlobalLock(*pH1++);
                m[i] -= ncl;
                }
        return m;
}

void free_dmatrix(LPLPDOUBLE m, int nrl, int nrh, HANDLE h)
{
 int i;
 LPHANDLE pH1;

        pH1=(LPHANDLE)&m[nrh+1];
        for(i=nrh;i>=nrl;i-,pH1++) {
                if(!GlobalUnlock(*pH1))
                        GlobalFree(*pH1);
                if(!GlobalUnlock(h))
                        GlobalFree(h);
                }
}
```

Once you are familiar with C++, you might want to take the code above as the springboard for an exercise: turn **dmatrix** and **free_dmatrix** into the constructor and destructor, respectively, of a C++ matrix class. How much more readable is your final C++ code than this C code? Can you measure a speed difference between your C++ code and this C code? Which is faster? Why? Try porting each version to Windows NT. Which is easier to port?

Unsafe Unions

Unions are another oft-abused C facility. How often have you seen code that used a union to defeat type-checking? For instance:

```
union sleazy_hack {
      int i;
      char *p;
      float f;
      } ush;

int ival = SOME_CONSTANT;
char *pval;
float fval;

      ush.i= ival;
      pval = ush.p; //probably will cause a fault
      fval = ush.f; //probably will not be a valid number
```

What's wrong with this code? Just about everything. It blithely assumes that the representation of some integer constant will have some meaning as a data pointer and as a floating point value.

Stroustrup gives an example of a useful union in *The C++ Programming Language*, section 5.4.6; the union holds lexical tokens for a C compiler. Even Bjarne's example is fraught with difficulties. Another useful union is in the SREGS structure used by many MS-DOS C compilers to represent the Intel 80x86 register set: since the byte registers AL and AH really do use the two halves of the word register AX, a union actually is the appropriate data structure. On the other hand, if you don't need to see a change to AL reflected in the lower half of AX, the union notation just makes the code harder to read and write than a simple **struct**.

How does C++ help save us from unsafe unions? As far as I can tell, it doesn't. Stroustrup's lexical token example evolves quickly from unions to class constructors and destructors, but the C++ language is sufficiently compatible with C that the sort of nonsense typified by **union sleazy_hack** can make it into compiled code.

I guess it all just goes to show that you can write FORTRAN in any language. In FORTRAN, the equivalent sleazy hack is done with EQUIVALENCE statements.

Type Safety and The Perils of `printf` and `scanf`

FORTRAN, of course, also gave us the READ, PRINT, and FORMAT statements. In C, the READ and FORMAT are rolled into the **scanf** library routine, while PRINT and FORMAT are rolled into the **printf** library routine.

What remains wrong with **printf**, **scanf**, and their brethren is that (1) you must manually match format strings to variable types,[5] and (2) you can't use them to print a user-defined type. C++ gives us **iostream** instead.

---

[5] Format strings themselves are useful but archaic and less than natural. If I had a nickel for every time I messed up a format string width and precision . . .

Meyers makes an eloquent case for the benefits of << and >> over C standard I/O functions in *Effective C++*, section 2; Meyer's argument appears to be loosely based on Stroustrup's exposition of streams in Chapter 10 of *The C++ Programming Language*. The overloaded << and >> operators are *type-safe*, flexible, and extensible. They don't, however, do you much good when you're writing display or printing code for Windows or Win32.[6]

The need to manually match **%s** to a **char *** and **%d** to an **int** implies that **printf** and **scanf** are not type-safe. I'm afraid that "type-safe" is one of the more abused terms in the object-oriented lexicon (second only to *object-oriented* itself);[7] it means that the compiler and linker enforce strong typing.

Perhaps an example will make this clearer. Suppose we have two separately compiled modules written in K&R C:

Module 1

```
main() {
int x;
float y;
      y=f(x);
      printf("%d",y);
}
```

Module 2

```
int f(double y) {
      return((int)floor(y*y));
}
```

I'm sure you're already laughing at the errors: the mismatch in function **f**'s argument and return types between modules as well as the mismatch between the **%d** format string and the **float** value **y** in the **printf** statement. As I'm sure you know, K&R compilers allow such errors to pass uncommented.

ANSI C compilers will complain of an undeclared function **f** in module 1, but it will be at a warning level rather than an error level. C++ compilers will refuse to compile the **y=f(x)** line until you've added a prototype for **f**; then they'll generate a decorated name for **f** that reflects its argument and return types, so that linkages with mismatched arguments simply won't be resolved. What I'm saying is that C++ will protect you from this kind of error at compile time and link time: C will let you find it at runtime, if you're lucky.

---

[6] While Microsoft supplies **iostream** classes with both their 16-bit and 32-bit compilers, **cin** and **cout** are bound to **stdin** and **stdout**, which are less than meaningful in a true Windows application. It is possible, as noted in the Microsoft **iostream** documentation, for a knowledgeable C++ programmer to derive custom stream classes that interact directly with the Windows environment, but it isn't easy. You can, of course, use **iostream** classes freely for disk I/O from Windows or Win32.

[7] Type safety is an important feature of C++. I object only to the overuse of the term in "OOP" (Object-Oriented Programming) jargon.

Even C++ won't necessarily find the type mismatch in the **printf** format string at compile time. That is why **cout << y**, in which the type of **y** is automatically applied to the output format, is preferable to **printf**.

Dynamic Memory Management

In standard C, as you know, dynamic memory management is done with the **malloc** and **free** library functions. In 16-bit Windows the native dynamic memory management functions are **LocalAlloc**, **GlobalAlloc**, **LocalLock**, **GlobalLock**, **LocalUnlock**, **GlobalUnlock**, **LocalFree**, and **GlobalFree**. In Win32, any of the above can be used.

In C++, you don't have to fuss with any of that stuff. In any environment you use **new** and **delete**, and you rely on the compiler library to call the appropriate underlying system functions.

It gets better: **new** automatically determines the size of the structure you wish to allocate, so you don't have to code silly repetitive things like **sizeof(x)**. You do, however, have to remember to use the array form of **delete** if you used **new** to allocate an array. For instance:

```
const int ARRAY_SIZE = 20;
float *x = new float;
float *Array = new float[ARRAY_SIZE];
//...
delete x;
delete[] Array;
```

Even keeping **delete** and **delete[]** straight needn't be a problem, as you can hide the complicated parts of your memory management inside class definitions. Secondary memory allocations go in the class *constructor*, and secondary deallocations go in the class *destructor*.

Error Handling

The C language has limited error-handling capabilities. The standard C library offers **signal**, which allows you to declare functions to handle seven major error conditions,[8] and allows you to have the system ignore selected error conditions. The C library also offers the **setjmp** and **longjmp** function pair for nonlocal jumps, which are sometimes used to handle more predictable synchronous error conditions, like being unable to find a file.

---

[8]
SIGABRT	Abnormal termination
SIGFPE	Floating-point error
SIGILL	Illegal instruction
SIGINT	CTRL+C signal
SIGSEGV	Illegal storage access
SIGTERM	Termination request

I find **setjmp** and **longjmp** among the least readable and most unsafe C functions. The mechanism used is just returning to a saved stack frame, so that the code immediately following a **setjmp** has to distinguish between normal execution (the **setjmp** just happened) or abnormal execution (a **longjmp** returned to the point immediately after the **setjmp**). It's incredibly difficult to write safe **longjmp** code: there always seems to be something that isn't cleaned up properly.

Not every environment and operating system supports **signal**, **setjmp**, and **longjmp**. In Windows 3.x, for instance, **signal** is supported, but the kernel API functions **catch** and **throw** replace the library functions **setjmp** and **longjmp**. Some other systems fail to support **signal** for lack of a hardware exception mechanism.

The errors caught by **signal** handlers are generally serious problems that would otherwise cause the program to crash. The errors handled by **setjmp**/**longjmp** or Windows' **catch**/**throw** need not be fatal: if they are not handled, the program can often manage to bumble along for a while without doing any serious damage.

The ANSI C++ exception-handling mechanism, which is so new that it hasn't been implemented properly in most compilers as of this writing,[9] uses a structured **throw**/**catch** mechanism with **try** blocks. Called functions can **throw** named exceptions (note that the C++ **throw** and **catch** keywords are quite distinct from the Windows **throw** and **catch** kernel functions) when passed bad arguments or encountering other error conditions; calling functions can declare their interest in handling such exceptions by enclosing the code that might trigger them in a **try** block followed by **catch** block. When a function throws an exception, the C++ runtime library looks for the lowest-level handler for the exception, starting with the immediate calling function and working back. If there is no **try** block in scope, the exception is passed back to the default handler, which will terminate the program.

Windows NT has its own structured exception-handling mechanism that is similar in philosophy and nomenclature but different in implementation from ANSI C++ exceptions. NT also has a termination-handling mechanism. Both mechanisms are language-independent: they are not specific to C++. In fact, they work in Microsoft C for Windows NT as well as C++.

The Windows NT exception handling mechanism uses a **try** block followed by an **except** block. The termination handling mechanism uses a **try** block followed by a **finally** block. Be careful: Windows NT's **try** might look a bit like ANSI C++ **try**, but it does *not* use the C++ **throw** or **catch**. We'll explain and demonstrate exception and termination handling in a later chapter.

Just to add to the confusion, the Microsoft Foundation Classes include a set of classes derived from **CException**, which implement a variation on the ANSI C++

---

[9] According to Stroustrup, ANSI C++ exceptions are currently implemented in compilers from IBM (for the RS/6000) and HP/USL.

exception handling mechanism with heavy reliance on the macros **TRY**, **THROW**, and **CATCH**. Note that these macros are uppercased, and the Windows NT **try**, **except**, and **finally** keywords are lowercased.

For reasons of efficiency, we'll prefer the Windows NT system-level structured exception- and termination-handling mechanisms to the MFC macros throughout this book, except when portability is of paramount importance. If ANSI-standard exceptions were available and built into a C++ for Windows NT in an efficient way, they might be an option—but they aren't as of this writing.

I think that's probably enough about the subject of C++ as a better C. Let's move on to Bjarne's second goal.

"Support Data Abstraction"

Data abstraction is another abused member of object-oriented lexicon. It's basically an outgrowth of the modular programming style, and of the precept of information hiding as a strategy to insure maintainable code.

Let's go back to basics for a few minutes. You certainly know that if you want to describe some sort of real-world object in C, you can usually represent it as a data structure. And you know that once you have data structures that reflect enough of the properties of the real-world object you need to model, you can apply algorithms that manipulate the data structures and wind up with a program. So you know what data abstraction is, at least in principle.

An Isotope Inventory in C

Even though you know all that, let's work through a concrete example just to have something to talk about. Suppose we need to write an inventory program that will track a nuclear reactor facility's stock of isotopes. We can describe each isotope with a structure:

```
struct isotope {
        char element[3];
        int atomic_number;
        int atomic_weight;
        float half_life;
        struct isotope *pDecaysTo;
        struct isotope *pNextIsotope;
        struct isotope_stock *pStockOfThisIsotope;
        };
```

And we can describe our stock of each isotope with another structure:

```
struct isotope_stock {
```

```
        double grams;
        long as_of_date;
        long as_of_time;
        enum location_number stock_location;
        struct isotope *pIsotope;
        struct isotope_stock *pNextStockOfThisIsotope;
        }
```

We need to define some operations: setting an isotope's properties, adding an isotope to stock, removing an isotope from stock, and calculating the decay of an isotope over time. The decay involves decreasing the stock of the mother isotope, and adding stock of a daughter isotope, then updating the inventory time for the mother.[10] You need to maintain multiple stock records for each isotope to reflect the different locations: in the reactor, in the chemistry area, in the separation facility, and so on. You also need to maintain multiple stock records when there are decays, so that you can update the times and amounts properly.

It's clear that we can do all that in C. We'd have one module, perhaps ISOTOPE.C, that contained all the isotope functions: **define_isotope**, **add_isotope**, **remove-**
_isotope, **decay_isotope**. Then we'd have a design decision to make.

Data Hiding in C

We could allow other modules to access the members of the **isotope_stock** and **isotope** stuctures, or we could hide the members. Allowing other modules to see the structure definitions automatically allows them to change the structure members. That makes it relatively simple for a module to get the current inventory of an isotope, by looking at the **grams** field of the right structure instance. On the other hand, this set of structures with pointers among them is just complicated enough that not everybody would write the code correctly every time: we'd really like to keep the maintainance of the pointers to ourselves.

In addition, we don't want some user-written module to accidentally change the value of the half-life of Americium or "accidentally" reduce the stock of weapons-grade Plutonium by 10 kilograms. Which means that we have to hide the structures, and write functions to initialize the structure lists, to set and retrieve values, and all that stuff. Anyone should be able to call the query function

```
double get_current_stock_of_isotope(element,
      atomic_number, atomic_weight);
```

but only trusted code, run by trusted users, leaving a verifiable audit trail, should be able to change the inventory amounts.

---

[10] In real life there can be multiple decay paths. We'll defer that detail until later.

Data Hiding in C++: The `class`

What we need is a structure that can't be accessed indiscriminately, a structure that has associated with it some public functions and some private functions. And that, dear reader, is what C++ calls a **class**.

C allows you to code with data hiding in mind; C++ actually supports data hiding. The C++ class is a *user-defined type*: it not only has its own data structure, but it has its own functions and operators, which can be made to look like ordinary arithmetic operators, if that is appropriate. Another term for a user-defined type is an *abstract data type*. Using such types is called *data abstraction*.

User-defined operators help to take the sting out of data hiding. For instance, you could, as part of the **isotope_stock** class, define the **+=** operation to increment the stock of an isotope at a location by some amount and return the new inventory, passing the stock by reference:[11]

```
double operator+=(isotope_stock& is,const double add)
{
        is.grams += add;
        return(is.grams);
}
```

Then you could express adding stock in an intuitive way that looks just like ordinary incrementation:

```
isotope_stock is;
double dAmt;

        is += dAmt;
```

With simple syntax like that, it is no burden at all if the caller is unable to access the **grams** member directly. This protects us against accidental overwriting of the private data member, although it does not protect us against deliberate misuse of the public operator. We'd express hiding the data representation and exposing the addition operator when we declare the class:

```
enum location {received, reactor, daughter,
            cells, refined, dock, shipped};

class isotope_stock {
        double grams;
        long as_of_date;
```

---

[11] Operator overloading requires more space than we can give it here. I recommend that you consult Stroustrup if you're not already comfortable with the concept.

```
        long as_of_time;
        location stock_location;
        isotope& Isotope;
        isotope_stock* pNextStockOfThisIsotope;
        isotope_stock* pPreviousStock;

//NOTE: everything above 'public' is private by default *
public:
        //constructor declaration
        isotope_stock(double g,long d, long t, location s,
                isotope& i, isotope_stock* previous);
        //destructor declaration
        ~isotope_stock();
        //addition declaration
        friend double operator+(isotope_stock& is,const double add);
        //<more declarations here>
        friend class isotope;   //isotope class members have access
        }; //class isotope_stock

//constructor implementation: initialize and add to linked list
isotope_stock::isotope_stock(double g,long d, long t, location s,
        isotope& i, isotope_stock* previous) {
        grams=g;
        as_of_date=d;
        as_of_time=t;
        stock_location=s;
        Isotope = i;
        pNextStockOfThisIsotope=0;
        pPreviousStock=previous;
        if(previous) {
                pNextStockOfThisIsotope
                        =previous->pNextStockOfThisIsotope;
                previous->pNextStockOfThisIsotope=this;
                }
        }

//destructor: remove from linked list
isotope_stock::~isotope_stock() {
        if(pPreviousStock)
        pPreviousStock->pNextStockOfThisIsotope
                =pNextStockOfThisIsotope;
        if(pNextStockOfThisIsotope)
        pNextStockOfThisIsotope->pPreviousStock
                =pPreviousStock;
        }
```

---

* It's important for you to know that a **class** is private by default and a **struct** is public by default, just as it is important to know the precedence of operators. On the other hand, you can be of service to people reading your classes by explicitly specifying your **private** section, just as you can sometimes make your mathematical code more readable by judiciously adding parentheses.

There are several things to understand here. Let's start with the options for class member access control. The ARM (*The Annotated C++ Reference Manual*) tells us that a member of a class can be

- **private**; that is, its name can be used only by member functions and friends of the class in which it is declared.
- **protected**; that is, its name can be used only by member functions and friends of the class in which it is declared and by member functions and friends of classes derived from this class.
- **public**; that is, its name can be used by any function.

In a C++ **struct**, members are public by default; in a **class**, members are private by default. Note that a C++ **struct** can do quite a bit more than a C **struct**. C++ is "as close to C as possible, but no closer."[12]

Constructors and Destructors

The function **isotope_stock()** is a *member* of **class isotope_stock**. The names are the same: that means that **isotope_stock()** is a *constructor*, which you can think of as a function that turns the class structure from raw memory into a valid object. **~isotope_stock()**, on the other hand, is the *destructor* for the class, which turns the object back into raw memory. You'll note that we've built the overhead of maintaining a doubly linked list into the class constructor and destructor. The allocation and deallocation of raw memory for a class object are handled automatically by the compiler or the runtime library, depending on whether the object is automatic, static, or dynamic.

As you'd expect, knowing C, an automatic variable is allocated on the stack when it comes into scope and popped off the stack when it goes out of scope. In C++, coming into scope also invokes a constructor, and going out of scope also invokes a destructor.

Static variables are allocated before control is passed to **main()**, and deallocated after a **return**, **exit**, or after **main()** goes out of scope. Constructors for static variables are therefore invoked before **main()** begins, and destructors for static variables are invoked after **main()** ends.

Dynamic variables in C++ are allocated using **new** and deallocated using **delete**. Constructors are invoked automatically after **new** allocates memory, and destructors are invoked automatically before **delete** deallocates memory.

Operators, Members, and Friends

In our example above we declared **double operator+(isotope_stock& is, const double add)** a **friend** of **class isotope_stock**. What's the difference

---

[12] "As close to C as possible, but no closer" is, among other things, the title of a paper in the July/August 1989 issue of the *C++ Report* by Bjarne Stroustrup and Andy Koenig.

between a member function, a friend function, and an operator? Does it matter which you use?

A member function is an actual part of a class, and has access to all of the other members of the class, even private members. A friend function is *not* a part of the class, but still has access to all the members of the class, even private members. A member function is inherited by derived classes (we'll explain inheritance in the next section), but a friend function is not inherited.

An operator is just a special kind of function: most operators can either be a member of a class or a friend of the class. There are a few exceptions: certain standard operators are always members of the class.

There are two reasons to make an operator a friend rather than a member of a class. The first reason is that an operator might need to work with more than one class at the implementation level: the classic example is a multiplication operator that gives the dot product of a matrix and a vector, which needs to access both the vector and matrix elements directly for efficiency. The second reason is that an operator might not be appropriate to inherit: making it a friend precludes inheritance, and precludes the use of a virtual function.

"Support Object-Oriented Programming"

Inheritance and virtual functions are at the core of the way C++ supports object-oriented programming. Before we explain what they are, let's see why we need them.

We saw something of the expressive power of user data types when we defined the **isotope** and **isotope_stock** classes. Let's consider the **isotope** class further.

We defined one fairly simple structure to represent an isotope. Suppose we now need to implement the function that calculates the decay of the isotope over time. We'll need to add a **decay** function to the class, which might now look like:

```
class isotope {
     char element[3];
     int atomic_number;
     int atomic_weight;
     float half_life;
     struct isotope *pDecaysTo;
     struct isotope *pNextIsotope;
     struct isotope_stock *pStockOfThisIsotope;
public:
     decay(time_t t);
     };
```

Since the **decay** function is a member of the class, and the **isotope** class is a friend of **isotope_stock**, the function should be able to navigate the list of stocks through the **pStockOfThisIsotope** pointer. But there's a problem: while many isotopes decay by only one mechanism, some isotopes decay with multiple mechanisms or into multiple channels. That means, unfortunately, that the single **pDecaysTo** pointer is inadequate for some isotopes.

Well, we could add extra pointers to accommodate more decay paths, and an integer to tell us how many decay paths are in use. We could additionally add a **float** to hold the percentage of the decay that goes into each path. The net effect would be that we'd have a bloated structure with a lot of elements unused in most instances, and we'd have an unnecessarily complicated **decay** function with all sorts of internal logic to handle different cases.

To quote Stroustrup, describing a simpler example:[13]

> *This is a mess. Functions such as **draw()** must "know about" all the kinds of shapes there are. Therefore the code for any such function grows each time a new shape is added to the system. If you define a new shape, every operation on a shape must be examined and (possibly) modified. You are not able to add a new shape to a system unless you have access to the source code for every operation.*

Substitute **decay()** for **draw()** and *isotope* for *shape* above and you'll have a succinct statement of our dilemma: to wit, data abstraction can be inflexible. The solution is to allow *inheritance*—something C++ borrowed from Simula.

Basically, we want to proceed from the general to the specific. All isotopes have an atomic weight and an atomic number. Some isotopes—the radionuclides—decay. Some radionuclides decay by emitting an α (alpha) particle (a ^{4}He nucleus), some by emitting a β^- (beta) particle (an electron), some by emitting a β^+ particle (a positron), and some by capturing an electron. Excited daughter nuclei emit γ (gamma) rays (photons) in a process called an isomeric transition when they decay to a lower energy state. They may also emit internal conversion electrons. The details of these decay processes are fascinating if you happen to have been trained in nuclear physics; I'll spare you the gory details.[14] Even without understanding the physics, you can certainly understand the interest one might have in calculating the emitted radioactivity as well as the updated isotope inventories.

---

[13] Stroustrup, B., op. cit., pp. 20-21.

[14] I was trained as a particle physicist, but worked at New England Nuclear Corporation for several years as a nuclear and accelerator physicist. I've introduced this admittedly rather knotty example because (1) I *know* the subject area and (2) I'm sick of the very simple **class shape** example that Stroustrup uses. Physicists note: I have deliberately left out some of the more interesting complexities of the subject, such as neutrino emission and forbidden transitions, to avoid totally losing the general reader.

How would we relate the underlying physics of the problem to a class design? Our *base class* is the **isotope**. From the base **isotope** class we can *derive* classes describing α-emitters, β⁻-emitters, and so on. β⁻-emitters with two branches can have their own *subclass* derived from plain β⁻-emitters. Finally, each isotope will have its own *instance* of one of these classes. The instance is also known as an *object*. This whole way of thinking about hierarchical classes is called *object-oriented programming*.

Let's stop and look at the class hierarchy as it stands:

```
#include <string.h>

class isotope {
      short int atomic_weight;    //A
      short int atomic_number;    //Z
      char name[3];
      //other stuff common to all isotopes would go here
      //such as the pointers to stock (which might need to
      //be protected rather than private
      //...
public:
      //constructor
      isotope(short int aw,short int an,char *szN);
      //read-only access function for private members
      char * get_isotope(short int& A,short int&Z,char *nm);
//the interface for decay() can be defined for the base clase,
//but the implementation cannot: therefore make it virtual
      virtual double decay(time_t); //return fraction decayed
      //...
      };

class stable_nuclide: public isotope {
public:
      stable_nuclide();
      double decay(time_t) {return 1.0; }; //isotope is stable
      };

class radionuclide: public isotope {
protected:
      double half_life; //in seconds
      isotope *daughter;
public:
      radionuclide();
//put common functionality for all radionuclides here
      double decay(time_t t);
      //...
      };

class alpha_emitter: public radionuclide {
protected:
```

```
        float alpha_energy;
public:
        alpha_emitter();
        double decay(time_t t);
        //...
        };

class beta_minus_emitter: public radionuclide {
protected:
        float beta_minus_energy;
public:
        beta_minus_emitter();
        double decay(time_t t);
        //...
        };

class beta_plus_emitter: public radionuclide {
protected:
        float beta_plus_energy;
public:
        beta_plus_emitter();
        double decay(time_t t);
        //...
        };

class electron_capturer: public radionuclide {
protected:
        float captured_electron_energy;
public:
        electron_capturer();
        double decay(time_t t);
        //...
        };

class isomeric_transition: public radionuclide {
protected:
        float gamma_energy;
public:
        isomeric_transition();
        double decay(time_t t);
        //...
        };

class two_branch_beta: public beta_minus_emitter {
        double larger_fraction;
        isotope *daughter2; //second isomeric state
        float energy2;
public:
        two_branch_beta();
        double decay(time_t t);
        //...
        };
isotope::isotope(short int aw,short int an,char *szN) {
```

```
            if(aw<1 || an<1 || aw>260 || an>130)
                    throw range();
//NB: throw not supported in some current C++ compilers
            atomic_weight=aw;
            atomic_number=an;
            if(szN) strncpy(name,szN,3);
            else throw null_element();
//NB: throw not supported in some current C++ compilers
            };

char * isotope::get_isotope(short int& A,short int&Z,char *nm) {
            A=atomic_weight;
            Z=atomic_number;
            if(nm) strcpy(nm,name);
            return nm;
            };

double radionuclide::decay(time_t t) {
            //do actual exponential decay calculation
            double f=1.0;
            //use time and half_life to calculate decay fraction
            //...
            return f;
            };

double alpha_emitter::decay(time_t t) {
            //rely on base class to do math
            double f = radionuclide::decay(t);
            //update amount of mother isotope and
            //amount of daughter isotope (Z-2,A-4)
            //...
            //emit alpha
            //...
            return f;
            };

double beta_minus_emitter::decay(time_t t) {
            //rely on base class to do math
            double f = radionuclide::decay(t);
            //update amount of mother isotope and
            //amount of daughter isotope (Z+1,A)
            //...
            //emit electron
            //...
            return f;
            };

double beta_plus_emitter::decay(time_t t) {
            //rely on base class to do math
            double f = radionuclide::decay(t);
            //update amount of mother isotope and
            //amount of daughter isotope (Z-1,A)
            //...
```

```
      //emit positron
      //...
      return f;
      };

double electron_capturer::decay(time_t t) {
      //rely on base class to do math
      double f = radionuclide::decay(t);
      //update amount of mother isotope and
      //amount of daughter isotope (Z-1,A)
      //...
      //absorb electron
      //...
      return f;
      };

double isomeric_transition::decay(time_t t) {
      //rely on base class to do math
      double f = radionuclide::decay(t);
      //update amount of mother isotope and
      //amount of daughter isomer (Z, A)
      //...
      //emit gamma rays
      //...
      return f;
      };

double two_branch_beta::decay(time_t t) {
      //rely on base class to do math
      double f = radionuclide::decay(t);
      //update amount of mother isotope and
      //amount of daughter isotopes (Z+1,A)
      //...
      //emit electron fracton of proper energy for
      //each branch
      //...
      return f;
      };
```

We still have a problem. (Pardon me if this gets too technical. This is real life, and in real life details have a nasty habit of getting technical and messing up the computer scientist's happy simplifications.) The 71.9 second halflife state of Indium isotope ^{114}In decays by β^--emission to the Tin isotope ^{114}Sn 99.46% of the time, and by electron capture to the Cadmium isotope ^{114}Cd 0.54% of the time.[15]

---

[15] There is also a 49.51 day halflife state of ^{114}In, which decays to the shortlived form of ^{114}In by isomeric transition 95.5% of the time, and by electron capture to ^{114}Cd 4.5% of the time. To handle this we need to allow multiple isotope objects with different halflives, and we need to have an isotope class which inherits both from isomeric transitions and from electron capture.

How do we handle that? We have to create a special class for isotopes that decay both by β⁻-emission and electron capture. Should we derive it from the β⁻-emitters or from the electron-capturers? Actually, we want to derive it from both parents. C++ allows this: it's called *multiple inheritance*.

```
class beta_and_EC:  public beta_minus_emitter, // 2 base classes
                    public electron_capturer {
     double beta_fraction;
     isotope *daughter2; //electron capture daughter
//the beta and EC energy are inherited from the base classes
public:
     beta_and_EC();
     double decay(time_t t);
     //...
     };

double beta_and_EC::decay(time_t t) {
     //rely on base class to do math
     double f = radionuclide::decay(t); //might be ambiguous
     //update amount of mother isotope and
     //amount of daughter isotopes (Z+1,A) and
     // (Z-1,A)
     //...
     //emit and capture electron fractions
     //...
     return f;
     };
```

One aspect worth noting in this version of the **isotope** class hierarchy is the use of a **virtual** function **decay()** in the abstract base class, **isotope**, coupled with a nonvirtual function **decay()** in each of the classes derived from **isotope**. Note also that the general decay calculation is isolated at the **radionuclide** class level, and that **radionuclide::decay(t)** is explicitly invoked by the lower-level derived classes. The derived classes have to worry about the mechanics of emitting the correct particles and updating the correct isotopes, but they can rely on the **radionuclide** class to crunch the decay numbers.

We've taken the **isotope** class hierarchy as far as we need to for purposes of discussion: you should now have a good gut feeling for the meaning of all the major terms related to object-oriented programming and C++. On the other hand, you might find it a useful exercise to finish and test the class implementation yourself, and then revise the design based on any problems you find. And there are problems; oh yes, there are problems indeed.

By the way, I have no intention of using multiple inheritance in the rest of this book unless absolutely, positively necessary. C++ is complicated enough without bending your mind with the ins and outs of multiple inheritance.

Why C++?

We've seen how C++ is a better C, how it supports data abstraction, and how it supports object-oriented programming. The question remaining is what that means to us.

That C++ is a better C means that we can switch our code from C to C++ incrementally: it is not necessary to go through a long transition period, it is not necessary to rewrite or restructure all our code, and it is not necessary to adopt object-oriented programming. This one aspect of C++ has contributed to its general acceptance.

On the other hand, once we switch to C++ we can gain some leverage from data abstraction and object-oriented programming. For instance, we can hide all the differences between Win16 and Win32 in classes: or, even better, we can use a class library that already hides the differences for us.

Some would argue that the most important benefit of C++ is not its compatibility with C, but its incompatibility with C. That is, the argument goes, to get the full benefit of C++ you must liberate yourself from the modular design process and start thinking in terms of classes and objects. In the long term, that is certainly correct; in the short term, though, preserving a large base of working C code is probably a pretty important consideration for most people.

At the same time, I have to admit that reusing C code is problematic at best. Well-designed C++ classes that really encapsulate their implementation details are much easier to reuse than C functions. And maybe that's the best reason of all to make the substantial effort needed to reorganize functions into objects.

Why Not C++?

That is not to imply that there aren't costs and risks involved in switching to C++. First of all, it's hard: C++ is a much bigger language than C, with many more subtle nooks and crannies to master. Second, many new C++ projects fail for lack of restraint, a side effect of the enthusiasm with which converts embrace a new religion.

Yes, I think object-oriented programming is a religion. I've seen programming religions come and go: structured programming, modular programming, top–down programming, bottom-up programming. Each religion has its obvious merits; none is complete, permanent, or perfect. Some people are more easily saved than others; I've seen enough of these religions rise and fall to have developed some cynicism about them, despite their attractions. It's the too-easily saved souls with a messianic gleam in their eyes and an utter lack of practical experience, who scare me.

Let me say it again: it is not necessary, or even desirable, to immerse yourself in object-oriented programming immediately and completely. Take your time, be pragmatic, learn as you go.

Remember: it's always the wrong time to have the program apart on the floor. Sure, you want to clean it up, but not at the expense of having it never work right again. At the same time, you *do* want to clean it up to improve its long-term maintainability and reusability. Distinguish between your real short-term goals, your real long-term goals, and your natural impulse to throw out all that old code and start fresh.

You'll need new design skills if you want to build your own class libraries, and you'll have to learn about other people's designs if you want to use commercial class libraries. Object-oriented programming is a new paradigm, which you can't learn just by reading a book. Do read the books, but then give yourself a chance to get comfortable with it.

When you do adopt C++ and object-oriented programming in your organization, you'll find that new social structures are needed. C programming lends itself to a horizontal division of labor by module; C++ stratifies the tasks more. There's a major difference between the skill and experience required to use a class library in an application, and the skill and experience required to design and implement a class library.

In a large enough organization, the most senior people can analyze requirements and design classes, and slightly less senior people can flesh out the classes and apply them. Truly junior people might not be allowed to do application development in this sort of environment until they've learned the ropes.

For some organizations, that's a natural division that uses the existing staff more effectively; other organizations will find themselves top- or bottom-heavy. Nevertheless, the isolation of design from implementation gained by such a structure can have long-term benefits to the organization: on the next project, you *won't* have to start from scratch.

Worldwide, the population of C++ programmers is doubling each year. That's good news for C++ tool vendors, but it also means that half of all C++ programmers have less than one year of experience. From a management point of view, that's *really* scary.

A Plan for Converting to C++

With that in mind, we can come up with several plans for converting a project from C to C++, ranging from "rewrite everything from scratch as classes" (high risk, high payoff) to "let's stick with C" (low risk, no payoff). My favorite plan for *existing* applications, because of its minimal risk and moderate payoff, is incremental switchover. It assumes you have a working application written entirely in C, with no known bugs.

For incremental switchover, you start by making backups; then you rename all your .C files to .CPP and try to rebuild your application. You edit only the files that won't compile, and you clean up only the lines that generate error messages. If you have a problem with a function that can't be cleaned up easily, you can revert that function to C, by surrounding it and its prototype with **extern "C" {   }**. Resist the temptation to restructure the code at this point; as you see modules that should become classes, write them on a list for future development.

Once you have the application rebuilt as C++ with the minimal required changes, you can start thinking about turning modules or groups of modules into classes. Spend the time to design your classes carefully, and only then start implementing them. That's where the real benefits will come, because that's the point where the code will start to become more compact, more readable, and more reusable.

If, however, you should be so fortunate as to become involved in a new project, you probably shouldn't think incrementally. Instead, you should try to design your project in as object-oriented a fashion as you can muster.

I'll let Bjarne Stroustrup have the last word on the subject of learning C++, as is only proper. He posted the following essay on BIX on December 29, 1992; it is Copyright © Bjarne Stroustrup, 1992, and reprinted here by kind permission of the author.

Learning C++

There have—under various headings—been several related discussions about the proper way to learn C++, C++'s relation to C, C++'s relation to Smalltalk, the difference (or not) between data abstraction and object-oriented programming, etc.

I think the practical concern underlying many of these discussions is: Given that I don't have much time to learn new techniques and concepts, how do I start using C++ effectively?

It is clear that to use C++ "best" in an arbitrary situation you need a deep understanding of many concepts and techniques, but that can only be achieved through years of study and experiments. It is little help to tell a novice (a novice with C++, typically not a novice with programming in general), first to gain a thorough understanding of C, Smalltalk, CLOS, Pascal, ML, Eiffel, assembler, capability based systems, OODMBSs, program verification techniques, etc., and then apply the lessons learned to C++ on his or her next project. All of those topics are worthy of study and would—in the long run—help, but practical programmers (and students) cannot take years off from whatever they are doing for a comprehensive study of programming languages and techniques.

On the other hand, most novices understand that "a little knowledge is a dangerous thing" and would like some assurance that the little they can afford time to learn before/while starting their next project will be of help and not a distraction or a hindrance to the success of that project. They would also like to be confident that the little new they can absorb immediately can be part of a path that can lead to the more comprehensive understanding actually desired rather than an isolated skill leading nowhere further.

Naturally, more than one approach can fulfill these criteria and exactly which to choose depends on the individual's background, immediate needs, and the time available. I think many educators, trainers, and posters to the net underestimate the importance of this: after all, it appears so much more cost effective—and easier—to "educate"' people in large batches rather than bothering with individuals.

Consider a few common questions:

- *I don't know C or C++, should I learn C first?*
- *I want to do OOP, should I learn Smalltalk before C++?*
- *Should I start using C++ as an OOPL or as a better C?*
- *How long does it take to learn C++?*

I don't claim to have "the (only) right answers" to these questions. As I said, the "right" answer depends on the circumstances. Most C++ textbook writers, teachers, and programmers have their own answers. For example, I seem to remember that the C++ FAQ discusses these questions.[16] My answers are based on years of programming in C++ and other languages, teaching short C++ design and programming courses (mainly to professional programmers), consulting about the introduction of and use of C++, discussing C++, and generally thinking about programming, design, and C++.

I don't know C or C++; should I learn C first?

*No. Learn C++ first. The C subset of C++ is easier to learn for C/ C++ novices and easier to use than C itself. The reason is that C++ provides better guarantees than C (stronger type checking). In addition, C++ provides many minor features, such as the **new** operator, that are notationally more convenient and less error-prone than their C alternatives. Thus, if you plan to learn C and C++ (or just C++) you shouldn't take the detour through C.*

---

[16] FAQ is an Internet acronym for Frequently Asked Questions. Most news groups post a FAQ list regularly to try to avoid having people constantly asking the same things.

To use C well, you need to know tricks and techniques that aren't anywhere near as important or common in C++ as they are in C. Good C textbooks tend (reasonably enough) to empha-size the techniques that you will need for completing major projects in C. Good C++ textbooks, on the other hand, emphasize techniques and features that lead to the use of C++ for data abstraction and object-oriented programming. Knowing the C++ constructs, their (lower-level) C alternatives are trivially learned (if necessary).

To show my inclinations:

- *To learn C use:*
  *Kernighan and Ritchie, **The C programming Language** (2nd edition), Prentice Hall, 1988 as the primary textbook.*

- *To learn C++ use:*
  *Stroustrup, **The C++ programming Language** (2nd edition), Addison-Wesley, 1991.*

Both books have the advantage of combining a tutorial pres-entation of language features and techniques with a complete reference manual. Both describe their respective languages rather than particular implementations and neither attempts to describe particular libraries shipped with particular imple-mentations.

There are many other good textbooks and many other styles of presentation, but these are my favorites for compre-hension of concepts and styles. It is always wise to look care-fully at at least two sources of information to compensate for bias and possible shortcomings.

I want to do OOP; should I learn Smalltalk before C++?

No. If you plan to use C++, learn C++. Languages such as C++, Smalltalk, Simula, CLOS, Eiffel, etc., each have their own view of the key notions of abstraction and inheritance and each support them in slightly different ways to support different notions of design. Learning Smalltalk will certainly teach you valuable lessons, but it will not teach you how to write pro-grams in C++. In fact, unless you have the time to learn and digest both the Smalltalk and the C++ concepts and techniques, using Smalltalk as a learning tool can lead to poor C++ designs.

Naturally, learning both C++ and Smalltalk so that you can draw from a wider field of experience and examples is the ideal, but people who haven't taken the time to digest all the new ideas often end up "writing Smalltalk in C++"—that is, applying Smalltalk design notions that don't fit well in C++. This can be as sub-optimal as writing C or Fortran in C++.

One reason often quoted for learning Smalltalk is that it is "pure" and thus forces people to think and program "object oriented." I will not go into the discussion about "purity" beyond mentioning that I think that a general purpose programming language ought to and can support more than one programming style ("paradigm").

The point here is that styles that are appropriate and well supported in Smalltalk are not necessarily appropriate for C++. In particular, a slavish following of Smalltalk style in C++ leads to inefficient, ugly, and hard to maintain C++ programs. The reason is that good C++ requires design that takes advantage of C++'s static type system rather than fights it. Smalltalk supports a dynamic type system (only) and that view translated into C++ leads to extensive unsafe and ugly casting.

I consider most casts in C++ programs signs of poor design. Some casts are essential, but most aren't. In my experience, old-time C programmers using C++ and C++ programmers introduced to OOP through Smalltalk are among the heaviest users of casts of the kind that could have been avoided by more careful design.

In addition, Smalltalk encourages people to see inheritance as the sole or at least primary way of organizing programs and to organize classes into single-rooted hierarchies. In C++, classes are types and inheritance is by no means the only means of organizing programs. In particular, templates is the primary means for representing container classes.

I am also deeply suspicious of arguments proclaiming the need to force *people to write in an object-oriented style. People who don't want to learn, on average, cannot be taught with reasonable effort and there is in my experience no shortage of people who* do *want to learn. Unless you manage to demonstrate the principle behind data abstraction and object-oriented programming all you'll get is inappropriate "baroque" misuses of the language features that support these notions—in C++, Smalltalk, or whatever.*

See ***The C++ Programming Language*** *(2nd Edition) and in particular Chapter 12 for a more thorough discussion of the relation between C++ language features and design.*

Should I start using C++ as an OOPL or as a better C?

That depends. Why do you want to start using C++? The answer to that question ought to determine the way you approach C++; not some one-size-fits-all philosophy. In my experience the safest bet is to learn C++ "bottom up," that is, first learn the features C++ provides for traditional procedural programming, the "better C" subset, then learn to use and appreciate the data abstraction features, and then learn to use class hierarchies to organize sets of related classes.

It is—in my opinion—dangerous to rush through the earlier stages because there is too high a probability of missing some key point.

For example, an experienced C programmer might consider the "better C" subset of C "well known" and skip the 100 pages or so of a textbook that describes it. However, in doing so he might miss the ability to overload functions, the difference between initialization and assignment, the use of the **new** *operator for allocation, the explanation of references, or some other minor feature in such a way that it will come back to haunt him at a later stage where sufficient new concepts are in play to complicate matters. If the concepts used in the better C subset are known the 100 pages will only take a couple of hours to learn and some details will be interesting and useful. If not, the time spent is essential.*

Some people have expressed fear that this "gradual approach" leads people to write in C style forever. This is of course a possible outcome, but not as likely as proponents of "pure" languages and proponents of the use of "force" in teaching programming like to believe. The key thing to realize is that using C++ well as a data abstraction and/or object-oriented language requires the understanding of a few new concepts that have no direct counterpart in languages such as C and Pascal.

C++ isn't just a new syntax for expressing the same old ideas—at least not for most programmers. This implies a need for education, rather than mere training. New concepts have to be learned and mastered through practice. Old and well-tried habits of work have to be re-evaluated, and rather than dashing off doing things "the good old way" new ways have to be considered—and often doing things a new way will be harder and more time-consuming than the old way, when tried for the first time.

The overwhelming experience is that taking the time and making the effort to learn the key data abstraction and object-oriented techniques is worth while for almost all programmers and yields benefits not just in the very long run but also on a three to twelve month timescale. There are benefits in using C++ without making this effort, but most benefits require the extra effort to learn new concepts—I would wonder why anyone not willing to make that effort would switch to C++.

*When approaching C++ for the first time, or after some time, take the time to read a good textbook or a few well chosen articles (the **C++ Report** and the **C++ Journal** contain many). Maybe also have a look at the definition or the source code of some major library and consider the techniques and concepts used. This is also a good idea for people who have used C++ for some time. Many could do with a review of the concepts and techniques. Much has happened to C++ and its associated programming and design techniques since C++ first appeared. A quick comparison of the 1st and the 2nd edition of **The C++ Programming Language** should convince anyone of that.*

How long does it take to learn C++?

Again, that depends. It depends both on your experience and on what you mean by "learning C++." The syntax and basics for writing C++ in the better C style plus defining and using a few simple classes takes a week or two for a programmer. That's the easy part. The main difficulty, and the main fun and gain comes from mastering new design and programming techniques. Most experienced programmers I have talked with quote times from a half year to one and a half years for becoming really comfortable with C++ and the key data abstraction and object-oriented techniques it supports. That assumes that they learn on the job and stay productive—usually by programming in a "less adventurous" style of C++ during that period. If one could devote full time to learning C++ one would be comfortable faster, but without actual application of the new ideas on real projects that degree of comfort could be misleading. Object-

oriented programming and object-oriented design are essentially practical—rather than theoretical—disciplines. Unapplied, or applied only to toy examples, these ideas can become dangerous "religions."

Note that learning C++ is then primarily learning programming and design techniques, not language details. Having worked through a good textbook I would suggest a book on design such as Grady Booch, **Object Oriented Design with Examples** (Benjamin Cummings, 1990), which has the nice property of having longish examples in five different languages (Ada, CLOS, C++, Smalltalk, and Object Pascal) and is therefore somewhat immune to the language bigotry that mars some design discussions. The parts of the book I like best are the presentation of the design concepts and the example chapters.

Looking at design contrasts sharply with the approach of looking very carefully at the details of the definition of C++— usually using the ARM: Ellis & Stroustrup, **The Annotated C++ Reference Manual** (Addison-Wesley, 1990), which is a book containing much useful information, but no information about how to write C++ programs. A focus on details can be very distracting and lead to poor use of the language. You wouldn't try to learn a foreign language from a dictionary and grammar, would you?

When learning C++, it is essential to keep the key design notions in mind so that one doesn't get lost in the language's technical details. That done, learning and using C++ can be both fun and productive. A little C++ can lead to significant benefits compared to C; further efforts to understand data abstraction and object-oriented techniques yield further benefits.

In which we clean up our ported
code, and think about reorganizing it as C++ code with classes.

A Higher Standard

· ·

We have a working Win32 program in IMAGE3 after the work we did in Chapter 2, but the code isn't what I'd call pretty. I'm not at all sure I'd want to maintain or expand it from this code base.

It's time to clean it up, time to adhere to a higher standard. As I hope I convinced you in Chapter 3, the higher standard is C++.

Given that we already have working code, it may or may not make sense to use an application framework like Microsoft's MFC (Microsoft Foundation Classes), Borland's OWL (Object Windows Library), or Inmark Development's zApp. You'd think that, unlike "real life," we could allow ourselves the luxury here of trying out all the application frameworks without worrying about a production schedule: but even book authors face deadlines, and the application frameworks for Windows NT are still under development as I write, making it difficult to work with any of them, much less all of them.[1]

---

[1] In particular, Borland let me know that OWL for Windows NT would be significantly different from OWL for Windows 3.1, but did not provide me with the implementation in time to include it in this chapter. Some of the later parts of this chapter talk heavily about Microsoft's MFC 2.0: I didn't have much choice under the circumstances.

So what do we need to do? First, we need to make all our code compile as C++. Then we'll try to reorganize at least some of the code we have into C++ classes and application code: that by itself will be more than a little instructive. Then we'll at least think about how much additional leverage we could get from application frameworks.

In terms of our wagon train metaphor, this chapter represents some scouting around to find the trail. We might not get where we're going in the most direct way, but we'll still get there safely.

A Better C: Image3a

As you might expect, the changes needed to make IMAGE3 compile as C++ are fairly simple, if rather boring. On the whole, there are fewer changes needed to make the bulk of the code compile as C++ than were needed to bring the code from 16-bit Windows to Win32.

One section that I could not make compile as C++ was the TIFF code. I rolled merrily along—that's a lie, I plodded grumpily along—converting K&R prototypes to ANSI prototypes. Boring, yes. Difficult, no. I could certainly have converted all the prototypes to ANSI, but I could not convert the compression hook function pointers in the **TIFF** struct:

```
typedef struct {
  charFAR *tif_name;    /* name of open file */
  short tif_fd;         /* open file descriptor */
  short tif_mode;       /* open mode (O_*) */
  char  tif_fillorder;  /* natural bit fill order for machine */
  char  tif_options;    /* compression-specific options */
  short tif_flags;
#define TIFF_DIRTYHEADER   0x1 /*header must be written on close*/
#define TIFF_DIRTYDIRECT   0x2 /*current directory must be written*/
#define TIFF_BUFFERSETUP   0x4 /* data buffers setup */
#define TIFF_BEENWRITING   0x8 /* written 1+ scanlines to file */
#define TIFF_SWAB          0x10 /* byte swap file information */
#define TIFF_NOBITREV      0x20 /* inhibit bit reversal logic */
  long  tif_diroff;     /* file offset of current directory */
  long  tif_nextdiroff; /* file offset of following directory */
  TIFFDirectory tif_dir; /* internal rep of current directory */
  TIFFHeader tif_header; /* file's header block */
  int   tif_typeshift[6]; /* data type shift counts */
  long  tif_typemask[6]; /* data type masks */
  long  tif_row;        /* current scanline */
  int   tif_curstrip;   /* current strip for read/write */
  long  tif_curoff;     /* current offset for read/write */
/* compression scheme hooks */
```

```
   int    (*tif_stripdecode)();  /* strip decoding routine (pre) */
   int    (*tif_decoderow)();    /* scanline decoding routine */
   int    (*tif_stripencode)();  /* strip encoding routine (pre) */
   int    (*tif_encoderow)();    /* scanline encoding routine */
   int    (*tif_encodestrip)();  /* strip encoding routine (post) */
   int    (*tif_close)();        /* cleanup-on-close routine */
   int    (*tif_seek)();         /* position within a strip routine */
   int    (*tif_cleanup)();      /* routine called to cleanup state */
   char   FAR *tif_data;         /* compression scheme private data */
/* input/output buffering    */
   int    tif_scanlinesize;      /* # of bytes in a scanline */
   char   FAR *tif_rawdata;      /* raw data buffer */
   long   tif_rawdatasize;       /* # of bytes in raw data buffer */
   char   FAR *tif_rawcp;        /* current spot in raw buffer */
   long   tif_rawcc;             /* bytes unread from raw buffer */
} TIFF;
```

The problem I had was that the C++ compiler would refuse to match things like
(***tif_stripdecode**) with actual function calls: I found it practically impossible
to get the prototypes right. Then I discovered that the TIFF header files already
account for use of the package with C++ code: they surround the function prototypes with:

```
#if defined(__cplusplus)
extern "C" {
#endif
//...<prototypes here>
#if defined(__cplusplus)
}
#endif
```

That was enough for me: clearly someone else had already faced and abandoned
this particular Sisyphean task.

I should point out here that using **extern "C"** is not in any sense a cop-out—in
fact, it's one of the most important things someone learning C++ can ever know. You
can use **extern "C"** whenever you have C code that really won't compile as C++,
especially working code that you don't have any good reason to rewrite. You can
also use it as a first step toward converting C code to C++, even if you're planning to
rewrite the code later: anything that gets you up and running quickly will ease your
transition.

Except for where I got bored halfway through the TIFF code (which had to stay in
C because of the function pointer prototypes), I turned all the remaining K&R
prototypes in C code into ANSI prototypes, since C++ absolutely requires ANSI
prototypes. I had to do a few other things as well. What I had to do most was to add
explicit casts.

In DIB.CPP, for instance, I had to add a cast to get the result of **GlobalLock** to **LPBITMAPINFOHEADER** before the assignment to **lpbi** (in multiple places), add a cast to get the result of **GetStockObject** to the correct handle type, and change **(LPSTR)** to **(LPBYTE)** or add a cast to **LPBYTE**:

```
lpbi = (LPBITMAPINFOHEADER)GlobalLock(hdib);
//...
hpal = (HPALETTE)GetStockObject(DEFAULT_PALETTE);
//...
hbm = CreateDIBitmap(hdc,
    (LPBITMAPINFOHEADER)lpbi,
    (LONG)CBM_INIT,
    (LPBYTE)lpbi + lpbi->biSize + PaletteSize(lpbi),
    (LPBITMAPINFO)lpbi,
     DIB_RGB_COLORS );
//...
    BYTE HUGE_T *hp = (LPBYTE)pv;   //added cast for C++
```

In DLGOPEN.CPP, I had to add a cast to **(LPSTR)** to make the pathname **FAR** for **lstrcpy**:

```
lstrcpy(szFileName,(LPSTR)of.szPathName);
```

In DRAWDIB.CPP, I needed to cast the result of **SelectObject** and to cast **lpbi**, as well as casting generic handles to explicit handles:

```
hbm = (HBITMAP)SelectObject (hdcBits, hbm);
//...
lpbi = (LPBITMAPINFOHEADER)GlobalLock(hbiCurrent);
//...
hbm = CropBitmap ((HBITMAP)h,&rcClip);
```

In GIF.CPP, I added some casts, changed others, and fixed a prototype or two. In IMAGE3.CPP, I changed the type of **hAccelTable** to **HACCEL**, and added some casts to the results of **GlobalLock** and **GetStockObject**. The code for reading VICAR images in general needed ANSI prototypes, and functions that were supposed to return an integer had to actually do so, even if they always returned zero

In PARSED.CPP I had to initialize an **enum** with an valid value **(NULL_TOKEN)** instead of relying on the integer equivalent **(0)**. And the balance of the functions I converted from C to C++ had more of the above, basically needing explicit casts for functions that return generic types and an occasional ANSI prototype.

Overall, C++ turned out to be fussier than C, but the results were worthwhile. For instance, at link time I discovered that a couple of global variables didn't match type across modules. When they were compiled as C, the linker simply linked the variables despite their mismatched types; when compiled as C++, the linker generated an error since each variable name was decorated with its type, and therefore variables with different types had different external names. C++'s type-safe linkage really does work.

I found little if any runtime cost for compiling as C++ rather than C: the executable file is a tad bigger in at least one version of 32-bit Microsoft C++, but the execution speed is the same as far as I can measure. In some cases C++ code might even compile a bit smaller than the same code compiled as C—it depends very much on the specific compiler and library implementation.

Making Image3 Object-Oriented

So much for the "better C" part of the project. We've gotten more protection from errors using C++ than we did with C, but we haven't yet made any significant gains in abstraction, encapsulation, or object-orientation. Our minimal port simply doesn't take advantage of any of the expressive power of C++, nor does it contribute anything to our original goal, which was to hide the differences between 16-bit and 32-bit Windows.

Let's now think about Objects. We'll talk about different kinds of objects—objects in Windows NT, objects in your conceptual application model, and objects in C++ classes. The game we'll play is often part of the object-oriented design process: it's called *Find the Objects.*

For purposes of argument, let us consider the proposition "An object is something with a handle."

Handle as Object

By this definition a window is an object, by virtue of **HWND**. An application instance is an object, by virtue of **HINSTANCE**. A device context is an object, by virtue of **HDC**. A pen is an object, on the strength of **HPEN**. And so it goes: brushes, bitmaps, icons, cursors, atoms, DDE conversations—all the things we instantiate and work with in Windows are objects.

Of course, there are more kinds of handles than just Windows handles. A file is an object by virtue of its handle—and it could be a Win32 object, a Windows object, a C library low-level I/O object, a C library stream object, or a C++ stream object. In Windows NT, different flavors of file handle are not interchangeable, as we saw when we ported the TIFF-reading code.

It helps if we can convert one kind handle into another—and one kind of object into another. We might also want to derive objects from other objects.

Let's get more specific. IMAGE3 does four major things: it reads a variety of raster image formats and converts them into memory DIBs (device-independent bitmaps), it displays DIBs, it processes DIBs, and it writes DIB files.

A DIB Class Design

A DIB in memory is already a sort of Windows and Win32 object, by virtue of the **BITMAPINFO** and **BITMAPINFOHEADER** structures, and by virtue of Windows and Win32 functions like **SetDIBits**, **SetDIBitsToDevice**, **StretchDIBits**, **GetDIBits**, **CreateDIBitmap**, and **CreateDIBSection** (which last is new for Win32). We could create an enhanced DIB class that uses those system functions, and which additionally contains member functions to perform image processing. Such a DIB class—which would contain most of the code now in IMAGE3A, albeit in reorganized form—could be the foundation for the image-processing portion of IMAGE4, and would also be fairly easy to reuse in other projects.

Writing a DIB file could be another member function in the DIB class, or perhaps it could be an overloaded << operator for the DIB class. Displaying a DIB could be expressed as the **paint** or **draw** member function for the class, which might automatically sense whether it was rendering the DIB to the screen, the printer, or to a metafile.

Displaying a 24-bit true-color DIB is a bit different from displaying an 8-bit palette-based DIB, especially on an 8-bit display device, so perhaps the DIB class could have derived classes for the various possible formats, including the compression formats as well as the different bit packings.

What about reading all those file formats? As you probably remember from *Advanced Windows Programming*, the general idea is that we

1. Identify the file format from the extension.
2. Verify the file format from signatures in the file.
3. Read the file header.
4. Convert the file header to a DIB header.
5. Create an empty DIB of the correct size.
6. Read the image bits from the file line by line.
7. Convert the image bits to DIB bits.

When we're done, we have a DIB object in memory. Basically, this process looks like it is a conversion constructor or >> operator. So our DIB class should have conversion constructors or >> operators that work from DIB files, GIF files, PCX files, TIFF files, Targa files, VICAR files, and raw image files. Again, we should be able to reuse the DIB class in another application more easily than we could the equivalent C functions, because the class will encapsulate its own code and data and offer a narrower, better-defined interface. We should also find the DIB class hierarchy easier to develop and maintain than our current C application, since we can work on isolated member functions for specific cases rather than large, confusing **switch** statements.

How might a DIB class hierarchy look? Let's sketch it out a bit. We start with a general class specification that references existing structures. Note that this implementation stores pointers. An alternate or supplemental choice would be to store handles. Of course, we can always get handles from pointers and pointers from handles using Windows API functions, so in some sense the choice is a matter of taste.

```
#include <windows.h>
class DIB {
private:
    LPBITMAPINFOHEADER lpbmi;
    LPRGBQUAD lprgb;
    LPBYTE pixels;
public:
    DIB();
    ~DIB();
    void GetPointers(LPBITMAPINFOHEADER& lpbmiExt,
        LPRGBQUAD& lprgbExt,LPBYTE& pixelsExt) {
        lpbmiExt=lpbmi;
        lprgbExt=lprgb;
        pixelsExt=pixels;
        }
    };
```

What have we done? We've put the three pointers needed to deal with a DIB in one convenient but hidden place; we've given the class a prototype default constructor and destructor; and we've given the user a way to retrieve copies of the three DIB pointers from any class or function, without allowing the pointers themselves to be modified.

That's the easy part. Now let's think about the various forms of DIB constructor we'll need.

First we'll want to beef up the constructor so that it builds a new DIB object from up to three pointers:

```
DIB(LPBITMAPINFOHEADER lpbmiExt=NULL, LPRGBQUAD lprgbExt=NULL,
    LPBYTE pixelsExt=NULL);
```

The implementation of this constructor would compute **lprgb** and **pixels** if they were not specified, and accept them if they were given. If **lpbmi** was not given, the constructor would set all three pointers to NULL.

We'll also want a member function that initializes an existing DIB object from pointers. Why? You might want to construct a static DIB object, and initialize it dynamically. So we add:

```
fromPointers(LPBITMAPINFOHEADER lpbmiExt=NULL,
  LPRGBQUAD lprgbExt=NULL, LPBYTE pixelsExt=NULL);
```

Such a member function might have to be careful about existing pointers. Three possible strategies come to mind: make the user manage the underlying memory DIB, take responsibility for the underlying memory DIB, or throw an error if the user tries to overwrite nonnull pointers.

I can think of at least one way we can allow for user preference. We can add an explicit member function that forgets the current DIB pointers:

```
void forgetPointers() {
   lpbmi=NULL;
   lprgb=NULL;
   pixels=NULL;
   }
```

That done, it becomes reasonable to throw an error if **fromPointers** tries to overwrite existing pointers; it would also be reasonable to automatically free the memory DIB in that case. I personally prefer encapsulating the donkey work in the class, so I would add a member function to free the memory DIB, and I would automatically free existing DIBs rather than throwing errors. The **freeDIB** member function is pretty simple:

```
void freeDIB() {
   if(lpbmi) {
      GlobalFreePtr(lpbmi);
      }
   forgetPointers();
   }
```

GlobalFreePtr is of course defined in WINDOWSX.H, so we will have to include that file. Now that we've implemented **freeDIB** in a safe way, the class destructor becomes trivial:

```
~DIB(){
   freeDIB();
   }
```

We could of course go on and define the implementation of the constructors, but I think the key points have been made. In any case, it is not yet clear that building a monolithic DIB class is the best way to go about making IMAGE3 more robust, maintainable, and reusable. So let's take a step back, and think about class hierarchies.

Class Hierarchy Granularity

There are classes, and classes. The classic Smalltalk class hierarchy has many generations of child classes that descend from a single ancestor. You sometimes hear such a structure referred to as *bushy*—laid out on paper, the hierarchy looks like an upside-down bush. Such topologies tend also to be *strongly coupled*, meaning that each class has a high degree of interrelationship with the other classes in its hierarchy. The NIH class library described in *Data Abstraction and Object-Oriented Programming in C++* (see the Recommended Reading section at the end of this book), inspired by the standard Smalltalk classes, is an example of this kind of bushy hierarchy in C++: all the NIH classes descend from class `Object`.

A bushy or monolithic class hierarchy has the big advantage that powerful features can be implemented once in a base class and apply to all derived classes. The principal disadvantage of this sort of hierarchy is that it can be constricting, intimidating, and difficult to understand: you might not want to import all the clanking machinery in the class hierarchy for one little function. A large, bushy class hierarachy is *coarse-grained*, meaning that the smallest usable class (the individual grain) pulls in a lot of code (is coarse).

At the other extreme of class design lies the non–member function, or *free subprogram*. Obviously, free subprograms are as fine-grained as you can get. At the same time, they offer no advantage in leverage over a C function—they *are* just functions.

The class designer is always faced with a choice for the relationships among classes and objects, and a choice for whether to contract out functionality to one method or many methods. As Bertrand Meyer says, "A good designer knows how to find the appropriate balance between too much contracting, which produces fragmentation, and too little, which yields unmanageably large modules."[2]

Booch suggests five metrics for evaluating a class design:[3]

- Coupling
- Cohesion
- Sufficiency
- Completeness
- Primitiveness

Coupling, as we mentioned earlier, has to do with the interactions between classes. In modular programming, weak coupling is generally considered better than strong coupling. In object-oriented programming, however, coupling can also be a

---

[2] Meyer, B. *Eiffel: Programming for Reusability and Extendability.* SIGPLAN Notices vol. 22, 1987.

[3] Booch, G. *Object-Oriented Design with Applications.* Benjamin-Cummings, 1991.

byproduct of inheritance. When strong coupling is a byproduct of inheritance, the benefits of inheritance—such as exploiting the commonality among abstractions—can outweigh the problems of strong coupling. Booch speaks of this as "a tension between the concepts of coupling and inheritance."

Cohesion measures the degree of connectivity among the elements of a single class. A class that models, say, radionuclide decay, is likely to have better cohesion than a class that models shoes, ships, sealing wax, cabbages, and kings. Functional cohesion is good; coincidental cohesion is less good. The DIB class we've been discussing will mostly likely have good functional cohesion because it deals with one well-defined kind of object. A class that modeled kings of countries, king crabs, checker kings and playing card kings would have only coincidental cohesion. A class that modeled checkerboards, checker pieces, checker kings, and checker moves would have functional cohesion.

A class is *sufficient* if it contains enough detail about the abstraction to be useful, and it is *complete* if it captures *all* of the meaningful detail about the abstraction. For instance, a specialized class to read only Class P TIFF files produced from one scanning program will be *sufficient* for reading those files, but it will not be a *complete* TIFF reader. Writing a complete TIFF reader is a much harder job. A *sufficient* image-processing class for scanners might only perform color adjustment, image rotation, and removal of stray pixels; a *complete* image-processing class would contain every image-processing operation in the known universe.

Booch points out: "Completeness is a subjective matter, and can be overdone. Providing all meaningful operations for a particular abstraction overwhelms the user and is generally unnecessary, since many high-level operations can be composed from low-level ones. For this reason, we also suggest that classes and modules be primitive."[4] Primitive operations require access to the low-level representation for efficient implementation; complex operations can be efficiently implemented in terms of primitive operations.

Consider reading a GIF file. The primitive operations might be reading the GIF header, reading the GIF palette, and reading the GIF image. A GIF file can have multiple blocks, of which an image block is only one type, so the second-level operation would be reading a GIF block. Reading a whole GIF file would be a third-level complex operation, since it decomposes to reading blocks, and reading the image block (the most complex type of block) decomposes to reading the image header, palette, and bits.

Other cases might be even less clear cut. Finding the next record in a database is probably a primitive operation, but finding a specific record in a database might or might not be primitive: if the database is indexed, finding the record should be implemented as a primitive operation to take advantage of the index structure;

---

[4] Ibid.

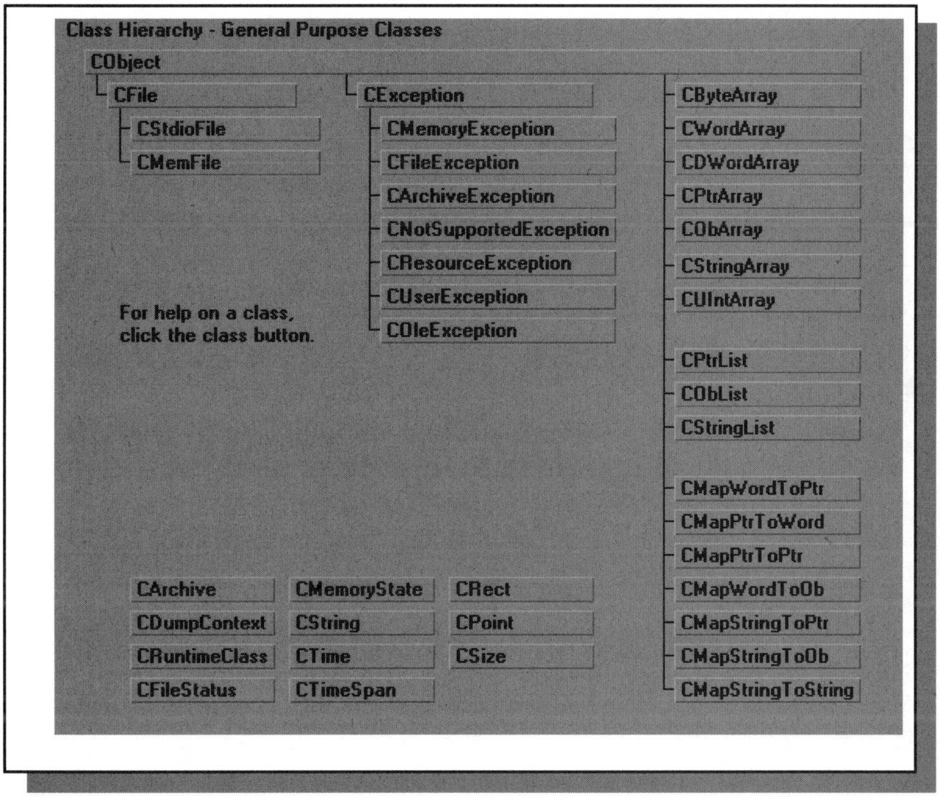

```
Class Hierarchy - General Purpose Classes
 CObject
  └ CFile              CException           CByteArray
    - CStdioFile         - CMemoryException   CWordArray
    - CMemFile           - CFileException     CDWordArray
                         - CArchiveException  CPtrArray
                         - CNotSupportedException  CObArray
                         - CResourceException CStringArray
     For help on a class, - CUserException    CUIntArray
     click the class button. - COleException
                                             - CPtrList
                                             - CObList
                                             - CStringList

                                             - CMapWordToPtr
                                             - CMapPtrToWord
                                             - CMapPtrToPtr
     CArchive    CMemoryState  CRect         - CMapWordToOb
     CDumpContext CString      CPoint        - CMapStringToPtr
     CRuntimeClass CTime       CSize         - CMapStringToOb
     CFileStatus  CTimeSpan                  - CMapStringToString
```

Figure 4-1 MFC hierarchy for general purpose classes.

otherwise, the search operation could be implemented just as efficiently in terms of the primitive "get next record."

We keep coming back to image files— funny thing about that. You might recall that we were talking about IMAGE3A earlier in the chapter. You might, if you have read *Advanced Windows Programming*, recall that IMAGE2 and IMAGE1 trace their lineage back to the Microsoft SHOWDIB sample program.

It might be interesting to have a look at the Microsoft Foundation Classes (MFC) at this point, to see how another class designer has tackled the problem of designing an image-reading class for a Windows application. Specifically, we should look at the MFC class hierarchy, and at a Visual C++ MFC sample, DIBLOOK, which is also a descendent of SHOWDIB.

MFC and a DIB API

The Microsoft Foundation Classes offer examples at several points in the class complexity spectrum. At one extreme, we have the complicated hierarchy built on **CObject**, illustrated in Figures 4-1 through 4-4.

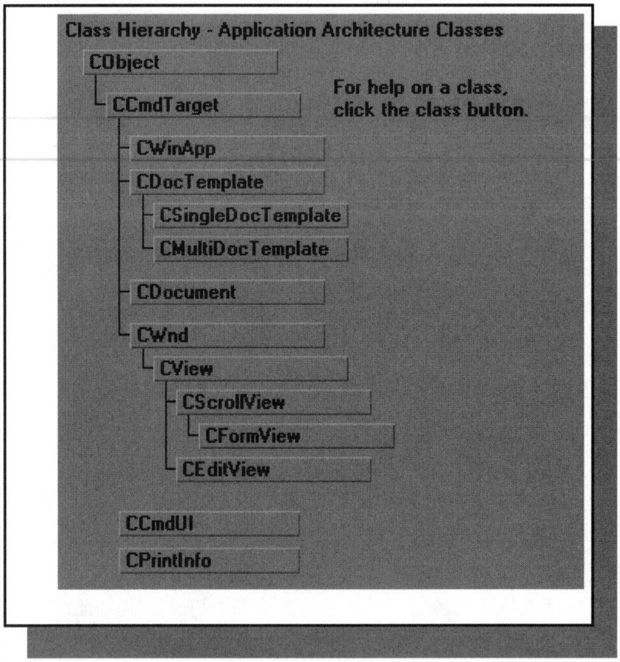

Figure 4-2   MFC hierarchy for application architecture classes.

The **CObject** hierarchy deserves some discussion: in particular we should introduce the MFC application and document architecture (Figure 4-2) before we dive into source code. The document architecture is new in MFC 2.0: a document is a data file, which is associated with one or more views. The views are displayed in frames. Documents, views, and frames are coordinated by document templates. Reading and writing documents is called *serializing* them. We'll add more detail about this stuff later on: if you find yourself lost in the source code at any point, you might want to skip ahead to the exposition and then return to the code.

Somewhat lower on the complexity spectrum than **CObject**, we have simple but useful free-standing utility classes like **CString** (Figure 4-1, near the bottom). And, at the other extreme, we have free subroutines, such as the "DIB API" functions implemented in mfc\src\diblook\dibapi.h, DIBAPI.CPP, and MYFILE.CPP. These have been made to look like native Windows functions, as you can clearly see from the interface:

DIBAPI.H

```
// This is a part of the Microsoft Foundation Classes C++ library.
// Copyright (C) 1992 Microsoft Corporation
// All rights reserved.
```

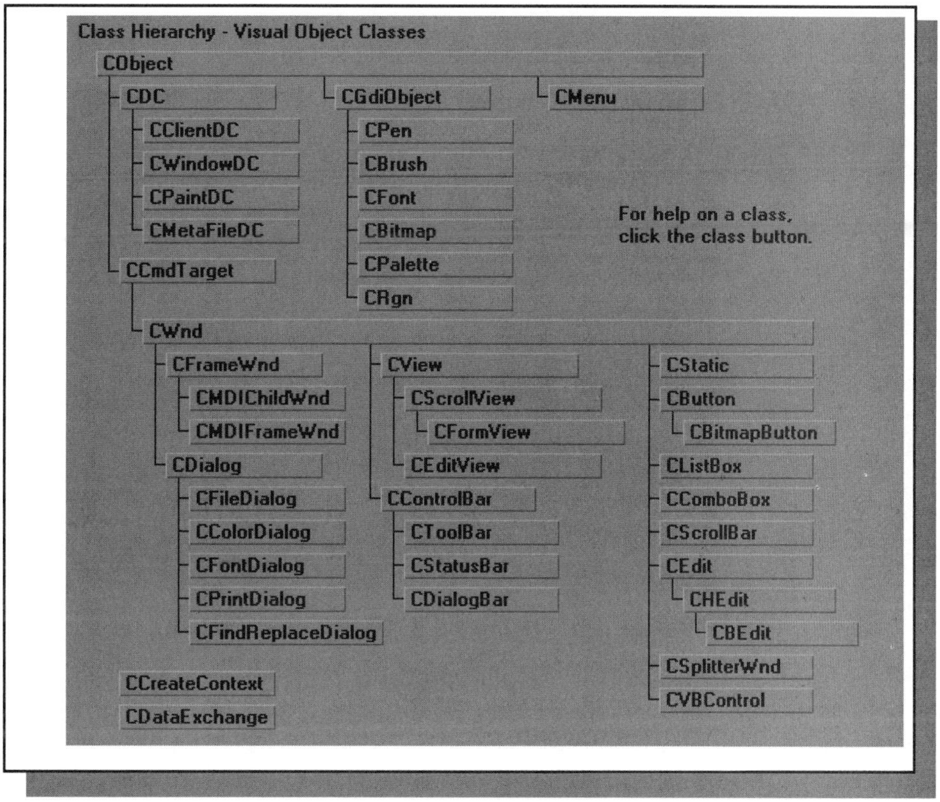

Figure 4-3 MFC hierarchy for visual object classes.

```
//
// This source code is only intended as a supplement to the
// Microsoft Foundation Classes Reference and Microsoft
// QuickHelp and/or WinHelp documentation provided with the
//  library.
// See these sources for detailed information regarding the
// Microsoft Foundation Classes product.

#ifndef _INC_DIBAPI
#define _INC_DIBAPI

/* Handle to a DIB */
DECLARE_HANDLE(HDIB);

/* DIB constants */
#define PALVERSION    0x300

/* DIB Macros*/

#define IS_WIN30_DIB(lpbi) /
```

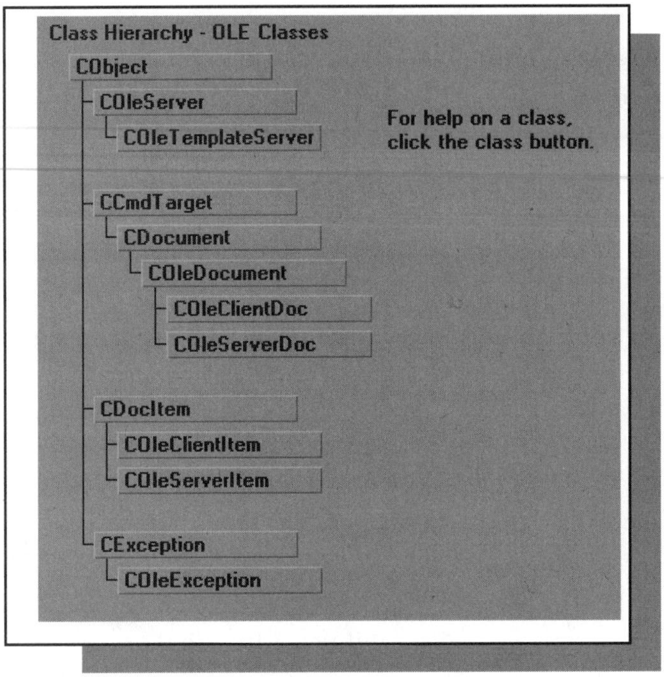

Figure 4-4   MFC hierarchy for OLE classes.

```
       ((*(LPDWORD)(lpbi))==sizeof(BITMAPINFOHEADER))
#define RECTWIDTH(lpRect)      ((lpRect)->right - (lpRect)->left)
#define RECTHEIGHT(lpRect)     ((lpRect)->bottom - (lpRect)->top)

// WIDTHBYTES performs DWORD-aligning of DIB scanlines.  The "bits"
// parameter is the bit count for the scanline
// (biWidth * biBitCount), and this macro returns the number of
// DWORD-aligned bytes needed to hold those bits.

#define WIDTHBYTES(bits)     (((bits) + 31) / 32 * 4)

/* Function prototypes */
BOOL      WINAPI  PaintDIB (HDC, LPRECT, HDIB, LPRECT,
                    CPalette* pPal);
BOOL      WINAPI  CreateDIBPalette(HDIB hDIB, CPalette* cPal);
LPSTR     WINAPI  FindDIBBits (LPSTR lpbi);
DWORD     WINAPI  DIBWidth (LPSTR lpDIB);
DWORD     WINAPI  DIBHeight (LPSTR lpDIB);
WORD      WINAPI  PaletteSize (LPSTR lpbi);
WORD      WINAPI  DIBNumColors (LPSTR lpbi);
HANDLE    WINAPI  CopyHandle (HANDLE h);
BOOL      WINAPI  SaveDIB (HDIB hDib, CFile& file);
HDIB      WINAPI  ReadDIBFile(CFile& file);

#endif //!_INC_DIBAPI
```

Anyone familiar with IMAGE3, or with *Advanced Windows Programming*, or with the Microsoft C language SHOWDIB sample will recognize this stuff without any further explanation. The point of showing you the prototypes, though, is to make you think about how you'd use such functions.

Is it necessary to have these functions in a class to make them useful? Obviously, the person designing the DIBLOOK sample didn't think so: he or she made them free subroutines, but did feel it was worthwhile to use classes—and in fact to use an application framework.

Object orientation is not an end in itself—it is a tool. Remember Booch's observations on completeness and making members primitive? Now, Microsoft sample writers might not necessarily be the best programmers in the world, or the best object-oriented stylists in the world, but somebody familiar with the bushy complexity of **CObject** thought that turning the DIB functions into free subroutines rather than the monolithic class we were working toward earlier was a good idea.

Let's consider the notion that he, she, or they knew their business, and also the notion that perhaps Dr. Heller was getting carried away with his monolithic image class, and read a bit more. We can also consider the notion that the sample writer was simply lazy: turning C functions into free subroutines requires less thought than turning them into a more coupled class. Think about Booch's five principles—coupling, cohesion, sufficiency, completeness, and primitiveness—as we look further into DIBLOOK and MFC. Let's browse a bit now.

ReadDIBFile obviously reads the DIB file. Who uses it? A little browsing (with the Visual C++ for NT class browser) tells us that it is called only from **CDibDoc::-OnOpenDocument**, in DIBDOC.CPP. Even without knowing anything about the architecture of MFC version 2 (the version of MFC shipped with Visual C++) we could certainly guess that **CDibDoc** has something to do with a DIB document. Let's examine its interface:

DIBDOC.H

```
//
// This is a part of the Microsoft Foundation Classes C++ library.
// Copyright (C) 1992 Microsoft Corporation
// All rights reserved.
//
// This source code is only intended as a supplement to the
// Microsoft Foundation Classes Reference and Microsoft
// QuickHelp and/or WinHelp documentation provided with the
// library.
// See these sources for detailed information regarding the
// Microsoft Foundation Classes product.

#include "dibapi.h"

class CDibDoc : public CDocument
{
```

```
protected: // create from serialization only
   CDibDoc();
   DECLARE_DYNCREATE(CDibDoc)

// Attributes
public:
   HDIB GetHDIB() const
       { return m_hDIB; }
   CPalette* GetDocPalette() const
       { return m_palDIB; }
   CSize GetDocSize() const
       { return m_sizeDoc; }

// Operations
public:
   void ReplaceHDIB(HDIB hDIB);
   void InitDIBData();

// Implementation
protected:
   virtual ~CDibDoc();

   virtual BOOL OnSaveDocument(const char* pszPathName);
   virtual BOOL OnOpenDocument(const char* pszPathName);

protected:
   HDIB m_hDIB;
   CPalette* m_palDIB;
   CSize m_sizeDoc;

#ifdef _DEBUG
   virtual void AssertValid() const;
   virtual void Dump(CDumpContext& dc) const;
#endif
protected:
   virtual BOOL     OnNewDocument();

// Generated message map functions
protected:
   //{{AFX_MSG(CDibDoc)
   //}}AFX_MSG
   DECLARE_MESSAGE_MAP()
};
```

CDibDoc is certainly a class, and certainly derived from the MFC hierarchy—specifically, from **CDocument**, which we saw in the MFC application class hierarchy in Figure 4-2. We see that **OnSaveDocument** matches **OnOpenDocument**; and, as we'd expect, **OnSaveDocument** calls **SaveDIB**:

from DIBDOC.CPP

```
BOOL CDibDoc::OnOpenDocument(const char* pszPathName)
{
```

```
   CFile file;
   CFileException fe;
   if (!file.Open(pszPathName,
       CFile::modeRead | CFile::shareDenyWrite, &fe))
   {
       ReportSaveLoadException(pszPathName, &fe,
           FALSE, AFX_IDP_FAILED_TO_OPEN_DOC);
       return FALSE;
   }

   DeleteContents();
   BeginWaitCursor();

   // replace calls to Serialize with ReadDIBFile function
   TRY
   {
       m_hDIB = ::ReadDIBFile(file);
   }
   CATCH (CFileException, eLoad)
   {
       file.Abort(); // will not throw an exception
       EndWaitCursor();
       ReportSaveLoadException(pszPathName, eLoad,
           FALSE, AFX_IDP_FAILED_TO_OPEN_DOC);
       m_hDIB = NULL;
       return FALSE;
   }
   END_CATCH

   InitDIBData();
   EndWaitCursor();

   if (m_hDIB == NULL)
   {
       // may not be DIB format
       MessageBox(NULL, "Couldn't load DIB", NULL,
               MB_ICONINFORMATION | MB_OK);
       return FALSE;
   }
   SetPathName(pszPathName);
   SetModifiedFlag(FALSE);      // start off with unmodified
   return TRUE;
}


BOOL CDibDoc::OnSaveDocument(const char* pszPathName)
{
   CFile file;
   CFileException fe;

   if (!file.Open(pszPathName, CFile::modeCreate |
     CFile::modeReadWrite | CFile::shareExclusive, &fe))
   {
       ReportSaveLoadException(pszPathName, &fe,
```

```
            TRUE, AFX_IDP_INVALID_FILENAME);
    return FALSE;
}

// replace calls to Serialize with SaveDIB function
BOOL bSuccess = FALSE;
TRY
{
    BeginWaitCursor();
    bSuccess = ::SaveDIB(m_hDIB, file);
    file.Close();
}
CATCH (CException, eSave)
{
    file.Abort(); // will not throw an exception
    EndWaitCursor();
    ReportSaveLoadException(pszPathName, eSave,
        TRUE, AFX_IDP_FAILED_TO_SAVE_DOC);
    return FALSE;
}
END_CATCH

EndWaitCursor();
SetModifiedFlag(FALSE);        // back to unmodified

if (!bSuccess)
{
    // may be other-style DIB (load supported but not save)
    //  or other problem in SaveDIB
    MessageBox(NULL, "Couldn't save DIB", NULL,
            MB_ICONINFORMATION | MB_OK);
}

return bSuccess;
}
```

What data members do we find in **CDibDoc**? One handle to a DIB (HDIB is made a specific kind of handle by the **DECLARE_HANDLE** macro invoked in DIBAPI.H), one pointer to a **CPalette** (a class for the Windows palette, defined in AFXWIN.H), and one **CSize** (an extent, similar to a Windows SIZE structure, and also defined in AFXWIN.H). Apparently this implementation doesn't keep a device-dependent bitmap in memory. **PaintDIB** should tell us more about that. Recall that its prototype includes a handle to a DIB and a pointer to a **CPalette**, but no reference of any sort to a device-dependent bitmap:

```
BOOL WINAPI PaintDIB (HDC, LPRECT, HDIB, LPRECT, CPalette* pPal);
```

This is quite interesting. But we might make more progress if we knew a little more about the design of the Microsoft Foundation Classes.

The MFC 2.0 Application Architecture

As we have started to discover, an application built with MFC's framework consists of exactly one application object derived from class C, one or more document objects derived from class **CDocument** and associated with a window, and one or more view objects derived from class **CView**. Each view object is attached to a document object, and therefore associated with a window.

The Application Object and Command Targets

CWinApp encapsulates what would normally go into **WinMain**, with hooks for a lot more functionality. Its interface is defined in AFXWIN.H:

```
///////////////////////////////////////////////////////////////////
// CWinApp - the root of all Windows applications

#define _AFX_MRU_COUNT    4
// default support for 4 entries in file MRU

class CWinApp : public CCmdTarget
{
    DECLARE_DYNAMIC(CWinApp)
public:

// Constructor
    CWinApp(const char* pszAppName = NULL);
// app name defaults to EXE name

// Attributes
    // Startup args (do not change)
    HINSTANCE m_hInstance;
    HINSTANCE m_hPrevInstance;
    LPSTR m_lpCmdLine;
    int m_nCmdShow;

    // Running args (can be changed in InitInstance)
    CWnd* m_pMainWnd;              // main window (optional)
    const char* m_pszAppName;      // human readable name
        //   (from constructor or AFX_IDS_APP_TITLE)

    // Support for Shift+F1 help mode.
    BOOL m_bHelpMode;              // are we in Shift+F1 mode?

public:  // set in constructor to override default
    const char* m_pszExeName;      // executable name (no spaces)
    const char* m_pszHelpFilePath;// default based on module path
    const char* m_pszProfileName; // default based on app name

// Initialization Operations - should be done in InitInstance
protected:
    void LoadStdProfileSettings();
        // load MRU file list and last preview state
    void EnableVBX();
```

```
    void EnableShellOpen();

    void SetDialogBkColor(COLORREF clrCtlBk = RGB(192, 192, 192),
            COLORREF clrCtlText = RGB(0, 0, 0));
        // set dialog box and message box background color

    void RegisterShellFileTypes();
        // call after all doc templates are registered

// Helper Operations - usually done in InitInstance
public:
    // Cursors
    HCURSOR LoadCursor(LPCSTR lpszResourceName) const;
    HCURSOR LoadCursor(UINT nIDResource) const;
    HCURSOR LoadStandardCursor(LPCSTR lpszCursorName) const;
        // for IDC_ values
    HCURSOR LoadOEMCursor(UINT nIDCursor) const;
        // for OCR_ values

    // Icons
    HICON LoadIcon(LPCSTR lpszResourceName) const;
    HICON LoadIcon(UINT nIDResource) const;
    HICON LoadStandardIcon(LPCSTR lpszIconName) const;
        // for IDI_ values
    HICON LoadOEMIcon(UINT nIDIcon) const;
        // for OIC_ values

    // Profile settings (to the app specific .INI file)
    UINT GetProfileInt(LPCSTR lpszSection, LPCSTR lpszEntry,
        int nDefault);
    BOOL WriteProfileInt(LPCSTR lpszSection, LPCSTR lpszEntry,
        int nValue);
    CString GetProfileString(LPCSTR lpszSection,
        LPCSTR lpszEntry, LPCSTR lpszDefault = NULL);
    BOOL WriteProfileString(LPCSTR lpszSection, LPCSTR lpszEntry,
        LPCSTR lpszValue);

// Running Operations - to be done on a running application
    // Dealing with document templates
    void AddDocTemplate(CDocTemplate* pTemplate);

    // Dealing with files
    virtual CDocument* OpenDocumentFile(LPCSTR lpszFileName);
        // open named file
    virtual void AddToRecentFileList(const char* pszPathName);
        // add to MRU

// Printer DC Setup routine, 'struct tagPD' is a PRINTDLG structure
    BOOL GetPrinterDeviceDefaults(struct tagPD FAR* pPrintDlg);

    // Preloading/Unloading VBX files and checking for existance
    HMODULE LoadVBXFile(LPCSTR lpszFileName);
    BOOL UnloadVBXFile(LPCSTR lpszFileName);
```

```
// Overridables
  // hooks for your initialization code
  virtual BOOL InitApplication();
  virtual BOOL InitInstance();

  // running and idle processing
  virtual int Run();
  virtual BOOL PreTranslateMessage(MSG* pMsg);
  virtual BOOL OnIdle(LONG lCount);
      // return TRUE if more idle processing

  // exiting
  virtual BOOL SaveAllModified(); // save before exit
  virtual int ExitInstance(); // return app exit code

  // Advanced: to override message boxes and other hooks
  virtual int DoMessageBox(LPCSTR lpszPrompt, UINT nType,
    UINT nIDPrompt);
  virtual BOOL ProcessMessageFilter(int code, LPMSG lpMsg);
  virtual LRESULT ProcessWndProcException(CException* e,
    const MSG* pMsg);
  virtual void DoWaitCursor(int nCode);
      // 0 => restore, 1=> begin, -1=> end

  // Advanced: process async DDE request
  virtual BOOL OnDDECommand(char* pszCommand);

  // Help support (overriding is advanced)
  virtual void WinHelp(DWORD dwData, UINT nCmd = HELP_CONTEXT);
      // general

// Command Handlers
protected:
  // map to the following for file new/open
  afx_msg void OnFileNew();
  afx_msg void OnFileOpen();

  // map to the following to enable print setup
  afx_msg void OnFilePrintSetup();

  // map to the following to enable help
  afx_msg void OnContextHelp();   // shift-F1
  afx_msg void OnHelp();          // F1 (uses current context)
  afx_msg void OnHelpIndex();
      // ID_HELP_INDEX, ID_DEFAULT_HELP
  afx_msg void OnHelpUsing();     // ID_HELP_USING

// Implementation
protected:
  MSG m_msgCur;                        // current message

  CPtrList m_templateList;             // list of templates
  HGLOBAL m_hDevMode;                  // printer Dev Mode
  HGLOBAL m_hDevNames;                 // printer Device Names
```

```
    DWORD m_dwPromptContext;
            // help context override for message box
    int m_nWaitCursorCount;      // for wait cursor (>0 => waiting)
    HCURSOR m_hcurWaitCursorRestore;
            // old cursor to restore after wait cursor

    CString m_strRecentFiles[_AFX_MRU_COUNT];
            // default MRU implementation
    void (CALLBACK* m_lpfnCleanupVBXFiles)();

    void UpdatePrinterSelection(BOOL bForceDefaults);
    void SaveStdProfileSettings();  // save options to .INI file
    BOOL ProcessHelpMsg(MSG& msg, DWORD* pContext);
    HWND SetHelpCapture(POINT ptCursor);

public: // public for implementation access
    ATOM m_atomApp, m_atomSystemTopic;   // for DDE open
    HCURSOR m_hcurHelp;   // always loaded if m_bHelpMode == TRUE
    UINT m_nNumPreviewPages; // number of default printed pages

    // memory safety pool
    size_t  m_nSafetyPoolSize;       // ideal size
    void*   m_pSafetyPoolBuffer;     // current buffer

    void SetCurrentHandles();
    BOOL PumpMessage();       // low level message pump
    int GetOpenDocumentCount();

    // helpers for standard commdlg dialogs
    BOOL DoPromptFileName(CString& fileName, UINT nIDSTitle,
            DWORD lFlags, BOOL bOpenFileDialog,
            CDocTemplate* pTemplate);
    int DoPrintDialog(CPrintDialog* pPD);

public:
    virtual ~CWinApp();
#ifdef _DEBUG
    virtual void AssertValid() const;
    virtual void Dump(CDumpContext& dc) const;
    int m_nDisablePumpCount;
        // Diagnostic trap to detect illegal re-entrancy
#endif //_DEBUG

#ifdef _AFXDLL
    // force linkage to AFXDLL startup code and special stack
    //     segment for applications linking with AFXDLL
    virtual void _ForceLinkage();
#endif //_AFXDLL

protected: // standard commands
    //{{AFX_MSG(CWinApp)
    afx_msg void OnAppExit();
    afx_msg void OnUpdateRecentFileMenu(CCmdUI* pCmdUI);
```

```
   afx_msg BOOL OnOpenRecentFile(UINT nID);
   //}}AFX_MSG
   DECLARE_MESSAGE_MAP()
};
```

You'll note that class **CWinApp** is derived from **CCmdTarget**, which serves as the base class for all objects that can receive or respond to messages:

```
/////////////////////////////////////////////////////////////////////
// CCmdTarget

// private structures
struct AFX_CMDHANDLERINFO;
   // info about where the command is handled

class CCmdTarget : public CObject
{
   DECLARE_DYNAMIC(CCmdTarget)
protected:
   CCmdTarget();

public:
// Operations
   void BeginWaitCursor();
   void EndWaitCursor();
   void RestoreWaitCursor();       // call after messagebox

// Overridables
   // route and dispatch standard command message types
   //    (more sophisticated than OnCommand)
   virtual BOOL OnCmdMsg(UINT nID, int nCode, void* pExtra,
      AFX_CMDHANDLERINFO* pHandlerInfo);

// Implementation
private:
   static CView* pRoutingView;
   friend class CView;

protected:
   CView* GetRoutingView();
   DECLARE_MESSAGE_MAP()           // base class - no {{ }} macros
};
```

Note that every **CCmdTarget**-derived class contains a static pointer to a **CView**. This is how a view is associated with a window and a document: the list of classes derived from **CCmdTarget** includes not only **CWinApp** but **CWnd**, **CDocTemplate**, and **CDocument**. **CView**, in turn, derives from **CWnd**.

Note also that **OnCmdMsg** is virtual in **CCmdTarget**, meaning that it can be overridden in derived classes. However, the implementation of **CCmdTarget::- OnCmdMsg**, found in CMDTARG.CPP in the MFC source directory, contains significant functionality: it is this **OnCmdMsg** that implements all the grubbing through message maps that is at the heart of MFC's message dispatching system:

```
BOOL CCmdTarget::OnCmdMsg(UINT nID, int nCode, void* pExtra,
  AFX_CMDHANDLERINFO* pHandlerInfo)
{
  ASSERT(nID != 0);    // 0 command IDs are not allowed !

  // Now look through message map to see if it applies to us
  AFX_MSGMAP* pMessageMap;
  AFX_MSGMAP_ENTRY FAR* lpEntry;
  for (pMessageMap = GetMessageMap(); pMessageMap != NULL;
    pMessageMap = pMessageMap->pBaseMessageMap)
  {
    ASSERT(pMessageMap != pMessageMap->pBaseMessageMap);
      //NOTE: catches BEGIN_MESSAGE_MAP(CMyClass,CMyClass)!

    // Constant code...
    if ((UINT)nCode < 0xC000 || (UINT)nCode > 0xFF00)
    {
      lpEntry =_AfxFindMessageEntry(pMessageMap>lpEntries,
              nCode, nID);
    }
    else
    {
      // registered notification code:  E.g. VBX_EVENTs
      lpEntry = pMessageMap->lpEntries;

      while ((lpEntry = _AfxFindMessageEntry(lpEntry, 0xC001,
            nID))
        != NULL)
       {
#ifndef _WINDLL
        int NEAR* pnCode = (int NEAR*)(lpEntry->nSig);
#else
        // if SS!=DS, then REGISTERED message must be
        //   in same data segment as the message map
        int FAR* pnCode = (in FAR*)MAKELONG(lpEntry->nSig,
          _AFX_FP_SEG(pMessageMap));
#endif
        ASSERT(((UINT)*pnCode) >= 0xC000);
              // must be successfully registered

        if (*pnCode == nCode)
          break;     // found it

        lpEntry++;     // keep looking past this one
      }
    }

    if (lpEntry != NULL)
    {
```

```
            // found it
#ifdef _DEBUG
            if (afxTraceFlags & 8)   // if command reporting
            {
                if (nCode == 0)
                {
                    TRACE2("SENDING command id 0x%04X to %Fs
                        target\n", nID,
                      GetRuntimeClass()->m_lpszClassName);
                }
                else if (nCode > 0)
                {
                    if (afxTraceFlags & 4)
                    {
                    TRACE3("SENDING control notification %d from"
                    "control id 0x%04X to %Fs window\n",
                        nCode, nID,
                      GetRuntimeClass()->m_lpszClassName);
                    }
                }
            }
#endif //_DEBUG
        if ((UINT)nCode < 0xC000 || (UINT)nCode > 0xFF00)
        {
            return DispatchCmdMsg(this, nID, nCode,
                lpEntry->pfn, pExtra, lpEntry>nSig, pHandlerInfo);
        }
        else
        {
            // Force VBX signature
            return DispatchCmdMsg(this, nID, nCode,
                lpEntry->pfn, pExtra, AfxSig_vbx, pHandlerInfo);
        }
    }
  }

  return FALSE;    // not handled
}
```

Another class, **CCmdUI**, provides a way to update user-interface objects, such as menu items and control-bar buttons. A command target can use a **CCmdUI** to help it enable, disable, check, and uncheck menu items and buttons.

```
class CCmdUI        // simple helper class
{
public:
// Attributes
   UINT m_nID;
   UINT m_nIndex;              // menu item or other index
```

```
    // if a menu item
    CMenu* m_pMenu;          // NULL if not a menu
    CMenu* m_pSubMenu;       // sub containing menu item
            // if a popup sub menu - ID is for first in popup

    // if from some other window
    CWnd* m_pOther;          // NULL if a menu or not a CWnd

// Operations to do in ON_UPDATE_COMMAND_UI
    virtual void Enable(BOOL bOn = TRUE);
    virtual void SetCheck(int nCheck = 1);
            // 0, 1 or 2 (indeterminate)
    virtual void SetRadio(BOOL bOn = TRUE);
    virtual void SetText(LPCSTR lpszText);

// Advanced operation
    void ContinueRouting();

// Implementation
    CCmdUI();
    BOOL m_bEnableChanged;
    BOOL m_bContinueRouting;
    UINT m_nIndexMax;        // last + 1 for iterating m_nIndex

    void DoUpdate(CCmdTarget* pTarget, BOOL bDisableIfNoHndler);
};

// special CCmdUI derived classes are used for other UI paradigms
//  like toolbar buttons and status indicators
```

You may have noticed that **CCmdTarget::OnCmdMsg** calls **CCmdTarget::-DispatchCmdMsg** before returning. In fact, that is how a **CCmdUI** is linked to a **CCmdTarget**, as well as how messages get passed to their handler functions:

```
static BOOL DispatchCmdMsg(CCmdTarget* pTarget, UINT nID,
    int nCode, AFX_PMSG pfn, void* pExtra, UINT nSig,
    AFX_CMDHANDLERINFO* pHandlerInfo)
    // return TRUE to stop routing
{
    ASSERT_VALID(pTarget);

    union MessageMapFunctions mmf;
    mmf.pfn = pfn;
    BOOL bOK = TRUE; // default is ok

    if (pHandlerInfo != NULL)
    {
        // just fill in the information, don't do it
        pHandlerInfo->pTarget = pTarget;
        pHandlerInfo->pmf = mmf.pfn;
        return TRUE;
```

```
}

switch (nSig)
{
case AfxSig_vv:
   // normal command or control notification
   ASSERT(CN_COMMAND == 0);   // CN_COMMAND same as BN_CLICKED
   ASSERT(pExtra == NULL);
   (pTarget->*mmf.pfn_COMMAND)();
   break;

case AfxSig_bw:
   // extended command (passed ID, returns bContinue)
   ASSERT(pExtra == NULL);
   bOK = (pTarget->*mmf.pfn_COMMAND_EX)(nID);
   break;

case AfxSig_cmdui:
   {
       // ON_UPDATE_COMMAND_UI case
       ASSERT(nCode == CN_UPDATE_COMMAND_UI);
       ASSERT(pExtra != NULL);
       CCmdUI* pCmdUI = (CCmdUI*)pExtra;
       ASSERT(pCmdUI->m_nID == nID);               // sanity assert
       ASSERT(!pCmdUI->m_bContinueRouting);   // idle - not set
       (pTarget->*mmf.pfn_UPDATE_COMMAND_UI)(pCmdUI);
       bOK = !pCmdUI->m_bContinueRouting;
       pCmdUI->m_bContinueRouting = FALSE;     // go back to idle
   }
   break;

case AfxSig_vbx:
   {
       // ON_VBX_EVENT case
       ASSERT(((WORD)nCode) >= 0xC000);
                   // must be a registered VB event
       AFX_VBXEVENTPARAMS FAR* lpEvent =
                   *(AFX_VBXEVENTPARAMS FAR**)pExtra;
       (pTarget->*mmf.pfn_VBXEVENT)(lpEvent->nNotifyCode,
           lpEvent->nEventIndex, lpEvent->pControl,
           lpEvent->lpUserParams);
   }
   break;

// general extensibility hooks
case AfxSig_vpv:
   (pTarget->*mmf.pfn_OTHER)(pExtra);
   break;
case AfxSig_bpv:
   bOK = (pTarget->*mmf.pfn_OTHER_EX)(pExtra);
   break;

default:    // illegal
```

```
        ASSERT(FALSE);
        return 0;
    }
    return bOK;
}
```

With the **ASSERT** macros removed, the case in **CCmdTarget::DispatchCmd-Msg** that connects to a **CCmdUI** reads:

```
case AfxSig_cmdui:
    {
        // ON_UPDATE_COMMAND_UI case
        CCmdUI* pCmdUI = (CCmdUI*)pExtra;
        (pTarget->*mmf.pfn_UPDATE_COMMAND_UI)(pCmdUI);
        bOK = !pCmdUI->m_bContinueRouting;
        pCmdUI->m_bContinueRouting = FALSE;       // go back to idle
    }
    break;
```

The first executable line just casts the **pExtra** argument to a **CCmdUI ***. The next line invokes the current command target's **UPDATE_COMMAND_UI** handler on the passed pointer to a **CCmdUI**. In other words, it asks the current window to update the current menu item or button.

The third executable line sets the return value for this message, **bOK**, based on the value of the **CCmdUI** object's **bContinueRouting** member. Returning **TRUE** from **CCmdTarget::DispatchCmdMsg** means that the menu item or button state has been set; returning **FALSE** means that the system should keep looking for a handler for this menu item or button.

Why all this overhead? Well, it's not as much as it could be: the message map mechanism appears to give most of the benefits of virtual functions, without all the overhead of virtual functions. I shudder to think how big a virtual function table would have to be to handle every possible Windows message, and shudder yet again to think how many instances of this virtual function table would exist in even a moderately complex program.

Why, then, is **DispatchCmdMsg** working so hard? It is making sure that it finds the correct handlers for the menu items and buttons. Suppose the user clicks on the Edit menu item of an MFC program. Windows will generate a **WM_INITMENUPOPUP** message and send it to the application's main window procedure, which is handled by MFC. For each item on the menu, MFC then follows a standard command routing: it looks for an update handler for the command ID of the menu item.

If an update handler is found, it is called. If there is no update handler, the framework looks for a command handler for the current command ID. If a command handler is found, the menu item is enabled; if not, it is disabled.

You'll notice that it is a little easier to follow this sort of code without the **ASSERT** macros. Yet, the **ASSERT** macros are quite important: they provide all the sanity checking for the debugging version of the MFC libraries. You can and should put **ASSERT** macros in your own code.

ASSERT, Message Maps, and other MFC Macro Magic

The MFC **ASSERT** macro is implemented within an **#ifdef _DEBUG** clause, so that it does nothing in production code:

from AFX.H

```
#ifdef _DEBUG
//...
#define TRACE              ::AfxTrace
#define THIS_FILE          __FILE__
#define ASSERT(f)          ((f) ? (void)0 : \
                ::AfxAssertFailedLine(THIS_FILE, __LINE__))
#define VERIFY(f)          ASSERT(f)
#define ASSERT_VALID(pOb)  (::AfxAssertValidObject(pOb, \
                THIS_FILE, __LINE__))
//...
#elseif
#define ASSERT(f)          ((void)0)
#define VERIFY(f)          ((void)(f))
#define ASSERT_VALID(pOb)  ((void)0)
//...
#endif
```

You'll note that the **VERIFY** macro does the same thing as the **ASSERT** macro when you are debugging; in production, it executes the conditional expression without reporting if it evaluates **FALSE**. Thus, you would code

```
ASSERT(THIS_EXPRESSION_IS_JUST_A_DEBUGGING_CHECK);
```

for an expression that matters only for debugging, but

```
VERIFY(THIS_EXPRESSION_SHOULD_ALWAYS_RETURN_TRUE);
```

for an expression that also needs evaluation in production code.

The **ASSERT_VALID** macro, like **ASSERT**, disappears in production code. In debugging code it determines whether an MFC object of a class derived from **CObject** is valid. How does it do that? First it makes sure that the pointer is not **NULL**. Then it calls the object's **AssertValid** member function: that is, it asks the object to check itself, which the object class normally implements by (surprise!) running a number of **ASSERT** macros.

You probably noticed the **DECLARE_DYNAMIC** and **DECLARE_DYNCREATE** macros in some of the MFC code above. **DECLARE_DYNAMIC** lets you identify classes derived from **CObject** at runtime, by defining a **GetRuntimeClass()** member. **DECLARE_DYNCREATE** lets the framework create the objects of the class dynamically at runtime—a necessity for document, view, and frame classes. A third macro, **DECLARE_SERIAL**, adds the capability to serialize objects of the class—that is, read them from disk and write them to disk.

from AFX.H

```
#define DECLARE_DYNAMIC(class_name) \
public: \
    static CRuntimeClass AFXAPP_DATA class##class_name; \
    virtual CRuntimeClass* GetRuntimeClass() const;

// not serializable, but dynamically constructable
#define DECLARE_DYNCREATE(class_name) \
    DECLARE_DYNAMIC(class_name) \
    static void PASCAL Construct(void* p);

#define DECLARE_SERIAL(class_name) \
    DECLARE_DYNCREATE(class_name) \
    friend CArchive& AFXAPI operator>> \
    (CArchive& ar, class_name* &pOb);
```

If you use any of these three macros in your header file, you also need to use the corresponding **IMPLEMENT** macro in your class body:

```
#define IMPLEMENT_DYNAMIC(class_name, base_class_name) \
_IMPLEMENT_RUNTIMECLASS(class_name, base_class_name, 0xFFFF, NULL)

#define IMPLEMENT_DYNCREATE(class_name, base_class_name) \
    void PASCAL class_name::Construct(void* p) \
        { new(p) class_name; } \
    _IMPLEMENT_RUNTIMECLASS(class_name, base_class_name, 0xFFFF, \
        class_name::Construct)

#define IMPLEMENT_SERIAL(class_name, base_class_name, wSchema) \
    void PASCAL class_name::Construct(void* p) \
        { new(p) class_name; } \
    _IMPLEMENT_RUNTIMECLASS(class_name, base_class_name, wSchema, \
        class_name::Construct) \
    CArchive& AFXAPI operator>>(CArchive& ar, class_name* &pOb) \
        { pOb = (class_name*) \
ar.ReadObject(RUNTIME_CLASS(class_name)); \
```

```
                return ar; } \
// end of IMPLEMENT_SERIAL
```

So, for instance, in AFXWIN.H we find the definition

```
class CWnd : public CCmdTarget
{
    DECLARE_DYNCREATE(CWnd)
//...
```

and in WINCORE.CPP we find the corresponding implementation

```
IMPLEMENT_DYNCREATE(CWnd, CCmdTarget)
```

Immediately after, in WINCORE.CPP, we encounter:

```
BEGIN_MESSAGE_MAP(CWnd, CCmdTarget)
    //{{AFX_MSG_MAP(CWnd)
    ON_WM_COMPAREITEM()
    ON_WM_MEASUREITEM()
    ON_WM_DRAWITEM()
    ON_WM_DELETEITEM()
    ON_WM_CTLCOLOR()
    ON_WM_NCDESTROY()

    // VBX support and control reflection
    ON_MESSAGE(WM_VBXEVENT, OnVBXEvent)

    // VBX support
    ON_WM_HSCROLL()
    ON_WM_VSCROLL()
    ON_WM_PARENTNOTIFY()
    //}}AFX_MSG_MAP
END_MESSAGE_MAP()
```

There are several things here that need explanation. One is that the message map implementation corresponds, as you might expect, to a message map declaration in the class, which is normally as simple as

```
DECLARE_MESSAGE_MAP
```

But the message map macros themselves are not simple:

```
#define DECLARE_MESSAGE_MAP() \
private: \
```

```
    static AFX_MSGMAP_ENTRY BASED_CODE _messageEntries[]; \
protected: \
    static AFX_MSGMAP AFXAPP_DATA messageMap; \
    virtual AFX_MSGMAP* GetMessageMap() const;

#define BEGIN_MESSAGE_MAP(theClass, baseClass) \
    AFX_MSGMAP* theClass::GetMessageMap() const \
        { return &theClass::messageMap; } \
    AFX_MSGMAP AFXAPP_DATA theClass::messageMap = \
    { &(baseClass::messageMap), \
        (AFX_MSGMAP_ENTRY FAR*) &(theClass::_messageEntries) }; \
    AFX_MSGMAP_ENTRY BASED_CODE theClass::_messageEntries[] = \
    {

#define END_MESSAGE_MAP() \
    { 0, 0, AfxSig_end, (AFX_PMSG)0 } \
    };
```

Now, what about these funny comments?

```
//{{AFX_MSG_MAP(CWnd)
//...
//}}AFX_MSG_MAP
```

These can't have any significance for the generated code. In fact, they are put there as markers by the Visual C++ Class Wizard tool. Message map entries between such comments can be maintained visually and semiautomatically using Class Wizard; but Class Wizard will not touch message map entries outside the **AFX_MSG_MAP** comments.

Class Wizard is one of the elements that makes Visual C++ usable by mere mortals. To manually code and maintain the message maps in a hierarchy of classes derived from MFC classes is a nightmare: there is just too much to remember.

For instance, a message map entry like **ON_WM_CTLCOLOR()** has a name in a form established by convention, that is **ON_WM_XXXX**, where **WM_XXXX** represents a predefined Windows message, and where the **ON_WM_XXXX** macro has no arguments. On the other hand, an entry like **ON_MESSAGE(WM_VBXEVENT, OnVBXEvent)** follows a different pattern: the first argument is a user-defined message ID, and the second argument is a handler name. There are seven such macro patterns in all: Class Wizard knows which to use when. Class Wizard also knows how to derive new classes and set up member functions that will safely override and/or call back to the corresponding class parent's member functions.

We'll come back to the Class Wizard tool. Right now we still need to understand more about MFC: specifically, more about the **CDocument** class that initially spurred this discussion.

Documents, Templates, Views, and Frames

You'll recall that the **CDibDoc** class of DIBLOOK is derived from **CDocument**, and that the **OnOpenDocument** and **OnSaveDocument** members of **CDibDoc** handle reading and writing files for the class. You'll also recall that documents are associated with views, and views are associated with frames.

To be more explicit, frame windows contain and manage your views; documents manage your application's data; and views both display your documents and manage the user's interaction with the documents. That means that we can look for code that defines and manipulates data in the document class, and code that displays and interacts with the data in the view class.

In a Single Document Interface (SDI, not to be confused with the Strategic Defense Initiative) application like Image3a, a single frame window that is also the application's main window serves as the container for a single view. In a Multiple Document Interface (MDI) application like DIBLOOK, the main application window contains several child windows: each MDI child window serves as the frame for a view.

Frames contain views. In MFC 2, a frame window class manages the frame, and a view class manages the contents; the view window is actually a child of the frame window, even though it might—in a different implementation—be conceptually simpler to make the view correspond to nothing more than the client area of the frame. Each frame window instance is managed by a frame object, each view window instance by a view object, and each document by a document object. The document object interacts with the view object.

The document template establishes the connection between the application, its documents, its frames, and its views; the framework uses the document template internally. **CDocTemplate** is an abstract base class for document templates; the derived class **CSingleDocTemplate** sets up the associations for an SDI application, and the derived class **CMultiDocTemplate** sets them up for an MDI application. The MFC function **AddDocTemplate** registers a document template with the application:

```
// example for CSingleDocTemplate::CSingleDocTemplate
BOOL CMyApp::InitInstance()
{
        // ...
        // Establish the document type
        // supported by the application

        AddDocTemplate( new CSingleDocTemplate( IDR_MAINFRAME,
                          RUNTIME_CLASS( CSheetDoc ),
                          RUNTIME_CLASS( CFrameWnd ),
                          RUNTIME_CLASS( CSheetView ) ) );

        // ...
}
```

The **RUNTIME_CLASS** macro retrieves the **CRuntimeClass** runtime class structure from the name of a C++ class that is derived from CObject and declared with **DECLARE_DYNAMIC**, **DECLARE_DYNCREATE**, or **DECLARE_SERIAL**. You can register more than one document template for an application, if your application supports more than one kind of data, although that makes more sense in an MDI application than it does in an SDI application:

```
//example for CMultiDocTemplate
BOOL CMyApp::InitInstance()
{
        // ...
        // Establish all of the document types
        // supported by the application

        AddDocTemplate( new CMultiDocTemplate( IDR_SHEETTYPE,
                           RUNTIME_CLASS( CSheetDoc ),
                           RUNTIME_CLASS( CMDIChildWnd ),
                           RUNTIME_CLASS( CSheetView ) ) );

        AddDocTemplate( new CMultiDocTemplate( IDR_NOTETYPE,
                           RUNTIME_CLASS( CNoteDoc ),
                           RUNTIME_CLASS( CMDIChildWnd ),
                           RUNTIME_CLASS( CNoteView ) ) );
        // ...
}
```

What does a frame window object actually do? Let's again consider DIBLOOK.CPP, and look at **CDibLookApp::InitInstance**, where **CMainFrame** is instantiated:

```
BOOL CDibLookApp::InitInstance()
{

   SetDialogBkColor();          // set dialog background color
   LoadStdProfileSettings();    // Load standard INI file options
// Register document templates which serve as connection between
//  documents and views.  Views are contained in the specified view

   AddDocTemplate(new CMultiDocTemplate(IDR_DIBTYPE,
          RUNTIME_CLASS(CDibDoc),
          RUNTIME_CLASS(CMDIChildWnd), // standard MDI child frame
          RUNTIME_CLASS(CDibView)));

   // create main MDI Frame window
   CMainFrame* pMainFrame = new CMainFrame;
   if (!pMainFrame->LoadFrame(IDR_MAINFRAME))
      return FALSE;
   pMainFrame->ShowWindow(m_nCmdShow);
   pMainFrame->UpdateWindow();
   m_pMainWnd = pMainFrame;
...
```

CMainFrame is a child of **CMDIFrameWnd**, defined in MAINFRM.H:

```
class CMainFrame : public CMDIFrameWnd
{
    DECLARE_DYNAMIC(CMainFrame)
public:
    CMainFrame();

// Implementation
public:
    virtual ~CMainFrame();

protected:  // control bar embedded members
    CStatusBar  m_wndStatusBar;
    CToolBar    m_wndToolBar;

// Generated message map functions
protected:
    //{{AFX_MSG(CMainFrame)
    afx_msg int OnCreate(LPCREATESTRUCT lpCreateStruct);
    afx_msg void OnPaletteChanged(CWnd* pFocusWnd);
    afx_msg BOOL OnQueryNewPalette();
    //}}AFX_MSG
    DECLARE_MESSAGE_MAP()
};
```

What does **CMainFrame::OnCreate** do? Looking in MAINFRM.CPP, we see that it calls **CMDIFrameWnd::OnCreate**, creates a toolbar, and creates a status bar:

```
int CMainFrame::OnCreate(LPCREATESTRUCT lpCreateStruct)
{
    if (CMDIFrameWnd::OnCreate(lpCreateStruct) == -1)
        return -1;

    if (!m_wndToolBar.Create(this) ||
        !m_wndToolBar.LoadBitmap(IDR_MAINFRAME) ||
        !m_wndToolBar.SetButtons(buttons,
          sizeof(buttons)/sizeof(UINT)))
    {
        TRACE("Failed to create toolbar\n");
        return -1;      // fail to create
    }

    if (!m_wndStatusBar.Create(this) ||
        !m_wndStatusBar.SetIndicators(indicators,
          sizeof(indicators)/sizeof(UINT)))
    {
        TRACE("Failed to create status bar\n");
        return -1;      // fail to create
    }

    return 0;
}
```

In fact, **CMDIFrameWnd** has no **OnCreate** member of its own: it inherits **OnCreate** from **CFrameWnd**:

```
int CFrameWnd::OnCreate(LPCREATESTRUCT lpcs)
{
    CCreateContext* pContext = (CCreateContext*)
        _AfxGetPtrFromFarPtr(lpcs->lpCreateParams);

    return OnCreateHelper(lpcs, pContext);
}

int CFrameWnd::OnCreateHelper(LPCREATESTRUCT lpcs,
                 CCreateContext* pContext)
{
    if (CWnd::OnCreate(lpcs) == -1)
        return -1;

    // create special children first
    if (!OnCreateClient(lpcs, pContext))
    {
        TRACE0("Failed to create client pane/view for frame\n");
        return -1;
    }

    // post message for initial message string
    PostMessage(WM_SETMESSAGESTRING, (WPARAM)AFX_IDS_IDLEMESSAGE,
             0L);
    return 0;   // create ok
}
```

Wheels within wheels: **CFrameWnd::OnCreate** calls **OnCreateHelper**, which in turn calls back to **CWnd::OnCreate**, and then calls **OnCreateClient**. **CFrameWnd::OnCreateClient**, in its own turn, attempts to create a view object for the frame:

```
BOOL CFrameWnd::OnCreateClient(LPCREATESTRUCT, CCreateContext*
pContext)
{
    // default create client will create a view if asked for it
    if (pContext != NULL)
    {
        // try to create view object from RuntimeClass
        if (pContext->m_pNewViewClass != NULL)
        {
            CWnd* pView = (CWnd*)pContext->
                    m_pNewViewClass->CreateObject();
                // NOTE: can be a CWnd with PostNcDestroy self cleanup

            if (pView == NULL)
            {
```

```
            TRACE1("Warning: Dynamic create of view type %Fs failed\n",
                pContext->m_pNewViewClass->m_lpszClassName);
            return FALSE;
        }
        ASSERT(pView->IsKindOf(RUNTIME_CLASS(CWnd)));
        // Views are always created with a border !
        if (!pView->Create(NULL, NULL, AFX_WS_DEFAULT_VIEW,
            CRect(0,0,0,0), this, AFX_IDW_PANE_FIRST, pContext))
        {
            TRACE0("Warning: couldn't create view for frame\n");
            return FALSE;          // can't continue without a view
        }
    }
}

return TRUE;
}
```

It would be interesting to see if **CMDIFrameWnd** has its own **OnCreateClient** member. It does, with an implementation in WINMDI.CPP:

```
BOOL CMDIFrameWnd::OnCreateClient(LPCREATESTRUCT lpcs,
    CCreateContext* /*pContext*/)
{
    CMenu* pMenu = NULL;
    if (m_hMenuDefault == NULL)
    {
// default implementation for MFC V1 backward compatibility
        pMenu = GetMenu();
        ASSERT(pMenu != NULL);
// This is attempting to guess which sub-menu is the Window menu.
// The Windows user interface guidelines say that the right-most
// menu on the menu bar should be Help and Window should be one
// to the left of that.
        int iMenu = pMenu->GetMenuItemCount() - 2;

// If this assertion fails, your menu bar does not follow the
// guidelines so you will have to override this function and call
// CreateClient appropriately or use the MFC V2 MDI functionality.
        ASSERT(iMenu >= 0);
        pMenu = pMenu->GetSubMenu(iMenu);
        ASSERT(pMenu != NULL);
    }
    return CreateClient(lpcs, pMenu);
}
```

As you can see, **CMDIFrameWnd::OnCreateClient** finds the Window menu and calls **CreateClient**, which actually creates a MDI client window using Windows API calls:

```
BOOL CMDIFrameWnd::CreateClient(LPCREATESTRUCT lpCreateStruct,
   CMenu* pWindowMenu)
{
   ASSERT(m_hWnd != NULL);
   ASSERT(m_hWndMDIClient == NULL);
   DWORD dwStyle = WS_VISIBLE | WS_CHILD | WS_BORDER |
      WS_CLIPCHILDREN | MDIS_ALLCHILDSTYLES;
   // allow children to be created invisible
   // will be inset by the frame

   CLIENTCREATESTRUCT ccs;
   ccs.hWindowMenu = pWindowMenu->GetSafeHmenu();
   // set hWindowMenu for MFC V1 backward compatibility
   // for MFC V2, window menu will be set in OnMDIActivate
   ccs.idFirstChild = AFX_IDM_FIRST_MDICHILD;

   if (lpCreateStruct->style & (WS_HSCROLL | WS_VSCROLL))
   {
      // parent MDIFrame's scroll styles move to the MDICLIENT
      dwStyle |= (lpCreateStruct->style &
            (WS_HSCROLL | WS_VSCROLL));

      // fast way to turn off the scrollbar bits (without a resize)
      ::SetWindowLong(m_hWnd, GWL_STYLE,
         ::GetWindowLong(m_hWnd, GWL_STYLE) &
            ~(WS_HSCROLL | WS_VSCROLL));
      ::SetWindowPos(m_hWnd, NULL, 0, 0, 0, 0,
         SWP_NOSIZE | SWP_NOMOVE | SWP_NOZORDER | SWP_NOREDRAW |
            SWP_NOACTIVATE | SWP_FRAMECHANGED);
   }

   // Create MDICLIENT control with special IDC
   static char BASED_CODE _szMdiClient[] = "mdiclient";

   if ((m_hWndMDIClient = ::CreateWindowEx(0, _szMdiClient, NULL,
      dwStyle, 0, 0, 0, 0, m_hWnd, (HMENU)AFX_IDW_PANE_FIRST,
      AfxGetInstanceHandle(),
      (LPSTR)(LPCLIENTCREATESTRUCT)&ccs)) == NULL)
   {
   TRACE0("Warning: CMDIFrameWnd::OnCreateClient: failed to create"
         " MDICLIENT\n");
      return FALSE;
   }

   return TRUE;
}
```

Now that we've browsed the code, we know what a frame window object does. When created itself, it takes care of creating all its children, including (if appropriate) a toolbar, a status bar, an MDI child window, and a view. In other words, it's a convenient place to hang everything.

A view, in turn, takes care of displaying and interacting with a document. Again, let's start with DIBLOOK: the relevant class is **CDibView**, as we saw in **CDibLook-App::InitInstance.CDibView** is derived from **CScrollView**, and declared in DIBVIEW.H:

```
class CDibView : public CScrollView
{
protected: // create from serialization only
   CDibView();
   DECLARE_DYNCREATE(CDibView)

// Attributes
public:
   CDibDoc* GetDocument()
      {
         ASSERT(m_pDocument->IsKindOf(RUNTIME_CLASS(CDibDoc)));
         return (CDibDoc*) m_pDocument;
      }

// Operations
public:

// Implementation
public:
   virtual ~CDibView();
   virtual void OnDraw(CDC* pDC);  // overridden to draw this view

   virtual void OnInitialUpdate();
   virtual void OnActivateView(BOOL bActivate,
      CView* pActivateView, CView* pDeactiveView);

   // Printing support
protected:
   virtual BOOL OnPreparePrinting(CPrintInfo* pInfo);

// Generated message map functions
protected:
   //{{AFX_MSG(CDibView)
   afx_msg void OnEditCopy();
   afx_msg void OnUpdateEditCopy(CCmdUI* pCmdUI);
   afx_msg void OnEditPaste();
   afx_msg void OnUpdateEditPaste(CCmdUI* pCmdUI);
   afx_msg LRESULT OnDoRealize(WPARAM wParam, LPARAM lParam);
                           // user message
   //}}AFX_MSG
   DECLARE_MESSAGE_MAP()
};
```

CScrollView is only one of many possible specialized view classes. It allows either scrolling of the image in the frame or automatic scaling of the image to the frame size. **CDibView** uses the scrolling option by calling its **SetScrollSizes** member (inherited from **CScrollView**):

```
void CDibView::OnInitialUpdate()
{
    CScrollView::OnInitialUpdate();
    ASSERT(GetDocument() != NULL);

    SetScrollSizes(MM_TEXT, GetDocument()->GetDocSize());
}
```

To automatically scale the image to the frame, we could instead call **CScroll-View::SetScaleToFitSize**. That would make a nice "zoom" capability. What we'd really want, though, for normal image display, would be to automatically scale the *frame* to fit the size of the *picture*, when possible. If that wasn't possible, we'd scale the frame as large as possible in the directions that were limited by the main window size, and set a scroll size for that direction. Implementing this scheme will take a little bit of work, since it doesn't quite conform to what is provided in the **CScrollView** class.

What other derived view classes *are* provided in MFC 2? **CEditView** is set up to be the basis of a simple text editor, and **CFormView** is a scrollable view for displaying a dialog, much like a Visual Basic form.

Views generally belong to a simple frame window. Sometimes, though, you might want to look at multiple views of a document: one way to do that is to embed a multipaned *splitter window* (see Figure 4-5), implemented in class **CSplitter-Wnd**, in the parent **CFrameWnd** or **CMDIChildWnd**. Then, make each view one pane of the splitter window. When a **CScrollView** sees that it resides in a splitter pane, it automatically uses the shared scroll-bars provided by the splitter. The source code for splitter windows (in WINSPLIT.CPP) makes interesting reading, if you like learning about the user-interface parts of the Windows API.

If we're serious about overriding the automatic scrolling scaling behavior, we'll have more interesting reading: the implementation of **CScrollView** resides in VIEWSCRL.CPP. But for now, let's finish our survey of MFC so we can get back to our original goal: making IMAGE3 more object-oriented.

Dialogs and Controls

We've covered most of the parts of the Microsoft Foundation Classes that are new in version 2—the parts that comprise the document-frame-view application model. You might not, however, be up to speed on the older, less abstract parts of MFC, so the next few sections provide a lightning introduction. Feel free to skip it if you are already familiar with MFC; also please refer to the Microsoft Visual C++ *Class Library Reference* for more detail. It doesn't matter, by the way, whether you have the documentation for the Windows version or the Windows NT version.

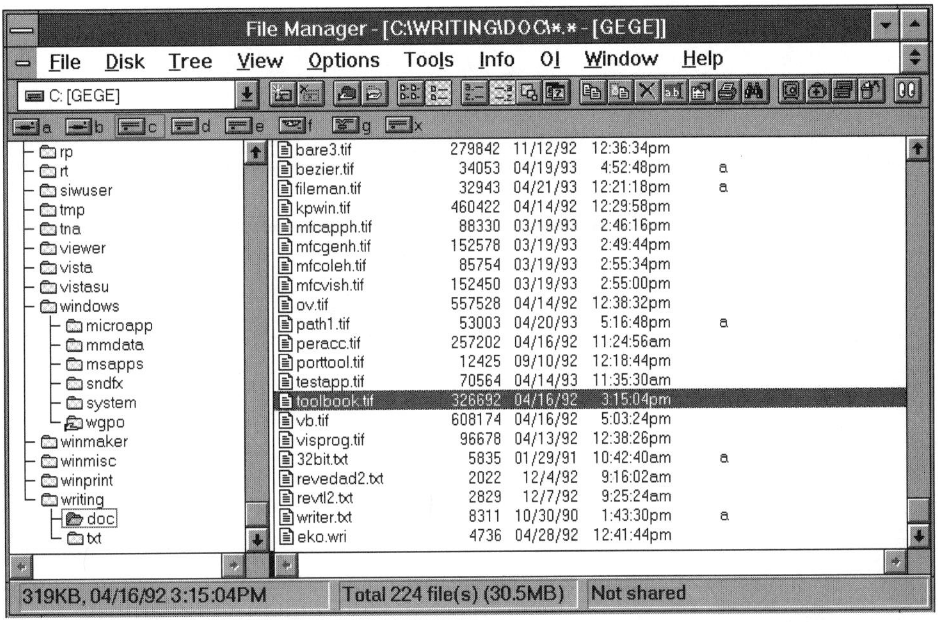

Figure 4-5 The Windows File Manager demonstrates the use of inhomogeneous splitter windows in a multiple-document user interface. It also demonstrates the use of icon bars, status bars, and extendible menus.

The **CDialog** class in MFC acts as a wrapper for both modal and modeless dialogs, and works in conjunction with the dialog resource as interpreted by the Windows dialog manager. One interesting improvement that **CDialog** makes to the standard way of implementing dialog box procedures is embodied in the **DoDataExchange** member function. This provides a standard mechanism for dialog data exchange and dialog data validation. If you've read *Advanced Windows Programming* or worked extensively with dialog boxes, you know that data validation is absent from the basic Windows API set: **CDialog** adds useful functionality here. You won't find **DoData-Exchange** in the definition of **CDialog**, however:

```
//////////////////////////////////////////////////////////////////
// CDialog - a modal or modeless dialog

class CDialog : public CWnd
{
    DECLARE_DYNAMIC(CDialog)

    // Modeless construct
    // (protected since you must subclass to implement a
    //    modeless Dialog)
```

```
protected:
   CDialog();

   BOOL Create(LPCSTR lpszTemplateName, CWnd* pParentWnd = NULL);
   BOOL Create(UINT nIDTemplate, CWnd* pParentWnd = NULL);
   BOOL CreateIndirect(const void FAR* lpDialogTemplate,
      CWnd* pParentWnd = NULL);

   // Modal construct
public:
   CDialog(LPCSTR lpszTemplateName, CWnd* pParentWnd = NULL);
   CDialog(UINT nIDTemplate, CWnd* pParentWnd = NULL);

   BOOL InitModalIndirect(HGLOBAL hDialogTemplate);
                // was CModalDialog::Create()

// Attributes
public:
   void MapDialogRect(LPRECT lpRect) const;
   void SetHelpID(UINT nIDR);

// Operations
public:
   // modal processing
   virtual int DoModal();

   // message processing for modeless
   BOOL IsDialogMessage(LPMSG lpMsg);

   // support for passing on tab control -
   //    use 'PostMessage' if needed
   void NextDlgCtrl() const;
   void PrevDlgCtrl() const;
   void GotoDlgCtrl(CWnd* pWndCtrl);

   // default button access
   void SetDefID(UINT nID);
   DWORD GetDefID() const;

   // termination
   void EndDialog(int nResult);

// Overridables (special message map entries)
   virtual BOOL OnInitDialog();
   virtual void OnSetFont(CFont* pFont);
protected:
   virtual void OnOK();
   virtual void OnCancel();

// Implementation
public:
   virtual ~CDialog();
#ifdef _DEBUG
```

```
    virtual void AssertValid() const;
    virtual void Dump(CDumpContext& dc) const;
#endif
    virtual BOOL PreTranslateMessage(MSG* pMsg);
    virtual WNDPROC* GetSuperWndProcAddr();
    virtual BOOL OnCmdMsg(UINT nID, int nCode, void* pExtra,
       AFX_CMDHANDLERINFO* pHandlerInfo);

protected:
    UINT m_nIDHelp; // Help ID (0 for none, see HID_BASE_RESOURCE)

    // parameters for 'DoModal'
    LPCSTR m_lpDialogTemplate;   // name or MAKEINTRESOURCE
    HGLOBAL m_hDialogTemplate;
                     // Indirect if (lpDialogTemplate == NULL)
    CWnd* m_pParentWnd;

protected:
    //{{AFX_MSG(CDialog)
    afx_msg HBRUSH OnCtlColor(CDC* pDC, CWnd* pWnd, UINT nCtlColor);
    afx_msg LRESULT OnCommandHelp(WPARAM wParam, LPARAM lParam);
    afx_msg LRESULT OnHelpHitTest(WPARAM wParam, LPARAM lParam);
    //}}AFX_MSG
    DECLARE_MESSAGE_MAP()
};

// all CModalDialog functionality is now in CDialog
#define CModalDialog    CDialog
```

Where *is* **DoDataExchange**? It's in **CWnd**. You also need to override it in your own dialog classes. If you don't have any data, for instance in an **About** box, you don't have to do anything of interest in this member function, but you do need to have it call back to the parent class's member function:

```
void CAboutDlg::DoDataExchange(CDataExchange* pDX)
{
    CDialog::DoDataExchange(pDX);
    //{{AFX_DATA_MAP(CAboutDlg)
    //}}AFX_DATA_MAP
}
```

On the other hand, the **DoDataExchange** member function for a complicated dialog can be quite substantial. Fortunately, much of the donkey work needed to create such a function can be done graphically using Class Wizard. You'll note that the **AFX_DATA_MAP** comment macros bracket Class Wizard's automatic data exchange mappings.

By the way, never call **DoDataExchange** directly. If you want **DoDataExchange** to be invoked, call the **CWnd::UpdateData** member function. Actually, you won't even have to do that if you use modal dialogs: the framework automatically calls **UpdateData** with **bSaveAndValidate** set to **FALSE** (meaning to load the data into the dialog box) when a modal dialog box is created in the default implementation of **CDialog::OnInitDialog**; in addition, the default implementation of **CDialog::OnOK** calls **UpdateData** with **bSaveAndValidate** set to **TRUE** to retrieve the data. If **UpdateData** is successful, **OnOK** will close the dialog box.

As you might expect, popping up a dialog whose class is derived from **CDialog** is a simple matter. For a modal dialog, just create an instance of the class, and call its **DoModal** member. You'd normally do this in a command handler, which can belong to your application class, your frame class, or your view class, depending on what is appropriate for your design. The command handler would of course be bound to a menu item and/or a button.

```
void CMyApplicationOrFrameOrViewClass::OnMyDialog()
{
    CMyDlg myDlg;     //create instance of the dialog class
    //To do: initialize the dialog class member variables

    if(myDlg.DoModal()==IDOK){
        //To do: retrieve the dialog class member variables

    }
}
```

A modeless dialog takes a little more work: you'll need to create your own dialog class derived from **CDialog**, and call **Create** in its constructor. Naturally, the easiest way to set this up is to use App Studio and Class Wizard.

In most circumstances, you create controls visually at design time for a specific dialog, using App Studio, and create the code you need to manage the controls with Class Wizard. This is not at all difficult, since Class Wizard already knows what variable types are appropriate for most controls.

In some cases, though, you might want to add a control to your application at runtime. For this situation, MFC has C++ classes that encapsulate the Windows control classes, which you can instantiate or subclass as necessary. For instance, you can add a static text control to the client area of an MFC application (see Figure 4-6) by constructing a **CStatic** object, and then calling the object's **Create** member. In the listings below, the few lines of code I added over and above the code generated by AppWizard are marked by **//MH** comments.

MAINFRM.H

```
class CMainFrame : public CFrameWnd
{
protected: // create from serialization only
```

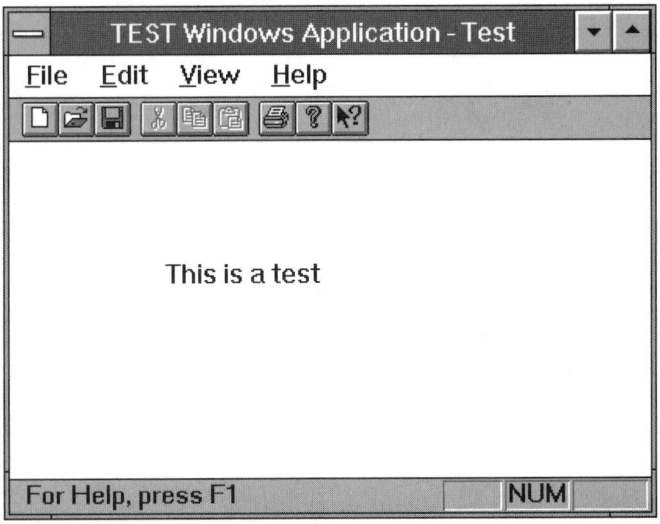

Figure 4-6 Test MFC application with static text control in client area.

```
    CMainFrame();
    DECLARE_DYNCREATE(CMainFrame)

// Attributes
public:

// Operations
public:

// Implementation
public:
    virtual ~CMainFrame();
#ifdef _DEBUG
    virtual  void AssertValid() const;
    virtual  void Dump(CDumpContext& dc) const;
#endif


protected:   // control bar embedded members
    CStatusBar    m_wndStatusBar;
    CToolBar  m_wndToolBar;

// Generated message map functions
protected:
    //{{AFX_MSG(CMainFrame)
    afx_msg int OnCreate(LPCREATESTRUCT lpCreateStruct);
    // NOTE - the ClassWizard will add and remove member
    //     functions here.
    //DO NOT EDIT what you see in these blocks of generated code!
    //}}AFX_MSG
    DECLARE_MESSAGE_MAP()
```

```
//MH: member for static text control in client area
protected:
CStatic    text1;
};
```

MAINFRM.CPP

```cpp
int CMainFrame::OnCreate(LPCREATESTRUCT lpCreateStruct)
{
   if (CFrameWnd::OnCreate(lpCreateStruct) == -1)
      return -1;

   if (!m_wndToolBar.Create(this) ||
      !m_wndToolBar.LoadBitmap(IDR_MAINFRAME) ||
      !m_wndToolBar.SetButtons(buttons,
         sizeof(buttons)/sizeof(UINT)))
   {
      TRACE("Failed to create toolbar\n");
      return -1;     // fail to create
   }

   if (!m_wndStatusBar.Create(this) ||
      !m_wndStatusBar.SetIndicators(indicators,
         sizeof(indicators)/sizeof(UINT)))
   {
      TRACE("Failed to create status bar\n");
      return -1;     // fail to create
   }
//MH: create static text control in client area
   RECT r={100,100,250,130};
   text1.Create((LPCSTR)"This is a test",
      SS_LEFT|WS_CHILD|WS_VISIBLE,
      r,               //control location
      this,            //pointer to parent window
      1001);           //control ID

   return 0;
}
```

While I haven't finished describing all the facilities of MFC, I think I've given you enough of a sampling to whet your interest. Actually, I'm beginning to tire of writing about MFC. At this point, you should probably read the Visual C++ *Class Libraries User's Guide* and go through the tutorial; then you should at least browse through the Visual C++ *Class Libraries Reference*, to get a feel for the features available in the system.

How does MFC rate on Booch's five principles? It varies, as I'm sure you'll agree. The application architecture shows good coupling, cohesion, sufficiency, and completeness, but it doesn't look quite as strong on primitiveness: you really have to buy into a lot of stuff to use the framework. On the other hand, the "DIB API" we found in DIBLOOK is sufficient, cohesive, and quite primitive, but lacks coupling and completeness. Or at least that's the way it looks to me.

We'll come back to MFC as needed in the following chapters. However, I don't think MFC and DIBLOOK provide the only way to work with DIBs in an object-oriented fashion.

Remember the image class I started designing at the beginning of this chapter? As it happens, a class written along similar lines fell into my lap before I finished my implementation.

An Image Class

This class comes to us courtesy of Mr. Chris Marriott, the author of the shareware astronomy program SkyMap, and a scientist at one of Britain's atomic energy establishments. Chris writes:

> *Dear Martin,*
>
> *Please find enclosed my C++ version of the GIF reading class, and sample code showing how it's used. I grant you permission to use this in any way you see fit—goodness knows, it's based on your code in the first place! All the code compiles cleanly with no warnings at /W3 with MSC++ v7.*
>
> *Files GIFCLS.H and GIFCLS.CPP contain the actual GIF reader. I've simplified this quite a bit from the original code in IMAGE2 by making it specifically a class to read a GIF image and return a handle to a CF_DIB memory block. I handle all the palette and DDB creation externally, as you'll see later. This makes the class application-independent and, I hope, portable.*
>
> *I've added a lot of comments to the code—purely so that I could understand what it did myself. I got a copy of the GIF spec from CompuServe which helped tremendously. I hope you'll forgive me hacking the code like this—this code was written for use with my "SkyMap" code with no thought, at the time, of anyone else ever seeing or using it. Feel free to put back the original comments with your modifications in, which I've removed. I've also renamed all the functions and most of the variables to the standard "Hungarian" notation and capitalization that the Windows API uses—simply because it's what the rest of "SkyMap" uses, and I found it easier to understand that way.*
>
> *This code **unconditionally** reads the DIB into memory. That's what I needed for SkyMap so I took out all the tests for whether*

to read the pixel data or not—that hugely simplified the code.

Anyway, I have another **ImageClass** *class which I've included in this archive, but you won't want to use because it's a fundamental part of SkyMap rather than being a standalone class. It lets you see how I use the* **GIF** *class though. That's in files IMAGECLS.H and IMAGECLS.CPP.*

The way the code works is basically this:

In my main program I have an "Open Image" menu item. This invokes a standard file selector and gets the name of an image file to open. The program then essentially says:

```
pImage = new ImageClass( hWnd, szFileName );
```

where **hWnd** *is the handle of the window the image should be displayed in, and* **szFileName** *is the full path name of the image. All the work is done in the constructor of the image class. Omitting all the SkyMap-specific stuff, the constructor says:*

```
//   ImageClass::ImageClass
//   Read an image into memory.

ImageClass::ImageClass( HWND hWindow, LPSTR
szFileName )

//   Input arguments:
//   szFileName              Pointer to filename buffer.

{
    // Initialize the global data.

    nUpdateCount = 0;          // image update counter

    bDIBToDevice = FALSE;  // blit image to device
    bImageValid = FALSE;    // image data is valid

    hpalCurrent = NULL;     // palette handle
    hdibCurrent = NULL;     // handle to current
                                    memory DIB
    hbmCurrent  = NULL;     // handle to current
                                    memory BITMAP

    // Make a copy of the file name.

    lstrcpy( achFileName, szFileName );

    // Identify the file format.

    IdentifyFileFormat();
```

```
    // The action to take depends what the file
    format is:

    switch (nFileFormat) {

        // GIF file:

        case FI_GIF:
            ReadGIF();
            break;

        // DIB:

        case FI_DIB:
        default:
            ReadDIB();
            break;
    }
}
```

The **ImageClass** *holds three handles:*

- **hpalCurrent**   *Handle of GDI palette*
- **hdibCurrent**   *Handle of CF_DIB memory block*
- **hbmCurrent**   *Handle of DDB*

You may well recognize this from your original code! What the constructor does is to call a function to get the file type—that comes straight from IMAGE2. It then calls a function to read the file based on the type. The GIF reading code says:

```
//  ImageClass::ReadGIF
//  Attempt to read a GIF file.

BOOL ImageClass::ReadGIF()

//  Return value:
//  TRUE    if the file is successfully read.
//  FALSE   if an error occurred.

{
    GIF GIF;                        // GIF information

    // Attempt to read the GIF file. Return a
    // failure code if we are unable to do so.

    hdibCurrent = GIF.Read( achFileName );
    if (hdibCurrent==NULL) return FALSE;

    // Create a GDI palette to match the bitmap
    // colours.
```

```
    // If we fail to create a palette, return an
    // error code.

    hpalCurrent = CreateDibPalette( hdibCurrent );
    if (hpalCurrent == NULL) {
        FreeData();
        return FALSE;
    }

    // Create a memory DDB from the DIB.

    if (hdibCurrent && !bDIBToDevice){
        hbmCurrent =
          (HBITMAP)BitmapFromDib(hdibCurrent,
            hpalCurrent);
        if (!hbmCurrent){
            FreeData();
            return FALSE;
        }
    }

// Set the flag — we now have a valid image in
// memory.

    bImageValid = TRUE;

// Return a success code.

    return TRUE;
}
```

i.e., it:

1. *Reads the GIF into a DIB*
2. *Creates a GDI palette from the DIB*
3. *Creates a DDB from the DIB*

The SkyMap program then displays the DDB in the window using the palette.

If I add any other file formats, such as TIFF or VICAR, the first step is just replaced by "Reads the XXXXX into a DIB"—an idea that comes from IMAGE2, of course!

The reason I do things this way is so that the GIF class, which has a lot of data, and so uses a lot of stack, is only in scope for the lifetime of the **ReadGIF** function. The declaration:

```
GIF GIF;
```

at the top of the class creates an instance of the class. Note that it's just used to call the **GIF.Read()** function—the **Read** func-

tion is the only *public function that the class has—all its data is private.*

If you compare this with the original IMAGE2 I hope you'll agree it's better [I do —mh], *because in IMAGE2 all the global data for GIF, VICAR, TIFF, etcetera hangs around for the lifetime of the program. If I add, as I probably will at some stage, a* **ReadVICAR** *function, I'll have a separate* **VICARClass** *and, once again, the class and all its data will only exist while a VICAR image is actually being read—the only thing that persists outside the constructor is the DIB, DDB, and palette.*

Anyway, I hope that's enough to explain the concept of what I've done.

When I was a Windows "novice" you solved no end of problems for me, Martin, and I'm delighted to finally be in a position where I can repay some small part of the generosity you've shown to me over the years on BIX.

Let me know if you need any more information, or if you'd like me to write this up in a more "formal" manner—anything I can do to help you with your book will be a pleasure—I honestly mean that!

BTW, just so you can see that my interlaced GIF reading code works, I've included a small interlaced GIF image of the spiral galaxy "M74." It's a public domain image, so feel free to use it as you wish.

Best wishes,

Chris

Object, Objects, Objects

You'll find Chris Marriott's GIF and image classes, as well as the sample GIF image mentioned in his letter, in the CHAP4\CAMGIF directory on your companion disk. I think you'll find the code easy reading, given his introduction.

So, where are we? We started this chapter with C code for an image-processing program. We made some of the C code compile as C++, and isolated the TIFF code that resisted translation. Then we discussed object-oriented design and object-oriented programming as they apply to our image-processing program. We started the design of a bushy DIB class, had a look at the Microsoft DIB APIs as implemented in DIBLOOK, explored the MFC application model, and finally looked at Chris Marriott's image classes.

Along the way, we learned a lot about class design, and about the Microsoft Foundation Classes. But we never did actually make Image3 object-oriented.

To be completely honest, I originally intended to complete that exercise myself before completing the writing of this chapter, thinking that there would be one best way to do it. Along the way, however, I realized that there are many good solutions, and that no single solution would be best from all viewpoints.

And so I leave the exercise to you: using the IMAGE3A code and anything else you deem fit for use, write an object-oriented IMAGE4 program. I'll be doing the exercise, too. If I can come up with an answer (not *the* answer, but *an* answer) before the master companion disk is produced, an answer that I consider worth your time to examine, it'll be IMAGE4 on your companion disk. If it takes me longer than the disk production schedule allows, I'll post the code where you can download it—send me electronic mail (to **mheller@bix.com** or any of the other aliases listed in the preface) and I'll let you know the status of IMAGE4 and where it can be found.

5

In which we learn to use some of
the advanced features of Win32.

Total Immersion

. . . .

Win32 is a lot more than a straight expansion of 16-bit Windows to a 32-bit environment. So far, though, our code uses only those Win32 functions that are also supported in Windows 3.1. That's good if we plan to maintain a single set of sources for
Windows 3.x and Windows NT, but it doesn't take maximum advantage of the
Windows NT system.

And we should learn to take full advantage of Windows NT. Writing to a lowest
common denominator might give you maintainable code with acceptable performance on both systems. But, supporting key features of Windows NT can give you
major performance benefits that will make your program more marketable.

We'll be looking at a *lot* of source code in this chapter. Consider it the wagon
train's day log. It's not all fascinating, by any means, but the highlights make the
reading worthwhile.

Threads, Processes, and Synchronization

Supporting multiple threads of execution can make an *enormous* difference in how
your application behaves. This is most obvious on a machine that has multiple
processors: a properly written multithreaded application running on a machine with,
for example, four processors, will run nearly four times as fast as a single-threaded

application running on the same hardware. On a machine with eight processors, it could run as much as eight times as fast. The ability of a system to improve its speed as you add processors is called *scaling*; it's not easy to achieve, but it can be done, as we'll show later in this chapter when we look at a draft version of the *WINDOWS Magazine* Windows NT benchmarks (the Hellstones).

Formally, a thread is "the basic entity to which the operating system allocates CPU time. A thread can execute any part of the application's code, including a part currently being executed by another thread. All threads of a process share the virtual address space, global variables, and operating system resources of the process."[1]

Threads can have substantial benefits even on a machine with a single CPU. With multiple threads, user input can continue without interference during processing and printing. By contrast, a single-thread application's input queue is locked during processing. Do you want to run the word processor that ignores you while it is printing, or the one that lets you edit while you print?

If you use threads, you'll also have to synchronize them. Win32 includes quite a variety of events, semaphores, and critical sections—everything needed to synchronize threads, as you can see in Table 5-1.

We see here several mechanisms with overlapping uses: the event, the mutex, the semaphore, and the critical section can all be used for synchronization, but each has its own special purpose. Understanding the differences will take some work: we'll go over them later in this chapter. All four are *waitable objects*—and in fact threads and processes are also waitable objects: they signal when they terminate.

By the way, it's easy to confuse Win32 objects with C++ objects, but they're quite different, despite the similar terminology and intent. A C++ object is an instance of a C++ class; a Win32 object is an instance of a Win32 type. It would be easy to create C++ classes to manipulate Win32 objects as C++ objects, but you can use Win32 objects from any 32-bit language that runs in Windows NT and can access functions in DLLs.

For completeness we should list the thread and process APIs. We do so in Table 5-2. In case you were wondering, a process is "an executing application that consists of a private virtual address space, code, data, and other operating system resources, such as files, pipes, and synchronization objects that are visible to the process. A process also contains one or more threads that run in the context of the process."[2]

Beyond using and coordinating multiple threads, we might eventually want to write systems that use and coordinate multiple processes. Interprocess communication is actually quite a large subject, which we will postpone until Chapter 11. Using and synchronizing multiple computers is another area that can offer obvious benefits: included in the Win32 networking APIs are Remote Procedure Calls (RPCs), which

---

[1] Windows NT API Help.

[2] Ibid.

Table 5-1   Win32 Synchronization APIs

API Call	Function
CreateEvent	Returns a handle to a new event object
CreateMutex	Returns a handle to a new mutex object
CreateSemaphore	Returns a handle to a new semaphore
DeleteCriticalSection	Deletes an unowned critical section
EnterCriticalSection	Enters a critical section
GetOverlappedResult	Returns last overlapped result
InitializeCriticalSection	Initializes critical section object
InterlockedDecrement	Decrements a LONG
InterlockedIncrement	Increments a LONG
LeaveCriticalSection	Leaves a previously entered critical section
MsgWaitForMultipleObjec ts	Waits for mulitple object handles
OpenEvent	Opens an event object
OpenMutex	Opens a named mutex object
OpenSemaphore	Opens a named semaphore object
PulseEvent	Sets and resets an event
ReleaseMutex	Releases a mutex object
ReleaseSemaphore	Releases a semaphore object
ResetEvent	Resets an event object
SetEvent	Sets an event object
WaitForMultipleObjects	Waits for multiple waitable objects
WaitForMultipleObjectsEx	Waits for multiple objects or I/O completion
WaitForSingleObject	Waits for single waitable object
WaitForSingleObjectEx	Waits for single object or I/O completion

allow client-server coordination over a network, and security APIs, which allow safe use of multiple machines without multiple logins. We'll discuss RPCs and the other Win32 networking APIs, along with security, in Chapter 11.

Applications intended for international use should support Unicode, another new feature of Win32, which we discuss in Chapter 9. Remember, at least half the market for most programs is outside the United States.

A few more areas—multimedia and pen support, and support for OLE 2—are essentially the same in Win32 and Win16. None of these was ready for prime time when I was writing *Advanced Windows Programming*, though. I introduce multimedia

Table 5-2 Win32 Process and Thread APIs

API Call	Function
AttachThreadInput	Attaches one thread to another
CreateProcess	Creates a new process and thread object
CreateRemoteThread	Creates a thread in another process
CreateThread	Creates a new thread
DuplicateHandle	Duplicates an object handle
ExitProcess	Exits the current process
ExitThread	Exits the current thread
GetCommandLine	Returns a pointer to the command line
GetCurrentProcess	Returns a handle to the current process
GetCurrentProcessId	Returns the current process ID
GetCurrentThread	Returns a handle to the current thread
GetCurrentThreadId	Returns the current thread ID
GetEnvironmentStrings	Returns a pointer to the environment block
GetEnvironmentVariable	Returns process environment variable
GetExitCodeProcess	Retrieves process termination code
GetExitCodeThread	Returns thread termination code
GetPriorityClass	Returns priority class for a process
GetProcessShutdownParameters	Retrieves process shutdown parameters
GetStartupInfo	Gets startup information for current process
GetThreadPriority	Returns specified thread priority

programming in Chapter 7, pen programming in Chapter 8, and OLE 2 programming in Chapter 10. Each of these areas probably deserves a whole book, but perhaps my introductions will get you going in the right direction.

But we're getting a little ahead of ourselves. First we should discuss the advanced graphics functions of Win32, and after that we should develop a sample program to illustrate the use of threads, synchronization, and some of the other advanced Win32 features.

Advanced Graphics

In 16-bit Windows, people who wanted to draw smooth curves often did their own calculations to generate an array of closely spaced points. They then either called the

Table 5-2   continued

API Call	Function
LoadModule	Loads and executes a program
OpenProcess	Returns a handle to a process object
ResumeThread	Restarts a suspended thread
SetEnvironmentVariable	Sets an environment variable
SetPriorityClass	Sets priority class for a process
SetProcessShutdownParameters	Sets process shutdown parameters
SetThreadPriority	Sets thread priority
Sleep	Suspends a thread for a set time
SleepEx	Suspends a thread until I/O completes
SuspendThread	Suspends a thread
TerminateProcess	Kills a process and its threads
TerminateThread	Kills a thread
TlsAlloc	Allocates thread local storage index
TlsFree	Frees thread local storage index
TlsGetValue	Returns a TLS value
TlsSetValue	Sets a TLS value
WaitForInputIdle	Waits until a process is idle
WinExec	Runs a program
Yield	Obsolete

MoveTo function for the first point and **LineTo** for each subsequent point, or they used **Polyline** to connect the entire array of points.

While this approach does work, it raises several issues. If you use many calls to **LineTo** and wish to draw dotted or dashed lines, you'll find out quickly that the dot pattern for each segment starts over at the beginning with each call: you won't be able to draw a smooth, dotted curve this way, although you will be able to draw a smooth, solid curve, or a jagged, dotted curve.

Using the **Polyline** API enables you to draw smooth dotted lines, but you'll find that you have to generate far more points than you'd like in order to guarantee a smooth appearance: you have the choice between generating a lot of points and drawing a smooth line very slowly, or generating relatively few points and drawing a jagged line quickly. Neither is really satisfactory, although in most cases it *is* possible to find a heuristic that allows you to generate "enough" but not "too many" points.

Bézier Curves

Win32's built-in Bézier functions—**PolyBezier**, **PolyBezierTo**, and **PolyDraw**—allow you to draw smooth curves quickly without a lot of fuss. The Bézier curve itself is a form of cubic polynomial curve segment. A single Bézier curve is specified by two end points, through which it passes, and two control points, through which it need not pass. When two Bézier curves are joined at a point and have the control points and the join point collinear, they are C^0 and C^1 continuous—meaning they form a curve without breaks or cusps. You can make a cusp at a join between Bézier curves by making the control points noncollinear.

The mathematical basis of Bézier curves is fairly simple: you'll find it covered thoroughly in four pages of *Computer Graphics*.[3] Nevertheless, as a *user* of the Win32 Bézier curve facility, you needn't know anything at all about the mathematics of Bézier curves—all you need to know is that the Bézier curve will be generally smooth and pass through the starting point and every third point thereafter, with the curvature determined by the nearest two control points.

PolyBezier takes three arguments: a device context, a long pointer to an array of points, and an integer count of the number of points in the array. The number of points needs to be three times the number of curve segments desired, plus one, since the first point is counted as the starting point. **PolyBezier** does not use or update the GDI current position.

PolyBezierTo, which is otherwise identical to **PolyBezier**, uses the GDI current position as its starting point, and updates the GDI current position to its ending point. **PolyBezierTo** requires exactly three times as many points as the number of curve segments desired.

PolyDraw is a bit more complicated: it draws a set of line segments and Bézier curves. It takes four arguments: a device context, a long pointer to an array of points, a long pointer to an array of line and curve identifiers, and a point count. The **PT_MOVETO** identifier means that GDI should move the current position to the specified point; the **PT_LINETO** identifier means that GDI should draw a line from the current position to the specified point; the **PT_BEZIERTO** identifier means that GDI should use the specified point as either a control point or end point for a Bézier curve; and setting the **PT_CLOSEFIGURE** bit on a **PT_LINETO** or **PT_BEZIERTO** identifier means that the figure should be closed with a straight line after drawing the current line or curve segment.

---

[3] Foley, van Dam, Feiner, & Hughes. *Computer Graphics*, Second Edition. Addison-Wesley, 1990, pp. 488–491. The first edition of this classic was by Foley & van Dam, and you'll find that old hands still refer to the new volume as "Foley and van Dam." I couldn't bring myself to use all four names in every reference to this book in the text, and "Foley and van Dam" isn't technically correct: I hope all you old graphics hackers can get over the culture shock of hearing the book called by its title.

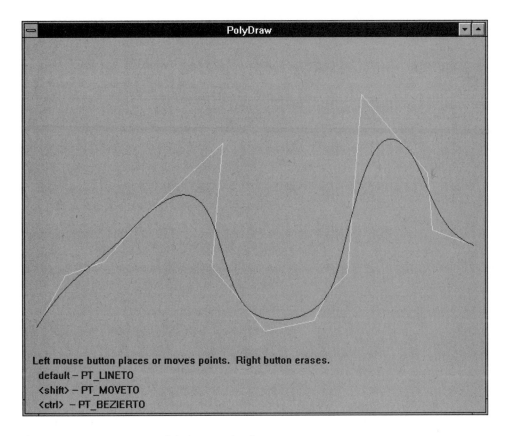

Figure 5-1 Bézier curves and their control points.

As you might expect from the mathematics of Bézier curves, **PT_BEZIERTO** identifiers, like all good things, come in threes. **PolyDraw** does use and update the current GDI position.

As you can see in Figure 5-1, a rather complex smooth Bézier curve can be drawn using relatively few end and control points. To get the same smooth curve using line segments, you'd have to use at least ten times as many points. Since Windows NT's Bézier curve drawing is well optimized, using them will not only improve your rendering, it will speed up your drawing of smooth curves.

Paths

Bézier curves and lines are two of the many possible GDI objects (including ellipses, arcs, text, and polygons) that can be used to make up *paths*. A path is itself a GDI object that belongs to a device context in much the same way as a pen, brush, or font, although a device context does not have a path by default.

Table 5-3 Win32 Path Functions

API Call	Function
AbortPath	Aborts and discards any paths in a DC
BeginPath	Starts a path bracket
CloseFigure	Closes a figure in a path
EndPath	Ends a path bracket
ExtCreatePen	Creates a logical pen
FillPath	Fills the current path
FlattenPath	Transforms curves to lines
GetMiterLimit	Returns current miter-join length
GetPath	Returns all lines and curves in path
PathToRegion	Creates a region from a path
SetMiterLimit	Sets miter-join length
StrokeAndFillPath	Closes, strokes, and fills a path
StrokePath	Renders a path with the current pen
WidenPath	Sets the current path to pen width

What is a path? If you are familiar with graphics systems other than Windows (for instance, PostScript and GKS) you probably already understand this simple yet powerful concept, sometimes also called a *segment*; if not, you might have a bit of trouble with it. A path is basically a stored sequence of graphical figures: that's the simple part. The powerful part is that the path can be as complex as you like, and that you can do a lot of things once you have a stored path: you can draw the outline of a path, or *stroke* the path, with the current pen; you can fill it with the current brush; you can widen a path and apply transformations (discussed in the next section) to a path; you can use the path as a clipping region or an ordinary region; you can convert the path to line segments, or *flatten* the path; and you can retrieve the line segments from a flattened path or the line and Bézier curve segments from an unflattened path. The path functions are listed in Table 5-3.

How does one actually use paths? You start a *path bracket* by calling **BeginPath**; then you call the GDI functions that define the path; and you end the path bracket by calling **EndPath**. When you end the path bracket, GDI automatically selects the path into the current device context and deletes any path that was already resident in the device context.

The GDI calls you make within the path bracket do *not* draw in the device context: they only serve to define the path. Once you've defined the path, you can render it in a number of ways. For example, the display of Figure 5-2 was produced by this code:

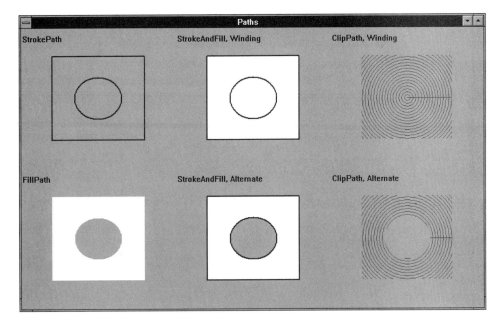

Figure 5-2   Six path renderings in search of an author.

from PATHS.C (in Q_A\SAMPLES)

```
/* 1. Just stroke the path */
SetViewportOrgEx (hdc, 0, 0, NULL);
TextOut (hdc, 2, 10, STROKEPATH, sizeof (STROKEPATH)-1);
DrawPath(hdc, &rect);
StrokePath (hdc);

/* 2. Fill the path */
SetViewportOrgEx (hdc, 0, rect.bottom, NULL);
TextOut (hdc, 2, 10, FILLPATH, sizeof (FILLPATH)-1);
DrawPath(hdc, &rect);
FillPath (hdc);

/* 3. Stroke and fill the path */
SetViewportOrgEx (hdc,rect.right, 0, NULL);
SetPolyFillMode (hdc, WINDING);
TextOut (hdc, 2, 10, STROKEANDFILLWIND,
      sizeof (STROKEANDFILLWIND)-1);
DrawPath(hdc, &rect);
StrokeAndFillPath (hdc);

/* 4. Stroke and fill it again, but with different mode. */
SetViewportOrgEx (hdc,rect.right, rect.bottom, NULL);
SetPolyFillMode (hdc, ALTERNATE);
TextOut (hdc, 2, 10, STROKEANDFILLALT,
      sizeof (STROKEANDFILLALT)-1);
```

```
DrawPath(hdc, &rect);
StrokeAndFillPath (hdc);

/* 5. Set the clipping region based on the path. */
SetViewportOrgEx (hdc,rect.right*2, 0, NULL);
SetPolyFillMode (hdc, WINDING);
TextOut (hdc, 2, 10, CLIPPATHWIND, sizeof (CLIPPATHWIND)-1);
SelectObject(hdc, hPenFill);
DrawPath(hdc, &rect);
hrgn = PathToRegion(hdc);
SelectClipRgn (hdc, hrgn);
DeleteObject (hrgn);
MoveToEx (hdc, rect.right/2, rect.bottom/2, NULL);
for (i = 0; i < rect.right; i += 5)
   AngleArc (hdc, rect.right/2, rect.bottom/2, i,
      (FLOAT)0.0, (FLOAT)360.0);

/* 6. Set the clipping region based on the path,
   with different mode. */
SetViewportOrgEx (hdc,rect.right*2, rect.bottom, NULL);
SetPolyFillMode (hdc, ALTERNATE);
/* clear the clip region so that TextOut() shows up. */
ExtSelectClipRgn (hdc, NULL, RGN_COPY);
TextOut (hdc, 2, 10, CLIPPATHALT, sizeof (CLIPPATHALT)-1);
DrawPath(hdc, &rect);
hrgn = PathToRegion(hdc);
SelectClipRgn (hdc, hrgn);
DeleteObject (hrgn);
MoveToEx (hdc, rect.right/2, rect.bottom/2, NULL);
for (i = 0; i < rect.right; i += 5)
   AngleArc (hdc, rect.right/2, rect.bottom/2, i,
      (FLOAT)0.0, (FLOAT)360.0);
//...
/************************************************************\
*
*   function:  DrawPath()
*
* The path used here is a simple rectangle with an ellipse inside
* of it. The InflateRect() calls have nothing to do with the path,
* but are just used for convenience.
\************************************************************/
void DrawPath(HDC hdc, PRECT prect)
{
RECT destRect;

    /* make a copy that we can modify with impunity. */
    CopyRect (&destRect, prect);

    BeginPath (hdc);

    InflateRect (&destRect, ((destRect.left- destRect.right)/5),
                     ((destRect.top- destRect.bottom)/5));
```

Table 5-4 GDI Functions that Can Be Used in a Path Bracket

AngleArc	LineTo	Polyline
Arc	MoveToEx	PolylineTo
ArcTo	Pie	PolyPolygon
Chord	PolyBezier	PolyPolyline
CloseFigure	PolyBezierTo	Rectangle
Ellipse	PolyDraw	RoundRect
ExtTextOut	Polygon	TextOut

```
    Rectangle (hdc, destRect.left, destRect.top,
                    destRect.right, destRect.bottom);

    InflateRect (&destRect, ((destRect.left- destRect.right)/4),
                      ((destRect.top- destRect.bottom)/4));

    Ellipse (hdc, destRect.left, destRect.top,
                  destRect.right, destRect.bottom);

    EndPath (hdc);
}
```

Now, this is a very simple path. Because of the wide variety of GDI calls that can be used to make up a path—including calls to **TextOut** using whatever font you've selected into the device context—you can easily make a path that has some real interest. Table 5-4 lists all the GDI functions that can be used to define paths.

Not every function used in a path bracket works quite as you'd expect it to. For instance, when you use **TextOut** in a path bracket with the default (opaque) background mode, the path you get is not the text itself, but the text's bounding box minus the text. If you want the path to be the text itself, you must first set the background mode to transparent with **SetBkMode(hDC,TRANSPARENT)**, as in the following example:

```
// obtain the window's client rectangle
GetClientRect(hwnd, &r);

// THE FIX: by setting the background mode
// to transparent, the region is the text itself
SetBkMode(hdc, TRANSPARENT);

 // bracket begin a path
BeginPath(hdc);
```

Figure 5-3 Use of a clip path based on an arial font.

```
// send some text on out into the world
TextOut(hdc, r.left, r.top, "Windows NT Rules Well & Wisely", 4);

// bracket end a path
EndPath(hdc);

// derive a region from that path
SelectClipPath(hdc, RGN_AND);

// this generates the same result as SelectClipPath()
// SelectClipRgn(hdc, PathToRegion(hdc));

// okay, fill the region with grayness

FillRect(hdc, &r, GetStockObject(GRAY_BRUSH));
```

When you use clip paths correctly, you can get results that would be difficult to obtain any other way, as you can see in Figure 5-3. The code that produced Figure 5-3 follows. It is a Microsoft example that you can find in the Win32 help; I've edited the code to emphasize the part that actually deals with paths.

```
CHOOSEFONT cf;              /* common dialog box font structure */
LOGFONT lf;                 /* logical font structure */
HFONT hfont;                /* new logical font handle */
HFONT hfontOld;             /* original logical font handle */
HDC hdc;                    /* display DC handle */
int nXStart, nYStart;       /* drawing coordinates */
RECT rc;                    /* rectangle structure for window */
SIZE sz;                    /* size structure for text extents */
double aflSin[90];          /* sine of 0-90 degrees */
double aflCos[90];          /* cosine of 0-90 degrees */
double flRadius,a;          /* radius of circle */
int iMode;                  /* clipping mode */
HRGN hrgn;                  /* clip region handle */
//...

case IDM_CLIP_PATH:
   hdc = GetDC(hwnd);
```

```
    hfont = CreateFontIndirect(cf.lpLogFont);
    hfontOld = SelectObject(hdc, hfont);
    GetTextExtentPoint(hdc, "Clip Path", 9, &sz);
    hrgn = CreateRectRgn(nXStart, nYStart,
                         nXStart + sz.cx,
                         nYStart + sz.cy);
    SelectClipRgn(hdc, hrgn);
/*
 * Create a clip path using text drawn with
 * the user's requested font.
 */
    BeginPath(hdc);
    TextOut(hdc, nXStart, nYStart, "Clip Path", 9);
    EndPath(hdc);
    SelectClipPath(hdc, iMode);
/* Compute the sine of 0, 1, 2, ... 90 degrees. */
    for (i = 0; i < 90; i++) {
        aflSin[i] = sin( (((double)i) / 180.0) * 3.14159);
        }
/* Compute the cosine of 0, 1, 2, ... 90 degrees. */
    for (i = 0; i < 90; i++) {
        aflCos[i] = cos( (((double)i) / 180.0) * 3.14159);
        }
/* Set the radius value. */
    flRadius = (double)(2 * sz.cx);

/*
 * Draw the 90 rays extending from the
 * radius to the edge of the circle.
 */
    for (i = 0; i < 90; i++) {
        MoveToEx(hdc, nXStart, nYStart, (LPPOINT) NULL);
        LineTo(hdc, nXStart + ((int) (flRadius * aflCos[i])),
                    nYStart + ((int) (flRadius * aflSin[i])));
                    }

    SelectObject(hdc, hfontOld);
    DeleteObject(hfont);
    ReleaseDC(hwnd, hdc);
    break;
```

Note that when Windows NT uses a TrueType font to generate a path, it first gets the character glyph outlines for the current font in the device context: the resulting path no longer has the benefits of the scaling hints built into TrueType fonts.

You can scale a path—any path, whether generated from a TrueType font or not—but not in quite the same way that TrueType fonts scale. The usual way to scale a path is to use a world transform. In fact, world transforms can scale, translate, rotate, and/or shear any Win32 graphic display on any device.

World Transforms

To understand world transforms, we should first understand Windows coordinates and mapping modes. You'll recall that in 16-bit Windows there are eight possible mapping modes that can be used by **SetMapMode**: **MM_TEXT**, **MM_HIENGLISH**, **MM_HIMETRIC**, **MM_LOENGLISH**, **MM_LOMETRIC**, **MM_TWIPS**, **MM_ISOTROPIC**, and **MM_ANISOTROPIC**. **MM_TEXT** mode uses device coordinates (pixels); the English, Metric, and twips modes attempt to use physically meaningful units; the **MM_ISO-TROPIC** and **MM_ANISOTROPIC** modes are scalable.

You control the scaling in **MM_ISOTROPIC** and **MM_ANISOTROPIC** modes with **SetWindowExt** and **SetViewportExt**: essentially, you adjust the ratio between two rectangles. These provide a linear magnification capability: in **MM_ISOTROPIC** mode the magnification is constrained to be the same in the x and y directions, and in **MM_ANISOTROPIC** mode the axes are scaled independently.

World coordinates provide an additional transformation layer. When a world transform is in effect, Win32 maps from *world space* to *page space* before doing the other two mappings that are similar to those done by Win16: page space (logical coordinates) to *device space* (device coordinates), and device space to the physical device. World space measures 2^{32} units in each direction; in Win32, page space measures 2^{32} units in each direction and device space measures 2^{27} units in each direction. In Win16, the logical and physical coordinate systems measure 2^{16} units in each direction.

Win32 maintains full compatibility with the Win16 mapping modes in the default **GM_COMPATIBLE** *graphics mode*. You can enable world coordinates by switching Win32 to **GM_ADVANCED** graphics mode. Note that the *graphics* mode determines how the *mapping* mode will be interpreted and whether or not an attempt to instate a world transform will succeed; and, if a world transform is in effect, you cannot return to **GM_COMPATIBLE** graphics mode until you've removed it:

```
//start in default (compatible) mapping mode
bFlag=SetWorldTransform(hDC,lpXform); //bFlag will be false
//didn't work

iPreviousMode=SetGraphicsMode(hDC,GM_ADVANCED);
//advanced mapping now enabled, iPreviousMode==GM_COMPATIBLE

bFlag=SetWorldTransform(hDC,lpXform); //bFlag will be true
//World transform is now in effect

//....
//try to disable advanced mapping mode
iPreviousMode=SetGraphicsMode(hDC,GM_COMPATIBLE);
//Didn't work: iPreviousMode==0

//World transform still in effect: you can't go back to
//compatible mode until you've returned to the default world //
```

```
transform – the identity matrix
bFlag=ModifyWorldTransform(hDC,lpXform,MWT_IDENTITY);

//Now we can reset the graphics mode
iPreviousMode=SetGraphicsMode(hDC,GM_COMPATIBLE);
//OK, iPreviousMode==GM_ADVANCED
```

World transforms are not only able to scale an image, they can rotate, shear, and translate, or any combination of the four. All world transforms are expressed as the multiplication of the world coordinate vector by a 3 x 3 transformation matrix using what's known in the literature as *homogeneous coordinates*. You can find a full discussion of this system, the reasons for using it, and how it applies to world coordinates in *Computer Graphics*.[4]

Basically, instead of using (x, y) pairs for the transformation calculations, the homogeneous coordinate system uses $(x, y, 1)$ triples: that is, the calculations are done in three dimensions, but restricted to the z=1 plane. (This is actually referred to as the w=1 plane in the literature.) This trick enables translation (normally an addition operation) to be expressed in the same way as rotation and scaling (normally multiplication operations).

In *Computer Graphics*, the homogeneous translation equations are expressed as left-multiplication of a column vector by the transformation matrix:

$$
\begin{bmatrix} x' \\ y' \\ 1 \end{bmatrix} = \begin{bmatrix} r_{11} & r_{12} & t_x \\ r_{21} & r_{22} & t_y \\ 0 & 0 & 1 \end{bmatrix} \bullet \begin{bmatrix} x \\ y \\ 1 \end{bmatrix}
$$

In Microsoft's documention the opposite convention is used, and the world transform equations are expressed as right-multiplication of a row vector by a transposed transformation matrix, using a slightly different notation for the matrix elements:

$$
\begin{bmatrix} x' & y' & 1 \end{bmatrix} = \begin{bmatrix} x & y & 1 \end{bmatrix} \bullet \begin{bmatrix} eM_{11} & eM_{12} & 0 \\ eM_{21} & eM_{22} & 0 \\ eD_x & eD_y & 1 \end{bmatrix}
$$

In any case, the equations used multiply out to:

$$x' = x \cdot eM_{11} + y \cdot eM_{21} + eD_x$$

$$y' = x \cdot eM_{12} + y \cdot eM_{22} + eD_y$$

---

[4] Ibid., pp. 204–213.

As you can see from the equations, a null transformation has **eM11** and **eM22** set to 1, and all the other components set to zero. This of course gives an identity matrix, and is the default world transform. As we showed above when we gave a world transform code example, you can always return to the identity matrix with:

```
ModifyWorldTransform(hDC, lpXform, MWT_IDENTITY);
```

For scaling, set the **eM11** and **eM22** components of the **XFORM** structure to the desired horizontal and vertical magnification factors. For translation, set the **eDx** and **eDy** components to the desired horizontal and vertical offsets. For reflection about the horizontal axis, negate **eM22**; for reflection about a vertical axis, negate **eM11**.

For a shear transformation along the horizontal axis, set **eM12** nonzero; for a shear transformation along the vertical axis, set **eM21** nonzero. For rotation, set **eM11** and **eM22** to *cosine(θ)*, where θ is the desired rotation angle, **eM12** to *sine(θ)*, and **eM21** to *−sine(θ)*.

The **SetWorldTransform** function sets the current world transform to whatever values you pass in the **XFORM** structure. The **ModifyWorldTransform** function, which we used earlier to reset the world transform to an identity matrix, can also be used for *composition* of transformations. Use **MWT_LEFTMULTIPLY** for the third argument to **ModifyWorldTransform** if you want your passed transformation to be applied before the currently set transformation, and **MWT_RIGHTMULTIPLY** if you want your passed transform matrix to be applied after the currently set world transform. As I'm sure you know, matrix multiplication is not commutative: a rotation followed by a translation gives a different result from a translation followed by a rotation.

You can apply a world transform within a path bracket, if you wish; it will affect only those objects drawn after it is set. You can also apply world transforms when rendering a path. It doesn't make a lot of sense to do both, though, unless the transform embedded in the path modifies rather than sets the current state. As an amusing exercise, you might want to see what happens if you embed a right-multiplied rotation and size reduction in a path and render the path repeatedly.

By now, you should have a pretty good idea what you can do with world transforms and paths, including clip paths. Clip paths, as we've seen, act like stencils. Win32 has another function, masking, that does the same sort of thing for bitmaps.

Masking and Parallelogram Blitting

The Win32 **MaskBlt** and **PlgBlt** functions extend the functionality of the standard Windows **BitBlt**, **PatBlt**, and **StretchBlt** functions. **MaskBlt** adds a masking capability to the raster operations of **BitBlt**; **PlgBlt** adds both masking and mapping from a rectangle to a parallelogram but lacks a choice of raster operation. It is worthwhile to compare the argument lists of these five functions:

```
BOOL PatBlt(hdc, nXLeft, nYLeft, nWidth, nHeight, dwRop)
```

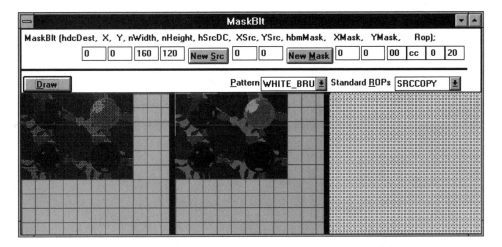

Figure 5-4 The MaskBlt function demonstrated combines the source bitmap (center) with the mask (right) using the SRCCOPY raster operation to produce the result (left). The Microsoft MaskBlt sample program shown is found in the Q_A\SAMPLES directory tree. Note that in this figure the right panel is the mask, the middle panel is the source, and the left panel is the result.

```
BOOL BitBlt(hdcDest, nXDest, nYDest, nWidth, nHeight, hdcSrc,
      nXSrc, nYSrc, dwRop)
BOOL StretchBlt(hdcDest, nXOriginDest, nYOriginDest, nWidthDest,
      nHeightDest, hdcSrc, nXOriginSrc, nYOriginSrc,
      nWidthSrc, nHeightSrc, dwRop)
BOOL MaskBlt(hdcDest, nXDest, nYDest, nWidth, nHeight, hdcSrc,
      nXSrc, nYSrc, hbmMask, xMask, yMask, dwRop)
BOOL PlgBlt(hdcDest, lpPoint, hdcSrc, nXSrc, nYSrc, nWidth,
      nHeight, hbmMask, xMask, yMask)
```

As you can see, the arguments to **MaskBlt** are identical to the arguments to **Bit-Blt** except for the addition of **hbmMask**, **xMask**, and **yMask** prior to **dwRop**. **Mask-Blt** combines the color data for the source and destination bitmaps using the given monochrome bit mask and the given raster operation. As with **BitBlt**, the raster operation code determines how the source and destination will be combined: the difference is that the mask is used to choose between two ROP codes on a pixel-by-pixel basis.

A value of 1 in the mask means that the destination pixel color should be combined with the source pixel color by using the high-order word of the **dwRop** value; 0 in the mask indicates that the destination pixel color should be combined with the source pixel color by using the low-order word. Note that if the mask rectangle is smaller than the source and destination rectangles, the function replicates the mask pattern. The standard ROP codes have appropriately different values in their high and low words. Figure 5-4 demonstrates the use of one of the more common ROP codes, SRCCOPY.

The **PlgBlt** function uses an **LPPOINT** argument to specify the destination location. This argument points to an array of three points in logical space that identify

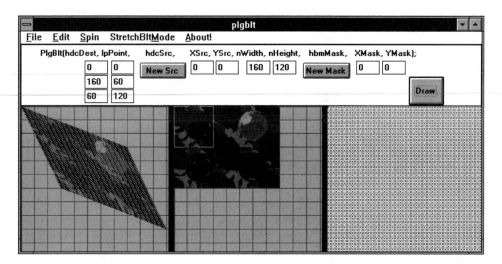

Figure 5-5 The PlgBlt function demonstrated combines the source bitmap (center) with the mask (right) into a parallelogram (left). The PlgBlt sample program shown is found in the MSTOOLS-\SAMPLES directory tree.

three corners of the destination parallelogram. The upper-left corner of the source rectangle is mapped to the first point in this array, the upper-right corner to the second point in this array, and the lower-left corner to the third point. The lower-right corner of the source rectangle is mapped to the implicit fourth point in the parallelogram, which is computed by treating the first three points as vectors **A**, **B**, and **C** and calculating $D = B + C - A$.

You can use the **PlgBlt** function for rapid shear and rotation of bitmaps (see Figure 5-5). Note that you cannot use either a **PlgBlt** or **MaskBlt** function when the *source* device context has a rotation or shearing world transformation in effect. You can however, use scaling, reflection, and translation transforms in the source device context, and any transform in the destination device context of both functions.

Well, that's enough new material to chew on for a while. Now we'll try to put together something useful: a benchmark program.

The WINMAG NT Benchmarks: The Hellstones

I don't remember exactly why I started writing a Windows NT benchmark suite. I had the idea that it would be good to do benchmarks "right" for quite a while, and had proposed the project to several people—none of whom wanted to pay for it. I think what spurred me to start it on my own was that I had to test a symmetric multiprocessing machine for an article in *WINDOWS Magazine* in the absence of any shipping 32-bit threaded applications for Windows NT. In any event the project, like Topsy, "just growed." Eventually, I wrote both Windows 3.1 and Windows NT benchmarks, discussing them and publishing the code in my monthly column as I progressed. After a lot of testing and extension, they were adopted by *WINDOWS Magazine*.

One distinguishing element of the *WINDOWS Magazine* low-level benchmarks is that they include predictions, based on my multiple linear regression studies of results produced at the magazine's testing lab, of how the machine under test would perform on the magazine's high-level application benchmarks. I don't include that functionality in the Hellstone version included with the book because it belongs, at least partially, to the magazine. You can, of course, get the full benchmarks (at least the executables) on disk from the magazine.

I started with standard, C language, public domain measurements of integer and floating point processor performance, the Dhrystone and Whetstone synthetic benchmarks. I quickly found that it was impossible to get two copies of a benchmark program running truly simultaneously from the Windows NT command shell: one would always start after the other. After trying and discarding batch files and C-Shell scripts, I eventually built the standard CPU benchmarks into a small graphical application.

I found no standard code to test disk performance, so I wrote that part from scratch, with the goal that I could test both sequential and random access reading and writing using a variety of file sizes. Because I was concerned that the standard C file I/O functions might not map into the most efficient possible code (and also because I was interested in learning something about Win32), I wrote the NT disk benchmarks to the Win32 API; later I went back and wrote a separate module using the Windows API, for use in the 16-bit Windows benchmarks.

Finally, I added video benchmarks that I felt would reflect the way real applications use the screen in Windows. I wanted the video benchmarks to exercise a variety of GDI functions in meaningful ways: the problem with a lot of other low-level video benchmarks is that vendors can (and do) write device drivers that cheat by, for instance, detecting multiple sequential calls to the same function with the same parameters and ignoring all but the first.

I used a case tool—WindowsMaker Professional, by Blue Sky Software—to design a common interface for the Windows and NT benchmarks. I hoped the generated ANSI C code would work correctly in both Windows and Windows NT, but I was disappointed: the code worked in 16-bit Windows, but failed miserably in Windows NT. It took several hours of going through the compiler diagnostics and working with PORTTOOL to make the code run in Windows NT: clearly, I didn't want to redo that effort every time I generated new code from WindowsMaker.

So, I switched to MFC. With WindowsMaker, this was a matter of installing the "MFC Switch-It Code Generation Module," selecting the new module from a menu, and generating new code. I had to change only a couple lines of generated code to make the MFC code compile and run correctly in Windows NT; that experience, more than

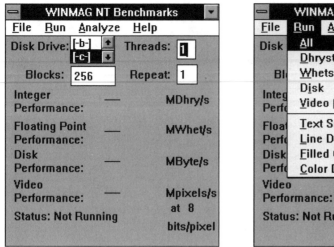 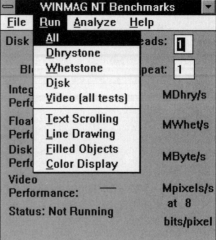

Figure 5-6 NT Hellstones when first launched. **Figure 5-7** NT Hellstones: The Run Menu.

anything else, convinced me of the advantage of using the Microsoft Foundation Classes for work that has to be portable between 16-bit and 32-bit Windows.[5]

Windowing and Message Handling in the Hellstones

The client area of the main window in this application is invisible: it is completely covered by a dialog box (see Figures 5-6, 5-7, and 5-8). The code that sets up the dialog box on top of the Window is rather instructive, especially as it was generated automatically by WindowsMaker:

from WINHELL.WMC

```
// ***************************************************************
//      FUNCTION FOR CREATING CONTROLS IN MAIN WINDOW
// ***************************************************************

// Startup procedure for controls in the client area
// This routine loads the dialog from the resources,
// and then changes the style bits to make it displayable
// in the main window.
```

---

[5] The code displayed in the following sections was generated using the MFC 1.0 Switch-It module. Code generated using the MFC 2.0 Switch-It module is similar in structure, although different in detail. For instance, the MFC 2.0 code for message maps uses the **ON_COMMAND** macro, where the MFC 1.0 code explicitly writes out lines like:

```
afx_msg void wmIDM_SaveCM () {BLD_SaveUDCFunc (this);};
```

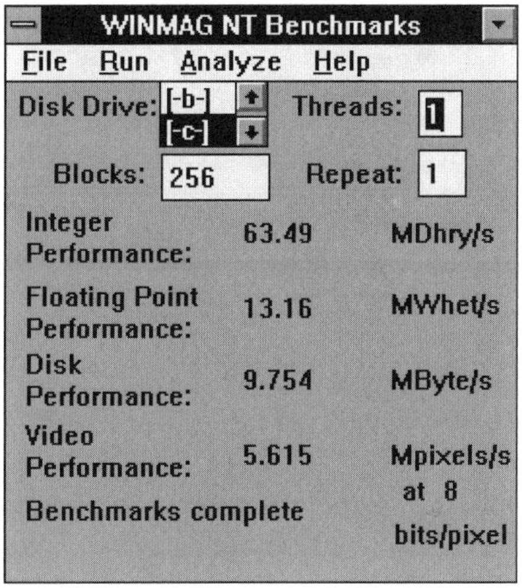

WINMAG NT Benchmarks

File   Run   Analyze   Help

Disk Drive: [-b-] / [-c-]   Threads: 1

Blocks: 256   Repeat: 1

Integer Performance:	63.49	MDhry/s
Floating Point Performance:	13.16	MWhet/s
Disk Performance:	9.754	MByte/s
Video Performance:	5.615	Mpixels/s at 8 bits/pixel
Benchmarks complete		

Figure 5-8 NT Hellstones: after running.

```
BOOL BLDCreateClientControls (char *pTemplateName,
                              CWinMakerClientDlg* pDlg)
{
    RECT   rClient, rMain, rDialog;
    int    dxDialog, dyDialog, dyExtra, dtXold, dtYold;
    HANDLE hRes, hMem;
    LPBLD_DLGTEMPLATE lpDlg;
    unsigned long styleold,style;

    if( !IsWindow (TheApp.m_pMainWnd->GetSafeHwnd ()) )
        return 0;
    if( TheApp.m_pMainWnd->IsZoomed () )
        TheApp.m_pMainWnd->ShowWindow (SW_RESTORE);

    if( IsWindow (TheApp.pWndClient->GetSafeHwnd ()) )
        TheApp.pWndClient->DestroyWindow ();
                // Destroy Previous window in client area

    // Get access to data structure of dialog box containing
    //  layout of controls
    if( !(hRes = FindResource (AfxGetInstanceHandle (),
                              (LPSTR)pTemplateName, RT_DIALOG)) )
        return 0;
    if( !(hMem = LoadResource (AfxGetInstanceHandle (), hRes)) )
        return 0;
    if( !(lpDlg = (LPBLD_DLGTEMPLATE)LockResource (hMem)) )
        return 0;

    // Change dialog box data structure so it can be used as a
    //  window in client area
```

```
    styleold        = lpDlg->dtStyle;
    style           = lpDlg->dtStyle&(CLIENTSTRIP);
    lpDlg->dtStyle = lpDlg->dtStyle^style;
    lpDlg->dtStyle = lpDlg->dtStyle | WS_CHILD | WS_CLIPSIBLINGS;
    dtXold          = lpDlg->dtX;
    dtYold          = lpDlg->dtY;

/* NOTE: the following two lines were commented out by MH to make
the application work. They don't work in Windows NT because the
dialog description structure in Win32 is different from the dialog
description structure in Win16. */
/*  lpDlg->dtX   = 0;
    lpDlg->dtY   = 0;
*/

    if( !(pDlg->doCreateIndirect ((const BYTE FAR *)lpDlg)) )
        return 0;
    HWND   hNew = pDlg->GetSafeHwnd ();

    // Restore dialog box data structure.
    lpDlg->dtStyle = styleold;
    lpDlg->dtX    = dtXold;
    lpDlg->dtY    = dtYold;

    UnlockResource (hMem);
    FreeResource (hMem);

    // Move and size window in client area and main window
    TheApp.m_pMainWnd->GetClientRect (&rClient);
    TheApp.m_pMainWnd->GetWindowRect (&rMain);
    GetWindowRect (hNew, &rDialog);
    dxDialog = (rDialog.right - rDialog.left) -
            (rClient.right - rClient.left);
    dyDialog = (rDialog.bottom - rDialog.top) -
            (rClient.bottom - rClient.top);
    BLDMoveWindow (TheApp.m_pMainWnd->GetSafeHwnd (),
        rMain.left, rMain.top,
        (rMain.right - rMain.left) + dxDialog,
        (rMain.bottom - rMain.top) + dyDialog,
        TRUE);
    pDlg->MoveWindow (0, 0,
        (rDialog.right - rDialog.left),
        (rDialog.bottom - rDialog.top),
        TRUE);
    TheApp.m_pMainWnd->GetClientRect (&rClient);

    // Compensate size if menu bar is more than one line.
    if( (rDialog.bottom - rDialog.top) >
        (rClient.bottom - rClient.top) )
    {
        dyExtra = (rDialog.bottom - rDialog.top) -
                    (rClient.bottom - rClient.top);
```

```
        BLDMoveWindow (TheApp.m_pMainWnd->GetSafeHwnd (),
            rMain.left, rMain.top,
            (rMain.right - rMain.left) + dxDialog,
            (rMain.bottom - rMain.top) + dyDialog + dyExtra,
            TRUE);
    }

    pDlg->InvalidateRect (NULL, TRUE);
    TheApp.pWndClient = (CWinMakerClientDlg*)pDlg;
    pDlg->ShowWindow (SW_SHOW);
    return TRUE;
}


// Ensure that window is within screen.
void BLDMoveWindow(HWND hWnd, int x, int y,
   int nWidth, int nHeight, BOOL bRepaint)
    {
    int xMax,yMax,xNew,yNew;

    xMax = GetSystemMetrics(SM_CXSCREEN);
    yMax = GetSystemMetrics(SM_CYSCREEN);

    if ((nWidth<=xMax)&&(x+nWidth>xMax))
        xNew=xMax-nWidth;
    else
        xNew=x;

    if ((nHeight<=yMax)&&(y+nHeight>yMax))
        yNew=yMax-nHeight;
    else
        yNew=y;

    MoveWindow(hWnd,xNew,yNew,nWidth,nHeight,bRepaint);
    return;
    }
```

The hack that Blue Sky Software accomplishes here is quite clever. Basically, they find the dialog resource, load it, lock it, diddle the window style bits so it will work as a child of the application's main window, set the window position to (0, 0), and finally run it as a modeless dialog box: **doCreateIndirect** is nothing more than a WindowsMaker **CWinMakerClientDlg** class member function that acts as a wrapper to **CreateIndirect**. The **BLDCreateClientControls** function also resizes the main window so that it exactly fits the dialog, and calls **BLDMoveWindow** to nudge the window onscreen after resizing if necessary.

You'll note that I had to comment out two lines of their code to make it work in Windows NT, the two lines that set the window position to (0, 0). The dialog description structure changed from Win16 and Win32; in Win32 there is some extra stuff before the Window position.

The WindowsMaker Class Hierarchy

The main source file generated by WindowsMaker, NTHELL.CPP, contains precious little code of its own, although it does contain **#include** lines for AFXWIN.H, NTBENCH.H, and NTHELL.WMC:

NTHELL.CPP

```
//Filename: NTHELL.CPP
//"NTHELL" Generated by WindowsMAKER Professional
//Author: Martin Heller

//
// ****************************************************************
// Code in this file is initially generated  by WindowsMAKER
// Professional. This file contains member functions you can change
// to provide whatever functionality you require. This file
// also contains the message maps for the classes.
// You can add functionality to all the functions referred to in
// the message map - however be careful to call the equivalent
// functions in the WindowsMAKER base classes if you overload any
// of the WindowsMAKER member functions. For more information, see
// the section "How code is generated" in the documentation.
// ****************************************************************
//
// Classes:
//        Cwm_Application
//        Cwm_MainWnd
//
//
// -----------------
// |  MFC CLASS    |
// | |             |
// -----------------
//        |
// -----------------
// | WindowsMAKER  |
// | Common Class  |
// -----------------
//        |
// -----------------
// | WindowsMAKER  |
// |  Base Class   |
// -----------------
//        |
// -----------------
// |  USER CLASS   |   <- You are here
// | |             |
// -----------------


#include <afxwin.h>
#include "NTBENCH.H"
```

```
WMPDEBUG
#include "NTHELL.WMC"

// a simple way to reduce the size of C run times
// disables the use of the getenv and argv/argc
extern "C" void _setargv() { }
extern "C" void _setenvp() { }

// ****************************************************************
// Create the window application object.  Sets the ball in
// motion for the entire application.
// ****************************************************************

Cwm_Application TheApp;

// ****************************************************************
//             MAIN APPLICATION CLASS: Cwm_Application
// ****************************************************************

// The User window application. In this class, you can override any
// member functions in parent classes you need to, and add your own
// functionality.

// Initialize the application
BOOL Cwm_Application::InitApplication ()
{

// Base Class processing of InitApplication
    return CWinMakerApp::InitApplication ();
}


// Initialize this instance of the application
BOOL Cwm_Application::InitInstance ()
{

// Base Class processing of InitInstance
    return CWinMakerApp::InitInstance ();
}


// Exit for this instance of the application
BOOL Cwm_Application::ExitInstance ()
{

// Base Class processing of ExitInstance
    return CWinMakerApp::ExitInstance ();
}


// ****************************************************************
//          MAIN WINDOW CLASS: Cwm_MainWnd
// ****************************************************************

// this is the message map for the generated window class,
// Cwm_MainWnd.  You can define whatever message handlers you need
```

```
// to here.  Note that some messages are already handled
// by the Cwm_MainBaseWnd base class, and unless you want to
// overload their functionality, it is not necessary to handle
// those messages here.

BEGIN_MESSAGE_MAP(Cwm_MainWnd,Cwm_MainBaseWnd)
    ON_WM_SETFOCUS()
END_MESSAGE_MAP()

void Cwm_MainWnd::OnSetFocus (CWnd* pOldWnd)
{

// Base Class processing of OnSetFocus
    Cwm_MainBaseWnd::OnSetFocus (pOldWnd);
}

// Procedure for processing message WM_CREATE
int Cwm_MainWnd::BLD_WM_CREATEMsg(LPCREATESTRUCT lpCreateStruct)
{

    return CWinMakerFrameWnd::OnCreate (lpCreateStruct);
}
```

What's happening here? The program creates a global instance, **TheApp**, of the **Cwm_Application** class, which is derived from a WindowsMaker base class. Where? NTBENCH.H declares the classes but does not define them:

NTBENCH.H

```
// Filename: NTBENCH.H
// "NTHELL" Generated by WindowsMAKER Professional
// Author: Martin Heller

#define WMPDEBUG

// WindowsMAKER class definitions.
class CWinMakerApp;
class CWinMakerFrameWnd;
class CWinMakerModelessDlg;
class CWinMakerModalDlg;
class CWinMakerClientDlg;
class Cwm_MainBaseWnd;
class Cwm_Application;
class Cwm_MainWnd;

class Cwm_MainWinControlsBaseDlg;
class Cwm_MainWinControlsDlg;
class Cwm_AboutBaseDlg;
class Cwm_AboutDlg;
class Cwm_ShowDetailsBaseDlg;
class Cwm_ShowDetailsDlg;
```

```
class Cwm_Menu41BaseDlg;
class Cwm_Menu41Dlg;

// ************************************************************
// WindowsMAKER ID Values

#define id_cb_drive                              10000
#define id_ed_threads                            10001
#define id_ed_blocks                             10002
#define id_ed_repeat                             10003
#define id_tx_dhrys                              10004
#define id_tx_whets                              10005
#define id_tx_kbytes                             10006
#define id_tx_status                             10007
#define id_tx_video                              10008
#define id_text_bpp                              10009
#define id_tx_bpp                                10010
#define id_tx_rpt                                10011
#define id_tx_seqrd                              10012
#define id_tx_seqwrite                           10013
#define id_tx_seqread                            10014
#define id_tx_randwrite                          10015
#define id_tx_randread                           10016
#define id_tx_textscroll                         10017
#define id_tx_linedraw                           10018
#define id_tx_filledobj                          10019
#define id_tx_colordisp                          10020
#define id_ed_describe                           10021
#define id_tx_version                            10022


// ************************************************************
// WindowsMAKER Pro automatically generated ID Values

#define IDM_Save                                 4000
#define IDM_Saveas                               4001
#define IDM_Print                                4002
#define IDM_Exit                                 4003
#define IDM_All                                  4004
#define IDM_Dhrystone                            4005
#define IDM_Whetstone                            4006
#define IDM_Disk                                 4007
#define IDM_Videoalltests                        4008
#define IDM_TextScrolling                        4009
#define IDM_LineDrawing                          4010
#define IDM_FilledObjects                        4011
#define IDM_ColorDisplay                         4012
#define IDM_Details                              4013
#define IDM_Charts                               4014
#define IDM_Comparisons                          4015
#define IDM_Predictions                          4016
#define IDM_About                                4017
```

```
// Constants for error message strings
#define BLD_CannotRun          4000
#define BLD_CannotCreate       4001
#define BLD_CannotLoadMenu     4002
#define BLD_CannotLoadIcon     4003
#define BLD_CannotLoadBitmap   4004

#if !defined(THISISBLDRC)

// Give access to handles in all code modules
extern Cwm_Application TheApp;

// WindowsMaker internal functions
BOOL    BLDCreateClientControls (char *, CWinMakerClientDlg*);
int     BLDDisplayMessage (HWND, unsigned, char *, int);
BOOL    BLDDrawBitmap (LPDRAWITEMSTRUCT, char *, BOOL);
BOOL    BLDDrawIcon (LPDRAWITEMSTRUCT, char *);
void    BLDMoveWindow (HWND, int, int, int, int, BOOL);
BOOL    BLDSwitchMenu (CWnd* pWnd, char *pTemplateName);

BOOL BLD_RunBenchMarksUDCFunc (CWnd *pWnd);
BOOL BLD_ExitUDCFunc (CWnd *pWnd);
BOOL BLD_PrintUDCFunc (CWnd *pWnd);
BOOL BLD_SaveUDCFunc (CWnd *pWnd);
BOOL BLD_SaveasUDCFunc (CWnd *pWnd);
CWnd * BLD_MainWinControlsClFunc (CWnd *pWnd);
BOOL   BLD_AboutDlgFunc (CWnd *pWnd);
BOOL BLD_RunDhrystoneUDCFunc (CWnd *pWnd);
BOOL BLD_RunWhetstoneUDCFunc (CWnd *pWnd);
BOOL BLD_RunDiskUDCFunc (CWnd *pWnd);
BOOL BLD_RunVideoUDCFunc (CWnd *pWnd);
BOOL BLD_TextScrollingUDCFunc (CWnd *pWnd);
BOOL BLD_LineDrawingUDCFunc (CWnd *pWnd);
BOOL BLD_FilledObjectsUDCFunc (CWnd *pWnd);
BOOL BLD_ColorDisplayUDCFunc (CWnd *pWnd);
BOOL   BLD_ShowDetailsDlgFunc (CWnd *pWnd);
BOOL   BLD_Menu41DlgFunc (CWnd *pWnd);

// ****************************************************************
// Variables, types and constants for controls in main window.
// ****************************************************************

#define CLIENTSTRIP WS_MINIMIZE|WS_MAXIMIZE|WS_CAPTION|WS_BORDER /
      |WS_DLGFRAME|WS_SYSMENU|WS_POPUP|WS_THICKFRAME|DS_MODALFRAME

typedef struct
{
    unsigned long dtStyle;
    BYTE dtItemCount;
    int dtX;
    int dtY;
    int dtCX;
```

```
   int dtCY;
} BLD_DLGTEMPLATE;

typedef BLD_DLGTEMPLATE far      *LPBLD_DLGTEMPLATE;

#include "NTHELL.WMH"
#endif
```

Aha! NTBENCH.H, in turn, includes NTHELL.WMH, which does the actual base class definitions:

NTHELL.WMH

```
//Filename: NTHELL.WMH
//"NTHELL" Generated by WindowsMAKER Professional
//Author: Martin Heller

//
// ****************************************************************
// Do not add code here. Add code in the .HPP file.
//
// This file is maintained by WindowsMAKER Professional.
// As you make changes in your application using WindowsMAKER
// Professional, this file is automatically updated, therefore you
// never modify this file. This file contains the base classes for
// the application and the main window class. It also contains the
// WindowsMAKER common classes - which is the basis for common
// WindowsMAKER functionality (eg. menu handling)
// For more information, see the section "How code is generated"
// in the documentation.
// ****************************************************************
//
// Classes:
//          CWinMakerApp
//          CWinMakerFrameWnd
//          CWinMakerModelessDlg
//          CWinMakerModalDlg
//          CWinMakerClientDlg
//          Cwm_MainBaseWnd
//
//
// ----------------
// |  MFC CLASS   |
// | |           . |
// ----------------
//          |
// ----------------
// | WindowsMAKER |   <- You are here
// | Common Class |
// ----------------
```

```
//            |
// ----------------
// | WindowsMAKER |
// |  Base Class  |
// ----------------
//            |
// ----------------
// |  USER CLASS  |
// |              |
// ----------------


#ifndef __WMP_INCLUDED__
#define __WMP_INCLUDED__


// *************************************************************
//                     CLASS: CWinMakerApp
// *************************************************************

// This is a WindowsMAKER class that encapsulates all the
// functionality for a WindowsMAKER application.  The user's
// application class must inherit from this class.  This class
// handles initialization and termination of the application, the
// creation of windows and registration of windows classes.

class CWinMakerApp : public CWinApp
{
public:

    CWinMakerApp (const char* pName = NULL);

    virtual ~CWinMakerApp() {} ;

    virtual BOOL InitInstance ();
    virtual BOOL InitApplication ();
    virtual CString RegisterCustClass ();
    virtual BOOL ExitInstance ();

    HBRUSH                 hbrBack;

    CWinMakerClientDlg* pWndClient;
    Cwm_MainWnd*        pWndMain;


private:
    CString strWndClass;

protected:
    virtual BOOL PreTranslateMessage(MSG* pMsg);
} ;


// Prototypes for User Class
#define WMPROTO_Application()
```

```
// **************************************************************
//                    CLASS: CWinMakerFrameWnd
// **************************************************************

// This is a WindowsMAKER class that encapsulates all the
// functionality of the applications frame windows.  The
// initialization of the windows are done by this class, and all
// the menu commands for the windows come through this class. User
// windows should inherit from this class to gain default
// WindowsMAKER functionality.

class CWinMakerFrameWnd : public CFrameWnd
{
public:
    CWinMakerFrameWnd () : CFrameWnd() {} ;
    virtual ~CWinMakerFrameWnd() {} ;

    virtual BOOL LoadAccelTable (const char *szTable)
            {return TRUE;};
    friend BLDSwitchMenu (CWnd* pWnd, char *pTemplateName);

    // a buffer function so that a window can be created by any
    // function, public or private.
    virtual BOOL doCreate (const char *strClass, const char *szCap,
        DWORD dwStyle, const CRect& rc, const CWnd *pParent,
                    const char FAR *szMenu)
        { return Create (strClass, szCap, dwStyle, rc,
                        pParent, szMenu); } ;

protected:

// Menu command functions in menu: MAINMENUBAR
    afx_msg void wmIDM_SaveCM () {BLD_SaveUDCFunc (this);} ;
    afx_msg void wmIDM_SaveasCM () {BLD_SaveasUDCFunc (this);} ;
    afx_msg void wmIDM_PrintCM () {BLD_PrintUDCFunc (this);} ;
    afx_msg void wmIDM_ExitCM () {BLD_ExitUDCFunc (this);} ;
    afx_msg void wmIDM_AllCM () {BLD_RunBenchMarksUDCFunc (this);} ;
    afx_msg void wmIDM_DhrystoneCM ()
        {BLD_RunDhrystoneUDCFunc (this);} ;
    afx_msg void wmIDM_WhetstoneCM ()
        {BLD_RunWhetstoneUDCFunc (this);} ;
    afx_msg void wmIDM_DiskCM () {BLD_RunDiskUDCFunc (this);} ;
    afx_msg void wmIDM_VideoalltestsCM ()
        {BLD_RunVideoUDCFunc (this);} ;
    afx_msg void wmIDM_TextScrollingCM ()
        {BLD_TextScrollingUDCFunc (this);} ;
    afx_msg void wmIDM_LineDrawingCM ()
        {BLD_LineDrawingUDCFunc (this);} ;
    afx_msg void wmIDM_FilledObjectsCM ()
        {BLD_FilledObjectsUDCFunc (this);} ;
    afx_msg void wmIDM_ColorDisplayCM ()
        {BLD_ColorDisplayUDCFunc (this);} ;
```

```
    afx_msg void wmIDM_DetailsCM ()
        {BLD_ShowDetailsDlgFunc (this);} ;
    afx_msg void wmIDM_AboutCM () {BLD_AboutDlgFunc (this);} ;
    DECLARE_MESSAGE_MAP()
} ;

// ****************************************************************
//                    CLASS: Cwm_MainBaseWnd
// ****************************************************************

// This is a WindowsMAKER class that encapsulates all the
// functionality for the applications main window. The
// initialization of the window are done by this class, and all the
// messages for the window come through this class.  User windows
// should inherit from this class to gain default WindowsMAKER
// functionality.

class Cwm_MainBaseWnd : public CWinMakerFrameWnd
{
public:
    Cwm_MainBaseWnd () : CWinMakerFrameWnd() {};
    virtual ~Cwm_MainBaseWnd() {} ;

    virtual BOOL InitWindow (const char *strClass);
    virtual BOOL InitMainMenu ();
    virtual BOOL LoadAccelTable (const char *szTable);


protected:
    virtual int  BLD_WM_CREATEMsg(LPCREATESTRUCT lpCreateStruct)
        {return 0;};

// Prototypes for Message Handling Functions
    afx_msg int OnCreate (LPCREATESTRUCT lpCreateStruct);
    afx_msg void OnSetFocus (CWnd* pOldWnd);

    friend class CWinMakerApp;    // for PreTranslate access

    DECLARE_MESSAGE_MAP()
} ;


// Prototypes for User Class
#define WMPROTO_MainWnd() \
    virtual int  BLD_WM_CREATEMsg(LPCREATESTRUCT lpCreateStruct);\



// ****************************************************************
//                    CLASS: CWinMakerModalDlg
// ****************************************************************

// This is a WindowsMAKER modal dialog class that encapsulates all
```

```
// the base functionality that WindowsMAKER provides for modal
// dialogs.  Every modal dialog box in the system inherits from
// this class, and redefines attributes for that specific dialog
// box.

class CWinMakerModalDlg : public CModalDialog
{
public:
    CWinMakerModalDlg(const char FAR* AName,
                      CWnd* pParentWnd = NULL)
    : CModalDialog (AName, pParentWnd) {} ;

    virtual ~CWinMakerModalDlg() {} ;

    friend BLDSwitchMenu (CWnd* pWnd, char *pTemplateName);

protected:

// Menu command functions in menu: MAINMENUBAR
    afx_msg void wmIDM_SaveCM () {BLD_SaveUDCFunc (this);} ;
    afx_msg void wmIDM_SaveasCM () {BLD_SaveasUDCFunc (this);} ;
    afx_msg void wmIDM_PrintCM () {BLD_PrintUDCFunc (this);} ;
    afx_msg void wmIDM_ExitCM () {BLD_ExitUDCFunc (this);} ;
    afx_msg void wmIDM_AllCM () {BLD_RunBenchMarksUDCFunc (this);};
    afx_msg void wmIDM_DhrystoneCM ()
      {BLD_RunDhrystoneUDCFunc (this);} ;
    afx_msg void wmIDM_WhetstoneCM ()
      {BLD_RunWhetstoneUDCFunc (this);} ;
    afx_msg void wmIDM_DiskCM () {BLD_RunDiskUDCFunc (this);} ;
    afx_msg void wmIDM_VideoalltestsCM ()
      {BLD_RunVideoUDCFunc (this);} ;
    afx_msg void wmIDM_TextScrollingCM ()
      {BLD_TextScrollingUDCFunc (this);} ;
    afx_msg void wmIDM_LineDrawingCM ()
      {BLD_LineDrawingUDCFunc (this);} ;
    afx_msg void wmIDM_FilledObjectsCM ()
      {BLD_FilledObjectsUDCFunc (this);} ;
    afx_msg void wmIDM_ColorDisplayCM ()
      {BLD_ColorDisplayUDCFunc (this);} ;
    afx_msg void wmIDM_DetailsCM ()
      {BLD_ShowDetailsDlgFunc (this);} ;
    afx_msg void wmIDM_AboutCM () {BLD_AboutDlgFunc (this);} ;
    DECLARE_MESSAGE_MAP()
} ;


// *************************************************************
//                   CLASS: CWinMakerModelessDlg
// *************************************************************

// This is a WindowsMAKER modeless dialog class that encapsulates
// all the base functionality that WindowsMAKER provides for
```

```
// modeless dialogs.  Every modeless dialog box in the system
// inherits from this class, and redefines attributes for that
// specific dialog box.

class CWinMakerModelessDlg : public CDialog

{
public:
    CWinMakerModelessDlg () : CDialog () {} ;

    virtual ~CWinMakerModelessDlg() {} ;

    friend BLDSwitchMenu (CWnd* pWnd, char *pTemplateName);
    virtual BOOL doCreateIndirect (const BYTE FAR *pDlgTmp,
            CWnd *pParent = NULL)
        { return CreateIndirect (pDlgTmp, pParent); } ;

protected:
// for custom cleanup after WM_NCDESTROY
    virtual void PostNcDestroy();

// Overridables (special message map entries)
    virtual void OnOK();
    virtual void OnCancel();

// Menu command functions in menu: MAINMENUBAR
    afx_msg void wmIDM_SaveCM () {BLD_SaveUDCFunc (this);} ;
    afx_msg void wmIDM_SaveasCM () {BLD_SaveasUDCFunc (this);} ;
    afx_msg void wmIDM_PrintCM () {BLD_PrintUDCFunc (this);} ;
    afx_msg void wmIDM_ExitCM () {BLD_ExitUDCFunc (this);} ;
    afx_msg void wmIDM_AllCM () {BLD_RunBenchMarksUDCFunc (this);};
    afx_msg void wmIDM_DhrystoneCM ()
      {BLD_RunDhrystoneUDCFunc (this);} ;
    afx_msg void wmIDM_WhetstoneCM ()
      {BLD_RunWhetstoneUDCFunc (this);} ;
    afx_msg void wmIDM_DiskCM () {BLD_RunDiskUDCFunc (this);} ;
    afx_msg void wmIDM_VideoalltestsCM ()
      {BLD_RunVideoUDCFunc (this);} ;
    afx_msg void wmIDM_TextScrollingCM ()
      {BLD_TextScrollingUDCFunc (this);} ;
    afx_msg void wmIDM_LineDrawingCM ()
      {BLD_LineDrawingUDCFunc (this);} ;
    afx_msg void wmIDM_FilledObjectsCM ()
      {BLD_FilledObjectsUDCFunc (this);} ;
    afx_msg void wmIDM_ColorDisplayCM ()
      {BLD_ColorDisplayUDCFunc (this);} ;
    afx_msg void wmIDM_DetailsCM ()
      {BLD_ShowDetailsDlgFunc (this);} ;
    afx_msg void wmIDM_AboutCM () {BLD_AboutDlgFunc (this);} ;
    DECLARE_MESSAGE_MAP()
} ;
```

```
// *************************************************************
//                  CLASS: CWinMakerClientDlg
// *************************************************************

// This is a WindowsMAKER Client dialog class that encapsulates all
// the base functionality that WindowsMAKER provides for client
// dialogs. Every client dialog box in the system inherits from
// this class, and redefines attributes for that specific dialog
// box.

class CWinMakerClientDlg : public CDialog
{
public:
    CWinMakerClientDlg () : CDialog () {} ;

    virtual ~CWinMakerClientDlg() {} ;

    friend BLDSwitchMenu (CWnd* pWnd, char *pTemplateName);
    virtual BOOL doCreateIndirect (const BYTE FAR *pDlgTmp,
        CWnd *pParent = NULL)
        { return CreateIndirect (pDlgTmp, pParent); } ;

protected:
// for custom cleanup after WM_NCDESTROY
    virtual void PostNcDestroy();

// Overridables (special message map entries)
    virtual void OnOK(){};
    virtual void OnCancel(){};

    DECLARE_MESSAGE_MAP()
} ;

// Include of user header file

#include "NTHELL.HPP"

#endif
```

Curiouser and curiouser: NTHELL.WMH, in turn, includes NTHELL.HPP. Fortunately, the **#include** nesting ends here, where the user classes are defined:

NTHELL.HPP

```
//Filename: NTHELL.HPP
//"NTHELL" Generated by WindowsMAKER Professional
//Author: Martin Heller

//
// *************************************************************
// Code in this file is initially generated  by WindowsMAKER
```

```
// Professional. This file contains classes for the main window and
// application itself. You can modify these classes to add your own
// functionality. If you need to, you can overload the member
// functions of the WindowsMAKER base classes to override the
// default functionality of a given class. Note that WindowsMAKER
// often provides functionality that is required for the program to
// function correctly - for instance the initialization of the
// application. For more information, see the section "How code is
// generated" in the documentation.
// ****************************************************************
//
// Classes:
//          Cwm_Application
//          Cwm_MainWnd
//
//
// ----------------
// |   MFC CLASS   |
// | |             |
// ----------------
//        |
// ----------------
// | WindowsMAKER  |
// | Common Class  |
// ----------------
//        |
// ----------------
// | WindowsMAKER  |
// |  Base Class   |
// ----------------
//        |
// ----------------
// |  USER CLASS   |   <- You are here
// | |             |
// ----------------

// ****************************************************************
//              MAIN APPLICATION CLASS: Cwm_Application
// ****************************************************************

// The User window application.  In this class, you can override
// any member functions in parent classes you need to, and add your
// own functionality.

class Cwm_Application : public CWinMakerApp
{
public:
    Cwm_Application (const char* pName = NULL)
    : CWinMakerApp (pName) {} ;
    virtual ~Cwm_Application () { } ;

    virtual BOOL InitApplication ();
    virtual BOOL InitInstance ();
```

```
    virtual BOOL ExitInstance ();

    WMPROTO_Application()

protected:

} ;

// **************************************************************
//          MAIN WINDOW CLASS: Cwm_MainWnd
// **************************************************************

// The main window user class.  This class handles all the
// processing for the main window.  In it, you can define whatever
// member functions are necessary to create your application.  You
// can override message handling for the main window in this class
// if you so choose.  You can also override any of the
// initialization routines if you need very flexible
// initialization.

class Cwm_MainWnd : public Cwm_MainBaseWnd
{
public:
    Cwm_MainWnd () : Cwm_MainBaseWnd () { } ;
    virtual ~Cwm_MainWnd () { } ;

    WMPROTO_MainWnd()

protected:
    afx_msg void OnSetFocus (CWnd* pOldWnd);
    DECLARE_MESSAGE_MAP()
} ;
```

Whew! We can fairly complain that WindowsMaker creates a lot of files, but remember: those files are generated automatically based on settings and drawings we did in the WindowsMaker application designer. We haven't yet started to look at my own application code.

It's interesting to compare the code WindowsMaker generated to the code generated by AppWizard and ClassWizard that we looked at in the last chapter. WindowsMaker creates several intermediate levels between your application classes and the base MFC classes, but uses only the MFC 1.0 functionality.[6] AppWizard and ClassWizard create application classes that are directly derived from base MFC 2.0 classes. Both the WindowsMaker approach and the VC++ approach free you from maintaining your own message map code, and both approaches give you a running application—albeit one that doesn't do anything useful—very quickly.

Let's take a step back, now, and look at the Dhrystones.

---

[6] As of this writing, WindowsMaker can currently generate code *compatible* with MFC 2.0, but the code does not use the frame-document-view architecture of MFC 2.0.

Integer CPU Performance: The Dhrystones

As I mentioned earlier, I chose the Dhrystone synthetic benchmark to measure integer CPU performance because it is a generally accepted standard. As you will see later, I had to bend the standard somewhat to make it work in a multithreaded application, but I did my best to minimize the changes I made.

The Dhrystone benchmark program is synthetic in that it does nothing useful: it just runs typical kinds of code sequences, which are intended to have the same sort of statistical distribution as you'll find in real code. The program is primarily the brainchild of Reinhold Weicker of Siemens AG; his paper in the *Communications of the ACM* in 1984 explains the genesis of the statistical distribution of statements, and presents the original benchmark in Ada. Since then, of course, C has become important, and optimizing compilers have become rather sophisticated: Weicker's current version is written in C, and uses three separate files (one include file and two C source files) to avoid having all the function calls optimized away.

The include file, DHRY.H, contains all the global definitions, the environment-dependent compilation switches, and the comments:

DHRY.H

```
/*
 *****************************************************************
 *
 *                 "DHRYSTONE" Benchmark Program
 *                 ----------------------------
 *
 * Version:    C, Version 2.1
 *
 * File:       dhry.h (part 1 of 3)
 *
 * Date:       May 17, 1988
 *
 * Author:     Reinhold P. Weicker
 *                  Siemens AG, E STE 35
 *                  Postfach 3240
 *                  8520 Erlangen
 *                  Germany (West)
 *                      Phone:  [xxx-49]-9131-7-20330
 *                      (8-17 Central European Time)
 *                      Usenet: ..!mcvax!unido!estevax!weicker
 *
 *        Original Version (in Ada) published in
 *        "Communications of the ACM" vol. 27., no. 10 (Oct. 1984),
 *        pp. 1013 - 1030, together with the statistics
 *        on which the distribution of statements etc. is based.
 *
 * In this C version, the following C library functions are used:
 *        - strcpy, strcmp (inside the measurement loop)
 *        - printf, scanf (outside the measurement loop)
```

```
*   In addition, Berkeley UNIX system calls "times ()" or "time ()"
*   are used for execution time measurement. For measurements
*   on other systems, these calls have to be changed.
*
*   Collection of Results:
*               Reinhold Weicker (address see above) and
*
*               Rick Richardson
*               PC Research. Inc.
*               94 Apple Orchard Drive
*               Tinton Falls, NJ 07724
*                       Phone:  (201) 389-8963 (9-17 EST)
*                       Usenet: ...!uunet!pcrat!rick
*
* Please send results to Rick Richardson and/or Reinhold Weicker.
* Complete information should be given on hardware and
* software used.
* Hardware information includes: Machine type, CPU, type and size
* of caches; for microprocessors: clock frequency, memory speed
* (number of wait states).
* Software information includes: Compiler (and runtime library)
* manufacturer and version, compilation switches, OS version.
* The Operating System version may give an indication about the
* compiler; Dhrystone itself performs no OS calls in the
* measurement loop.
*
*   The complete output generated by the program should be mailed
*     such that at least some checks for correctness can be made.
*
****************************************************************
*
*   History:    This version C/2.1 has been made for two reasons:
*
*   1) There is an obvious need for a common C version of
*      Dhrystone, since C is at present the most popular system
*      programming language for the class of processors
*      (microcomputers, minicomputers) where Dhrystone is used most.
*      There should be, as far as possible, only one C version of
*      Dhrystone such that results can be compared without
*      restrictions. In the past, the C versions distributed
*      by Rick Richardson (Version 1.1) and by Reinhold Weicker
*      had small (though not significant) differences.
*
*   2) As far as it is possible without changes to the Dhrystone
*      statistics, optimizing compilers should be prevented from
*      removing significant statements.
*      This C version has been developed in cooperation with
*      Rick Richardson (Tinton Falls, NJ), it incorporates many
*      ideas from the "Version 1.1" distributed previously by
*      him over the UNIX network Usenet.
*      I also thank Chaim Benedelac (National Semiconductor),
*      David Ditzel (SUN), Earl Killian and John Mashey (MIPS),
*      Alan Smith and Rafael Saavedra-Barrera (UC at Berkeley)
*      for their help with comments on earlier versions of the
*      benchmark.
```

```
 *
 *  Changes: In the initialization part, this version follows
 * mostly Rick Richardson's version distributed via Usenet, not
 * the version distributed earlier via floppy disk by Reinhold
 * Weicker.
 *  As a concession to older compilers, names have been made
 * unique within the first 8 characters.
 * Inside the measurement loop, this version follows the
 * version previously distributed by Reinhold Weicker.
 * At several places in the benchmark, code has been added,
 * but within the measurement loop only in branches that
 * are not executed. The intention is that optimizing compilers
 * should be prevented from moving code out of the measurement
 * loop, or from removing code altogether. Since the statements
 * that are executed within the measurement loop have NOT been
 * changed, the numbers defining the "Dhrystone distribution"
 * (distribution of statements, operand types and locality)
 * still hold. Except for sophisticated optimizing compilers,
 * execution times for this version should be the same as
 * for previous versions.
 *
 * Since it has proven difficult to subtract the time for the
 * measurement loop overhead in a correct way, the loop check
 * has been made a part of the benchmark. This does have
 * an impact - though a very minor one - on the distribution
 * statistics which have been updated for this version.
 *
 * All changes within the measurement loop are described
 * and discussed in the companion paper "Rationale for
 * Dhrystone version 2".
 *
 * Because of the self-imposed limitation that the order and
 * distribution of the executed statements should not be
 * changed, there are still cases where optimizing compilers
 * may not generate code for some statements. To a certain
 * degree, this is unavoidable for small synthetic benchmarks.
 * Users of the benchmark are advised to check code listings
 * whether code is generated for all statements of Dhrystone.
 *
 * Version 2.1 is identical to version 2.0 distributed via
 * the UNIX network Usenet in March 1988 except that it corrects
 * some minor deficiencies that were found by users of version 2.0.
 * The following corrections have been made in the C version:
 *     - The assignment to Number_Of_Runs was changed
 *     - The constant Too_Small_Time was changed
 *     - An "else" part was added to the "if" statement in Func_3;
 *       for compensation, an "else" part was removed in Proc_3
 *     - Shorter file names are used
 *
 ****************************************************************
 *
 * Defines:    The following "Defines" are possible:
 *    -DREG=register          (default: Not defined)
```

```
*                 As an approximation to what an average C programmer
*                 might do, the "register" storage class is applied
*                 (if enabled by -DREG=register)
*                 - for local variables, if they are used (dynamically)
*                   five or more times
*                 - for parameters if they are used (dynamically)
*                   six or more times
*              Note that an optimal "register" strategy is
*              compiler-dependent, and that "register" declarations
*              do not necessarily lead to faster execution.
*           -DNOSTRUCTASSIGN          (default: Not defined)
*                 Define if the C compiler does not support
*                 assignment of structures.
*           -DNOENUMS                 (default: Not defined)
*                 Define if the C compiler does not support
*                 enumeration types.
*           -DTIMES                   (default)
*           -DTIME
*              The "times" function of UNIX (returning process times)
*                 or the "time" function (returning wallclock time)
*                 is used for measurement.
*              For single user machines, "time ()" is adequate. For
*              multi-user machines where you cannot get single-user
*              access, use the "times ()" function. If you have
*              neither, use a stopwatch in the dead of night.
*             "printf"s are provided marking the points "Start Timer"
*              and "Stop Timer". DO NOT use the UNIX "time(1)"
*              command, as this will measure the total time to
*              run this program, which will (erroneously) include
*              the time to allocate storage (malloc) and to perform
*              the initialization.
*           -DHZ=nnn
*               In Berkeley UNIX, the function "times" returns process
*               time in 1/HZ seconds, with HZ = 60 for most systems.
*           CHECK YOUR SYSTEM DESCRIPTION BEFORE YOU JUST APPLY
*           A VALUE.
*
********************************************************************
*
*  Compilation model and measurement (IMPORTANT):
*
*  This C version of Dhrystone consists of three files:
*  - dhry.h (this file, containing global definitions and comments)
*  - dhry_1.c (containing the code corresponding to Ada package
*    Pack_1)
*  - dhry_2.c (containing the code corresponding to Ada package
*    Pack_2)
*
*  The following "ground rules" apply for measurements:
*  - Separate compilation
*  - No procedure merging
*  - Otherwise, compiler optimizations are allowed but should be
```

```
*    indicated
*    - Default results are those without register declarations
*    See the companion paper "Rationale for Dhrystone Version 2" for
*      a more detailed discussion of these ground rules.
*
*    For 16-Bit processors (e.g. 80186, 80286), times for all
*    compilation models ("small", "medium", "large" etc.) should be
*    given if possible, together with a definition of these models
*    for the compiler system used.
*
*********************************************************************
*
*    Dhrystone (C version) statistics:
*
*    [Comment from the first distribution, updated for version 2.
*     Note that because of language differences, the numbers are
*    slightly different from the Ada version.]
*
*    The following program contains statements of a high level
*    programming language (here: C) in a distribution considered
*    representative:
*
*      assignments                 52 (51.0 %)
*      control statements          33 (32.4 %)
*      procedure, function calls   17 (16.7 %)
*
*    103 statements are dynamically executed. The program is
*    balanced with respect to the three aspects:
*
*      - statement type
*      - operand type
*      - operand locality
*          operand global, local, parameter, or constant.
*
*    The combination of these three aspects is balanced only
*      approximately.
*
*    1. Statement Type:
*    -----------------           number
*
*      V1 = V2                   9
*        (incl. V1 = F(..)
*      V = Constant              12
*      Assignment,               7
*        with array element
*      Assignment,               6
*        with record component
*                                --
*                                34        34
*
*      X = Y +|-|"&&"|"|" Z       5
*      X = Y +|-|"==" Constant    6
*      X = X +|- 1                3
*      X = Y *|/ Z                2
```

```
*        X = Expression,            1
*            two operators
*        X = Expression,            1
*            three operators
*                                  --
*                                  18          18
*
*        if ....                   14
*          with "else"      7
*          without "else"   7
*                executed       3
*                not executed   4
*        for ...                    7  |  counted every time
*        while ...                  4  |  the loop condition
*        do ... while               1  |  is evaluated
*        switch ...                 1
*        break                      1
*        declaration with           1
*          initialization
*                                  --
*                                  34          34
*
*        P (...)  procedure call   11
*          user procedure      10
*          library procedure    1
*        X = F (...)
*               function  call      6
*          user function       5
*          library function    1
*                                  --
*                                  17          17
*                                             ---
*                                             103
*
* The average number of parameters in procedure or function calls
* is 1.82 (not counting the function values as implicit
* parameters).
*
*
*   2. Operators
*   ------------
*                              number     approximate
*                                         percentage
*
*   Arithmetic                  32          50.8
*
*       +                       21          33.3
*       -                        7          11.1
*       *                        3           4.8
*       / (int div)              1           1.6
*
*   Comparison                  27          42.8
*
```

```
*      ==                    9            14.3
*      /=                    4             6.3
*      >                     1             1.6
*      <                     3             4.8
*      >=                    1             1.6
*      <=                    9            14.3
*
*   Logic                    4             6.3
*
*      && (AND-THEN)         1             1.6
*      |  (OR)               1             1.6
*      !  (NOT)              2             3.2
*
*                           --           -----
*                           63           100.1
*
*
*  3. Operand Type (counted once per operand reference):
*  ----------------
*                        number      approximate
*                                    percentage
*
*   Integer              175           72.3 %
*   Character             45           18.6 %
*   Pointer               12            5.0 %
*   String30               6            2.5 %
*   Array                  2            0.8 %
*   Record                 2            0.8 %
*                        ---         -------
*                        242          100.0 %
*
*  When there is an access path leading to the final operand (e.g.
*  a record component), only the final data type on the access path
*  is counted.
*
*
*  4. Operand Locality:
*  -------------------
*                        number      approximate
*                                    percentage
*
*   local variable       114           47.1 %
*   global variable       22            9.1 %
*   parameter             45           18.6 %
*      value                    23         9.5 %
*      reference                22         9.1 %
*   function result        6            2.5 %
*   constant              55           22.7 %
*                         _           ___
*                        242          100.0 %
*
*
*  The program does not compute anything meaningful, but it is
*  syntactically and semantically correct. All variables have a
```

```
 * value assigned to them before they are used as a source operand.
 *
 * There has been no explicit effort to account for the effects of
 * a cache, or to balance the use of long or short displacements
 * for code or data.
 *
 ****************************************************************
 */

/* Compiler and system dependent definitions: */

#define TIME
#define MSC_CLOCK

#ifndef TIME
#ifndef TIMES
#define TIMES
#endif
#endif
                /* Use times(2) time function unless    */
                /* explicitly defined otherwise          */

#ifdef MSC_CLOCK
#undef HZ
#undef TIMES
#include <time.h>
#define HZ   CLOCKS_PER_SEC
#endif
      /* Use Microsoft C hi-res clock */

#ifdef TIMES
#include <sys/types.h>
#include <sys/times.h>
                /* for "times" */
#define HZ   150
#endif

#define Mic_secs_Per_Second     1000000.0
 /* Berkeley UNIX C returns process times in seconds/HZ */

#ifdef  NOSTRUCTASSIGN
#define structassign(d, s)        memcpy(&(d), &(s), sizeof(d))
#else
#define structassign(d, s)      d = s
#endif

#ifdef  NOENUM
#define Ident_1 0
#define Ident_2 1
#define Ident_3 2
#define Ident_4 3
#define Ident_5 4
  typedef int   Enumeration;
#else
```

```
      typedef enum {Ident_1, Ident_2, Ident_3, Ident_4, Ident_5}
            Enumeration;
#endif
/* for boolean and enumeration types in Ada, Pascal */

/* General definitions: */

#include <stdio.h>
#include <stdlib.h>
                  /* for strcpy, strcmp */

#define Null 0
                  /* Value of a Null pointer */
#define true  1
#define false 0

typedef int     One_Thirty;
typedef int     One_Fifty;
typedef char    Capital_Letter;
typedef int     Boolean;
typedef char    Str_30 [31];
typedef int     Arr_1_Dim [50];
typedef int     Arr_2_Dim [50] [50];

typedef struct record
    {
    struct record *Ptr_Comp;
    Enumeration    Discr;
    union {
        struct {
                Enumeration Enum_Comp;
                int         Int_Comp;
                char        Str_Comp [31];
                } var_1;
        struct {
                Enumeration E_Comp_2;
                char        Str_2_Comp [31];
                } var_2;
        struct {
                char        Ch_1_Comp;
                char        Ch_2_Comp;
                } var_3;
        } variant;
    } Rec_Type, *Rec_Pointer;
```

The first C source file, DHRY_1.C or DPACK1.C, contains most of the actual benchmark code:

DHRY_1.C (DPACK1.C)

```
/*
 **************************************************************
 *
```

```
 *                    "DHRYSTONE" Benchmark Program
 *                    ----------------------------
 *
 *  Version:   C, Version 2.1
 *
 *  File:      dhry_1.c (part 2 of 3)
 *
 *  Date:      May 17, 1988
 *
 *  Author:    Reinhold P. Weicker
 *
 *****************************************************************
 */

#include "dhry.h"

/* Global Variables: */

Rec_Pointer     Ptr_Glob,
                Next_Ptr_Glob;
int             Int_Glob;
Boolean         Bool_Glob;
char            Ch_1_Glob,
                Ch_2_Glob;
int             Arr_1_Glob [50];
int             Arr_2_Glob [50] [50];

//extern char    *malloc ();
Enumeration  Func_1 ();
/* forward declaration necessary since Enumeration may not simply be
int */

#ifndef REG
        Boolean Reg = false;
#define REG
        /* REG becomes defined as empty */
        /* i.e. no register variables */
#else
        Boolean Reg = true;
#endif

/* variables for time measurement: */

#ifdef TIMES
struct tms        time_info;
extern  int   times ();
                /* see library function "times" */
#define Too_Small_Time (2*HZ)
                /* Measurements should last at least about 2
seconds */
#endif
#ifdef TIME
extern time_t time();
                /* see library function "time"  */
```

```
#define Too_Small_Time 2
                  /* Measurements should last at least 2 seconds */
#endif
#ifdef MSC_CLOCK
extern clock_t clock();
#undef Too_Small_Time
#define Too_Small_Time (2*HZ)
#endif

long              Begin_Time,
                  End_Time,
                  User_Time;
float           Microseconds,
                  Dhrystones_Per_Second;

/* end of variables for time measurement */


main ()
/*****/

  /* main program, corresponds to procedures          */
  /* Main and Proc_0 in the Ada version               */
{
        One_Fifty       Int_1_Loc;
  REG   One_Fifty       Int_2_Loc;
        One_Fifty       Int_3_Loc;
  REG   char            Ch_Index;
        Enumeration     Enum_Loc;
        Str_30          Str_1_Loc;
        Str_30          Str_2_Loc;
  REG   int             Run_Index;
  REG   long            Number_Of_Runs;

  /* Initializations */

  Next_Ptr_Glob = (Rec_Pointer) malloc (sizeof (Rec_Type));
  Ptr_Glob = (Rec_Pointer) malloc (sizeof (Rec_Type));

  Ptr_Glob->Ptr_Comp                    = Next_Ptr_Glob;
  Ptr_Glob->Discr                       = Ident_1;
  Ptr_Glob->variant.var_1.Enum_Comp   = Ident_3;
  Ptr_Glob->variant.var_1.Int_Comp      = 40;
  strcpy (Ptr_Glob->variant.var_1.Str_Comp,
          "DHRYSTONE PROGRAM, SOME STRING");
  strcpy (Str_1_Loc, "DHRYSTONE PROGRAM, 1'ST STRING"");

  Arr_2_Glob [8][7] = 10;
 /* Was missing in published program. Without this statement, */
 /* Arr_2_Glob [8][7] would have an undefined value.          */
 /* Warning: With 16-Bit processors and Number_Of_Runs > 32000, */
 /* overflow may occur for this array element.                */
```

```
  printf ("\n");
  printf ("Dhrystone Benchmark, Version 2.1 (Language: C)\n");
  printf ("\n");
  if (Reg)
  {
    printf ("Program compiled with 'register' attribute\n");
    printf ("\n");
  }
  else
  {
    printf ("Program compiled without 'register' attribute\n");
    printf ("\n");
  }
/*
 printf ("Please give the number of runs through the benchmark: ");
  {
    int n;
    scanf ("%d", &n);
    Number_Of_Runs = n;
  }
  printf ("\n");
*/
#ifndef LOOPS
#define LOOPS 32000
#endif
  Number_Of_Runs = LOOPS;

  printf ("Execution starts, %d runs through Dhrystone\n",
          Number_Of_Runs);

  /***************/
  /* Start timer */
  /***************/

#ifdef TIMES
  times (&time_info);
  Begin_Time = (long) time_info.tms_utime;
#endif
#ifdef TIME
  Begin_Time = time ( (long *) 0);
#endif
#ifdef MSC_CLOCK
  Begin_Time = clock();
#endif

  for (Run_Index = 1; Run_Index <= Number_Of_Runs; ++Run_Index)
  {

    Proc_5();
    Proc_4();
      /* Ch_1_Glob == 'A', Ch_2_Glob == 'B', Bool_Glob == true */
    Int_1_Loc = 2;
```

```
    Int_2_Loc = 3;
    strcpy (Str_2_Loc, "DHRYSTONE PROGRAM, 2'ND STRING");
    Enum_Loc = Ident_2;
    Bool_Glob = ! Func_2 (Str_1_Loc, Str_2_Loc);
      /* Bool_Glob == 1 */
    while (Int_1_Loc < Int_2_Loc)  /* loop body executed once */
    {
       Int_3_Loc = 5 * Int_1_Loc - Int_2_Loc;
         /* Int_3_Loc == 7 */
       Proc_7 (Int_1_Loc, Int_2_Loc, &Int_3_Loc);
         /* Int_3_Loc == 7 */
       Int_1_Loc += 1;
    } /* while */
      /* Int_1_Loc == 3, Int_2_Loc == 3, Int_3_Loc == 7 */
    Proc_8 (Arr_1_Glob, Arr_2_Glob, Int_1_Loc, Int_3_Loc);
      /* Int_Glob == 5 */
    Proc_1 (Ptr_Glob);
    for (Ch_Index = 'A'; Ch_Index <= Ch_2_Glob; ++Ch_Index)
                            /* loop body executed twice */
    {
       if (Enum_Loc == Func_1 (Ch_Index, 'C'))
           /* then, not executed */
         {
         Proc_6 (Ident_1, &Enum_Loc);
         strcpy (Str_2_Loc, "DHRYSTONE PROGRAM, 3'RD STRING");
         Int_2_Loc = Run_Index;
         Int_Glob = Run_Index;
         }
    }
       /* Int_1_Loc == 3, Int_2_Loc == 3, Int_3_Loc == 7 */
    Int_2_Loc = Int_2_Loc * Int_1_Loc;
    Int_1_Loc = Int_2_Loc / Int_3_Loc;
    Int_2_Loc = 7 * (Int_2_Loc - Int_3_Loc) - Int_1_Loc;
       /* Int_1_Loc == 1, Int_2_Loc == 13, Int_3_Loc == 7 */
    Proc_2 (&Int_1_Loc);
       /* Int_1_Loc == 5 */

  } /* loop "for Run_Index" */

  /**************/
  /* Stop timer */
  /**************/

#ifdef TIMES
  times (&time_info);
  End_Time = (long) time_info.tms_utime;
#endif
#ifdef TIME
  End_Time = time ( (long *) 0);
#endif
#ifdef MSC_CLOCK
```

```
  End_Time = clock();
#endif

  printf ("Execution ends\n");
  printf ("\n");
  printf ("Final values of the variables used in the "
  "benchmark:\n");
  printf ("\n");
  printf ("Int_Glob:            %d\n", Int_Glob);
  printf ("        should be:   %d\n", 5);
  printf ("Bool_Glob:           %d\n", Bool_Glob);
  printf ("        should be:   %d\n", 1);
  printf ("Ch_1_Glob:           %c\n", Ch_1_Glob);
  printf ("        should be:   %c\n", 'A');
  printf ("Ch_2_Glob:           %c\n", Ch_2_Glob);
  printf ("        should be:   %c\n", 'B');
  printf ("Arr_1_Glob[8]:       %d\n", Arr_1_Glob[8]);
  printf ("        should be:   %d\n", 7);
  printf ("Arr_2_Glob[8][7]:    %d\n", Arr_2_Glob[8][7]);
  printf ("        should be:   Number_Of_Runs + 10\n");
  printf ("Ptr_Glob->\n");
  printf ("  Ptr_Comp:          %d\n", (int) Ptr_Glob->Ptr_Comp);
  printf ("        should be:   (implementation-dependent)\n");
  printf ("  Discr:             %d\n", Ptr_Glob->Discr);
  printf ("        should be:   %d\n", 0);
  printf ("  Enum_Comp:         %d\n",
      Ptr_Glob->variant.var_1.Enum_Comp);
  printf ("        should be:   %d\n", 2);
  printf ("  Int_Comp:          %d\n",
      Ptr_Glob->variant.var_1.Int_Comp);
  printf ("        should be:   %d\n", 17);
  printf ("  Str_Comp:          %s\n",
      Ptr_Glob->variant.var_1.Str_Comp);
  printf ("        should be: DHRYSTONE PROGRAM, SOME STRING\n");
  printf ("Next_Ptr_Glob->\n");
  printf ("  Ptr_Comp:          %d\n",
      (int) Next_Ptr_Glob->Ptr_Comp);
  printf ("        should be:   (implementation-dependent), "
  "same as above\n");
  printf ("  Discr:             %d\n", Next_Ptr_Glob->Discr);
  printf ("        should be:   %d\n", 0);
  printf ("  Enum_Comp:         %d\n",
      Next_Ptr_Glob->variant.var_1.Enum_Comp);
  printf ("        should be:   %d\n", 1);
  printf ("  Int_Comp:          %d\n",
      Next_Ptr_Glob->variant.var_1.Int_Comp);
  printf ("        should be:   %d\n", 18);
  printf ("  Str_Comp:          %s\n",
          Next_Ptr_Glob->variant.var_1.Str_Comp);
  printf ("        should be: DHRYSTONE PROGRAM, SOME STRING\n");
```

```c
    printf ("Int_1_Loc:              %d\n", Int_1_Loc);
    printf ("          should be:    %d\n", 5);
    printf ("Int_2_Loc:              %d\n", Int_2_Loc);
    printf ("          should be:    %d\n", 13);
    printf ("Int_3_Loc:              %d\n", Int_3_Loc);
    printf ("          should be:    %d\n", 7);
    printf ("Enum_Loc:               %d\n", Enum_Loc);
    printf ("          should be:    %d\n", 1);
    printf ("Str_1_Loc:              %s\n", Str_1_Loc);
    printf ("          should be:    DHRYSTONE PROGRAM, 1'ST STRING\n");
    printf ("Str_2_Loc:              %s\n", Str_2_Loc);
    printf ("          should be:    DHRYSTONE PROGRAM, 2'ND STRING\n");
    printf ("\n");

  User_Time = End_Time - Begin_Time;

  if (User_Time < Too_Small_Time)
  {
    printf ("Measured time too small to obtain meaningful"
      " results\n");
    printf ("Please increase number of runs\n");
    printf ("\n");
  }
  else
  {
#ifdef TIME

#ifdef SIMULATOR
/* time.c returns the simulator clock.  this need to be scaled by
/* the clock frequency to get the actual number of seconds */
    Microseconds = (float) User_Time * Mic_secs_Per_Second /
      (float) MHZ / (float) Number_Of_Runs;
    Dhrystones_Per_Second = (float) Number_Of_Runs * (float) MHZ
        / (float) User_Time;

#else
    Microseconds = (float) User_Time * Mic_secs_Per_Second
                      / (float) Number_Of_Runs;
    Dhrystones_Per_Second = (float) Number_Of_Runs /
        (float) User_Time;
#endif

#else
    Microseconds = (float) User_Time * Mic_secs_Per_Second
                      / ((float) HZ * ((float) Number_Of_Runs));
    Dhrystones_Per_Second = ((float) HZ * (float) Number_Of_Runs)
                      / (float) User_Time;
#endif
    printf ("Microseconds for one run through Dhrystone: ");
    printf ("%6.1f \n", Microseconds);
    printf ("Dhrystones per Second:                      ");
    printf ("%6.1f \n", Dhrystones_Per_Second);
```

```
   printf ("\n");
   }

   exit(0);   /* wyu */
}


Proc_1 (Ptr_Val_Par)
/*****************/

REG Rec_Pointer Ptr_Val_Par;
   /* executed once */
{
  REG Rec_Pointer Next_Record = Ptr_Val_Par->Ptr_Comp;
                                     /* == Ptr_Glob_Next */
  /* Local variable, initialized with Ptr_Val_Par->Ptr_Comp,  */
  /* corresponds to "rename" in Ada, "with" in Pascal         */

  structassign (*Ptr_Val_Par->Ptr_Comp, *Ptr_Glob);
  Ptr_Val_Par->variant.var_1.Int_Comp = 5;
  Next_Record->variant.var_1.Int_Comp
       = Ptr_Val_Par->variant.var_1.Int_Comp;
  Next_Record->Ptr_Comp = Ptr_Val_Par->Ptr_Comp;
  Proc_3 (&Next_Record->Ptr_Comp);
    /* Ptr_Val_Par->Ptr_Comp->Ptr_Comp
                          == Ptr_Glob->Ptr_Comp */
  if (Next_Record->Discr == Ident_1)
    /* then, executed */
  {
    Next_Record->variant.var_1.Int_Comp = 6;
    Proc_6 (Ptr_Val_Par->variant.var_1.Enum_Comp,
          &Next_Record->variant.var_1.Enum_Comp);
    Next_Record->Ptr_Comp = Ptr_Glob->Ptr_Comp;
    Proc_7 (Next_Record->variant.var_1.Int_Comp, 10,
          &Next_Record->variant.var_1.Int_Comp);
  }
  else /* not executed */
    structassign (*Ptr_Val_Par, *Ptr_Val_Par->Ptr_Comp);
} /* Proc_1 */


Proc_2 (Int_Par_Ref)
/*****************/
    /* executed once */
    /* *Int_Par_Ref == 1, becomes 4 */

One_Fifty *Int_Par_Ref;
{
  One_Fifty  Int_Loc;
  Enumeration Enum_Loc;

  Int_Loc = *Int_Par_Ref + 10;
  do /* executed once */
```

```
   if (Ch_1_Glob == 'A')
      /* then, executed */
   {
      Int_Loc -= 1;
      *Int_Par_Ref = Int_Loc - Int_Glob;
      Enum_Loc = Ident_1;
   } /* if */
  while (Enum_Loc != Ident_1); /* true */
} /* Proc_2 */


Proc_3 (Ptr_Ref_Par)
/******************/
    /* executed once */
    /* Ptr_Ref_Par becomes Ptr_Glob */

Rec_Pointer *Ptr_Ref_Par;

{
  if (Ptr_Glob != Null)
    /* then, executed */
    *Ptr_Ref_Par = Ptr_Glob->Ptr_Comp;
  Proc_7 (10, Int_Glob, &Ptr_Glob->variant.var_1.Int_Comp);
} /* Proc_3 */


Proc_4 () /* without parameters */
/*******/
    /* executed once */
{
  Boolean Bool_Loc;

  Bool_Loc = Ch_1_Glob == 'A';
  Bool_Glob = Bool_Loc | Bool_Glob;
  Ch_2_Glob = 'B';
} /* Proc_4 */


Proc_5 () /* without parameters */
/*******/
    /* executed once */
{
  Ch_1_Glob = 'A';
  Bool_Glob = false;
} /* Proc_5 */


        /* Procedure for the assignment of structures,        */
        /* if the C compiler doesn't support this feature      */
#ifdef  NOSTRUCTASSIGN
memcpy (d, s, l)
register char *d;
register char *s;
register int  l;
```

```
{
        while (1—) *d++ = *s++;
}
#endif
```

The second C source file, DHRY_2.C or DPACK2.C, contains only a few functions, ones that need to be protected from inlining by the compiler to keep the results meaningful:

DHRY_2.C (DPACK2.C)

```
/*
 ***************************************************************
 *
 *                    "DHRYSTONE" Benchmark Program
 *                    _____
 *
 *
 *  Version:    C, Version 2.1
 *
 *  File:       dhry_2.c (part 3 of 3)
 *
 *  Date:       May 17, 1988
 *
 *  Author:     Reinhold P. Weicker
 *
 ***************************************************************
 */

#include "dhry.h"

#ifndef REG
#define REG
        /* REG becomes defined as empty */
        /* i.e. no register variables    */
#endif

extern  int     Int_Glob;
extern  char    Ch_1_Glob;


Proc_6 (Enum_Val_Par, Enum_Ref_Par)
/******************************/
    /* executed once */
    /* Enum_Val_Par == Ident_3, Enum_Ref_Par becomes Ident_2 */

Enumeration  Enum_Val_Par;
Enumeration *Enum_Ref_Par;
{
  *Enum_Ref_Par = Enum_Val_Par;
  if (! Func_3 (Enum_Val_Par))
    /* then, not executed */
```

```
      *Enum_Ref_Par = Ident_4;
   switch (Enum_Val_Par)
   {
      case Ident_1:
        *Enum_Ref_Par = Ident_1;
        break;
      case Ident_2:
        if (Int_Glob > 100)
          /* then */
        *Enum_Ref_Par = Ident_1;
        else *Enum_Ref_Par = Ident_4;
        break;
      case Ident_3: /* executed */
        *Enum_Ref_Par = Ident_2;
        break;
      case Ident_4: break;
      case Ident_5:
        *Enum_Ref_Par = Ident_3;
        break;
   } /* switch */
} /* Proc_6 */


Proc_7 (Int_1_Par_Val, Int_2_Par_Val, Int_Par_Ref)
/*******************************************/
    /* executed three times                             */
    /* first call:      Int_1_Par_Val == 2, Int_2_Par_Val == 3,  */
    /*                  Int_Par_Ref becomes 7                     */
    /* second call:     Int_1_Par_Val == 10, Int_2_Par_Val == 5, */
    /*                  Int_Par_Ref becomes 17                    */
    /* third call:      Int_1_Par_Val == 6, Int_2_Par_Val == 10, */
    /*                  Int_Par_Ref becomes 18                    */
One_Fifty       Int_1_Par_Val;
One_Fifty       Int_2_Par_Val;
One_Fifty      *Int_Par_Ref;
{
  One_Fifty Int_Loc;

  Int_Loc = Int_1_Par_Val + 2;
  *Int_Par_Ref = Int_2_Par_Val + Int_Loc;
} /* Proc_7 */


Proc_8 (Arr_1_Par_Ref, Arr_2_Par_Ref, Int_1_Par_Val, Int_2_Par_Val)
/*******************************************************************/
    /* executed once      */
    /* Int_Par_Val_1 == 3 */
    /* Int_Par_Val_2 == 7 */
Arr_1_Dim       Arr_1_Par_Ref;
Arr_2_Dim       Arr_2_Par_Ref;
int             Int_1_Par_Val;
int             Int_2_Par_Val;
{
```

```
  REG One_Fifty Int_Index;
  REG One_Fifty Int_Loc;

  Int_Loc = Int_1_Par_Val + 5;
  Arr_1_Par_Ref [Int_Loc] = Int_2_Par_Val;
  Arr_1_Par_Ref [Int_Loc+1] = Arr_1_Par_Ref [Int_Loc];
  Arr_1_Par_Ref [Int_Loc+30] = Int_Loc;
  for (Int_Index = Int_Loc; Int_Index <= Int_Loc+1; ++Int_Index)
    Arr_2_Par_Ref [Int_Loc] [Int_Index] = Int_Loc;
  Arr_2_Par_Ref [Int_Loc] [Int_Loc-1] += 1;
  Arr_2_Par_Ref [Int_Loc+20] [Int_Loc] = Arr_1_Par_Ref [Int_Loc];
  Int_Glob = 5;
} /* Proc_8 */


Enumeration Func_1 (Ch_1_Par_Val, Ch_2_Par_Val)
/************************************************/
/* executed three times                                        */
/* first call:      Ch_1_Par_Val == 'H', Ch_2_Par_Val == 'R'   */
/* second call:     Ch_1_Par_Val == 'A', Ch_2_Par_Val == 'C'   */
/* third call:      Ch_1_Par_Val == 'B', Ch_2_Par_Val == 'C'   */

Capital_Letter   Ch_1_Par_Val;
Capital_Letter   Ch_2_Par_Val;
{
  Capital_Letter       Ch_1_Loc;
  Capital_Letter       Ch_2_Loc;

  Ch_1_Loc = Ch_1_Par_Val;
  Ch_2_Loc = Ch_1_Loc;
  if (Ch_2_Loc != Ch_2_Par_Val)
    /* then, executed */
    return (Ident_1);
  else  /* not executed */
  {
    Ch_1_Glob = Ch_1_Loc;
    return (Ident_2);
  }
} /* Func_1 */


Boolean Func_2 (Str_1_Par_Ref, Str_2_Par_Ref)
/************************************************/
    /* executed once */
    /* Str_1_Par_Ref == "DHRYSTONE PROGRAM, 1'ST STRING" */
    /* Str_2_Par_Ref == "DHRYSTONE PROGRAM, 2'ND STRING" */

Str_30  Str_1_Par_Ref;
Str_30  Str_2_Par_Ref;
{
  REG One_Thirty       Int_Loc;
      Capital_Letter   Ch_Loc;
```

```
Int_Loc = 2;
while (Int_Loc <= 2) /* loop body executed once */
  if (Func_1 (Str_1_Par_Ref[Int_Loc],
              Str_2_Par_Ref[Int_Loc+1]) == Ident_1)
    /* then, executed */
  {
    Ch_Loc = 'A';
    Int_Loc += 1;
  } /* if, while */
if (Ch_Loc >= 'W' && Ch_Loc < 'Z')
  /* then, not executed */
  Int_Loc = 7;
if (Ch_Loc == 'R')
  /* then, not executed */
  return (true);
else /* executed */
{
  if (strcmp (Str_1_Par_Ref, Str_2_Par_Ref) > 0)
    /* then, not executed */
  {
    Int_Loc += 7;
    Int_Glob = Int_Loc;
    return (true);
  }
  else /* executed */
    return (false);
} /* if Ch_Loc */
} /* Func_2 */


Boolean Func_3 (Enum_Par_Val)
/***************************/
    /* executed once         */
    /* Enum_Par_Val == Ident_3 */
Enumeration Enum_Par_Val;
{
  Enumeration Enum_Loc;

  Enum_Loc = Enum_Par_Val;
  if (Enum_Loc == Ident_3)
    /* then, executed */
    return (true);
  else /* not executed */
    return (false);
} /* Func_3 */
```

As is obvious from the code, the Dhrystones do nothing to test floating point performance. While many Windows programs do little or no floating point arithmetic, some programs (spreadsheets, for instance) can have their execution times dominated by the floating point component, especially on machines without floating point coprocessors.

Floating Point Performance: The Whetstones

The Whetstones actually predate the Dhrystones by a number of years: the original floating point Whetstone, in Algol, was published in *Computer Journal* in 1976. The term "whetstone," of course, actually has some physical meaning; the term "dhrystone" is just a pun based on "whetstone." Computer scientists often have a strange sense of humor when it comes to names.

The current Whetstone benchmark is of course written in C: I use the double-precision version (in which variables are **double**) rather than the single-precision version (which uses **float** variables) because my experience doing numeric computing tells me that the extra range and precision of **double** variables is often important. You'll note that the Whetstone does, of necessity, include some integer arithmetic and memory manipulation as well as pure floating point computations. You'll also note that the Whetstone does *not* do tight loops measuring the speed of simple instructions: it instead measures moderately complex sequences that stress the compiler as well as the hardware.

WHET_D.C

```
#include <stdio.h>
#include <math.h>
#include <time.h>

long DoBench(bname, strp, liters, funcp)
char *bname;
char *strp;           /* Pointer to benchmark name */
long liters;          /* Number of iterations */
int (*funcp)();       /* Pointer to benchmark function */
{

  long stime;      /* Start time */
  long etime;      /* End time */
  long time;       /* Elapse time */
  int secs;        /* Seconds */
  int hunds;       /* 1/100 seconds */

  printf("%4s %-22s  %6d  ", bname, strp, liters);
  stime = clock();
  (*funcp)();
  etime = clock();
  time = etime - stime;
  time = (long)(time / (CLOCKS_PER_SEC/100.0)); //was 60.0! WRONG!
  secs = time / 100;
  hunds = time % 100;
  printf("%4d.%02d secs\n", secs, hunds);
  return time;
}

main()
```

```
{
  extern whetd();
  long Wtime;

  printf("Code Benchmark                    Iters     Time\n");
  printf("--------------------------- ------  -------\n");
  Wtime = DoBench("WD","Whetstone (double)",100L,whetd);
  if (Wtime)
   printf("  (%d KWhets/sec).\n",(int)(10000 / (Wtime/100.0)));
  exit(0);
}


/****************************************************************
 Whetstone benchmark in C.  This program is a translation of the
 original Algol version in "A Synthetic Benchmark" by H.J. Curnow
 and B.A. Wichman in Computer Journal, Vol  19 #1, February 1976.
 Used to test compiler efficiency, optimization, and double
 precision floating-point performance.  This version is specific
 to the Turbo-Amiga and Amiga but it can be easily adapted to
 other systems by replacing the clock() routine with your own.
 ****************************************************************/

#define ITERATIONS   10 /* 1 Million Whetstone instructions    */

static double   D_e1[4];
static double   D_t, D_t1, D_t2;
static long     j, k, l;

whetd() {

    long        i;
    long        n1, n2, n3, n4, n5, n6, n7, n8, n9, n10, n11;
    long        m, loops;
    double      D_x, D_y, D_z, D_x1, D_x2, D_x3, D_x4;

    /***********************/
    /* initialize constants */
    /***********************/

    D_t   =   0.499975;
    D_t1  =   0.500250;
    D_t2  =   2.0;

    /***********************/
    /* Set Module Weights. */
    /***********************/
/* m = 10 is used to obtain better timing  */
/* accuracy only.  Slow systems should use */
/* m = 1.                                   */
    m = 10;
    loops = m * ITERATIONS;
    n1  =    0 * loops;
    n2  =   12 * loops;
    n3  =   14 * loops;
```

```
  n4  = 345 * loops;
  n5  =   0 * loops;
  n6  = 210 * loops;
  n7  =  32 * loops;
  n8  = 899 * loops;
  n9  = 616 * loops;
  n10 =   0 * loops;
  n11 =  93 * loops;

  /*******************************/
  /* MODULE 1:  simple identifiers */
  /*******************************/

  D_x1 =  1.0;
  D_x2 = -1.0;
  D_x3 = -1.0;
  D_x4 = -1.0;

  if( n1 > 0 )
  {
    for(i = 1; i <= n1; i++)
    {
      D_x1 = ( D_x1 + D_x2 + D_x3 - D_x4 ) * D_t;
      D_x2 = ( D_x1 + D_x2 - D_x3 - D_x4 ) * D_t;
      D_x3 = ( D_x1 - D_x2 + D_x3 + D_x4 ) * D_t;
      D_x4 = (-D_x1 + D_x2 + D_x3 + D_x4 ) * D_t;
    }
  }

  /*****************************/
  /* MODULE 2:  Array Elements */
  /*****************************/
  D_e1[0] =  1.0;
/* Start at element 0 in C, vice 1 in Fortran */
  D_e1[1] = -1.0;
  D_e1[2] = -1.0;
  D_e1[3] = -1.0;

  if( n2 > 0 )
  {
    for (i = 1; i <= n2; i++)
    {
      D_e1[0] = ( D_e1[0] + D_e1[1] + D_e1[2] - D_e1[3] ) * D_t;
      D_e1[1] = ( D_e1[0] + D_e1[1] - D_e1[2] + D_e1[3] ) * D_t;
      D_e1[2] = ( D_e1[0] - D_e1[1] + D_e1[2] + D_e1[3] ) * D_t;
      D_e1[3] = (-D_e1[0] + D_e1[1] + D_e1[2] + D_e1[3] ) * D_t;
    }
  }

  /*********************************/
  /* MODULE 3:  Array as Parameter */
  /*********************************/
  if( n3 > 0 )
```

```
{
  for (i = 1; i <= n3; i++)
  {
    D_pa(D_e1);
  }
}
/********************************/
/* MODULE 4:  Conditional Jumps */
/********************************/
j = 1;

if( n4 > 0 )
{
  for (i = 1; i <= n4; i++)
  {
   if (j == 1)
      j = 2;
   else
      j = 3;

   if (j > 2)
      j = 0;
   else
      j = 1;

   if (j < 1 )
      j = 1;
   else
      j = 0;
  }
}

/**********************/
/* MODULE 5:  Omitted */
/**********************/


/********************************/
/* MODULE 6:  Integer Arithmetic */
/********************************/
j = 1;
k = 2;
1 = 3;

if( n6 > 0 )
{
  for (i = 1; i <= n6; i++)
  {
   j = j * (k - j) * (1 -k);
   k = 1 * k - (1 - j) * k;
   1 = (1 - k) * (k + j);
```

```
   D_e1[1 - 2] = j + k + 1; /* Remember we started at D_e1[0].*/
   D_e1[k - 2] = j * k * 1; /* 1-2 in C, vice 1-1 in Fortran */
   }
}

/************************************/
/* MODULE 7:  Trigonometric Functions */
/************************************/
D_x = 0.5;
D_y = 0.5;

if( n7 > 0 )
{
  for(i = 1; i <= n7; i++)
  {
   D_x = D_t * atan(D_t2*sin(D_x)*cos(D_x)
      /(cos(D_x+D_y)+cos(D_x-D_y)-1.0));
   D_y = D_t * atan(D_t2*sin(D_y)*cos(D_y)
      /(cos(D_x+D_y)+cos(D_x-D_y)-1.0));
  }
}

/*****************************/
/* MODULE 8:  Procedure Calls */
/*****************************/

D_x = 1.0;
D_y = 1.0;
D_z = 1.0;

if( n8 > 0 )
{
  for (i = 1; i <= n8; i++)
  {
   D_p3(D_x, D_y, &D_z);
  }
}

/*****************************/
/* MODULE 9:  Array References */
/*****************************/

j = 1;
k = 2;
l = 3;

D_e1[0] = 1.0;
D_e1[1] = 2.0;
D_e1[2] = 3.0;

if( n9 > 0 )
{
  for(i = 1; i <= n9; i++)
```

```
      {
        D_p0();
      }
    }

    /**********************************/
    /* MODULE 10:  Integer Arithmetic */
    /**********************************/

    j = 2;
    k = 3;

    if( n10 > 0 )
    {
      for(i = 1; i <= n10; i++)
      {
        j = j + k;
        k = j + k;
        j = k - j;
        k = k - j - j;
      }
    }

    /**********************************/
    /* MODULE 11:  Standard Functions */
    /**********************************/

    D_x = 0.75;

    if( n11 > 0 )
    {
      for(i = 1; i <= n11; i++)
      {
        D_x = sqrt( exp( log(D_x) / D_t1) );
      }
    }

    /**************************/
    /* End of Whetstone Tests */
    /**************************/

#if 0 /* Done elsewhere now. */
    stoptime  = clock();
    benchtime = stoptime - starttime - nulltime;
    D_x1 = (double)benchtime/100.0;
    printf("   Benchtime(sec) = %lf\n",D_x1);
    D_x2 = 100.0 * (double)loops / D_x1;
    KWhets = (long)D_x2;
    printf("   KWhets/sec     = %ld\n\n",KWhets);
#endif

}
```

```
/******************/
/* Subroutine pa() */
/******************/

D_pa(e)        /* Exactly as in the Algol 60 version, but we */
               /* could do away with that 'goto'.            */
double e[4];

{
   int j;

   j = 0;
     lab:
   e[0] = (  e[0] + e[1] + e[2] - e[3] ) * D_t;
   e[1] = (  e[0] + e[1] - e[2] + e[3] ) * D_t;
   e[2] = (  e[0] - e[1] + e[2] + e[3] ) * D_t;
   e[3] = ( -e[0] + e[1] + e[2] + e[3] ) / D_t2;
   j ++;

   if (j < 6)
      goto lab;
}

/***********************/
/* Subroutine p3(x,y,z) */
/***********************/

D_p3(x, y, z)

double x, y, *z;

{
   x  = D_t * (x + y);
   y  = D_t * (x + y);
   *z = (x + y) /D_t2;
}

/******************/
/* Subroutine p0() */
/******************/

D_p0()
{
   D_e1[j] = D_e1[k];
   D_e1[k] = D_e1[l];
   D_e1[l] = D_e1[j];
}
```

Using Threads for Dhrystones and Whetstones

Putting the Dhrystones and Whetstones into a single framework wasn't too difficult: I chose the **DoBench** timer from the Whetstone and commented out the timing code in the Dhrystone. Then invoking the individual tests became a simple matter of calling

DoBench with the right arguments:

```
long Wtime=0;
for(int i=0;i<nreps;i++) {
   Wtime += DoBench("WD","Whetstone (double)",whetd,pDlg);
   }
if(Wtime<=0) Wtime=1000; //protect against divide by 0
sprintf(temp,"%.4g",(nreps * 10.0 / (Wtime/100.0)));
//display temp to see answer
//...
Wtime=0
for(int i=0;i<nreps;i++) {
   Wtime += DoBench("DR","Dhrystone",dhry,pDlg);
   }
//and so on
```

Calling a function as a separate thread is a little harder than just calling a function. To begin with, a thread gets only one 32-bit argument. In most cases, you use the argument as a **(void *)** pointer to an array or structure that holds all the real arguments. For the purpose of calling **DoBench** in its own thread so that **DoBench** would then call and time the proper function, I came up with a fairly straightforward structure:

```
struct Benchargs {
   char *bname;
   char *strp;
   void(*funcp)();
   CWnd *pDlg;
   HANDLE hWaitFor;
   };
```

The first three items in the **Benchargs** structure are just the arguments to **Do-Bench**: an abbreviation for the current benchmark, a description of the current benchmark, and a pointer to the benchmark function. The fourth argument is a pointer to an MFC **CWnd** object, which is needed by my Windows version of **DoBench** to display the current status and results:

```
long DoBench(char *bname,char *strp,void(*funcp)(),CWnd * pDlg)
{
   long stime;      /* Start time */
   long etime;      /* End time */
   long time;       /* Elapse time */
   int secs;  /* Seconds */
   int hunds;       /* 1/100 seconds */
   char temp1[100],temp2[20];
   MSG msg;

   sprintf(temp1,"%4s %-22s ", bname, strp);
   stime = clock();
```

```
    (*funcp)();
    etime = clock();
    time = etime - stime;
    time = (long)(time / ((double)CLOCKS_PER_SEC/100.0));
    secs = int(time / 100);
    hunds = int(time % 100);
    sprintf(temp2,"%4d.%02d secs\n", secs, hunds);
    strcat(temp1,temp2);
    pDlg->SetDlgItemText(id_tx_status,temp1);
    TRACE(temp1);
    PeekMessage(&msg,NULL,NULL,NULL,PM_NOREMOVE); //breathe a little
    return time;
}
```

The last item in the **Benchargs** structure is an event handle that I use to synchronize the threads. You might wonder why I need to synchronize the threads at all.

In fact, Windows NT does thread creation sequentially: it can only create one thread at a time, because all thread creation has to go through a common point deep inside the system. You can't create a bunch of threads in a tight loop and expect them to run simultaneously. You *can* have the threads wait for an event and then start their timed loops simultaneously, as I do in **DoBenchThread**:

```
unsigned long DoBenchThread(void *bargs)
{
    long TTime;
    Benchargs *args = (Benchargs *)bargs;

    DWORD rc=WaitForSingleObject(args->hWaitFor,10000);
    TRACE("DoBenchThread: done waiting for event, rc %d\n",rc);
    TTime=DoBench(args->bname,args->strp,args->funcp,args->pDlg);
    TRACE("DoBenchThread: bench done, time is %d\n",TTime);
    ExitThread(TTime);
    return(TTime);
}
```

Let's look at this function line by line. The argument **bargs** is of type **void *** because that's what a thread gets when it is created. The variable **TTime** holds the time for the current thread on the thread's stack: yes, every thread gets its own stack. **WaitForSingleObject** is a Win32 system function that says the current thread can't continue until the object whose handle is given in the first argument signals, or until the time given in milliseconds in the second argument expires.

So what's happening? The thread is created, and then it sits around waiting for the object **hWaitFor** to signal. **hWaitFor** is actually an event created by the same function that creates the threads:

```
hWaitFor=CreateEvent(
```

```
NULL,    //no security attributes for this event
TRUE,    //must manually reset event
FALSE,   //initial state is nonsignaled
NULL);   //create object without a name
```

Our purpose is to get all the threads to start at the same time. It's not obvious that an event is the right kind of synchronization object to do this, nor is it obvious why a manual event rather than an automatic event is what we need. Let's push the conversational stack for a little while and discuss synchronization objects.

The three principal objects that Win32 uses for synchronization are events, mutexes, semaphores. Each of these synchronization objects can be *signaled* or *nonsignaled*. A thread waits for one or more objects: when the objects signal, the wait function returns.

A *mutex*, or mutual exclusion object, can be owned by only one thread at a time: it is used to control access to a system resource that can't be shared simultaneously by more than one user. A mutex state is signaled when not owned by any thread, and nonsignaled when it is owned by some thread. For instance, you might protect access to a common bowl of spaghetti by requiring each dining philosopher to use the one and only serving fork: you could model the serving fork as a mutex.[7]

A *semaphore* maintains a count between zero and some maximum value: it is used to limit the number of threads that can simultaneously access some resource that doesn't need to be made exclusive. A semaphore's state is signaled when its count is greater than zero, and nonsignaled when its count is zero. You might, for instance, want only N philosophers to be able to eat simultaneously, and so you would set out only N individual pasta bowls on the table: a semaphore initialized to N could model the bowl dispenser.

An *event* simply signals that something has or hasn't happened. Its state is explicitly set, pulsed, or reset under program control. An automatic event is reset each time a waiting thread is released; a manual event stays signaled even when a thread is released.

Now it *is* obvious that we want to use a manual event to synchronize our threads: we start all the threads with the event in the nonsignaled state, then set or pulse the event so all the threads run simultaneously. And now we can pop the conversational stack frame and return to our discussion of the **DoBenchThread** function.

The **TRACE** macro sends **printf**-like output to the debugging terminal or debugging Window (**afxDump**) only when you've compiled for debugging. It is a facility of MFC that does nothing in the release environment:

```
TRACE("DoBenchThread: done waiting for event, rc %d\n",rc);
TTime=DoBench(args->bname,args->strp,args->funcp,args->pDlg);
```

---

[7] I'm assuming that you are familiar with the "dining philosophers" problem used in many computer science texts.

```
TRACE("DoBenchThread: bench done, time is %d\n",TTime);
ExitThread(TTime);
return(TTime);
```

We know what **DoBench** does: it times and calls the actual benchmark code. **ExitThread** is actually not required in this case, but I've included it here for clarity, since it might not be obvious to the reader that **return(TTime)** would end the thread. As written, the function never executes the **return(TTime)** line.

When I naively ran the threaded Whetstone and Dhrystone benchmarks, I found that the results didn't scale on machines with multiple processors—the results didn't even make sense. Then I realized—as I'm sure you already realize—that using unprotected global variables in multiple threads is a Bad Thing.

If you look at the code, you'll see that the Whetstone has only a few static variables, and no global variables:

```
static double    D_e1[4];
static double    D_t, D_t1, D_t2;
static long      j, k, 1;
```

The Dhrystone has only a few global variables that we need to handle:

```
Rec_Pointer    Ptr_Glob,
               Next_Ptr_Glob;
int            Int_Glob;
Boolean        Bool_Glob;
char           Ch_1_Glob,
               Ch_2_Glob;
int            Arr_1_Glob [50];
int            Arr_2_Glob [50] [50];
```

To make each thread run independently, all the variables need to be on the stack. If we absolutely positively had to keep global variables, we'd need one or more mutex objects to control access to them. Clearly we don't want each thread sitting around waiting for access to **Ptr_Glob**: we want each thread to have its own copy of the variable in its stack.

So, I rewrote both benchmarks to keep all variables on the stack. That meant passing more arguments to certain functions:

From the revised DPACK1.C

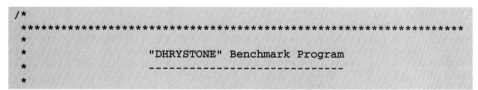

```
/*
 ************************************************************
 *
 *              "DHRYSTONE" Benchmark Program
 *              ------------------------------
 *
```

```
*   Version:  C, Version 2.1
*
*   File:     dhry_1.c (part 2 of 3)
*
*   Date:     May 17, 1988
*
*   Author:   Reinhold P. Weicker
*
*   ****************************************************************
*/

/* Modified to run in multiple threads
   M. Heller 9/92
*/

#include "dhry.h"

Enumeration   Func_1 ();
/* forward declaration necessary since Enumeration may not simply
   be int */
#ifndef REG
        Boolean Reg = false;
#define REG
        /* REG becomes defined as empty */
        /* i.e. no register variables */
#else
        Boolean Reg = true;
#endif

//...

Proc_1 (REG Rec_Pointer Ptr_Val_Par,int Int_Glob,
   Rec_Pointer Ptr_Glob);
Proc_2 (One_Fifty *Int_Par_Ref,int Int_Glob,char Ch_1_Glob);
Proc_3 (Rec_Pointer *Ptr_Ref_Par,int Int_Glob,
   Rec_Pointer Ptr_Glob);
Proc_4 (char *pCh_1_Glob,char *pCh_2_Glob, Boolean *Bool_Glob);
Proc_5 (char *pCh_1_Glob, Boolean *Bool_Glob);
Proc_6 (Enumeration Enum_Val_Par,Enumeration *Enum_Ref_Par,
   int Int_Glob);
Proc_8 ( Arr_1_Dim Arr_1_Par_Ref,
        Arr_2_Dim  Arr_2_Par_Ref,
         int Int_1_Par_Val,
         int Int_2_Par_Val,
         int Int_Glob);
Enumeration Func_1 (Capital_Letter Ch_1_Par_Val,
                    Capital_Letter Ch_2_Par_Val,char Ch_1_Glob);
Boolean Func_2 (Str_30 Str_1_Par_Ref,Str_30 Str_2_Par_Ref,char
Ch_1_Glob,int *Int_Glob);

void dhry(void)
/*****/
```

```
  /* main program, corresponds to procedures          */
  /* Main and Proc_0 in the Ada version               */
{
        One_Fifty        Int_1_Loc;
  REG   One_Fifty        Int_2_Loc;
        One_Fifty        Int_3_Loc;
  REG   char             Ch_Index;
        Enumeration      Enum_Loc;
        Str_30           Str_1_Loc;
        Str_30           Str_2_Loc;
  REG   int              Run_Index;
  REG   int              Number_Of_Runs;
  int           Int_Glob = 0; //mh
  char          Ch_1_Glob,
                   Ch_2_Glob;
Rec_Pointer    Ptr_Glob=NULL,
                 Next_Ptr_Glob=NULL;
int              Arr_1_Glob [50];
int              Arr_2_Glob [50] [50];
Boolean          Bool_Glob;  //mh

  /* Initializations */
  Next_Ptr_Glob = (Rec_Pointer) malloc (sizeof (Rec_Type));
  Ptr_Glob = (Rec_Pointer) malloc (sizeof (Rec_Type));
  Ptr_Glob->Ptr_Comp                      = Next_Ptr_Glob;
  Ptr_Glob->Discr                         = Ident_1;
  Ptr_Glob->variant.var_1.Enum_Comp    = Ident_3;
  Ptr_Glob->variant.var_1.Int_Comp     = 40;
  strcpy (Ptr_Glob->variant.var_1.Str_Comp,
          "DHRYSTONE PROGRAM, SOME STRING");
  strcpy (Str_1_Loc, "DHRYSTONE PROGRAM, 1'ST STRING");

  Arr_2_Glob [8][7] = 10;
/* Was missing in published program. Without this statement, */
/* Arr_2_Glob [8][7] would have an undefined value.          */
/* Warning: With 16-Bit processors and Number_Of_Runs > 32000 */
/* overflow may occur for this array element.                */

//...

#ifndef LOOPS
#if defined(WIN32) || defined (_NTWIN)
#define LOOPS 200000
#else
#define LOOPS 32000
#endif
#endif
  Number_Of_Runs = LOOPS;

  for (Run_Index = 1; Run_Index <= Number_Of_Runs; ++Run_Index)
  {
```

```
   Proc_5(&Ch_1_Glob,&Bool_Glob);
   Proc_4(&Ch_1_Glob,&Ch_2_Glob,&Bool_Glob);
      /* Ch_1_Glob == 'A', Ch_2_Glob == 'B', Bool_Glob == true */
   Int_1_Loc = 2;
   Int_2_Loc = 3;
   strcpy (Str_2_Loc, "DHRYSTONE PROGRAM, 2'ND STRING");
   Enum_Loc = Ident_2;
   Bool_Glob = ! Func_2 (Str_1_Loc, Str_2_Loc, Ch_1_Glob,
         &Int_Glob); //mh
      /* Bool_Glob == 1 */
   while (Int_1_Loc < Int_2_Loc)  /* loop body executed once */
   {
      Int_3_Loc = 5 * Int_1_Loc - Int_2_Loc;
        /* Int_3_Loc == 7 */
      Proc_7 (Int_1_Loc, Int_2_Loc, &Int_3_Loc);
        /* Int_3_Loc == 7 */
      Int_1_Loc += 1;
   } /* while */
      /* Int_1_Loc == 3, Int_2_Loc == 3, Int_3_Loc == 7 */
   Proc_8 (Arr_1_Glob, Arr_2_Glob, Int_1_Loc, Int_3_Loc,
         Int_Glob); //mh
      /* Int_Glob == 5 */
   Proc_1 (Ptr_Glob,Int_Glob,Ptr_Glob); //mh
   for (Ch_Index = 'A'; Ch_Index <= Ch_2_Glob; ++Ch_Index)
          /* loop body executed twice */
   {
      if (Enum_Loc == Func_1 (Ch_Index, 'C',Ch_1_Glob)) //mh
          /* then, not executed */
        {
        Proc_6 (Ident_1, &Enum_Loc,Int_Glob); //mh
        strcpy (Str_2_Loc, "DHRYSTONE PROGRAM, 3'RD STRING");
        Int_2_Loc = Run_Index;
        Int_Glob = Run_Index;
        }
   }
      /* Int_1_Loc == 3, Int_2_Loc == 3, Int_3_Loc == 7 */
   Int_2_Loc = Int_2_Loc * Int_1_Loc;
   Int_1_Loc = Int_2_Loc / Int_3_Loc;
   Int_2_Loc = 7 * (Int_2_Loc - Int_3_Loc) - Int_1_Loc;
      /* Int_1_Loc == 1, Int_2_Loc == 13, Int_3_Loc == 7 */
   Proc_2 (&Int_1_Loc,Int_Glob,Ch_1_Glob); //mh
      /* Int_1_Loc == 5 */

  } /* loop "for Run_Index" */

//...

  free(Ptr_Glob);
  free(Next_Ptr_Glob);

}
```

```
Proc_1 (REG Rec_Pointer Ptr_Val_Par,int Int_Glob,
  Rec_Pointer Ptr_Glob) {
//...
```

The Whetstones got similar treatment:

From WHET_D.C

```
/* These variables have been moved onto the stack:
static double   D_el[4];
static double   D_t, D_t1, D_t2;
static long     j, k, l;
*/

//These three functions have more parameters than in the standard
// Whetstone:
extern D_p0(double D_el[4],int j,int k,int 1);
extern D_pa(double e[4],double D_t,double D_t2);
extern D_p3(double x,double y,double *z,double D_t, double D_t2);

void whetd(void) {
    double   D_el[4];
    double   D_t, D_t1, D_t2;
    long     j, k, l;

    long      i;
    long      n1, n2, n3, n4, n5, n6, n7, n8, n9, n10, n11;
    long      m, loops;
    double   D_x, D_y, D_z, D_x1, D_x2, D_x3, D_x4;
//...
```

One more thing was necessary to make the floating point Whetstones scale properly on machines with multiple Pentium chips: I had to link with LIBCMT.LIB rather than LIBC.LIB. That was not as easy at it sounds.

In the Windows NT SDK, Microsoft supplies the file NTSAMPLE.MAK to help you build applications for Windows NT, specifically MFC applications. The general idea is that your own MAKE file will pull in a lot of details from NTSAMPLE.MAK with the line:

```
!include ntsample.mak
```

That's all well and good. But buried inside NTSAMPLE.MAK without any explicit documentation, at least in the SDK, is the assumption that MFC applications are single-threaded, and can safely link with LIBC.

Well, you've just seen that we break that assumption. The fix—linking with LIBCMT rather than LIBC—is simple enough. But NTSAMPLE.MAK is the sort of file you don't normally look inside of, so it's easy to miss the problem.

By the way, in Visual C++ for Windows NT you don't have this problem: you choose the single-thread, multithreaded, or multithreaded DLL runtime libraries from a dialog box, and there is no NTSAMPLE.MAK to worry about: the integrated environment generates a MAKE file based on your selections. You'll find that dialog under options/ project/compiler/runtime.

Now that we've been through the changes to the benchmark functions themselves, we are ready to look at the code that invokes each benchmark:

from BENCH1.CPP

```
//...
extern "C" void whetd(void);
const MAXTHREADS = 63;

CString DoWhetstone(CWnd *pDlg,int nthreads,int nreps)
{
  char temp[30];
  CString answer;
  long Wtime=0;
#ifdef WIN32
  MSG msg;
  DWORD dw;

  if(nthreads>1) {
    HANDLE hWait,hThread[MAXTHREADS];
    unsigned long id[MAXTHREADS];
    Benchargs args;

    hWait=CreateEvent(NULL,TRUE,FALSE,NULL);
                    //manual reset, initially false
    ASSERT(hWait);
    args.bname="WD";
    args.strp="Whetstone (double)";
    args.funcp=whetd;
    args.pDlg=pDlg;
    args.hWaitFor=hWait;

    for(int i=0;i<nreps;i++) {
      long avg;
      unsigned long exitcode;

      for(int j=0; j<nthreads; j++)
         hThread[j]=CreateThread(
            NULL,0,
            (LPTHREAD_START_ROUTINE)DoBenchThread,
            &args,NULL,&id[j]);
      PeekMessage(&msg,NULL,NULL,NULL,PM_NOREMOVE);
      Sleep(1000);                    //allow time for thread creation
      PeekMessage(&msg,NULL,NULL,NULL,PM_NOREMOVE);
      BOOL rc=SetEvent(hWait);//release all threads at once
      ASSERT(rc);
```

```
      //Wait for all threads to complete and get their results
      TRACE("DoWhetstone: about to wait for threads\n");

      for(j=0; j<nthreads; j++) {
          do
              {
              PeekMessage(&msg,NULL,NULL,NULL,PM_NOREMOVE);
              dw=WaitForSingleObject(hThread[j],200);
              }
          while (dw);
          }
      TRACE("DoWhetstone: done waiting for threads, dw %d\n",dw);

      avg = 0;
      for(j=0; j<nthreads; j++) {
          GetExitCodeThread(hThread[j],&exitcode);
          avg += exitcode;
          }
      avg /= nthreads;
      Wtime += avg;
      ResetEvent(hWait);

      } //for nreps

    sprintf(temp,"%.4g",
      (nreps * nthreads * 10.0 / (Wtime/100.0)));
    answer=temp;
    return(answer);

    } //if nthreads>1
#endif

  for(int i=0;i<nreps;i++) {
    Wtime += DoBench("WD","Whetstone (double)",whetd,pDlg);
    }
  if(Wtime<=0) Wtime=1000; //protect against divide by 0
  sprintf(temp,"%.4g",(nreps * 10.0 / (Wtime/100.0)));
  answer=temp;
  return(answer);
}

extern "C" void dhry(void);

CString DoDhrystone(CWnd *pDlg,int nthreads,int nreps)
{
  char temp[30];
  CString answer;
  long Wtime=0;
#ifdef WIN32
  MSG msg;
  DWORD dw;
```

```
if(nthreads>1) {
   HANDLE hWait,hThread[MAXTHREADS];
   unsigned long id[MAXTHREADS];
   Benchargs args;

   hWait=CreateEvent(NULL,TRUE,FALSE,NULL);
            //manual reset, initially false
   ASSERT(hWait);
   args.bname="DR";
   args.strp="Dhrystone";
   args.funcp=dhry;
   args.pDlg=pDlg;
   args.hWaitFor=hWait;

   for(int i=0;i<nreps;i++) {
    long avg;
    unsigned long exitcode;

    for(int j=0; j<nthreads; j++)
       hThread[j]=CreateThread(
          NULL,0,
          (LPTHREAD_START_ROUTINE)DoBenchThread,
          &args,NULL,&id[j]);
    PeekMessage(&msg,NULL,NULL,NULL,PM_NOREMOVE);
    Sleep(1000);                 //allow time for thread creation
    PeekMessage(&msg,NULL,NULL,NULL,PM_NOREMOVE);
    BOOL rc=SetEvent(hWait);//release all threads at once
    ASSERT(rc);

    //Wait for all threads to complete and get their results
    TRACE("DoDhrystone: about to wait for threads\n");

    for(j=0; j<nthreads; j++) {
       do
          {
          PeekMessage(&msg,NULL,NULL,NULL,PM_NOREMOVE);
          dw=WaitForSingleObject(hThread[j],200);
          }
       while (dw);
       }
    TRACE("DoDhrystone: done waiting for threads, dw %d\n",dw);

    avg = 0;
    for(j=0; j<nthreads; j++) {
       GetExitCodeThread(hThread[j],&exitcode);
       avg += exitcode;
       }
    avg /= nthreads;
    Wtime += avg;
    ResetEvent(hWait);

    } //for nreps
```

```
        sprintf(temp,"%.4g",
          (nreps * nthreads * 200.0 / (Wtime/100.0)));
        answer=temp;
        return(answer);

        } //if nthreads>1
#endif

    for(int i=0;i<nreps;i++) {
        Wtime += DoBench("DR","Dhrystone",dhry,pDlg);
        }
#ifdef WIN32
    double mulfact=200.0;
#else
    double mulfact=32.0;
#endif
    if(Wtime<=0) Wtime=1000; //protect against divide by 0
    sprintf(temp,"%.4g",(nreps * mulfact / (Wtime/100.0)));
    answer=temp;
    return(answer);
}
```

Let's consider what happens in **DoDhrystone** (since **DoWhetstone** is logically nearly identical) when the symbol WIN32 is defined and the number of threads to use, **nthreads**, is greater than one.

First we create an event, for synchronization of the threads as we discussed earlier. Then we create all the threads required—each of which will wait for the event to signal before it does anything—and save the thread handles and thread IDs in arrays. Then we go to sleep for a second to make sure all the threads have a chance to start, and when we wake up we set the event that all the threads are waiting for—sort of like dropping the checkered flag.

Then we wait for all the threads to finish. A thread is in a nonsignaled state when it is active, and in a signaled state when it exits: waiting for a thread object means you are waiting for the thread to exit.

Note that waiting for each thread in turn might not be as clean as waiting for all the threads simultaneously with a single call to **WaitForMultipleObjects**, and waiting for only 200 milliseconds at a time might not be as clean as waiting forever until the conditions are met.

In fact, I originally tried to do everything cleanly, but found it was unreliable. This way works all the time, and doesn't affect the timings in significant digits. Of course, I've worked with many alpha and beta test versions of Windows NT, so I might have encountered a temporary bug: you might want to do your own experiment in waiting for multiple threads.

Once all the threads have finished, we get their exit codes—that is, we get their saved return values, which in this case means getting their timing numbers. We add up

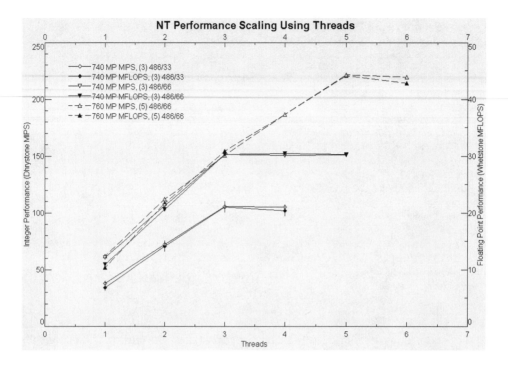

Figure 5-9 The multithreaded Whetstone and Dhrystone benchmarks demonstrate that symmetric multiprocessing (SMP) machines in Windows NT can effectively use several processors. In a perfect SMP system, the lines would be perfectly straight up to the number of installed processors, and then be perfectly flat. These results are excellent.

the times, divide by the number of threads, reset the synchronization event, and, if desired, repeat the process. Figure 5-9 shows the scaling of a 3-CPU and a 5-CPU machine measured with these multithreaded Dhrystones and Whetstones.

CPU speed is probably the most important performance indicator for most computers used as workstations, but it is hardly the only one. Some programs—database programs, for instance, and linkers—tend to be disk-bound rather than CPU-bound.

Measuring Disk I/O Performance

As I mentioned earlier, I could find no established standard measurement of disk performance, so I made up my own. I don't pretend there's any scientific or statistical basis for them as they stand.

On the other hand, they make sense. Some programs access the disk sequentially: word processors, image editing programs, and so on all read a whole file from disk, work on it in memory, and later write out a whole new file. Other programs—principally databases and programs that use databases—access the disk randomly. I don't know, *a priori*, which access pattern is more important to a given user, so I test them equally. I don't know, either, whether a given user will mostly read or mostly write to the disk, so I test reading and writing equally.

You could argue about how to balance the functions for various catagories of users, but it wouldn't matter too much: this rather cavalier partition of the testing seems to correlate fairly well with the real world. Purists, of course, can always look at the individual performance numbers.

There are seven functions in DISKNT.CPP. **OkMsgBox** should already be familiar to readers of my *Advanced Windows Programming* and/or Petzold's *Programming Windows.*[8] **diskio0** creates a temporary file on disk and checks for possible errors. **diskio1** tests sequential writes, **diskio2** sequential reads, **diskio3** random writes, and **diskio4** random reads. **diskio5** closes and deletes the file. More than half the code in the six **diskio** functions is devoted to error checking and reporting, although this has little effect on the timings.

Let's read this through: then I'll go back and discuss some of the more interesting points.

DISKNT.CPP

```
#include <afxwin.h>
#define BLOCKSIZE 4096
char drive[15];
char fillchar = 'm';
int filesize;
UINT blocksize = BLOCKSIZE;
char buffer[BLOCKSIZE];
char dummy[BLOCKSIZE];
HANDLE fh=NULL;
char filename[MAX_PATH];
int file_error=0;

void OkMsgBox (char *szCaption, char *szFormat,...)
    {
    char szBuffer [256] ;
    char *pArguments ;

    pArguments = (char *) &szFormat + sizeof (szFormat) ;
    vsprintf (szBuffer, szFormat, pArguments) ;
    MessageBox (GetActiveWindow(), szBuffer, szCaption, MB_OK) ;
    }


void diskio0(void)  //create file
{
DWORD SectorsPerCluster;
```

---

[8] Petzold, Charles. *Programming Windows.* Redmond, WA: MicroSoft Press, 1990.

```
DWORD BytesPerSector;
DWORD FreeClusters;
DWORD Clusters;
char root[15];

   file_error=0;
   SetErrorMode(SEM_FAILCRITICALERRORS | SEM_NOOPENFILEERRORBOX);
   strcpy(root,drive);
   strcat(root,"\\");
   BOOL bOK=GetDiskFreeSpace(root, &SectorsPerCluster,
      &BytesPerSector, &FreeClusters, &Clusters);
   if(!bOK) {
      MessageBeep(0);
      OkMsgBox("DISKIO0","Could not access Drive %s",root);
      file_error=12;
      return;
   }
   if(FreeClusters*SectorsPerCluster*BytesPerSector<
                                    blocksize*filesize) {
      MessageBeep(0);
      OkMsgBox("DISKIO0","Insufficient Space on Drive %s",drive);
      file_error=10;
      return;
      }
   UINT num=GetTempFileName(drive,"mhtest",0,filename);
   if(num==0) {
      MessageBeep(0);
      DWORD error=GetLastError();
      TRACE("DISKIO0: attempt to create temporary file %s, ERROR"
         " %d\n",filename,error);
      OkMsgBox("DISKIO0","Could not create temporary file %s, "
         "error %d",filename,error);
      file_error=1;
      return;
      }
   TRACE("DISKIO0: drive %s,filename %s\n",drive,filename);
   ASSERT(num>0);
   ASSERT(strlen(filename)>4);
   fh=CreateFile(filename,GENERIC_READ | GENERIC_WRITE,
      0,NULL,OPEN_EXISTING,FILE_ATTRIBUTE_NORMAL,NULL);
//NOTE: the CreateFile call above uses OPEN_EXISTING rather than
// CREATE_NEW because GetTempFileName actually creates the empty
// file. Using CREATE_NEW generates an invalid handle value with
// ERROR_FILE_EXISTS (80)
   ASSERT(fh);
   if(fh==INVALID_HANDLE_VALUE) {
      MessageBeep(0);
      DWORD error=GetLastError();
      TRACE("DISKIO0: attempt to open file %s, "
         "ERROR %d\n",filename,error);
      OkMsgBox("DISKIO0","Could not open file %s, "
```

```
            "error %d",filename,error);
        file_error=2;
        }
    else
    TRACE("DISKIO0: opened file %s,to write %d of"
        " %d\n",filename,filesize,blocksize);
}

void diskio1(void)   //sequential write test
{
    int i;
    BOOL flag=TRUE;
    DWORD written;

    if(file_error) return;
    SetFilePointer(fh,0,0,FILE_BEGIN);
    for(i=0;i<filesize && flag;i++) {
        flag=WriteFile(fh,buffer,blocksize,&written,NULL);
        }
    if(!flag) {
        MessageBeep(0);
        DWORD error=GetLastError();
        TRACE("DISKIO1: could not write block %d, "
            "error %d\n",i,error);
        OkMsgBox("Sequential Write Test","Could not write block %d,"
            " error %d",i,error);
        file_error=3;
        }
    else {
        TRACE("DISKIO1: wrote %d blocks normally, blocksize"
            " %d\n",i,blocksize);
        }
}

void diskio2(void)   //sequential read test
{
    int i;
    BOOL flag=TRUE;
    DWORD read;

    if(file_error) return;
    SetFilePointer(fh,0,0,FILE_BEGIN);
    for(i=0;i<filesize && flag;i++) {
        flag=ReadFile(fh,buffer,blocksize,&read,NULL);
        }
    if(!flag) {
        MessageBeep(0);
        TRACE("DISKIO2: could not read block %d\n",i);
        OkMsgBox("Sequential Read Test","Could not read block %d",i);
        file_error=5;
        }
}
```

```
void diskio3(void)   //random write test
{
    int i;
    BOOL flag=TRUE;
    DWORD written;
    long fp1=0L,fp2=0L;

    if(file_error) return;
    for(i=0;i<filesize && flag;i++) {
        fp1=long(rand()*float(filesize-1)/RAND_MAX*blocksize);
        //TRACE("DISKIO3: block %ld\n", fp1);
        SetFilePointer(fh,fp1,&fp2,FILE_BEGIN);
        flag=WriteFile(fh,buffer,blocksize,&written,NULL);
    }
    if(!flag) {
        MessageBeep(0);
        TRACE("DISKIO3: could not write %dth block(offset"
            " %ld)\n",i,fp1);
        OkMsgBox("Random Write Test","Could not write %dth"
            " block(offset %ld)",i,fp1);
        file_error=7;
    }

}

void diskio4(void)   //random read test
{
    int i;
    BOOL flag=TRUE;
    DWORD read;
    long fp1=0L,fp2=0L;

    if(file_error) return;
    for(i=0;i<filesize && flag;i++) {
        fp1=long(rand()*float(filesize-1)/RAND_MAX*blocksize);
        //TRACE("DISKIO4: block %ld\n", fp1);
        SetFilePointer(fh,fp1,&fp2,FILE_BEGIN);
        flag=ReadFile(fh,buffer,blocksize,&read,NULL);
    }
    if(!flag) {
        MessageBeep(0);
        TRACE("DISKIO4: could not read %dth block(offset"
            " %ld)\n",i,fp1);
        OkMsgBox("Random Read Test","Could not read %dth block"
            "(offset %ld)",i,fp1);
        file_error=9;
        }

}

void diskio5(void)   //close and delete file
```

```
{
  CloseHandle(fh);
  DeleteFile(filename);
}
```

The first interesting function comes early in **diskio0**:

```
SetErrorMode(SEM_FAILCRITICALERRORS | SEM_NOOPENFILEERRORBOX);
```

Why do we need *that*? Without it, we'd get error messages from Windows NT when we generated critical errors or couldn't find a file, and then *other* error messages from our program. That turns out to be less than aesthetically pleasing. With this setting, though, the program stays in control.

The **SetErrorMode** function has one more possible flag: **SEM_NOGPFAULT-ERRORBOX**. We can't use it, though: it's only for debugging applications that handle GP faults themselves.

The next system call attempts to avoid the most common error in the disk test, running out of disk space:

```
BOOL bOK=GetDiskFreeSpace(root, &SectorsPerCluster,
    &BytesPerSector, &FreeClusters, &Clusters);
```

The code that immediately follows this in the listing multiplies the 4 returned variables to get the bytes available, and compares the result to the bytes required for the full file. If the call cannot access the disk drive, or if the amount of free space is inadequate, the program sets the **file_error** flag and returns. Otherwise, it goes on to create a unique temporary file on the desired disk drive:

```
UINT num=GetTempFileName(drive,"mhtest",0,filename);
```

It's important to understand that **GetTempFileName** actually does create the file, because when we call **CreateFile** we need to tell it to open an existing file rather than to create a new file:

```
fh=CreateFile(filename,GENERIC_READ | GENERIC_WRITE,
    0,NULL,OPEN_EXISTING,FILE_ATTRIBUTE_NORMAL,NULL);
```

CreateFile has options coming out of its ears. The filename can specify a file, pipe, communications resource, or console. Access can be **GENERIC_READ**, **GENE-RIC_WRITE**, or both. You can share the file for reading, writing, both, or neither, and you can pass a security attributes structure. Your creation mode can be **CREATE_NEW**,

CREATE_ALWAYS, OPEN_EXISTING, OPEN_ALWAYS, or TRUNCATE_EXISTING. The file attributes and flags can be any combination of FILE_ATTRIBUTE_AR-CHIVE, FILE_ATTRIBUTE_NORMAL, FILE_ATTRIBUTE_HIDDEN, FILE_-ATTRIBUTE_READONLY, FILE_ATTRIBUTE_SYSTEM, FILE_ATTRI-BUTE_TEMPORARY, FILE_ATTRIBUTE_ATOMIC_WRITE, FILE_FLAG_-WRITE_THROUGH, FILE_FLAG_OVERLAPPED, FILE_FLAG_NO_BUFFERING, FILE_FLAG_RANDOM_ACCESS, FILE_FLAG_SEQUENTIAL_SCAN, FILE_FLAG_DELETE_ON_CLOSE, FILE_FLAG_BACKUP_SEMANTICS, FILE_FLAG_POSIX_SEMANTICS, SECURITY_ANONYMOUS, SECUR-ITY_IDENTIFICATION, SECURITY_IMPERSONATION, SECURITY_DELE-GATION, SECURITY_CONTEXT_TRACKING, and SECURITY_EFFECTIVE_ONLY. If you need extended attributes for the file, you can supply them by specifying the handle to a template file.

In our particular **CreateFile** call we specify an actual file, ask for both read and write access, allow no sharing, take the default security attributes, ask to open an existing file, mark this as a normal file, and pass no extended attributes. It might be tempting to try different file flags to optimize performance: I haven't done it because I don't think it is appropriate in a benchmark.

In the functions that do the actual reading and writing, you'll see that nothing will be done if **file_error** has been set: this saves us a lot of frustration for pathological cases, such as CD-ROM drives, write-protected floppy disks, and floppy disk drives with no disk in the drive. The actual sequential write loop sets the file pointer to the top of the file and then does a bunch of **WriteFile** calls:

```
if(file_error) return;
SetFilePointer(fh,0,0,FILE_BEGIN);
for(i=0;i<filesize && flag;i++) {
    flag=WriteFile(fh,buffer,blocksize,&written,NULL);
    }
```

Note that any error condition will be reflected in the value of **flag**. The sequential read loop is very similar:

```
SetFilePointer(fh,0,0,FILE_BEGIN);
for(i=0;i<filesize && flag;i++) {
    flag=ReadFile(fh,buffer,blocksize,&read,NULL);
    }
```

To test random writing, we set the file pointer to a random block before each write:

```
for(i=0;i<filesize && flag;i++) {
    fp1=long(rand()*float(filesize-1)/RAND_MAX*blocksize);
```

```
      //TRACE("DISKIO3: block %ld\n", fp1);
      SetFilePointer(fh,fp1,&fp2,FILE_BEGIN);
      flag=WriteFile(fh,buffer,blocksize,&written,NULL);
   }
```

Random reading uses essentially the same logic. Finally we close and delete the file, this time unconditionally, since we want to clean up even if there has been an error:

```
   CloseHandle(fh);
   DeleteFile(filename);
```

Interestingly enough, the **CloseHandle** call sometimes takes the bulk of the time. Why? Because it flushes the cache and forces a real write to disk.

That wasn't too hard, actually: we have a pretty solid disk benchmark, and you now know how to use the core Win32 file I/O functions. Of course, you can still use the C or C++ library I/O functions in Windows NT—and you can also use pretty much all of the Windows I/O functions. What you can't do is mix and match: a handle from one library or subsystem is probably not meaningful to another, as we saw when we were working on IMAGE3.

Actually timing the disk benchmarks is no big deal, since we have no need to run multithreaded disk benchmarks:

from BENCH1.CPP

```
extern char drive[];
extern int filesize;
extern UINT blocksize;
extern char buffer[];
extern char fillchar;
extern void diskio0(void);
extern void diskio1(void);
extern void diskio2(void);
extern void diskio3(void);
extern void diskio4(void);
extern void diskio5(void);
extern int file_error;
long DiskTimes[6];

CString DoDiskBench(CWnd *pDlg,int nblocks,int nreps,char *ddrive)
{
   CString answer;
   long Wtime;
   char temp[30];

   memset(buffer,fillchar,blocksize);
   filesize = nblocks;
   strcpy(drive,ddrive);
```

```
ASSERT(nblocks>1);
ASSERT(nreps>0);
ASSERT(blocksize==4096);

//accumulate time in hundredths of a second

Wtime = DiskTimes[0] = DoBench("IO","Create file",diskio0,pDlg);
for(int i=0;i<nreps;i++) {
   Wtime+= DiskTimes[1] = DoBench("I1",
       "Sequential Write Test",diskio1,pDlg);
   Wtime+= DiskTimes[2] = DoBench("I2",
       "Sequential Read Test ",diskio2,pDlg);
   Wtime+= DiskTimes[3] = DoBench("I3",
       "Random Write Test      ",diskio3,pDlg);
   Wtime+= DiskTimes[4] = DoBench("I4",
       "Random Read Test       ",diskio4,pDlg);
   }
Wtime+= DiskTimes[5] = DoBench("I5","Delete file",diskio5,pDlg);
if(file_error)
 strcpy(temp,"A disk error occurred");
else
 sprintf(temp,"Total Disk test time %ld.%ld s",
     Wtime/100,Wtime%100);
pDlg->SetDlgItemText(id_tx_status,temp);

//turn time into MBytes/second

if(Wtime<=0) Wtime=1000; //protect against divide by 0
double mbytes_per_sec =(nblocks * (double)blocksize *
                     0.0004 * nreps / (double)Wtime);
if(file_error)
 strcpy(temp,"Error");
else
 sprintf(temp,"%.4g",mbytes_per_sec);
answer=temp;
return(answer);
}
```

Measuring Video I/O Performance

In one of my magazine columns on the video portion of the Hellstones, I described my feelings and goal with a quotation from Shakespeare's Henry V:

> *Once more unto the breach, dear friends, once more;*
> *Or close the wall up with our English dead!*
> *In peace there's nothing so becomes a man*
> *As modest stillness and humility:*
> *But when the blast of war blows in our ears,*

Then imitate the action of the tiger;
Stiffen the sinews, summon up the blood,
Disguise fair nature with hard-favored rage;
Then lend the eye a terrible aspect.

I had good reasons for thinking of writing video benchmarks as bloody war, and for thinking of the goal of the benchmarks themselves as to "imitate the action of the tiger." Perhaps I should explain.

The video adapter market is nothing if not competitive. It's routine for a board manufacturer to claim their product is eight times faster than all competitors—with or without any legitimate basis. Several magazines and other organizations have published benchmark programs that attempt to test video performance—some from DOS, some from Windows, some based on raw operation speed, some based on simulated applications. Some of the video benchmark programs even gave reasonable results—for a while.

As the benchmarks became popular, device driver writers figured out how to cheat them. Does the benchmark draw the same line 10,000 times? Detect the 9,999 duplicate operations and ignore them. Does the benchmark write one bitmap all over the screen? Cache the bitmap in video memory so you can do fast onboard transfers instead of slow transfers over the computer's bus.

When caught at this, some of the manufacturers argued that these cheats can speed up real applications. Well, real applications don't display exactly the same thing over and over—only benchmarks do that. So, how to be a benchmark that doesn't act like a benchmark? Act like an application: "imitate the action of the tiger."

As with the disk tests, I had no formal statistics to use as a basis for my mix of video tests. All I had was my experience writing and using real Windows programs.

The first test of the video system to come to mind was scrolling text. I find that on many systems slow video scrolling speed limits the throughput of terminal emulation programs, and makes otherwise sprightly editing programs feel like they are operating in a pool of molasses. A typical sequence for a scrolling text display alternates calls to **TextOut**, **ScrollWindow**, and **UpdateWindow**.

To preclude cheating by the video device driver and to make the benchmark simulate a real application, I made each successive string displayed by **TextOut** slightly different. In a plain terminal or editing program, all lines would be in the same font and color; in a fancy word processor, there would be a number of changes of font; in a programmer's editor, there would be a number of changes of color. I decided to change color before each line, like a programmer's editor gone awry, and to change fonts only four times, since a good word processor will cache fonts. You'll find the text scrolling code in functions **video1** and **scroll1** of module VIDEOWIN.CPP, shown on the next page; some of the output is shown in Figure 5-10.

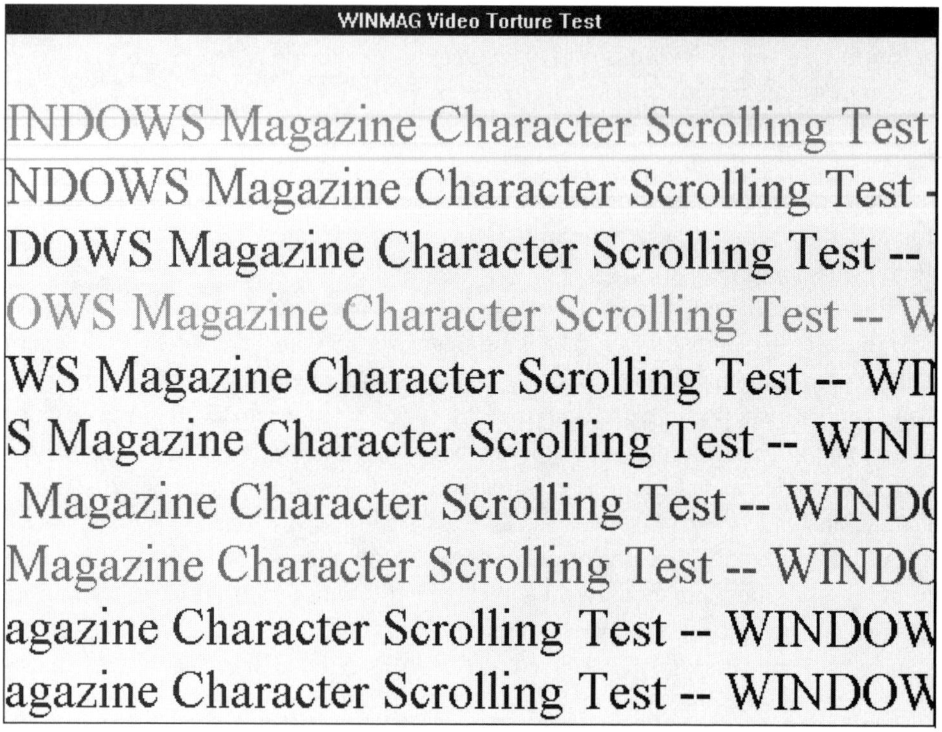

Figure 5-10 Video Test Window at the end of the text scrolling segment.

VIDEOWIN.CPP

```cpp
#include <afxwin.h>
#include <math.h>
#include <memory.h>
static CWnd VWnd;
static BOOL fCreated=FALSE;
extern CWnd *pParent;
long screenarea;
const int vid1reps=50;
const int vid2reps=2;
const int vid3reps=50;
const int vid4reps=1;
long vid1pix=0;
long vid2pix=0;
long vid3pix=0;
long vid4pix=0;
static RECT crect;
extern int bpp,rastercaps,sizepalette,numreserved;

void video0(void) //create window
{
```

```
   RECT r={0,0,640,480};
   fCreated=VWnd.Create(NULL,"WINMAG Video Torture Test",
      WS_POPUP|WS_CAPTION|WS_VISIBLE,r,pParent,NULL);
   if(!fCreated) MessageBeep(0);
   VWnd.GetClientRect(&crect);
   screenarea=(long)crect.right*(long)crect.bottom;
   TRACE("screenarea:%ld",screenarea);
}

void scroll1(CClientDC& vdc)
{
   TEXTMETRIC tm;
   vdc.GetTextMetrics(&tm);
   int yChar=tm.tmHeight + tm.tmExternalLeading;
   ASSERT(yChar>0);
   ASSERT(VWnd.GetSafeHwnd());
   int yLoc= crect.bottom-yChar;
   vdc.PatBlt(0,0,crect.right,crect.bottom,WHITENESS);
      //the PatBlt is to erase the background
   CString TestString("WINDOWS Magazine Character Scrolling Test"
   " —WINDOWS Magazine Character Scrolling Test — WINDOWS"
   " Magazine Character Scrolling Test");
   for(int i=0;i<vid1reps;i++) {
      vdc.SetTextColor(PALETTEINDEX(i%15));
      vdc.TextOut(0,yLoc,TestString.Mid(i%40,80));
      VWnd.ScrollWindow(0,-yChar);
      VWnd.UpdateWindow();
   }
   vid1pix += screenarea * (vid1reps+1);
   TRACE("vid1pix:%ld",vid1pix);
   vdc.SetTextColor(PALETTEINDEX(0));
}

void video1(void) //character scrolling
{
   vid1pix=0;
   if(!fCreated) return;
   CClientDC vdc(&VWnd); //construct device context for client area
   CFont cf;
   cf.CreateFont(20,0,0,0,0,0,0,0,1,
      OUT_TT_PRECIS,CLIP_TT_ALWAYS,
      PROOF_QUALITY,DEFAULT_PITCH,"Arial");
   CFont *poldf=vdc.SelectObject(&cf);
                    //poldf should point to SYSTEM
   scroll1(vdc); //scroll test with Arial 20
   vdc.SelectObject(poldf);
   cf.DeleteObject();
   cf.CreateFont(40,0,0,0,0,0,0,0,1,
      OUT_TT_PRECIS,CLIP_TT_ALWAYS,
      PROOF_QUALITY,DEFAULT_PITCH,"Arial");
   poldf=vdc.SelectObject(&cf);    //poldf should point to SYSTEM
   scroll1(vdc); //scroll test with Arial 40
```

```
   vdc.SelectObject(poldf);
   cf.DeleteObject();
   cf.CreateFont(20,0,0,0,0,0,0,0,1,
       OUT_TT_PRECIS,CLIP_TT_ALWAYS,
       PROOF_QUALITY,DEFAULT_PITCH,"Times New Roman");
   poldf=vdc.SelectObject(&cf);    //poldf should point to SYSTEM
   scroll1(vdc); //scroll test with Times 20
   vdc.SelectObject(poldf);
   cf.DeleteObject();
   cf.CreateFont(40,0,0,0,0,0,0,0,1,
       OUT_TT_PRECIS,CLIP_TT_ALWAYS,
       PROOF_QUALITY,DEFAULT_PITCH,"Times New Roman");
   poldf=vdc.SelectObject(&cf);    //poldf should point to SYSTEM
   scroll1(vdc); //scroll test with Times 40
   vdc.SelectObject(poldf);
   cf.DeleteObject();

}

void video2(void) //line/curve drawing
{
   int i,j;
   CPen *ppen,*ppenold;

   vid2pix=0;
   int hcenter=(crect.left+crect.right)/2;
   int vcenter=(crect.top+crect.bottom)/2;
   if(!fCreated) return;
   CClientDC vdc(&VWnd); //construct device context for client area
   for(j=0;j<vid2reps*2;j++) {              //line drawing tests
       vdc.PatBlt(0,0,crect.right,crect.bottom,WHITENESS);
       vid2pix += screenarea;
       for(i=crect.left;i<crect.right;i++) {//vertical black lines
           vdc.MoveTo(i,crect.top);
           vdc.LineTo(i,crect.bottom);
       }
       vid2pix += screenarea;
       ppenold=(CPen *)vdc.SelectStockObject(WHITE_PEN);
       for(i=crect.top;i<crect.bottom;i++) {//horizontal white lines
           vdc.MoveTo(crect.left,i);
           vdc.LineTo(crect.right,i);
       }
       vdc.SelectObject(ppenold);
       vid2pix += screenarea;
       for(i=0;i<3600;i+=5) {
           //colored clock wipe, half-degree increments
           double theta=i/572.96;
           ppen=new CPen(0,0,PALETTEINDEX((i/5)%15));
           vdc.SelectObject(ppen);
           vdc.MoveTo(hcenter,vcenter);
           vdc.LineTo(int(hcenter+hcenter*cos(theta)),
                     int(vcenter+vcenter*sin(theta)));
```

```
                vdc.SelectObject(ppenold);
                delete ppen;
          }
          vid2pix += screenarea;
}
    for(j=0;j<vid2reps;j++) {           //arc drawing tests
        vdc.PatBlt(0,0,crect.right,crect.bottom,WHITENESS);
        vid2pix += screenarea;
        for(i=0;i<hcenter;i++) {//solid-lined colored ellipses
            ppen=new CPen(0,0,PALETTEINDEX(i%15));
            vdc.SelectObject(ppen);
            vdc.Arc(crect.left+i,crect.top+i,
                    crect.right-i,crect.bottom-i,
                    crect.right,vcenter,crect.left,vcenter);
            vdc.Arc(crect.left+i,crect.top+i,
                    crect.right-i,crect.bottom-i,
                    crect.left,vcenter,crect.right,vcenter);
            vdc.SelectObject(ppenold);
            delete ppen;
        }
        vid2pix += screenarea;
    }
    TRACE("vid2pix:%ld",vid2pix);

}

void video3(void) //filled objects
{
    int i,j;
    int  xLeft, xRight, yTop, yBottom;
    BYTE nRed, nGreen, nBlue ;

    vid3pix=0;
    if(!fCreated) return;
    CClientDC vdc(&VWnd);//construct device context for client area
    vdc.PatBlt(0,0,crect.right,crect.bottom,WHITENESS);
    vid3pix += screenarea;
    for(j=0;j<vid3reps*2;j++) {       //random rectangles
      xLeft    = rand () % crect.right ;
      xRight   = rand () % crect.right ;
      yTop   = rand () % crect.bottom ;
      yBottom  = rand () % crect.bottom ;
      nRed   = rand () & 255 ;
      nGreen   = rand () & 255 ;
      nBlue    = rand () & 255 ;
      CBrush *cb = new CBrush(RGB (nRed, nGreen, nBlue)) ;
      CBrush *cbold = vdc.SelectObject(cb) ;
      vdc.Rectangle (min (xLeft, xRight), min (yTop, yBottom),
                      max (xLeft, xRight), max (yTop, yBottom));
      vdc.SelectObject(cbold);
      delete cb;
      vid3pix += labs(long(xLeft-xRight)*long(yTop-yBottom));
```

```
    }
    vdc.PatBlt(0,0,crect.right,crect.bottom,WHITENESS);
    vid3pix += screenarea;
    for(j=0;j<vid3reps;j++) {   //random rounded rectangles
      xLeft    = rand () % crect.right ;
      xRight   = rand () % crect.right ;
      yTop  = rand () % crect.bottom ;
      yBottom = rand () % crect.bottom ;
      nRed  = rand () & 255 ;
      nGreen = rand () & 255 ;
      nBlue    = rand () & 255 ;
      CBrush *cb = new CBrush(RGB (nRed, nGreen, nBlue)) ;
      CBrush *cbold = vdc.SelectObject(cb) ;
      vdc.RoundRect (min (xLeft, xRight), min (yTop, yBottom),
                      max (xLeft, xRight), max (yTop, yBottom),
                    20, 20);
      vdc.SelectObject(cbold);
      delete cb;
      vid3pix += labs(long(xLeft-xRight)*long(yTop-yBottom));
    }
    vdc.PatBlt(0,0,crect.right,crect.bottom,WHITENESS);
    vid3pix += screenarea;
    for(j=0;j<vid3reps;j++) {   //random ellipses
      xLeft    = rand () % crect.right ;
      xRight   = rand () % crect.right ;
      yTop  = rand () % crect.bottom ;
      yBottom = rand () % crect.bottom ;
      nRed  = rand () & 255 ;
      nGreen = rand () & 255 ;
      nBlue    = rand () & 255 ;
      CBrush *cb = new CBrush(RGB (nRed, nGreen, nBlue)) ;
      CBrush *cbold = vdc.SelectObject(cb) ;
      vdc.Ellipse (min (xLeft, xRight), min (yTop, yBottom),
                     max (xLeft, xRight), max (yTop, yBottom));
      vdc.SelectObject(cbold);
      delete cb;
      vid3pix += labs(long(xLeft-xRight)*long(yTop-yBottom));
            //NB:bad approximation, but fair enough
    }
    TRACE("vid3pix:%ld",vid3pix);
}

void video4(void) //color display
{
    int i;
    BYTE red,green,blue;
    CPalette cpal;
    vid4pix=0;
    if(!fCreated) return;
    CClientDC vdc(&VWnd);//construct device context for client area
    vdc.PatBlt(0,0,crect.right,crect.bottom,WHITENESS);
    vid4pix += screenarea;
```

```
//set up palette for gradient fill

int numcolors=sizepalette-numreserved;
if(numcolors<=0)
    if(bpp>=8)
        numcolors=255;
        //limited by number of levels of 1 color we can use
    else numcolors=2^bpp;
LOGPALETTE *plgpl = (LOGPALETTE*) LocalAlloc(LPTR,
 sizeof(LOGPALETTE) + 256 * sizeof(PALETTEENTRY));
plgpl->palVersion = 0x300;
for(int j=0;j<vid4reps;j++) {
    plgpl->palNumEntries = numcolors;
    for (i = 0,red = 0,green = 0,blue = 0; i < numcolors;
      i++, blue += 1) {
        plgpl->palPalEntry[i].peRed = red;
        plgpl->palPalEntry[i].peGreen = green;
        plgpl->palPalEntry[i].peBlue = blue;
        plgpl->palPalEntry[i].peFlags = PC_RESERVED;
    }
    BOOL fpal=cpal.CreatePalette(plgpl);
    CPalette *oldpal=vdc.SelectPalette(&cpal,FALSE);
    UINT numrealized=vdc.RealizePalette();

    //do gradient fill

    for(i=crect.top;i<crect.bottom;i++) {        //horizontal lines
        int ipal=i%numcolors;
        CPen *cp=new CPen(0,0,PALETTERGB(
            plgpl->palPalEntry[ipal].peRed,
            plgpl->palPalEntry[ipal].peGreen,
            plgpl->palPalEntry[ipal].peBlue));
        CPen *oldpen=vdc.SelectObject(cp);
        vdc.MoveTo(crect.left,i);
        vdc.LineTo(crect.right,i);
        vdc.SelectObject(oldpen);
        delete cp;
        }
    vid4pix += screenarea;

    //animate palette if there is one

    for(i=0;i<numcolors && sizepalette>0;i++) {
        PALETTEENTRY pe;
        pe=plgpl->palPalEntry[0];
        memmove(&plgpl->palPalEntry[0],
                &plgpl->palPalEntry[1],
                (numcolors-1)*sizeof(PALETTEENTRY));
        plgpl->palPalEntry[numcolors-1]=pe;
        cpal.AnimatePalette(0,numcolors,plgpl->palPalEntry);
        vid4pix += numcolors*sizeof(PALETTEENTRY);
        }
```

```
//load 24-bit DIB (BIRD BITMAP resource)

HINSTANCE hinst=AfxGetInstanceHandle();
ASSERT(hinst);
HRSRC hr=FindResource(hinst,"BIRD",RT_BITMAP);
ASSERT(hr);
if(!hr) {
    MessageBeep(0);
    LocalFree((HLOCAL) plgpl);
    return;
}
HGLOBAL hg=LoadResource(hinst,hr);
ASSERT(hg);
void FAR *pBird=LockResource(hg);
ASSERT(pBird);
LPBITMAPINFOHEADER lpbi=(LPBITMAPINFOHEADER)pBird;
LPSTR pixels=(LPSTR)pBird + *(LPDWORD)pBird +
            lpbi->biClrUsed*sizeof(RGBQUAD);

//if needed, set and realize a generalized palette for the
//  24-bit dib

vdc.PatBlt(0,0,crect.right,crect.bottom,WHITENESS);
vid4pix += screenarea;
if(sizepalette>0) {
    red = green = blue = 0;
    vdc.SelectPalette(oldpal,FALSE);
    cpal.DeleteObject(); //free our old palette explicitly
    plgpl->palNumEntries = 256;
    for (i = 0;  i < 256;  i++) {
        plgpl->palPalEntry[i].peRed = red;
        plgpl->palPalEntry[i].peGreen = green;
        plgpl->palPalEntry[i].peBlue = blue;
        plgpl->palPalEntry[i].peFlags = (BYTE) 0;
        if (!(red += 32))
            if (!(green += 32))
                blue += 64;
    }
    fpal=cpal.CreatePalette(plgpl);
    vdc.SelectPalette(&cpal,FALSE);
    numrealized=vdc.RealizePalette();
    }

//Actually display the 24-bit dib

ASSERT(vdc.GetSafeHdc());
SetDIBitsToDevice(vdc.GetSafeHdc(),0,0,lpbi->biWidth,
      lpbi->biHeight,0,0,0,
      lpbi->biHeight,pixels,
      (LPBITMAPINFO)lpbi,DIB_RGB_COLORS);
vid4pix += (long)lpbi->biWidth*lpbi->biHeight;
```

```
      //clean up

      UnlockResource(hg);
      FreeResource(hg);
      vdc.SelectPalette(oldpal,FALSE); //restore original palette
      cpal.DeleteObject(); //free our palette explicitly
      }
   LocalFree((HLOCAL) plgpl);
   TRACE("vid4pix:%ld",vid4pix);
}

void video5(void) //destroy window
{
   if(!fCreated) return;
   BOOL fDestroyed=VWnd.DestroyWindow();
   if(!fDestroyed)
      MessageBeep(0);
}
```

I decided to keep the window size for these tests fixed at 640 x 480 pixels, so that it would be easy to compare speeds from one system to another. Perhaps I should say easier rather than easy: there was no simple way I could bridge the difference between 4-bit, 8-bit, and 24-bit color displays, so I decided simply to report the current color depth. I discovered one anomaly when doing so: VGA displays report themselves as having one bit in four planes, not four bits in one plane.

Putting up a 640 x 480 window turned out to be fairly simple, as you can see in function **video0**. But beneath this simplicity lies an interesting trap. At one point my code read:

```
RECT r={0,0,640,480};
fCreated=VWnd.Create(NULL,"Video Test",
WS_POPUP|WS_CAPTION|WS_VISIBLE,r,pParent,3);
```

The reason for setting the last parameter to 3 was historical: I had previously tried to make this a **WS_CHILD** window rather than a **WS_POPUP** window. A child window has to have an ID number: I picked 3. The window was created fine, but I didn't like having the child window clipped to the parent window, so I switched the style to a popup.

To my consternation and surprise, running the new code made Windows very unhappy—Windows 3.1 crashed rather ignominiously. (Remember, this code is common to both the 16-bit and 32-bit Windows benchmarks.) Why should a **CreateWindow** API call (for that is what the **CWnd Create** member function does for you) crash Windows?

It isn't obvious from the MFC documentation for **CWnd::Create**, but the underlying **CreateWindow** API has a polymorphic ninth parameter: it is the window ID for a child window, and the menu handle for a popup or overlapped window. So somewhere

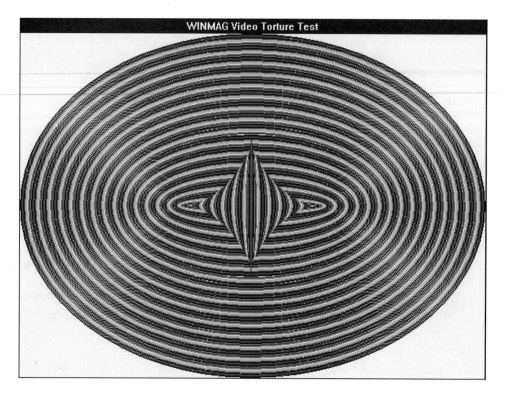

Figure 5-11   Video Test Window after line and arc drawing tests.

inside the USER portion of Windows, some code was trying to load menu 3 for my popup window without checking it for validity. Boom. Changing the ID parameter to NULL, of course, fixed the problem.

The second video test that I implemented exercises line and curve drawing. In **video2** you'll find three loops that use **MoveTo** and **LineTo** to fill the window: one draws vertical black lines, one draws horizontal white lines, and one draws colored radial lines at half-degree intervals—a *clock wipe* of sorts. A fourth loop uses two **Arc** calls per iteration to draw nested colored ellipses. The final display generated by the **Arc** sequence is shown in Figure 5-11.

On most machines the horizontal and vertical wipes are much faster than the clock wipe, for two reasons: the **LineTo** implementation in the video driver is generally much faster for the vertical and horizontal cases than it is for an arbitrary angle, and my code calculates floating point sines and cosines inside the clock wipe loop. I could certainly speed things up by coding an integer sine/cosine table lookup, and in my youth I certainly would have done so, but my intention is to imitate the action of the tiger: most applications don't bother with that sort of optimization in this day and age.

My third set of tests, in **video3**, exercises filled objects. The basic loop is my translation of Charlie Petzold's RANDRECT example from C with API calls to C++ with MFC:

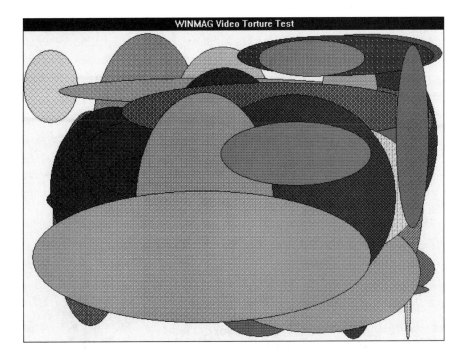

Figure 5-12   Video Test Window after running the filled object test.

```
for(j=0;j<vid3reps*2;j++) {      //random rectangles
   xLeft    = rand () % crect.right ;
   xRight   = rand () % crect.right ;
   yTop   = rand () % crect.bottom ;
   yBottom = rand () % crect.bottom ;
   nRed   = rand () & 255 ;
   nGreen   = rand () & 255 ;
   nBlue    = rand () & 255 ;
   CBrush *cb = new CBrush(RGB (nRed, nGreen, nBlue)) ;
   CBrush *cbold = vdc.SelectObject(cb) ;
   vdc.Rectangle (min (xLeft, xRight), min (yTop, yBottom),
                  max (xLeft, xRight), max (yTop, yBottom));
   vdc.SelectObject(cbold);
   delete cb;
   vid3pix += labs(long(xLeft-xRight)*long(yTop-yBottom));
}
```

The loops that follow in the listing extend the code from rectangles to rounded rectangles and ellipses. As you might expect, plain rectangles draw faster than rounded rectangles or ellipses. But I was surprised at how big the speed difference is on most machines: I suspect that drawing plain rectangles takes advantage of an optimized **PatBlt** for the patterned fill, where drawing rounded rectangles and ellipses uses a more time-consuming algorithm to extend the fill to the borders. The final appearance of the random ellipse test is shown in Figure 5-12.

My final test, in **video4**, exercises color display. The first section works properly only if the current video driver uses a color palette: it sets up a palette for a black to blue gradient fill, then performs the fill using **MoveTo** and **LineTo** to draw horizontal lines. Once the logical palette is filled in, the logic to activate the palette looks like:

```
BOOL fpal=cpal.CreatePalette(plgpl);
CPalette *oldpal=vdc.SelectPalette(&cpal,FALSE);
UINT numrealized=vdc.RealizePalette();
```

Once the lines are drawn, the program animates the color palette to give the illusion that the screen is scrolling upwards. Basically, that is just a matter of reordering the entries in the logical palette, then calling the **AnimatePalette** API:

```
for(i=0;i<numcolors && sizepalette>0;i++) {
    PALETTEENTRY pe;
    pe=plgpl->palPalEntry[0];
    memmove(&plgpl->palPalEntry[0],
            &plgpl->palPalEntry[1],
            (numcolors-1)*sizeof(PALETTEENTRY));
    plgpl->palPalEntry[numcolors-1]=pe;
    cpal.AnimatePalette(0,numcolors,plgpl->palPalEntry);
    vid4pix += numcolors*sizeof(PALETTEENTRY);
    }
```

The second section of the color test loads and displays a small 24-bit DIB: actually, it's the parrot image, BIRD.TIF, that you may recall from *Advanced Windows Programming*, which I converted to a DIB with IMAGE3A. The logic here is that we first find the DIB as a bitmap resource in the benchmark's EXE, then load and lock the resource. Locking the resource gives us a pointer, which we cast to a **LPBITMAPINFORHEADER**. We find the bits in the image just as we would for a DIB we'd loaded from a file: we jump over the header and the color table, using the sizes stored in the header:

```
LPSTR pixels=(LPSTR)pBird + *(LPDWORD)pBird +
             lpbi->biClrUsed*sizeof(RGBQUAD);
```

We set up a palette for the image if we need to, then actually display it with

```
SetDIBitsToDevice(vdc.GetSafeHdc(),0,0,lpbi->biWidth,
        lpbi->biHeight,0,0,0,
        lpbi->biHeight,pixels,
        (LPBITMAPINFO)lpbi,DIB_RGB_COLORS);
```

Finally, we unlock and free the bitmap resource and delete our palette. The display of the parrot, shown in Figure 5-13, takes up only a small portion of the test window.

Figure 5-13   The last of the video tests displays a 24-bit DIB.

On a 24-bit color display, the image appears in under a second; on an 8-bit color display, however, it can take as much as 100 seconds for the bird to draw, scan-line by scan-line. Some 8-bit Windows NT drivers cache the scan-lines: it can appear that nothing is happening for ten or twenty seconds at a time, and then a band of the image will be drawn.

I originally thought that it would make sense to time the color test along with the other three tests. I was wrong: the 100-second difference between the performance of a 24-bit driver and an 8-bit driver overwhelms the rest of the measurements. The color display test might correlate with image editing program performance, but it has little relevance to the behavior of a common business application like a word processor or a spreadsheet. So, I calculate the video throughput results only from the first three tests:

from BENCH1.CPP

```
extern void video0(void);
extern void video1(void);
extern void video2(void);
extern void video3(void);
extern void video4(void);
extern void video5(void);
CWnd *pParent;
extern long vid1pix,vid2pix,vid3pix,vid4pix;
extern long screenarea;
long VideoTimes[6];
```

```
CString DoVideoBench(CWnd *pDlg,int nreps)
{
  CString answer;
  long Wtime;
  long TotalPixels;
  char temp[30];

  ASSERT(nreps>0);
  pParent=pDlg;

  //accumulate time in hundredths of a second

  Wtime = VideoTimes[0] = DoBench("V0",
   "Create Window",video0,pDlg);
  for(int i=0;i<nreps;i++) {
    Wtime+= VideoTimes[1] = DoBench("V1",
      "Character Scrolling Test",video1,pDlg);
    Wtime+= VideoTimes[2] = DoBench("V2",
      "Line/Curve Drawing Test ",video2,pDlg);
    Wtime+= VideoTimes[3] = DoBench("V3",
      "Filled Object Test       ",video3,pDlg);
              VideoTimes[4] = DoBench("V4",
      "Color Display Test       ",video4,pDlg);
    //NB: color display excluded from total time
    }
  Wtime+= VideoTimes[5] = DoBench("V5",
     "Destroy Window",video5,pDlg);
  sprintf(temp,"Total Video test time %ld.%ld s",
     Wtime/100,Wtime%100);
  pDlg->SetDlgItemText(id_tx_status,temp);

  //turn time into KPixels/second
  if(Wtime<=0) Wtime=1000; //protect against divide by 0
  //count 1 screen each for window creation and destruction, plus
  //routines' record of number of pixels written
  TotalPixels=2L*screenarea + vid1pix*nreps
              //multiply by nreps since vid1pix reset each rep
     + vid2pix*nreps + vid3pix*nreps
     /* + vid4pix*nreps*/;
              //NB: color display excluded from total pixels
  double mpixels_per_sec =(1.0e-6 * TotalPixels /
                          ((double)Wtime/100.0));
  sprintf(temp,"%.4g",mpixels_per_sec);
  answer=temp;
  return(answer);
}
```

I might have liked to go on and dream up some Win32-specific video benchmarks: an image of a chambered nautilus built using world transforms and a stroked path came to mind, as did a Bézier curve test run with a complex clip path in effect. What stopped me is that there are not, at this writing, any high-level Win32 applications that use such complex effects, so I'd pretty much be guaranteed results that would not correlate with any possible application benchmarks.

Reporting the Hellstone Results

And remember, correlations are what makes the Hellstone benchmark different from all other benchmarks. For the sake of getting good correlations, we not only report the Hellstone results onscreen as we go, we let the user save them in a comma-delimited ASCII file:

from BENCH1.CPP

```
static int ResultThreads;
static int ResultBlocks;
static int ResultReps;
static char ResultDrive[4];
static CString ResultKDhrys;
static CString ResultKWhets;
static CString ResultKBytes;
static CString ResultKVideo;

BOOL RunBenchMarks(CWnd *pWnd, BOOL fDhry, BOOL fWhet, BOOL fDisk,
                   BOOL fVideo)
{
    char ddrive[4];
    int nthreads,nblocks,nreps;
    CString KDhrys,KWhets,KBytes,KVideo;

    //get handle for dialog window (child of main window)
    CWnd *pDlg = pWnd->GetTopWindow();
    ASSERT(pDlg);

    //get stuff from controls
    pDlg->DlgDirSelect(ddrive,id_cb_drive);
    nthreads=pDlg->GetDlgItemInt(id_ed_threads,NULL,FALSE);
    nblocks =pDlg->GetDlgItemInt(id_ed_blocks, NULL,FALSE);
    nreps   =pDlg->GetDlgItemInt(id_ed_repeat ,NULL,FALSE);
    if(nthreads>MAXTHREADS) {
        MessageBeep(0);
        pWnd->MessageBox("Maximum threads exceeded","Threads");
        pDlg->SetDlgItemInt(id_ed_threads,MAXTHREADS);
        nthreads=MAXTHREADS;
        }

    SetCursor(LoadCursor(NULL,IDC_WAIT));

    //post status and run dhrystones
    pDlg->SetDlgItemText(id_tx_status,"Running Dhrystones");
    if(fDhry)
        KDhrys=DoDhrystone(pDlg,nthreads,nreps);
```

```
    else
        KDhrys="";
    pDlg->SetDlgItemText(id_tx_dhrys,KDhrys);
    TRACE("%s MDhrys\n",KDhrys);

    //post status and run whetstones
    pDlg->SetDlgItemText(id_tx_status,"Running Whetstones");
    if(fWhet)
        KWhets=DoWhetstone(pDlg,nthreads,nreps);
    else
        KWhets="";
    pDlg->SetDlgItemText(id_tx_whets,KWhets);
    TRACE("%s MWhets\n",KWhets);

    //post status and run disk benchmark
    pDlg->SetDlgItemText(id_tx_status,"Running Disk Benchmark");
    if(fDisk)
        KBytes=DoDiskBench(pDlg,nblocks,nreps,ddrive);
    else
        KBytes="";
    pDlg->SetDlgItemText(id_tx_kbytes,KBytes);
    TRACE("%s MBytes\n",KBytes);

    //post status and run video benchmark
    pDlg->SetDlgItemText(id_tx_status,"Running Video Benchmark");
    if(fVideo)
        KVideo=DoVideoBench(pDlg,nreps);
    else
        KVideo="";
    pDlg->SetDlgItemText(id_tx_video,KVideo);
    TRACE("%s MChars\n",KVideo);

    //say that the benchmarks are done
    SetCursor(LoadCursor(NULL,IDC_ARROW));
#ifdef WIN32
    Sleep(1000);   //let them see last message
#endif
    pDlg->SetDlgItemText(id_tx_status,"Benchmarks complete");

    //enable reporting functions
    ResultThreads=nthreads;
    ResultReps=nreps;
    ResultBlocks=nblocks;
    strcpy(ResultDrive,ddrive);
    ResultKDhrys=KDhrys;
    ResultKWhets=KWhets;
    ResultKBytes=KBytes;
    ResultKVideo=KVideo;

    CMenu *main_menu=pWnd->GetMenu();
    ASSERT (main_menu);
    CMenu *file_menu=main_menu->GetSubMenu(0);
```

```
   ASSERT (file_menu);
   file_menu->EnableMenuItem(IDM_Save,  MF_ENABLED);
   file_menu->EnableMenuItem(IDM_Saveas,MF_ENABLED);
   file_menu->EnableMenuItem(IDM_Print, MF_ENABLED);
   CMenu *analyze_menu=main_menu->GetSubMenu(2);
   ASSERT (analyze_menu);
   analyze_menu->EnableMenuItem(IDM_Details,MF_ENABLED);

//The next three items are not implemented in this version
// analyze_menu->EnableMenuItem(IDM_Charts,MF_ENABLED);
// analyze_menu->EnableMenuItem(IDM_Comparisons,MF_ENABLED);
// analyze_menu->EnableMenuItem(IDM_Predictions,MF_ENABLED);
   return TRUE;
}

BOOL BLD_RunBenchMarksUDCFunc (CWnd *pWnd)
{
   return RunBenchMarks(pWnd,TRUE,TRUE,TRUE,TRUE);
}

// user defined code
BOOL BLD_ExitUDCFunc (CWnd *pWnd)
{
    PostQuitMessage(0);
    return TRUE;
}

void SaveResults(FILE *fh)
{
   fprintf(fh,"%d,%d,%d,%s,",
       ResultThreads,
       ResultReps,
       ResultBlocks,
       ResultDrive);
   fprintf(fh,"%s,",
       ResultKDhrys);
   fprintf(fh,"%s,",
       ResultKWhets);
   fprintf(fh,"%s,",
       ResultKBytes);
   fprintf(fh,"%s,",
       ResultKVideo);
   fprintf(fh,"%d,",
       bpp);
   for(int i=0;i<6;i++)
       fprintf(fh,"%ld.%ld,",DiskTimes[i]/100,DiskTimes[i]%100);
   for(i=0;i<6;i++)
       fprintf(fh,"%ld.%ld,",VideoTimes[i]/100,VideoTimes[i]%100);
   fprintf(fh,"\"%s\",",
       MachineDescription);
//Note: this checksum code will change from version to version
// to avoid cheating
```

```
    unsigned checksum = 3*ResultThreads+ResultReps+ResultBlocks/2+
        int(atof(ResultKDhrys)*10+atof(ResultKWhets)*10+
            atof(ResultKVideo)*bpp);
    for(i=0;i<6;i++)
        checksum += unsigned(DiskTimes[i]*2+VideoTimes[i]/3);
    fprintf(fh,"%g,%X\n",
        version,checksum);
    }
// user defined code
BOOL BLD_PrintUDCFunc (CWnd *pWnd)
{
    FILE *fh;

    fh=fopen("PRN","wt");
    ASSERT(fh);
    SaveResults(fh);
    fprintf(fh,"\f");
    fclose(fh);
    return TRUE;
}

#ifndef MAX_PATH
#define MAX_PATH 255
#endif

#ifdef WIN32
char CurrentFile[MAX_PATH]="NTHELL.DAT";
#else
char CurrentFile[MAX_PATH]="WINHELL.DAT";
#endif

// user defined code
BOOL BLD_SaveUDCFunc (CWnd *pWnd)
{
    FILE *fh;

    TRACE("BLD_SaveUDCFunc: about to open %s\n",CurrentFile);
    fh=fopen(CurrentFile,"at");
    ASSERT(fh);
    BLD_Menu41DlgFunc(pWnd);//get machine description
    SaveResults(fh);
    fclose(fh);
    return TRUE;
}

// user defined code
BOOL BLD_SaveasUDCFunc (CWnd *pWnd)
{
    TRACE("BLD_SaveasUDCFunc: about to start file open dialog\n");
    CFileDialog cfd(FALSE,"dat",CurrentFile,OFN_HIDEREADONLY,
    "Data Files (*.dat)|*.dat|All Files (*.*)|*.*||");
    if(cfd.DoModal()==IDCANCEL)
```

```
      return(FALSE);
   TRACE("BLD_SaveasUDCFunc: returned from file open dialog\n");
   CString name=cfd.GetPathName();
   if(strlen(name))
      strcpy(CurrentFile,name);
   BLD_SaveUDCFunc (pWnd);
   return TRUE;
}
```

You'll notice a few **#ifdef WIN32** lines in the above code. These flag source lines that work in the 32-bit Windows API but not in the 16-bit API. That isn't to say, though, that they won't work under Windows 3.1: they will, for the most part, work using the Win32s libraries. Many, but not all, of the benefits of Win32 can be yours using Win32s running on top of 16-bit Windows, as we'll see in the next chapter.

6

In which we learn to trade off between the advanced features of Windows NT and compatibility with Windows 3.1, using Win32s.

With a Shoehorn

. . . .

It's all very well to push the envelope and use all of the new Win32 features in a program intended to run on Windows NT, but there are also practical considerations in life: specifically, the market for Windows 3.1 programs is still much larger than the market for Windows NT programs.

Enter Win32s. The "s" stands for subset: we'll come to what kind of subset shortly. The important thing is that you can ship some DLLs and a VxD with your Win32 program that will allow it to run—within limits—on a 16-bit Windows 3.1 system equipped with an 80386 or better Intel processor and running in enhanced mode. The performance of Win32 programs running on Windows 3.1/Win32s systems is quite good: you get the full benefit of 32-bit pointers and 32-bit registers in your own code, with only a small "thunking" overhead when you make systems calls. If your program uses large data structures or does intensive computations, a Win32s version is likely to significantly outperform a 16-bit Windows version; if your program spends most of its time calling Windows APIs, the native 16-bit version will most likely outperform the Win32s version.

Win32s isn't the only announced subset of Win32: the "Chicago" system, which will probably be released as Windows 4 sometime in 1994, uses a larger and more capable subset, Win32c. Win32s programs will run on Windows NT (unless you use the Universal Thunk, which we will discuss shortly), Windows 3.1, and "Chicago";

Win32c programs will not run on Windows 3.1. Win16 programs will run on all Windows and Windows NT systems, even on RISC systems.

That's pretty confusing. Which Windows API is right for your application? If your application runs well as 16-bit code, then the 16-bit Windows 3.1 API will give you the largest market. If your program is CPU-bound and/or accesses large memory structures, it might run a lot faster as a 32-bit Win32s application. If your program requires threads, security, and/or interprocess communications, it should probably be a full-blown Win32 application that requires Windows NT. And sometime in the future, if your program can take advantage of threads but doesn't need security, it might do well as a Win32c application.

The Win32s Subset

From a programmer's point of view, the most important question about Win32s is "What's Missing?" The short answer to that is: threads, advanced graphics, asynchronous file I/O, Unicode, and security. But there is more to Win32s programming than just being aware of missing Win32 facilities: a program that is aware that it is really running on a 16-bit Windows system can take advantage of that.

Suppose you were writing an interactive programming system. Under Windows NT, you'd most likely use threads and processes and interprocess communications to make compilation occur in the background. Under Windows with Win32s, you could instead use a VxD or a piece of global memory to coordinate several virtual machines and accomplish pretty much the same goal. To access the VxD you'd probably have to build a 32-bit Win32s DLL to talk to a 16-bit Windows DLL which in turn called 32-bit VxD services through an interrupt: it's awkward, but it can be made to work.

What it Does

Before we list all the things that Win32s is missing, maybe we should look at what it does. First and foremost, it lets Win32 programs use the facilities of Windows 3.1 through a "thunking" layer—WIN32S16.DLL—which takes care of translating the call stack, expanding or truncating parameters, and mapping message parameters between the 32-bit application code and the 16-bit system. Windows 3.1 features supported by thunking include the following:

- All the windowing code in USER
- All the graphics code in GDI
- OLE 1.0
- DDE and DDEML
- TrueType fonts
- Common Dialogs

Those subjects are covered in my previous book, *Advanced Windows Programming*. Win32s version 1.1 also has support for several areas that were not supported in Win32s version 1.0:

- Network support (covered in Chapter 11 of this book)
- Multimedia Support (covered in Chapter 7)
- OLE Version 2.0 (covered in Chapter 10)
- MAPI (covered in Chapter 11)
- ODBC (not covered, since database connectivity is a rather specialized area)

Note that there *are* things in Windows 3.1 not supported by this mechanism: Pen functions, segment manipulation, DOS calls, and so on. Some of these things wouldn't make sense for a Win32 program, but others certainly would: in particular, it makes a lot of sense for programs working with pens to use 32-bit addressing, so it is a real shame that the pen APIs are not supported by Win32s.

In addition, Win32s provides—as a VxD, W32S.386—some features of Windows NT not normally present in Windows 3.1: structured exception handling, sparse virtual memory, growable heaps, named shared memory, and memory-mapped files. Those are certainly nice to have, but one could wish for a lot more: threads, for instance.

Still, there's enough in Win32s that you can build credible applications, as long as you are aware of what Win32 functions you won't be able to use. That will most likely change from version to version: Win32c adds thread support, for instance, and it is entirely possible that there will be a version of Win32s released between Win32s 1.1 and Win32c 1.0.

What's Missing

According to the official Microsoft documentation, Win32s has no planned support for:

- Console APIs (which I haven't covered in this book, since my emphasis is on applications with GUIs rather than character-mode applications)
- Unicode APIs (covered in Chapter 9 of this book)
- Security APIs (covered in Chapter 11)
- Communications APIs (not covered in this book, since I think communications programming is a specialized topic that really requires a whole book of its own)
- Asynchronous File I/O (an option for CreateFile, ReadFile, WriteFile, and the default for ReadFileEx and WriteFileEx, which I have not covered)
- Threads (covered in Chapter 5)
- Paths (covered in Chapter 5)
- Enhanced Metafiles (covered in Chapter 7)
- Bézier Curves (covered in Chapter 5)

Now, that's an interesting list. There are things in there that we certainly care about—but it's not a complete list, by any means. There are other areas that are not included in Win32 at all but can be found in 16-bit Windows systems, such as the Pen extensions, and there are a bunch of unsupported Win32 APIs omitted from the list. If you have the Windows NT SDK, the file WIN32API.CSV installed in the \MSTOOLS\LIB directory and the WIN32S.DAT file in \MSTOOLS\BIN both have current Win32s function lists. If you have a question as to whether you can use a given Win32 function in a Win32s application, you can search WIN32API.CSV for the function name and look at column D for a Y or N to indicate Win32s support. If you have a Win32 program that you want to check for Win32s compatibility, you can quickly flag unsupported APIs by using PORTTOOL (discussed in Chapter 1) with WIN32S.DAT renamed to PORTTOOL.INI.

For instance, **MaskBlt** and **PlgBlt**, which I covered in Chapter 5, are listed in the WIN32API spreadsheet as unsupported in Win32s, and are also flagged in WIN32S.DAT. If you try to run a Win32 program that blithely calls **MaskBlt** from Windows 3.1 using Win32s, you'll probably lock up Windows and have to reboot—at least, that's what happened when I tried to run the MASKBLT example program. Theoretically, Win32s programs can call any Win32 API; the catch is that they have to recover safely if the unsupported API fails. Maintaining that level of vigilance in a program is difficult, although not impossible.

What's Been Added

I mentioned earlier that we'd come to what kind of subset Win32s actually is. It is an *improper subset*, meaning that there are things in Win32s that are not in Win32.

The principal of these extra things is the *Universal Thunk*, which allows you to call 16-bit DLLs from 32-bit EXEs, after a fashion, but only in Win32s: the mechanism used by the Universal Thunk APIs *doesn't work in Windows NT.* Universal Thunks let you add bridges between the 32-bit code and the 16-bit system on a selective basis by writing pairs of DLLs: a 32-bit DLL that contains the 32-bit entry points and calls a 16-bit service dispatch routine, and a 16-bit DLL that includes the dispatch route and calls the actual desired services. We'll go over Univeral Thunks in more detail shortly.

Again, Universal Thunks work only on Windows 3.1 with the Win32s libraries. A Win32s application that uses Universal Thunks will *not* run under Windows NT.

Performance Issues

We mentioned earlier that thunks cause a small (typically 10%) overhead every time you make a system API call. That fact leads to a guiding principle: to optimize a Win32s program minimize the number of API calls you make. There are some obvious cases where you can actually follow this rule: you can use **Polyline** rather than **MoveTo** and **LineTo** to draw lines and curves, and you can use large blocks when you do

Table 6-1 Comparison of 16-bit and 32-bit Windows Benchmarks on a 486/50, Measured under Windows 3.1 with Win32s

Program	MDhry/s	MWhet/s	MB/s	MPixel/s *
WinHell (16-bit)	28	4.9	0.21	2.2
NTHell (32-bit)	63	10.6	0.21	1.8

* Video performance measured at 24 bits per pixel.

disk reads and writes. Minimizing the number of API calls isn't a bad rule for Win32 programs in general: there is some overhead every time you call into the system, even in Windows NT.

Most programs that do significant amounts of numeric computation or deal with substantial amounts of data will be faster as Win32s programs than as 16-bit Windows programs—according to experiments done by Microsoft, up to two times faster. You can get a feel for this from my benchmark results. On a 50 MHz 486 running Windows 3.1, I see the results shown in Table 6-1.

As you can clearly see, the integer (Dhrystone) and floating point (Whetstone) benchmarks come in just over twice as fast when running 32-bit code under Win32s (the NTHell line) as they do running 16-bit code (the WinHell line). The disk benchmarks are identical in both cases, and the 32-bit video benchmarks—which make a *lot* of API calls—are about 20 percent slower than the 16-bit video benchmarks.

My 20 percent degradation from thunking in the video measurements is worse than Microsoft's reported 10 percent degradation, but my tests are for a benchmark that does almost nothing but call video APIs, and Microsoft's tests were for applications. My CPU measurements show greater than the factor of two improvement reported by Microsoft.

By the way, NTHell running on the same machine under Windows NT reports 63 MDhry/s (the same as under Win32s), 13 MWhets/s (25 percent better than under Win32s), 9 MB/s (a *lot* better), and 5.6 MPixels/s at 8 bits per pixel (about the same raw transfer rate as the Win32s results, which were measured at 24 bits per pixel). The tremendous difference in disk performance is directly attributable to Windows NT's great disk caching implementation. The difference in floating point performance is probably because Windows NT handles floating point exception checking more efficiently than Win32s can. But we need to look a little deeper to understand that.

Look at Table 6-1 again and note the improvement in the Whetstone results between 16-bit Windows and Win32s. I expected the integer Dhrystone results, but the Whetstone results need some analysis. You'd think that, as Gertrude Stein might say, a coprocessor is a coprocessor is a coprocessor. Why should Win32s Whetstones be a factor of two faster than Windows Whetstones? Let's look at another set of measurements (Table 6-2).

Table 6-2 Floating Point Performance of a 25 MHx 80386 with 80387

Environment	MWhets/s	Ratio to DOS
DOS	2.3	1
Windows 3.1 Enhanced mode DOS box	1.98	0.86
Windows 3.1 Windows App	1.58	0.69
Windows 3.1 32-bit Win32s App	2.64	1.15

This raises even more questions. Why should Windows Whetstones run slower than DOS Whetstones, and why should Win32s Whetstones run faster?

First we have to understand what the Whetstone does: it consists of ten tight-loop tests that simulate the code found in real numerical programs. One test exercises floating point addition, subtraction, and multiplication with simple arguments; another does the same for array elements; a third passes the array to another function, and includes a little division as well; others test conditional jumps and integer arithmetic; yet others test trigonometric functions, logs, exponentials, and square roots. These are done in moderately complex expressions that exercise the compiler as well as the hardware—they aren't straight instruction timings.

In the 80x87 coprocessor family, several possible exception conditions can be flagged right in the floating point hardware, and results like "not a number" (NaN) or "negative infinity" can be represented. Good low-level floating point software has to test for such exception conditions and properly raise the appropriate signals; good high-level floating point software has to properly handle the signals when they occur.

On an 8087 or 80287, an invalid operation exception is raised automatically, and that generates an interrupt on the PC's 8259A interrupt controller. In this case, the low-level floating point software can rely on an interrupt handler to notify it of exceptions.

On an i486 CPU or a 387 NPX, no invalid operation exception is raised when encountering NaNs or denormals. On these processors, the low-level floating point software has to explicitly check for error conditions and clear them properly.

On DOS, that's not a big deal: there is only one process running, in real mode, and the overhead to check the floating point coprocessor for exceptions is minimal. On Windows, that could be a problem: many programs could be attempting to use the coprocessor, and if one program left an error condition on the floating point processor stack, another program might crash.

Windows manages—and if needed, emulates—the floating point coprocessor with WIN87EM.DLL. With a real floating point processor in place, most of the floating point library interrupts put in your code by the C compiler are replaced by inline floating point instructions. Why most? The FWAIT instructions are left as interrupts, which WIN87EM.DLL handles: it uses this opportunity to check the coprocessor for exceptions, which turns out to be a significant (30% in this measurement) overhead in enhanced mode.

The case of the enhanced mode DOS box also incurs overhead for coprocessor exception checking, but it is not quite as bad—only 15 percent—as you can see from the table. Apparently that is because the DOS box operates in the V86 mode of its virtual machine (VM), while Windows operates in protected mode. A DOS session in standard mode Windows runs in real mode with Windows suspended; it incurs no floating point overhead relative to plain DOS.

So now we understand why Windows floating point is slower than DOS floating point. Why is Win32s floating point faster than DOS floating point?

It isn't the floating point instructions themselves operating faster in 32-bit mode. The 80x87 family does all operations using 80-bit arithmetic. And it isn't just the exception handling, although that's part of it: W32SKRNL.DLL exports Load80387 and Un-load80387 functions. No, if it were just exception handling, Win32s floating point arithmetic would be exactly as fast as DOS floating point arithmetic.

Two other things are happening. One you could predict: the 32-bit integer code that supports the floating point coprocessor (for loading and storing numbers and doing index arithmetic) is more efficient than 16-bit for manipulating 64-bit quantities (double-precision floating point numbers). The other was a surprise: the Microsoft Windows NT compiler generates floating point code that makes better use of the coprocessor than its 16-bit cousins. Two snippets of code generated from the Whetstone will illustrate this fairly clearly:

```
Windows NT compiler output (32-bit code)

   mov    eax, 1200              ; 000004b0H
   fld    QWORD PTR _D_e1$S287+24
   fld    QWORD PTR _D_e1$S287+16
   fld    QWORD PTR _D_e1$S287
   fld    QWORD PTR _D_e1$S287+8
   jmp    SHORT $L321
$L445:

; 124   :
; 125   :   if( n2 > 0 )
; 126   :   {
; 127   :      for (i = 1; i <= n2; i++)

   fstp   ST(4)
$L321:

; 128   :      {
; 129   :          D_e1[0] = ( D_e1[0] + D_e1[1] + D_e1[2] - D_e1[3] )
;                      * D_t;
```

```
    fld     ST(0)
    fsub    ST(0), ST(4)
    fadd    ST(0), ST(3)
    fadd    ST(0), ST(2)
    fmul    QWORD PTR $T437
    fst     ST(2)
;....
; code continues and loops back to:
    jne     SHORT $L445


VC++ Compiler output (16-bit code)

    mov     ax,OFFSET DGROUP:$S434_D_e1+24
    mov     di,ax
    mov     si,OFFSET DGROUP:$T579
    movsd
    movsd
    mov     dx,1200 ;04b0H
    fld     QWORD PTR $T575
;|***
;|***    if( n2 > 0 )
;|***    {
;|***        for (i = 1; i <= n2; i++)
; Line 127
$F468:
;|*** {
;|***  D_e1[0] = ( D_e1[0] + D_e1[1] + D_e1[2] - D_e1[3] ) * D_t;
;|***  D_e1[1] = ( D_e1[0] + D_e1[1] - D_e1[2] + D_e1[3] ) * D_t;
; Line 130
    fld     QWORD PTR $S434_D_e1+8
    fsub    QWORD PTR $S434_D_e1+24
    fadd    QWORD PTR $S434_D_e1+16
    fadd    QWORD PTR $S434_D_e1
    fmul    ST(0),ST(1)
    fst     QWORD PTR $S434_D_e1
;....
; code continues and loops back to:
    jne     SHORT $F468
```

Do you see the difference? The 16-bit code constantly accesses memory; but the 32-bit code loads most of the variables onto the floating point coprocessor stack once and then uses them for arithmetic many times. And that accounts for the rest of the improvement in the speed of 32-bit code.

I'm afraid that there's a cheat here: Microsoft's best code generation technology has gone into its 32-bit compiler products, but hasn't been propogated back into its 16-bit products—at least not yet. I have no idea why this should be: it serves no rational purpose to make 16-bit Windows programs run slower than they need to.

Maybe nobody at Microsoft associated with Windows cares about floating point performance.[1]

We were originally talking about Win32s performance issues. There are two more considerations: you can improve performance if you tune your working set, and you can reduce your memory pointer thunking overhead by using local (stack) variables for parameters to system calls.

The working set—the region of memory a program uses in any given time span—can have a strong effect on performance in any virtual memory system. If your application constantly accesses code and data all over 2 GB of address space, the system will incur many page faults when trying to map this virtual address space into real RAM. If, on the other hand, your program uses a small region of memory continuously, there will be very few page faults, and your program will run at close to its theoretical speed. You can control the working set of your data by using algorithms with good *locality*—algorithms that don't jump all over memory. You can control the working set of your code by keeping functions that call each other heavily near each other in memory.

The Windows NT SDK provides the PVIEW process viewer, which can monitor the working set and other parameters of any process and its threads; it also provides a working set tuning utility (on the Intel platform) for reducing the working set of an executable. The working set tuner can't fix your algorithms, but it *can* reorder your functions in memory.

The working set tuner has several pieces: WST.DLL is used for data collection from programs built with the **-Gh** compiler option; WSTDUMP.EXE saves the collected snapshots to disk; WSTCAT.EXE can merge data collected from several runs of a program; WSTUNE.EXE analyzes the collected data, calculates a function ordering that will minimize the working set, and produces a file for the linker that specifies the new function ordering. In the Windows NT SDK, the working set tuner is documented in \MSTOOLS\BIN\WST.TXT.

Tuning your working set will improve the performance of your application both in Windows NT and in Win32s. How much it will improve the performance depends very much on how large and nonlocal the program was to begin with, and on whether or not the program fits entirely into physical RAM at the time it runs. Small programs will see little or no boost from working set tuning; large programs may get significant speedups.

---

[1] I am sensitive to floating point performance because I have a background in science and engineering: computer applications in those areas tend to use floating point arithmetic very heavily. On the other hand, the floating point component in mainstream productivity applications tends to be small. Word for Windows does not seem to do any measurable floating point computation; Excel does some floating point computation, but it is negligible compared with Excel's use of integer computations and screen I/O.

As we discussed earlier, Win32s has to translate any 32-bit near pointers it gets from the application to 16-bit far pointers that can be used by the Windows APIs. There is a difference in the time it takes to translate pointers to different memory areas: the global heap (`GlobalAlloc`), the local heap (`LocalAlloc`), private heaps (`HeapAlloc`), virtual memory pages (`VirtualAlloc`), global data, or local data. Win32s has some optimizations for translating the stack pointer, so local variables—which are on the application's stack—will always be translated fastest.

When you think about it, differing overheads for pointer translation does make some sense. The stack pointer should have the least overhead because the thunking layer will probably have a cached selector for the current stack. Translating a global heap pointer probably means adding a selector to the global descriptor table (GDT), and translating a local heap pointer probably means adding a selector to the local descriptor table (LDT).

Compatibility Issues

It's all very well to make a Win32s application run fast. It also has to run correctly. There are a number of issues to keep in mind when writing and testing a Win32s program.

The most important issue is that Win32s actually uses the facilities of Windows 3.1, which means that you are limited to the 16-bit Windows graphic coordinate system, 16-bit window identifiers, and 16-bit resource identifiers. You are also limited to 5 cached device contexts, 32KB of text in an edit control, and 64K of data in a list box.

You can't use **EM_SETHANDLE** and **EM_GETHANDLE** to manage text in edit controls, as these functions require 16-bit local heap handles that don't correspond to Win32s local handles: a Win32s application has a 32-bit local heap that is allocated from the global heap. If you want to use multiline edit controls in a Win32s application, use **WM_SETTEXT** and **WM_GETTEXT** to manage the controls of the control.

Win32s also uses Windows to pass messages. For standard messages, there is no problem: Win32s takes care of repacking the necessary parameters. For private messages, Win32s doesn't know how to repack the parameters, so it drops the high word of **wParam** going from the Win32 side to the Win16 side, and zero-extends **wParam** going from the Win16 side to the Win32 side. Even private messages between Win32s applications lose the high word of **wParam**. If you need to pass 32-bit pointers between Win32s applications, pass them in **lParam**.

If you write an application that is initially for Win32s and later want to run it under Windows NT, synchronization might be a problem for you. Win32s has no threads, and Windows 3.1 won't preempt an application while it is processing a message. Win32 does have threads, and Windows NT will preempt an application or thread while it is processing a message. That means you need to use mutex objects or critical sections to protect shared resources—even resources as apparently harmless as code in DLLs. If a DLL function uses only stack variables and the DLL is linked to CRTDLL or LIBCMT, you can use it safely from multiple threads; otherwise, the function should protect itself with critical sections or multiple exclusion semaphores under Windows NT. The synchronization functions will do nothing under Win32s.

Runtime Detection of Win32s

How can you tell you are running under Win32s? You could test the **CreateThread** function or some other function you know to be unsupported in Win32s, but there is a better way: you can check a bit in the value returned by **GetVersion**, as in this code from NTHELL\BENCH1.CPP:

```
#ifdef WIN32
   //Detect Win32s, suppress attempts to create threads if found
   DWORD Version = GetVersion();
   if(0x80000000 & Version) {
      //MessageBox("Win32s Detected","DEBUG");
      CEdit *ed_threads = (CEdit *)GetDlgItem(id_ed_threads);
      ed_threads->SetReadOnly();
      }
#else
      {
      CEdit *ed_threads = (CEdit *)GetDlgItem(id_ed_threads);
      ed_threads->SetReadOnly();
      }
#endif
```

This particular code, which is run inside **Cwm_MainWinControlsDlg::OnInitDialog()**, makes the edit control for the number of threads to use read-only if Win32s is detected or if the program is compiled for 16-bit operation. If the program is run under Windows NT, the user can change the number of threads, and the program will use multiple threads to run the Whetstone and Dhrystone benchmarks.

Another obvious strategy is to set a flag for the rest of your program to check:

```
BOOL bWin32sDetected=FALSE;
//...
DWORD Version = GetVersion();
if(0x80000000 & Version) {
   //MessageBox("Win32s Detected","DEBUG");
   bWin32sDetected=TRUE;
   }
//...
if(!bWin32sDetected) {
   //some action requiring full Windows NT
   }
else {
   //some fallback action
   }
```

Win32s Strategies

Deciding how much of the full Win32 functionality to use in a program can be tricky, especially if you also want to support Win32s. There are a number of strategies from which you can choose, each with its own advantages and shortcomings: sticking to the subset or lowest common denominator, conditional compilation, and runtime accommodation. If you choose runtime accommodation, you can try conditional execution (illustrated in the above example), delayed binding, or substituting for missing functions.

Sticking to the Subset and Conditional Compilation

If you restrict yourself to the Win32s subset, you will have a single executable that can run on Windows NT and Windows 3.1, but it won't support threads, advanced graphics, security, or any of the advanced features of Windows NT even though they might be available on a given system. Of course, just running in a 32-bit flat model might give you enough of a performance boost to justify doing your program this way, at least in the short term with the Windows 3.1/Win32s application market much larger than the Windows NT application market. If you have a mass-market application that benefits significantly from 32-bit code, sticking to the Win32s subset might make sense for you.

I'd like to convince you, though, that you can do better without inordinate effort. Conditional compilation is pretty easy: just define some symbol that flags code that won't work in Win32s:

```
#ifdef NATIVE_WIN32
   //code that uses threads
#else
   //code that doesn't use threads
#endif
```

The advantage of conditional compilation is that all the source is in one place, but only the code appropriate for the current target is compiled, which gives you the smallest possible application for Windows NT and for Win32s. The disadvantage is that you have two separate EXE files to ship, and a user who dual boots between Windows NT and Windows 3.1/Win32s has two separate EXE files on his or her hard disk. In the latter case, the user gets the best use of RAM at a pretty stiff cost in disk space.

Runtime Accommodation

It's probably better to decide what to do at runtime so that the user doesn't have to deal with two EXE files. Straight conditional execution requires a little more code, but the overall cost in RAM and execution time needn't be too horrendous. As we saw above you can reduce the repetitive burden of checking for Win32s to one test of a Boolean variable:

```
if(!bWin32sDetected) {
   //some action requiring full Windows NT
   }
else {
   //some fallback action
   }
```

If your program is fairly object-oriented, or at least fairly structured, you won't wind up with too much of this kind of code. If, on the other hand, your existing source code uses advanced Win32 APIs all over the place, adding conditional execution blocks might make your code unmaintainable.

Another option is to use delayed binding of your functions. In an object-oriented language like C++ you can do this with virtual functions; in either C or C++ you can use function pointers. If the RAM or virtual memory size cost of multiple functions is not an issue, it is easy to initialize function pointers:

```
DWORD Version = GetVersion();

if(0x80000000 & Version) {
   //use Win32s versions
   pFn1=&Fn1s;
   pFn2=&Fn2s;
   }
else {
   //use Windows NT versions
   pFn1=&Fn1Full;
   pFn2=&Fn2Full;
   }
```

If you want to avoid cluttering up memory with a lot of dead code, you can keep your system-dependent code in DLLs and load the correct DLL at runtime:

```
//Initialization code
DWORD Version = GetVersion();
HMODULE hDLL=NULL;
BOOL (CALLBACK *MyFirstFunc) (LPSTR acctid,
         struct account *acctrec,int by);
BOOL (CALLBACK *MySeondFunc) (int iArg, double dArg);
//... etc.

if(0x80000000 & Version) {
   bWin32sDetected=TRUE;
```

```
    //use Win32s version of DLL
    hDLL=LoadLibrary("my_w32s.dll");
    }
else {
    //use Windows NT versions
    hDLL=LoadLibrary("my_nt.dll");
    }

//handle possible LoadLibrary failure
if(!hDLL) {
    ErrMsg("Couldn't load the dll");
    return FALSE;
    }

//Get Function Pointers from loaded DLL
(FARPROC)MyFirstFunc=GetProcAddress(hDLL,"MyFirstFunc");
(FARPROC)MySecondFunc=GetProcAddress(hDLL,"MySecondFunc");
//... etc.

//Now we can use the DLL functions
MyFirstFunc(accid,accrec,i);   //call DLL function through pointer
MySecondFunc(1,3.14159);
//...
```

To be completely clean, you should remember to call **FreeLibrary(hDLL)** when the program ends.

You can do very well with this scheme for delayed binding. You can do the right thing for the current environment in the DLL functions, and maintain compatibility only at your well-defined high-level interface.

On the other hand you could, if you were ambitious, write DLLs that automatically used substitutes for missing API functions when needed. For instance, you could write a function **MyBezier**. The NT version of **MyBezier**, in BEZ_NT.DLL, would be trivial: it would just call the Win32 function **PolyBezier**. The Win32s version of **MyBezier**, in BEZ_W32.DLL, would compute the coefficients from the control points, interpolate the Bézier curve points from the coefficients, and call **PolyLine** to do the actual drawing.

You'd still have to use **LoadLibrary** and **GetProcAddress** to set up the pointer to **MyBezier** in this scheme, but it is completely kosher. A next logical step would be to intercept the dummy **PolyBezier** implementation in the Win32s GDI32.DLL and patch it to call your own implementation of **PolyBezier** instead.

Intercepting system DLLs is hard to do in a clean way, but it can be done. The usual technique is to rename the original DLL and write an interceptor DLL that replaces the original and duplicates all its exports; when the interceptor DLL initializes it dynamically loads the original, renamed DLL. Each unmodified entry point calls back to the original DLL. Each modified entry point implements the revised functionality itself, calling back to the original DLL only if needed.

I don't feel comfortable depending on interceptor DLLs for commercial products. Imagine being an end user who buys two Win32s applications that each want their own interceptor DLLs substituted for the original Win32s DLLs. Ouch.

Mixing 32-bit EXEs and 16-bit DLLs

I mentioned earlier that the *Universal Thunk* allows you to call 16-bit DLLs from 32-bit EXEs in Win32s, but not in Windows NT. Microsoft claims that the Universal Thunk is intended mainly to allow Win32s applications to call 16-bit Windows device drivers; under Windows NT the applications would call 32-bit device drivers. Microsoft also points out that the mechanism used by the Univeral Thunk is not supported under Windows NT, and claims that other methods that work on both systems, for example DDE, lack sufficient bandwidth for some applications.

I'll briefly outline how to use Universal Thunks. Then I'll go on to discuss alternative client-server methods to hook up 32-bit applications and 16-bit DLLs.

Using Universal Thunks

The Universal Thunk is basically a mutant form of **LoadLibrary** with a special way of handling procedure addresses. **UTRegister** can be used once by a 32-bit DLL to load a 16-bit DLL and create a thunk to mediate between the 16-bit and 32-bit DLLs. The 16-bit DLL can export only two functions: a function used for initialization that is required only if you need to call back to the 32-bit DLL, and a dispatch routine used to call other 16-bit DLL services. The names of the two 16-bit functions are specified in the **UTRegister** call.

When the 16-bit DLL is loaded and the thunk has been created, **UTRegister** calls the 16-bit initialization function and passes it a 16-bit FAR pointer to the 32-bit callback function; **UTRegister** returns a 32-bit pointer to the callable stub for the 16-bit dispatch function to the 32-bit DLL.

Once **UTRegister** has completed the 32-bit DLL can call the 16-bit dispatch function through its thunk and the 16-bit DLL can call back. The 32-bit dispatch function pointer has the following prototype:

```
typedef DWORD (WINAPI *UT32PROC)( LPVOID lpBuff,
                                  DWORD  dwUserDefined,
                                  LPVOID *lpTranslationList);
```

The first argument holds a pointer to a general-purpose memory buffer up to 32KB long. The second argument is generally used as a switch for the dispatch function, but could be anything the application wanted as long as the 32-bit client and the 16-bit server agreed on its meaning. The third argument points to a null-terminated array of 32-bit pointers that need to be converted to 16:16 pointers.

The 16-bit dispatch routine never sees the translation list. It sees a 16:16 alias for **lpBuff** and it sees **dwUserDefined** exactly as passed.

When the program is done with the 16-bit services, **UTUnRegister** can be used to destroy the thunk and unload the 16-bit DLL—or you can simply allow Win32s to clean up the libraries and thunks automatically.

The initialization part of the 32-bit DLL could look like this Microsoft example:

```
#define W32SUT_32

#include <windows.h>
#include <w32sut.h>
#include <db.h>

UT32PROC  pfnUTProc=NULL;
int       cProcessesAttached = 0;

BOOL
DllInit(HANDLE hInst, DWORD fdwReason, LPVOID lpReserved)
{
  if ( fdwReason == DLL_PROCESS_ATTACH ) {

    /*
     * Registration of UT need to be done only once for first
     * attaching process.
     */

    if ( cProcessesAttached++ ) {
       return(TRUE);
       }
    return UTRegister( hInst,         // DB32.DLL module handle
                       "DB16.DLL",    // name of 16bit thunk dll
                       NULL,          // no init routine
                       "UTProc",      // name of dispatch routine
                                      // exported from DB16.DLL
                       &pfnUTProc,    // variable for thunk address
                       NULL,          // no call back function
                       NULL           // no shared memroy
                     );
  } else if ( fdwReason == DLL_PROCESS_DETACH ) {

      if ( --cProcessesAttached == 0 ) {
         UTUnRegister( hInst );
      }
  }

}
```

There is no 16-bit side for this particular initialization—note that the third parameter to **UTRegister** is **NULL**. Also, there is no callback or shared memory: the fifth and sixth parameters are also **NULL**. Calling a 16-bit function from the 32-bit DLL is now a matter of calling through the function pointer and the thunk to the 16-bit dispatch routine:

```
/*
 * constants for dispatcher in 16bit side
 */

#define DB_SRV_GETVERSION   0
#define DB_SRV_SETTIME      1
#define DB_SRV_ADDUSER      2

int
DbGetVersion(void)
{

    /*
     * call the 16bit dispatch thru the 32bit thunk. no parameters
     * are passed.
     * returned value is the service result.
     */

    return( (int) (* pfnUTProc)(NULL, DB_SRV_GETVERSION, NULL) );

}

void
DbSetTime(LPDB_TIME pTime)
{

    /*
     * call the 16bit dispatch thru the 32bit thunk.
     * pass one pointer to a buffer which will be translated
     * to 16:16 address before passed to 16bit side.
     *
     */

    (* pfnUTProc)(pTime, DB_SRV_SETTIME, NULL);

}

short
DbAddUser(LPDB_NAME pName, DWORD Permission, LPDWORD pId)
{
    DWORD   Args[3];           // function has three arguments
    PVOID   TransList[4];      // Three pointers need translation:
                               //     pName
                               //     pName->str
                               //     pId
                               // plus null (end of list)
    char    *pSaveStr;
    int     Ret;
```

```
    /*
     * put arguments in buffer
     */

    Args[0] = (DWORD) pName;
    Args[1] = Permission;
    Args[2] = (DWORD) pId;

    /*
     * build translation list for all the flat pointers that need
     * to be translated to segmented form.
     */
    TransList[0] = & Args[0];
    TransList[1] = & pName->str;
    TransList[2] = & Args[2];
    TransList[3] = 0;

    /*
     * save the original pointer in the NAME struct so it can be
     * restored after the call to the thunk.
     * This is required only if the caller of the service expects
     * the structure to be left unmodified.
     */

    pSaveStr = pName->str;

    /*
     * call the 16bit dispatch thru the 32bit thunk.
     * pass arguments in buffer along with list of addresses
     * that need to be translated equivalent segmented format.
     *
     */

    Ret = (int) (* pfnUTProc)(Args, DB_SRV_ADDUSER, TransList);

    /*
     * restore flat pointer
     */
    pName->str = pSaveStr;

    return(Ret);
}
```

On the 16-bit side, the dispatch routine has to call the correct service. Win32s takes care of fixing the pointers in the translation list as part of the thunk:

```
#define W32SUT_16

#include <windows.h>
#include <w32sut.h>
#include "db.h"
```

```
/*
 * constants for dispatcher in 16bit side
 */

#define DB_SRV_GETVERSION   0
#define DB_SRV_SETTIME      1
#define DB_SRV_ADDUSER      2


/*
 * 16bit dispatcher function.
 * exported by DB16.DLL
 */

DWORD FAR PASCAL
UTProc(LPVOID lpBuf, DWORD dwFunc)
{
    /*
     * call 16bit DB services based on the function Id.
     */

    switch (dwFunc) {

    case DB_SRV_GETVERSION:
        return( (DWORD) DbGetVersion() );

    case DB_SRV_SETTIME:
        DbSetTime((LPDB_TIME) lpBuf);
        return(0);

    case DB_SRV_ADDUSER:
        return( (DWORD) DbAddUser((LPDB_NAME)((LPDWORD)lpBuf)[0] ,
                                  (DWORD)     ((LPDWORD)lpBuf)[1] ,
                                  (LPDWORD)   ((LPDWORD)lpBuf)[2]
                                 )
              );

    }

    return( 0 );
}
```

The 16-bit DLL can also translate pointers explicitly with **UTSelectorOffset-ToLinear** and **UTLinearToSelectorOffset**, if the translation buffer method proves excessively awkward or time-consuming.

Calling back to the 32-bit DLL from the 16-bit is very similar to the 32-bit to 16-bit call we just discussed. Note that you cannot use a 32-bit callback function from a 16-bit interrupt handler, since Win32s does not lock its memory pages.

As you can see, the Universal Thunk method is complicated but workable. Its major disadvantage is that it doesn't work in Windows NT.

Constructing a DDE or Other IPC Bridge

A DDE bridge will work on Windows NT as well as Win32s, but it is not likely to perform as well as the Universal Thunk. The general idea is this: just as in the case of the Universal Thunk, you write a 32-bit DLL and a 16-bit DLL. This time, however, you have the 32-bit DLL act as a DDE client using the 32-bit DDEML libraries, and the 16-bit DLL act as a DDE server using the 16-bit DDEML libraries.

You can confirm for yourself that 16-bit DDE works transparently with 32-bit DDE by running the 16-bit DDEML clock sample MSVC\SAMPLES\DDEML\CLOCK\-DDEMLCLK.EXE and the 32-bit DDEML client sample MSTOOLS\SAMPLES\-DDEML\CLIENT\CLIENT.EXE. In the CLIENT sample, open a conversation with CLOCK on the topic **Time**, and then open an advise on the item **Now**. It works for me.

How would you design a DDE bridge interface? The calls from the 32-bit application should look just like the calls to the 16-bit service desired, just as in the Universal Thunk example given above. On initialization, the 32-bit DLL would load the 16-bit DLL with **LoadLibrary** and establish a conversation on some topic, for example **BRIDGE**, and an advise on some item, for example **RESULTS**. When one of the 32-bit stub functions was called, it would build its ID and arguments into a DDE data block, and send the data block to the 16-bit server DLL using **DdeClientTransaction** with **XTYP_EXECUTE**. The server would copy the data block using **DdeGetData** and return **DDE_FACK** to the client. Then the server would unpack the data block and call the real 16-bit function.

When the function completed, the server would send the client the results using the open advise channel by calling **DdePostAdvise**, building the data into a block using **DdeCreateDataHandle**, and returning the data handle in response to the generated **XTYP_ADVREQ** transaction. Finally, the client would unpack the returned parameters from the advise and return them to the calling program.

Note that this protocol is actually asynchronous. The client sends an execute request, gets the acknowledgment, then goes into a **PeekMessage** loop until the advise comes back. The client can abort the transaction if it takes too long.

I'm not sure that such a two-transaction client-server interface will be fast enough for a lot of applications. It would probably be all right for functions that do a lot of work on the server side: nobody would mind an extra few hundred milliseconds of overhead for DDE transactions to facilitate a relational join of two large databases that might take several minutes or to give Win32 programs access to a 16-bit Windows scanner driver. But if each call only does a little work—a few milliseconds' worth—the overhead would be unacceptable.

One nice thing about the DDE bridge idea is that it can easily be extended to use NetDDE, and thus work over a network. Thus, it should be feasible to build a robust client-server application that works on Windows for Workgroups using Win32s as well as working on Windows NT. You wouldn't be limited to NetDDE, either:

sockets might be better for high-volume data transfers, and NetBIOS might extend the bridge over heterogeneous networks.

This discussion is, of course, leading us quickly to the rather large subject of inter-process communications, which we will cover in Chapter 11. Rather than get ahead of ourselves, let's return to the subject of writing substitutes for services missing in Win32s.

Loose Threads

If we had to, how could we simulate threads for Win32s programs? I've thought about this quite a bit.

No matter how you implement time-slicing among the threads, you'll have to set up a stack for each thread. You'll also need a safe mechanism for saving and restoring the state of each thread as you switch among them. Cooperative multithreading would be easier to implement than preemptive multithreading in the Windows environment.

My first idea was to use **PeekMessage** loops and messages to do cooperative multithreading. (See the function **SpinTheMessageLoop** in my earlier book, *Advanced Windows Programming*, for some discussion of this sort of approach.) That might work, but I discarded the idea as awkward. What would maintain granularity? How could you guarantee that one simulated thread wouldn't stomp another? What if one thread hogged the CPU? Ugh.

My second idea was to use a timer to do either cooperative or preemptive multithreading. I worried about how to guarantee the integrity of the interrupted thread, especially in the preemptive case. Using **WM_TIMER** messages coupled with **PeekMessage** loops might work: it's worth considering, anyway. Calling a timer handler that would preempt one thread and run the next would be a bit trickier, but could give better performance.

My next thought was to use nonlocal jumps for cooperative multitasking, either the Windows APIs **Catch** and **Throw** or the C library functions **setjmp** and **longjmp**. Better: **Catch** really does preserve the local execution state for **Throw** to restore. The folklore is that the C library functions **setjmp** and **longjmp** aren't supposed to be used under Windows, although I've never understood why. And the documentation for these functions says they shouldn't be used from C++ programs.

Catch and **Throw**, that's the ticket. But what's this? They aren't supported under Win32—they're obsolete. What replaces them? Why, structured exceptions. Implement threads with **try-except** and **RaiseException**? That sounds ugly.

What does the NT version of MFC use to implement its exceptions? Let's look in MFC\SRC\EXCEPT.CPP:

```
#if defined(_WINDOWS) && defined(_DOSWIN)
extern "C" void far pascal Throw(const int FAR*, int);
```

```
#define longjmp ::Throw
#else
extern "C" void __cdecl longjmp(jmp_buf, int);
#endif
```

MFC uses **Throw** when it is available—in 16-bit Windows—and otherwise uses **longjmp**. So much for consistency, and so much for all those warnings in the documentation: in this case I trust the code, not the documentation. But the comments in EXCEPT.CPP say that the code is written with the assumption that the application is single-threaded. Ouch.

So where are we? It looks like we might be able to build some sort of cooperative thread facility for Win32s using **setjmp** and **longjmp**, if we're very careful. Or we could build the facility with a timer. Or, we could build the facility with structured exceptions. All three approaches look like they will work—with some effort.

But none of these possibilities sounds like any fun, and none implements true preemptive threads. I am certainly beginning to see why Microsoft thinks that threads should be a system facility and not an add-on.

By the way, there is a shareware thread facility available for 16-bit Windows—EDI Threads, available from Eschalon Development, Inc., 110–2 Renaissance Square, New Westminster, B.C., V3M 6K3 Canada (604)520-1542. This product ships as a DLL with some sample code and seems to implement cooperative threads using a timer, **Catch**, and **Throw**. As we've seen, that won't work in Win32s—they'd have to switch to **setjmp** and **longjmp** or to structured exceptions. It certainly wouldn't make much sense to call the existing 16-bit facility through the Universal Thunk mechanism—there would be too much overhead. Which leaves us where we were.

It's clear that writing a thread facility for Win32s is possible: it's also clear that writing a good one would be a tricky piece of work. In my own Win32 programs, I take the easier road and use threads only when they are available on the system.

Through the Looking Glass

We saw that, under Win32s, the Universal Thunk allows 32-bit programs to call 16-bit DLLs. The Universal Thunk is a generalization of the thunking mechanism that allows Win32s to use the underlying 16-bit facilities of Windows 3.1.

Windows NT runs 16-bit Windows programs in the WOW (Windows on Windows) subsystem. For WOW to work at all, it has to have a way to thunk from 16-bit programs to the underlying 32-bit facilities of Windows NT. With some work, I was able to get Microsoft to provide me with documentation for the basic Windows NT thunking facility. There are five 16-bit functions in this facility, all of which live in the Windows NT kernel:

```
HINSTANCE FAR PASCAL LoadLibraryEx32W(lpszLibFile, hFile, dwFlags);
BOOL   FAR PASCAL FreeLibrary32W(HINSTANCE);
```

```
LPVOID FAR PASCAL GetProcAddress32W(HINSTANCE, LPCSTR);
DWORD FAR PASCAL GetVDMPointer32W(lpAddress, fMode);
DWORD FAR PASCAL CallProc32W(DWORD param1, DWORD param2,..,
  LPVOID lpProcAddress32,DWORD fAddressConvert,
  DWORD nParams);
```

Note that these functions, which allow 16-bit thunk DLLs to call 32-bit functions, are *not* Win32 API functions: they are specific to Windows NT. You probably won't ever find them in Win32s, Win32c, or other Microsoft 32-bit systems. **LoadLibraryEx32W** thunks to the Win32 **LoadLibraryEx** function, so that a 16-bit thunk DLL can load a 32-bit thunk DLL. **FreeLibrary32W** unloads a 32-bit DLL loaded with **LoadLibraryEx32W**. **GetProcAddress32W** lets a 16-bit thunk DLL get the 32-bit address of a function in a 32-bit DLL, which can be passed to **CallProc32W** to actually call the function. **GetVDMPointer32W** lets the 16-bit thunk DLL convert a 16-bit FAR pointer to a 32-bit linear address for use by a 32-bit function.

CallProc32W has an interesting set of parameters. The first *N* parameters, where *N* is in the range [0,32], are the parameters to be passed to the 32-bit function, cast into **DWORD**s without conversion; the last parameter gives the value of *N*—which is OK, since the last parameter is at the top of the stack in the Pascal calling convention. The second-to-last parameter, **fAddressConvert**, is bit-encoded: any set bit means that the corresponding parameter is a 16-bit FAR pointer that needs to be converted to a 32-bit linear address. Finally, the third-to-last parameter is the 32-bit function address obtained from **GetProcAddress32W**.

What can you do with the Windows NT generic thunk facility? Much the same thing as you can with the Win32s Universal Thunk: mix 16-bit and 32-bit code. The difference is that the Win32s Universal Thunk lets Win32 programs access facilities in 16-bit Windows, while the Windows NT generic thunk lets Win16 programs access 32-bit facilities in Windows NT.

By further analogy with Win32s, you might want to write 16-bit Windows programs that detect whether they're running under Windows NT or 16-bit Windows and then load the proper DLLs. You can accomplish this by testing the Windows flags against **0x4000**, as in the 16-bit function **IsNT**:

```
BOOL WINAPI IsNT(void) {
  DWORD dwFlags= GetWinFlags();
  return (dwFlags & 0x4000 ? TRUE:FALSE);
  }
```

Seize the Day

In this chapter we've seen that it is entirely possible to write a Win32 program that will also execute on 80386 and better systems running Windows 3.1, using the magic of the Win32s libraries. We've also seen that CPU-bound applications can realize a factor of two speed improvement between their 16-bit Windows versions and their 32-bit Win32s versions running on identical systems.

We've seen what is and isn't supported by Win32s. We've seen that taking full advantage of both systems requires some extra work, but that it can be done in a systematic way. And we've seen exactly how to write code that adapts to either Win32s or Windows NT without any extra RAM overhead.

There are a few more things you'll have to learn to use Win32s effectively, but they are well covered in the manuals. Debugging Win32s programs should be done in stages: first test and debug under Windows NT using WinDbg, then test and debug under Win32s. Use a remote copy of WinDbg (if you have two systems), the debugging versions of the Win32s libraries, and the Windows 3.1 kernel debugger to aid in debugging under Win32s.[2]

Finally, use the setup toolkit found in the WIN32S\SETUP directory tree. It can help you build a setup program that will automatically install Win32s components along with your program on Windows 3.1 systems, and automatically leave out the Win32s component when installing on a Windows NT system.

Win32s is a great opportunity for developers: *Carpe diem!*

---

[2] These instructions assume you have the Windows NT SDK. Follow the instructions provided by your compiler vendor for any other tools.

7

In which we learn and apply some multimedia programming.[1]

A Little Song, A Little Dance

· ·

I like music. I like movies. I like computers. Therefore. . .what?[2] There's a giant chasm between those three independent statements and any desire to use computers for sound and animation: but there we are, that's what multimedia computing is all about.

Don't get me wrong: as a composer, I wouldn't voluntarily give up my MIDI (Musical Instrument Digital Interface) sequencing program and my notation printing program to go back to pencil and paper. Being able to have the computer play arbitrarily complex music back to you with whatever voices you wish is invaluable: it's such wonderful feedback that I wonder how I ever composed or arranged without it.

At the same time, as a programmer, I wonder how useful it is to tie sound and animation capabilities to business applications. Is word processing improved by having "What *is* it, man?" spoken in the voice of a cartoon Chihuahua[3] when an error is encountered? Does it help the operation of the system if Commander Data[4] says

---

[1] The title for this chapter was inspired by the "Chuckles' Funeral" episode of *The Mary Tyler Moore Show*. Cognoscenti will recall the full quote, which was Chuckles the Clown's motto: "A little song, a little dance, a little seltzer down the pants."

[2] Recall Woody Allen's fractured syllogism in *Love and Death*: "All Greeks are men. Socrates is a man. Therefore all men are Socrates."

[3] Ren, of *Ren and Stimpy*, a somewhat warped cartoon that airs on Nickelodeon.

[4] Data is an android character on *Star Trek, The Next Generation.*

"Computer, execute complete shutdown of the holodeck" just before Windows shuts down? Does it really promote productivity to have Tribbles cascade down your screen at odd intervals?[5]

No, not really—but it *is* fun, at least for feeble minds like mine.[6] And it helps draw young users to the computer who wouldn't otherwise take an interest: for example, my own children. But I can't treat it any more seriously than that—or can I?

There are common situations when sound is a help, and special situations when sound is essential. For instance, different audible messages attached to various system sounds tell me what's happening on a system out of my direct line of sight but within earshot: I know without looking when a VC++ build has finished on this machine, and I know at the same time whether there were errors or warnings.

On another system, a synthesized voice reads back numbers from the spreadsheet on the screen. That allows the user to double-check the entries against the handwritten original without enlisting a second person to read the numbers aloud. On yet another system, anything that appears on the screen is also spoken: the user is blind. Elsewhere, the user wears a headset and speaks into the microphone: his wrists are badly swollen from repetitive stress, and every keystroke or mouse movement causes excruciating pain.

Then there's the kiosk at the mall. When you touch a box on the screen, you see the video product demonstration of your choice, complete with music and professional narration. What makes this better than an ordinary analog video loop is that you can interact with it, stopping, restarting, and selecting items of interest at will.

Then there's the training system, and the school recruitment system.... Maybe there is something to this multimedia business after all. So let's learn how to program media—program in the sense of telling the computer how to make it happen.

The Windows Multimedia Services Architecture

There is a great deal of commonality between Win32 and Win16 media services: you won't have any trouble writing programs that are portable between the two. The major differences are matters of driver availability: while almost every multimedia peripheral vendor has Windows 3.1 drivers, relatively few have their Windows NT drivers ready as I write. Real soon now, they promise. Right.

Drivers are the key to making anything audible or visible happen in Windows

---

[5] Tribbles are small furry purring objects that exist only to eat and breed. (*Consider the lilies of the field...*) They appeared in a favorite episode of the original *Star Trek* series, "The Trouble with Tribbles." Berkeley Systems currently sells a *Star Trek* screen saver that features Tribbles.

[6] Do you know any other programming author who would write footnotes about references to cartoons? I rest my case. The man is sick. He needs a rest. He needs higher royalties. He needs more people to buy his books.

(meaning both Windows 3.x and Windows NT). But drivers are pretty far removed from the application: the Windows multimedia services architecture has several layers.

At the highest level, the application can call the Media Control Interface (MCI, not to be confused with the homophonous long-distance carrier). You can access MCI by sending it text strings, or by sending it messages. In Win32, the text strings can use the Windows character set or the Unicode character set. Win16 has no Unicode support.

If MCI doesn't suit your needs, you can use high-level or low-level services. High-level services give you file-level control: play a waveform sound file, for example. Low-level services let you do pretty much anything the device driver can handle, but without having to worry about the differences between device drivers. Low-level audio services have the same API on a $100, 8-bit Sound Blaster as they do on a $600, 16-bit MultiSound board.

Media Control Interface

For most applications, MCI strings and messages offer plenty of control. If you are writing a application that does multimedia presentations, you should first determine if MCI will work for you. In fact, you'll find MCI the best choice for a lot of purposes: for instance, playing large wave files is a snap using MCI, but doesn't work using the high-level sound services **sndPlaySound** and **MessageBeep**, which require the entire file to fit into memory.

The high-level services do offer more convenience than MCI. For example, the following five snippets of code all accomplish the same thing, assuming that the **SystemExclamation** sound is currently set to OHOH.WAV, which exists in the current directory:

```
#include <windows.h>
#include <mmsystem.h>

//First method: MCI strings
mciSendString("open waveaudio!ohoh.wav",NULL,0,0);
mciSendString("play ohoh.wav wait",NULL,0,0);
mciSendString("close all",NULL,0,0);

//Second method: MCI commands
MCI_OPEN_PARMS mciOP;
mciOP.lpstrDeviceType="waveaudio";
mciOP.lpstrElementName="ohoh.wav"
mciSendCommand(0,MCI_OPEN, MCI_OPEN_TYPE|MCI_OPEN_ELEMENT,
          (DWORD)(LPVOID)&mciOP);
mciSendCommand(mciOP.wDeviceID, MCI_PLAY,MCI_WAIT,0);
mciSendCommand(mciOP.wDeviceID,MCI_CLOSE,0,0);

//Third method: High level audio using filename
sndPlaySound("ohoh.wav",SND_SYNC);
```

```
//Fourth method: High level audio, System alias
sndPlaySound("SystemExclamation",SND_SYNC);

//Fifth method: System alert audio playback
MessageBeep(MB_ICONEXCLAMATION);
```

The MCI string interface is obviously a lot easier to learn and use than the MCI command interface, but probably a little less efficient on the computer, since the strings have to be parsed and interpreted. On the other hand, serious multimedia applications move so much data around that their time is dominated by the storage and playback streaming rates, not by the CPU. Don't worry about the string interpretation time—it's not going to be noticeable.

Using MCI Command Strings

The syntax of **mciSendString** is:

```
MCIERROR mciSendString(lpszCommand, lpszReturnString,
                       cchReturn, hwndCallback)

LPCTSTR lpszCommand;    /* address of MCI command string  */
LPTSTR lpszReturnString;   /* address of return buffer    */
UINT cchReturn; /* size of return buffer, in characters  */
HANDLE hwndCallback;    /* callback-window handle    */
```

As we noted earlier, **mciSendString** sends a command string to a Media Control Interface (MCI) device. The first parameter, **lpszCommand**, points to a null-terminated string that specifies an MCI command string of the form:

```
    [command] [device] [parameters]
```

The second parameter, **lpszReturnString**, either points to a buffer that receives return information or contains **NULL**. The third parameter, **cchReturn**, contains the size of the return buffer specified by the **lpszReturnString** parameter. If **lpszReturnString** is **NULL**, **cchReturn** should be **0**. The final parameter, **hwndCallback**, passes the handle of a callback window if **"notify"** was specified in the command string.

If the **mciSendString** function succeeds, the return value is zero. Otherwise, the return value is an error code. The low-order word of the returned doubleword contains the error return value.

To get a text description of **mciSendString** return values, you can pass the return value to the **mciGetErrorString** function:

Table 7-1 Common MCI Command Strings

Command	Description
capability	Requests information about the capabilities of a device.
close	Closes a device after it has been used.
info	Requests information about a device (for example, a description of the hardware associated with the device).
open	Opens and initializes a device.
pause	Pauses playing or recording on a device.
play	Begins playing on a device.
record	Begins recording on a device.
resume	Resumes playing or recording on a paused device.
seek	Changes the current position in the media.
set	Changes control settings, such as the time format the device is using.
status	Requests information about the status of a device (for example, whether the device is playing or paused).
stop	Stops playing or recording on a device.
sysinfo	Obtains MCI system information.

```
BOOL mciGetErrorString(fdwError, lpszErrorText, cchErrorText)

DWORD fdwError;  /* error code */
LPTSTR lpszErrorText;  /* address of buffer for error string */
UINT cchErrorText;  /* size of buffer, in characters   */
```

Once you have a text description for an MCI error, you can display it for the user using **MessageBox**, or by using **TextOut** to place it in a status bar window or some other display device context.

It seems obvious to want to write a wrapper for **mciSendString** that automatically displays error messages, to avoid having three-quarters of your code dedicated to checking for errors. It also seems obvious to write a wrapper that sends multiple strings to MCI in sequence, aborting the sequence with a **"close all"** if one of the commands fails.

What isn't so obvious is how to handle return strings in such a sequence, or incorporate logic that depends on their contents. But I haven't explained why return strings are useful.

Let's look at some of the common MCI command strings in Table 7-1.

As you can see, the MCI **capability**, **info**, **status** and **sysinfo** commands provide information that might be returned as a string. Each MCI command has its own syntax for named parameters using keywords or flags; all MCI commands include **wait** and **notify** as optional flags.

Normally, MCI commands run asynchronously. For instance, when you issue **play mystuff** control returns to the program fairly quickly (i.e., in tens or hundreds of milliseconds), even if playing the file assigned to the **mystuff** alias takes seconds or minutes. That's good if you want to compute a few thousand digits of π while playing Beethoven's Ninth in the background; it's not so good if you want to bring up *The Merry-Go-Round Broke Down* when the animation of Elmer Fudd singing "kill the wabbit" to Wagner's *Ride of the Valkyries* finishes. And it's an absolute disaster when you first try an open/play/close sequence:

```
mciSendString("open waveaudio!ohoh.wav",NULL,0,0);
mciSendString("play ohoh.wav",NULL,0,0);
mciSendString("close all",NULL,0,0);
```

What happens when you run this sequence? Very little: the **close all** command runs before the **play ohoh.wav** command has actually made any sound. All that's required to make the sequence work properly, though, is a **wait** flag in the **play** command: **play ohoh.wav wait**.

But suppose you want to do something else during a **play** command? After all, we're talking about multimedia—more than one media device playing at a time. One simple thing to do is to add a **wait** flag to the last **play** command in a group that is to run simultaneously:

```
mciSendString("open waveaudio!wabbit.wav",NULL,0,0);
mciSendString("open autodesk!wabbit.fli",NULL,0,0);
mciSendString("play wabbit.wav",NULL,0,0);
mciSendString("play wabbit.fli wait",NULL,0,0);
mciSendString("close all",NULL,0,0);
```

In the second line of the **wabbit** example above, the reference to **autodesk** assumes that an Autodesk Animator .FLI file playback driver is installed in SYSTEM.INI, for instance in a section like this one, which also includes drivers for the Microsoft/Macromind animation (MMMovie) and Microsoft/Intel audio/visual interleave (AVIVideo) formats:

```
[mci]
CDAudio=mcicda.drv
Sequencer=mciseq.drv
WaveAudio=mciwave.drv
```

```
MMMovie=mcimmp.drv
Autodesk=mciaap.drv
AVIVideo=mciavi.drv
```

Of course, in Windows NT you won't find this information in SYSTEM.INI—you won't even find a SYSTEM.INI file. You'll find the information buried in the system registry. But that's an issue we can take up later. Let's return to the multimedia example we were examining.

If you're familiar with animation, you might be appalled at the approach taken in the **wabbit** example. Letting **wabbit.wav** and **wabbit.fli** run simultaneously is *not* the way to synchronize Elmer's lips with his singing. *That* requires a single driver to synchronize the sound and the visuals: Microsoft's AVI (audio/visual interleave) is supposed to do that, although its synchronization still leaves something to be desired.[7] By the way, playing AVI files is just as easy as playing WAVE files when you use MCI.

Synchronization aside, the use of **wait** might be inappropriate if you want to produce a smooth multimedia presentation with multiple segments. Why? For one thing, you really want to get the next segment open and ready to go while the current segment plays. On an ideal multimedia computer you'd never have to worry about such things, because files would open so fast the user would never notice, but on a real computer a smooth presentation takes some work. One way of getting background work done is to use the **notify** flag; another is to use a yield procedure, which we'll discuss later on, and still another would be to use multiple threads of execution—although using threads restricts us to Windows NT and opens up another can of worms having to do with process synchronization.

The MCI **notify** flag asks the media device driver to post an **MM_MCINOTIFY** message to your window when the device completes an action. Of course, your window procedure has to actually process the **MM_MCINOTIFY** message for notification to do you any good. For example, the Microsoft MCITEST sample program in the Win32 SDK includes this code to handle **MM_MCINOTIFY**:

```
case MM_MCINOTIFY:

    /*
     * Check the radio button corresponding to the notification
     * received.
     *
```

---

[7] What AVI does is essentially to free-run small bits of sound and visuals. When a particular machine can't keep up, animation frames are dropped to maintain some semblance of synchronization. Even on machines that can handle the full 15 frames per second specified by the AVI standard, the synchronization is less than compelling: one is reminded of a school assembly movie, the sort where the film has been run so many times that the sprocket holes have torn open and the projectionist has to stop and rethread the film periodically.

```
    */

        dprintf3((TEXT("MM_MCINOTIFY, wParam: %08XH"), wParam));
        wID = 0;
        switch (wParam) {
        case MCI_NOTIFY_SUCCESSFUL:

            wID = ID_NOT_SUCCESS;
            break;

        case MCI_NOTIFY_SUPERSEDED:

            wID = ID_NOT_SUPER;
            break;

        case MCI_NOTIFY_ABORTED:

            wID = ID_NOT_ABORT;
            break;

        case MCI_NOTIFY_FAILURE:

            wID = ID_NOT_FAIL;
            break;

        default:
            break;
        }

        if (wID) {

            CheckDlgButton (hwndDlg, wID, TRUE);
            SetFocus (GetDlgItem(hwndDlg, ID_INPUT));
        }

        break;
```

As you could guess from the code, **MM_MCINOTIFY** can indicate four possible results, which are flagged in **wParam**. A successful notification (**MCI_NOTIFY_SUC-CESSFUL**) means that the command completed without interruption. A superseded notification means that another notify request has come in while the device already has a pending notify request. Before registering the new notify request, the device sends a **MCI_NOTIFY_SUPERSEDED** notification to the window handling the prior request, to avoid a deadlock situation. An aborted notification (**MCI_NOTIFY_ABORTED**) means that the command was interrupted, as would happen in the following sequence:

```
mciSendString("open waveaudio!ohoh.wav",NULL,0,0);
mciSendString("play ohoh.wav notify",NULL,0,hWnd);
mciSendString("close all",NULL,0,0);
```

With the **notify** flag in the play command, we'd find out that the **close** command interrupted **ohoh.wav** by getting a **MM_MCINOTIFY** message with **wParam** set to **MCI_NOTIFY_ABORTED** rather than **MCI_NOTIFY_SUCCESSFUL**. That's better than getting a failure notification. A failure notification (**MCI_NOTIFY_FAILURE**) means that a device error—usually a hardware error—occured during the command.

When you're working with complicated scripts, especially scripts that can contain complicated filenames and paths, it is often worthwhile to use MCI's **alias** keyword to avoid having to do a lot of string substitution. For instance, the following function would be a bit more complicated without the use of **alias**:

```
void playwave(LPCSTR filename) {
  char temp[80];

  wsprintf(temp,"open waveaudio!%s alias theSound",filename);
  mciSendString(temp,NULL,0,0);
  mciSendString("play theSound wait",NULL,0,0);
  mciSendString("close theSound",NULL,0,0);
  }
```

You'll notice that I used a compound device specification here, as I have all along when talking about **waveaudio!ohoh.wav**. The **waveaudio** device requires a filename, and so it is a compound device. The **cdaudio** device does not require a filename, and so it is a simple device.

If you have a compound device, it is possible to avoid specifying the device name entirely—if the file extension matches the default extension for the device specified in WIN.INI (or the registry in the case of Windows NT):

```
[mci extensions]
wav=waveaudio
mid=sequencer
rmi=sequencer
fli=Autodesk
flc=Autodesk
avi=AVIVideo
```

So, assuming the filename passed includes a correctly registered extension, it is possible to extend our **playwave** function to be a generic function that plays any media file through MCI:

```
void playMCI(LPCSTR filename) {
  char temp[80];

  wsprintf(temp,"open %s alias theMedia",filename);
```

```
mciSendString(temp,NULL,0,0);
mciSendString("play theMedia wait",NULL,0,0);
mciSendString("close theMedia",NULL,0,0);
   }
```

Implicit device opening based on the file extension seems to obviate the necessity for finding out what devices are present on the system—but I'd suggest that shifting the burden for handling errors to the user doesn't constitute good design. It would be a better idea to ask the system what devices are loaded.

As we mentioned earlier, you don't want to look directly in SYSTEM.INI, since that file doesn't exist in a Windows NT system. A better alternative is to use the MCI **sysinfo** command:

```
#define STRICT
#include <windows.h>
#include <mmsystem.h>
#include <windowsx.h>
#include <stdlib.h>

LPSTR FAR *getMCInames(void) {
   char temp[80],answer[80];
   LPSTR FAR *lp=NULL;
   int i,n;

   mciSendString("sysinfo all quantity",answer,sizeof(answer),0);
   n=atoi(answer);
   if(n<1)
       return NULL;
   lp=(LPSTR FAR *)GlobalAllocPtr(GHND,(n+1)*sizeof(LPSTR));
   for(i=1;i<=n;i++) {
       wsprintf(temp,"sysinfo all name %d",i);
       mciSendString(temp,answer,sizeof(answer),0);
       lp[i-1]=(LPSTR)GlobalAllocPtr(GHND,lstrlen(answer));
       lstrcpy(lp[i-1],answer);
       }
   return lp;
}

void freeMCInames(LPSTR FAR *lp) {
   int i=0;

   while(lp[i]) {
       GlobalFreePtr(lp[i]);
       i++;
       }
   GlobalFreePtr(lp);
   }
```

You'll note that the **getMCInames** function allocates and returns an array of global strings. The program using **getMCInames** is responsible for calling **freeMCInames** to release the array when it is done with the device names. The implementation shown above is somewhat wasteful of selectors under Windows—it's a little silly to make all those global allocations, but we can get away with it because any given system will have a limited number of installed MCI devices. On the other hand, it works, it compiles as C or C++, it is usable in a DLL, and it is portable between 16- and 32-bit Windows.

So far we've been playing media elements. We can also record, at least on some devices.[8] The most common recording device is **waveaudio**: we could record using the following sequence of pseudo-MCI strings, to be sent with **mciSendString**:

```
open new type waveaudio alias theSound
set theSound time format ms bitpersample 16 channels 2
set theSound samplespersec 44100
cue theSound input
record theSound
<wait for user to press the stop button>
stop theSound
<ask the user to give a filename>
save theSound <filename>
close theSound
```

In the first line, the identifier **new** says that we want to record. The second line says we want 16-bit stereo recording, and the third line says that we want CD-quality 44 KHz frequency response. Of course, recording at this quality will chew up a *lot* of memory and disk space.

Cueing the device for input is an optional step that helps some drivers to respond to the **record** command more quickly. We record asynchronously so that the user can stop the recording. I'm not sure when the recording would stop if you issued **record theSound wait**—it might be when the system runs out of virtual memory, or there might be some lower limit built into your waveform device driver.

To ask the user to name the file we would most likely use the common dialog function **GetSaveFileName** with a default extension of WAV; then we could substitute the entered filename in the **save** command using **wsprintf** as shown in the **playwave** and **playMCI** functions above.

Error Handling

You'll note that we haven't as yet concerned ourselves with error handling. Let's correct that.

---

[8] Not every MCI device supports recording. For instance, the Microsoft AVIVideo driver does not record: you need to use the utilities supplied with your video capture board to record video in AVI format. In this particular case, resorting to low-level programming is not an option: the AVI-Video low-level functions have not been documented.

We mentioned earlier that it might make sense to write a wrapper for **mciSend-String** that would take care of error handling in one central place. Microsoft has actually provided an example of such a wrapper function, **sendstring** in MCITEST.C:

```
DWORD sendstring(HWND hwndDlg, PTSTR strBuffer)
{
    TCHAR   aszReturn[BUFFER_LENGTH]; /* string containing the
                                  message returned by MCI      */
    DWORD   dwErr;  /* variable containing the return
                      code from the MCI command     */
    dprintf2((TEXT("sendstring: %s"), strBuffer));

    /* Uncheck the notification buttons */

    CheckDlgButton (hwndDlg, ID_NOT_SUCCESS, FALSE);
    CheckDlgButton (hwndDlg, ID_NOT_SUPER, FALSE);
    CheckDlgButton (hwndDlg, ID_NOT_ABORT, FALSE);
    CheckDlgButton (hwndDlg, ID_NOT_FAIL, FALSE);

    /* Send the string command to MCI */

    dwErr = mciSendString(strBuffer, aszReturn,
        sizeof(aszReturn), hwndDlg);

    /* Put the text message returned by MCI into the
      'MCI Output' box */

    SetDlgItemText (hwndDlg, ID_OUTPUT, aszReturn);

    /* Decode the error # returned by MCI, and display the string
     in the 'Error' box. */

    mciGetErrorString(dwErr, strBuffer, BUFFER_LENGTH);
    SetDlgItemText(hwndDlg, ID_ERRORCODE, strBuffer);

    /* Update the internal list of currently open devices */

    update_device_list();
    return dwErr;
}
```

This isn't as clever a wrapper as we could write given a few more assumptions, but it isn't bad at all. Two unfamiliar functions are used here: **dprintf2** and **update_-device_list**. The former is a debugging output macro that you can safely ignore. The latter is a little more interesting: it maintains a list box of open MCI devices, with the aid of a helper function, **get_number_of_devices**:

```
int get_number_of_devices(void)
{
    MCI_SYSINFO_PARMS sysinfo;
```

```
      /* Parameter structure used for getting
   information about the MCI devices in
         the system                              */
   DWORD dwDevices; /* count of open devices  */

   /* Set things up so that MCI puts the number of open devices
      directly into <dwDevices>.  */

   sysinfo.lpstrReturn = (LPTSTR)(LPDWORD)&dwDevices;
   sysinfo.dwRetSize = sizeof(dwDevices);

   /* Send MCI a command querying all devices in the system to see
      if they are open. If the command was successful, return the
      number provided by MCI. Otherwise, return 0. */

   if (mciSendCommand (MCI_ALL_DEVICE_ID,
                       MCI_SYSINFO,
                       (MCI_SYSINFO_OPEN | MCI_SYSINFO_QUANTITY),
                       (DWORD)(LPMCI_SYSINFO_PARMS)&sysinfo) != 0)
      return 0;
   else
      return (int)dwDevices;
}

STATICFN void update_device_list(void)
{
   TCHAR aszBuf[BUFFER_LENGTH];
           /* string used for several things  */
   MCI_SYSINFO_PARMS sysinfo;
           /* Parameter structure used for getting
              information about the devices in the system */
   HWND hwndList;   /* handle to the Devices listbox window */
   int nDevices;
   int nCurrentDevice;

   /* If the Devices dialog is not present, then return */

   if (hwndDevices == 0) {
      return;
   }

/* Find out how many devices are currently open in the system */

   nDevices = get_number_of_devices();

   /* Update the dialog caption appropriately */

      wsprintf(aszBuf, aszDeviceTextFormat, nDevices);
      SetWindowText(hwndDevices, aszBuf);

   /* Get a handle to the dialog's listbox, and prepare it for
      updating */

   hwndList = GetDlgItem (hwndDevices, ID_DEVICE_LIST);
```

```
    SendMessage (hwndList, LB_RESETCONTENT, 0, 0L);

        if (nDevices) {
                SendMessage (hwndList, WM_SETREDRAW, FALSE, 0L);
        }

    /* Get the name of each open device in the system, one device
       at a time. Add each device's name to the listbox. */

    for (nCurrentDevice = 1;
         nCurrentDevice <= nDevices;
         ++nCurrentDevice) {

        sysinfo.dwNumber = nCurrentDevice;
        sysinfo.lpstrReturn = (LPTSTR)&aszBuf;
        sysinfo.dwRetSize = sizeof(aszBuf);

        /* If an error is encountered, skip to the next device. */
        if (mciSendCommand(MCI_ALL_DEVICE_ID, MCI_SYSINFO,
                    MCI_SYSINFO_OPEN | MCI_SYSINFO_NAME,
                    (DWORD)(LPMCI_SYSINFO_PARMS)&sysinfo) != 0) {
            continue;
            }

    /* Redraw the list when all device names have been added.*/
        if (nCurrentDevice == nDevices) {
        /* About to add the last device - allow redrawing */
            SendMessage(hwndList, WM_SETREDRAW, TRUE, 0L);
            }

        /* Add the device name to the listbox.*/
        SendMessage(hwndList, LB_ADDSTRING, 0,
                (LONG)(LPTSTR)aszBuf);
    } //for nCurrentDevice

    /* Remember the number of open devices we found this time */

    nLastNumberOfDevices = nDevices;
}
```

You'll note that these two functions make heavy use of command messages. It's not clear that there's anything that can be done with command messages that can't be done just as easily with command strings. Nevertheless, let's see what we can do with MCI command messages.

Using MCI Command Messages

We've already seen how to use **mciSendString** and **mciGetErrorString**. We've also seen that most of the functionality of **mciSendString** resides in the individual command strings, which then activate the appropriate device drivers.

mciSendCommand does roughly the same thing as **mciSendString**—only, instead of sending a raw ASCII string that will need to be interpreted, **mciSend-Command** sends a completely cooked command message to MCI. As I mentioned earlier, playing media takes enough time that you don't really have to worry about the overhead involved in interpreting a command string. Nevertheless, you may find that command messages suit your programming style better than command strings, that they fit your needs better, or that they are easier to use in situations that require substantial program logic.

The full specification of **mciSendCommand** is:

```
DWORD mciSendCommand(wDeviceID, wMessage, dwParam1, dwParam2)

UINT  wDeviceID  Specifies the device ID of the MCI device to
                 receive the command. This parameter is not used
                 with the MCI_OPEN command.

UINT  wMessage   Specifies the command message.

DWORD dwParam1   Specifies flags for the command.

DWORD dwParam2   Specifies a pointer to a parameter block for the
                 command.

Return Value     Returns zero if the function was successful.
                 Otherwise, it returns error information. The low-
                 order word of the returned DWORD is the error
                 return value. If the error is device-specific, the
                 high-order word contains the driver ID; otherwise
                 the high-order word is zero.
```

That doesn't look any worse than **mciSendString**, but in practice **mciSend-Command** calls tend to be rather verbose. The principal reason is that there are often a number of flags to be specified. In addition, setting up a parameter block can be complicated.

For instance, let's review the command to determine the number of open devices from function **get_number_of_devices**:

```
MCI_SYSINFO_PARMS sysinfo;
DWORD dwDevices; /* count of open devices  */

sysinfo.lpstrReturn = (LPTSTR)(LPDWORD)&dwDevices;
sysinfo.dwRetSize = sizeof(dwDevices);
if (mciSendCommand (MCI_ALL_DEVICE_ID,
                    MCI_SYSINFO,
                    (MCI_SYSINFO_OPEN | MCI_SYSINFO_QUANTITY),
                    (DWORD)(LPMCI_SYSINFO_PARMS)&sysinfo) != 0)
```

```
    return 0;
else
    return (int)dwDevices;
```

What would be the equivalent MCI string? Something like this:

```
char answer[80];
int n;

mciSendString("sysinfo open quantity",answer,sizeof(answer),0);
n=atoi(answer);
```

The command form of this will undoubtedly run a few milliseconds faster than the string form, but the command code is much more verbose than the string code. More importantly, the command code takes longer to write and debug than the string code.

Most of the content of the MCI system is held in the messages themselves. There are many kinds of MCI messages: system command messages, required command messages, basic command messages, extended commands for windowed video devices, window notification messages, joystick messages, file I/O messages, and so on.

System command messages are interpreted directly by MCI. These two messages do not rely on the ability of a device to respond to them. **MCI_BREAK** is sent by an application to set a break key for a specified device, and **MCI_SYSINFO** is sent by an application to obtain system-related information about a device.

The required command messages are supported by all MCI devices—hence the designation "required."

- **MCI_OPEN** is sent by an application to open a device and get an MCI device identifier for use with other commands.

- **MCI_CLOSE** is sent by an application to request that the specified device be closed.

- **MCI_GETDEVCAPS** is sent by an application to obtain information about device capabilities.

- **MCI_INFO** is sent by an application to obtain information about a device.

- **MCI_STATUS** is sent by an application to obtain status information about a device.

Basic command messages are *recognized* by all MCI devices, but not necessarily supported by all devices. If a device does not support a basic command, it returns **MCIERR_UNSUPPORTED_FUNCTION**, which your application should handle gracefully.

- **MCI_LOAD** is sent by an application to load a file.

- **MCI_PAUSE** is sent by an application to pause a device.

- **MCI_PLAY** is sent by an application to start a device playing.

- **MCI_RECORD** is sent by an application to start recording with a device.

- **MCI_RESUME** is sent by an application to resume playback or recording after a pause.

- **MCI_SAVE** is sent by an application to save the current file.

- **MCI_SEEK** is sent by an application to change locations within a media element.

- **MCI_SET** is sent by an application to set parameters for a device.

- **MCI_STOP** is sent by an application to stop a device from playing or recording.

Some MCI devices let you edit MCI data; they have extended commands for manipulating data. If a device supports editing, it can recognize **MCI_COPY**, and respond by copying data from the MCI element to the Clipboard.

- **MCI_CUT** asks the device to move data from the MCI element to the Clipboard.

- **MCI_DELETE** says to remove data from the MCI element.

- **MCI_PASTE** asks the device to paste data from the Clipboard to the MCI element.

Some MCI devices have additional operating features. They can optionally support **MCI_CUE**, which askes them to cue or prepare themselves for playback or recording; **MCI_ESCAPE**, which lets them receive a string command directly from the application, without any interpretation by MCI; **MCI_SPIN**, which tells a rotating media device such as a laserdisc to start or stop spinning; and/or **MCI_STEP**, which asks a frame-oriented device such as an animation player to advance one or more frames.

Animation players, video overlay devices, and Video for Windows (AVI) players all display data in a window. They support another set of MCI commands, to control the windowed display. **MCI_WINDOW** is sent by an application to specify a window and the characteristics of the window for a graphic device to use for its display. **MCI_WHERE** asks the device for the extent of a clipping rectangle, and **MCI_PUT** defines a source or destination clipping rectangle. **MCI_FREEZE** stops video capture, and **MCI_UN-FREEZE** restores capture that has been frozen. **MCI_REALIZE** tells the graphic device to realize its palette, and **MCI_UPDATE** tells the graphic device to update or paint the current frame.

We mentioned the **MM_MCINOTIFY** message earlier: it notifies the window function of the status of the currently executing MCI command. The **wParam** parameter of

MM_MCINOTIFY contains the status of the command. See the earlier example and discussion for the meanings of the four possible command status values.

If you support a joystick, there are a number of messages that the joystick driver can send to your window. You'll find the documentation for the **MM_JOY*** messages in the Joystick Messages topic of the Windows 3.1 Multimedia Reference help file, or by searching the Win32 help file for **MM_JOY1BUTTONDOWN**. By the way, you won't get joystick messages unless you capture a joystick with **joySetCapture**.

There are four more MCI functions that we haven't mentioned: I guess this is as good a place as any. The first, **mciGetDeviceID**, returns the device ID assigned when the device was opened. Why would you use this? You need the device identifier when you call **mciSendCommand**. In the normal situations we've discussed, you get the ID when you open the device. But you might have a function that didn't open the device—it might not even be in the same process as the function that opened the device—yet it needs to use the open device. Knowing only the ASCII device name, the function can call **mciGetDeviceID(lpstrName)** to get the ID.

The second function, **mciGetCreatorTask**, returns a handle to the process that opened a device, given a device ID. One imagines an amnesiac process wondering "Did I open that device? I'm sure I never did." Calling **mciGetCreatorTask(uDeviceID)** gets the task handle, which can then be compared with the current task's handle.

In 16-bit Windows, the task can find out its own handle with **GetCurrentTask**. In Win32, a task can get a "pseudohandle" to itself with **GetCurrentProcess** or **GetCurrentThread**, and it can find its process ID with **GetCurrentProcessID**. It's not clear to me which of these, if any, would correspond to the handle returned by **mciGetCreatorTask**. On the other hand, I haven't yet needed to know, and never expect to.

In our earlier discussion of MCI strings we raised the issues of background processing and media synchronization. MCI has a facility for background processing on a device-by-device basis, in which the devices call yield procedures.

The **mciSetYieldProc** function specifies a callback or yield procedure to be called periodically while an MCI device is completing a command specified with the **wait** flag. This allows you to do background processing in little gulps even though the major program logic that controls your media is synchronous. The specification is:

```
UINT mciSetYieldProc(IDDevice, yp, dwYieldData)

MCIDEVICEID IDDevice;   /* device to set yield procedure for  */
YIELDPROC yp;           /* address of yield procedure  */
DWORD dwYieldData;      /* yield-procedure data */
```

You'd most likely use the **dwYieldData** parameter to tell the yield procedure what to do. For instance, you could use it in a **switch** statement to control which one of several possible background activities should be worked on. If you wanted to give the yield procedure a little more authority, you could bit-encode the **dwYieldData** parameter to give the yield procedure permissions and priorities for different background activities.

mciGetYieldProc returns the curent yield procedure for an MCI device. Its specification is:

```
YIELDPROC mciGetYieldProc(IDDevice, lpdwYieldData)

MCIDEVICEID IDDevice;    /* device being monitored  */
LPDWORD lpdwYieldData;   /* address of yield data to be passed  */
```

Naturally, you use **mciGetYieldProc** to find out about the current yield procedure. If you wanted to add a background task, you could save the **YIELDPROC** and yield data returned by **mciGetYieldProc**, set your own yield procedure, and have your yield procedure call back to the original yield procedure.

The yield procedure itself is of the form:

```
int CALLBACK YieldProc(UINT wDeviceID,DWORD dwData)
```

YieldProc is a placeholder for the application-supplied function name. Export the actual name by including it in the **EXPORTS** statement in your module-definition file. The first parameter, **wDeviceID**, is the device ID of the MCI device; the second parameter, **dwData**, is the application-supplied yield data originally supplied in the **dwYieldData** parameter to **mciSetYieldProc**.

The **YieldProc** should normally return zero to continue the current operation. To cancel the current operation, it can return a nonzero value. One advantage of relying on **YieldProc** rather than coding with multiple threads of execution is that code using **YieldProc** works the same in Windows and Windows NT. If you are writing a Windows NT–only multimedia application, you have the freedom to ignore the **YieldProc** mechanism and use Win32 thread and synchronization APIs.

As we discussed earlier, the majority of the content of MCI is in the actual strings and messages. Complete coverage of all MCI strings and messages would take an entire book: you have enough background now, however, that you should be able to get started writing MCI code productively given the standard help files and tools.

And now, let's move down a level and look briefly at some of the media devices supported by Windows and Windows NT.

Windows and Win32 Audio

Near the beginning of this chapter, we demonstrated five ways to say "oh-oh." We'll repeat them now:

```
#include <windows.h>
#include <mmsystem.h>

//First method: MCI strings
mciSendString("open waveaudio!ohoh.wav",NULL,0,0);
mciSendString("play ohoh.wav wait",NULL,0,0);
mciSendString("close all",NULL,0,0);

//Second method: MCI commands
MCI_OPEN_PARMS mciOP;
mciOP.lpstrDeviceType="waveaudio";
mciOP.lpstrElementName="ohoh.wav"
mciSendCommand(0,MCI_OPEN, MCI_OPEN_TYPE|MCI_OPEN_ELEMENT,
        (DWORD)(LPVOID)&mciOP);
mciSendCommand(mciOP.wDeviceID, MCI_PLAY,MCI_WAIT,0);
mciSendCommand(mciOP.wDeviceID,MCI_CLOSE,0,0);


//Third method: High level audio using filename
sndPlaySound("ohoh.wav",SND_SYNC);

//Fourth method: High level audio, System alias
sndPlaySound("SystemExclamation",SND_SYNC);

//Fifth method: System alert audio playback
MessageBeep(MB_ICONEXCLAMATION);
```

We've already covered the first and second methods in the section on MCI. The third through fifth use high-level audio.

Using High-Level Audio

You already know how to use **MessageBeep**, of course. What you might not know—since the functionality was only added in Windows 3.1—is that the parameter to **MessageBeep** can be used to play system sounds. The standard message box flags, such as **MB_OK**, select different system sounds, and a value of –1 selects a standard beep using the system speaker. The Win32 version of the **MessageBeep** parameter table looks like Table 7-2.

Table 7-2 MessageBeep Parameters and Corresponding System Sounds

Parameter	System Sound Played
0xFFFFFFFF	Standard beep using the computer speaker
MB_ICONASTERISK	SystemAsterisk
MB_ICONEXCLAMATION	SystemExclamation
MB_ICONHAND	SystemHand
MB_ICONQUESTION	SystemQuestion
MB_OK	SystemDefault

sndPlaySound is not much more difficult to use than **MessageBeep**: the only trick is to use the flags correctly. In the previous example we used **SND_SYNC**, which means that the sound is played synchronously—the function does not return until the sound ends. That's fine for short sounds, and it's fine if you don't want your program to do anything else while the sound plays.

If you are playing a lengthy selection, like a piece of narration, you might want it to play in the background, so you would instead specify **SND_ASYNC**, which means that the sound is played asynchronously and the function returns immediately after beginning the sound.

That raises a potential problem. Suppose you want to give the user the opportunity to stop the sound? How do you do that? To terminate an asynchronously played sound, call **sndPlaySound** again with a **NULL** name for the sound.

So, how do you stop a synchronously played sound? You can't. Oops: better remember that **SND_ASYNC** flag.

There are a few more possible flags you can set for **sndPlaySound**. **SND_NO-DEFAULT** means that you don't want the function to play the default sound if the sound you specify can't be found. **SND_MEMORY** means that the first parameter to the function is *not* a pointer to a string specifying the filename or the system sound event, but rather a pointer to an in-memory image of a waveform sound. **SND_LOOP** means that you want the sound to play repeatedly until **sndPlaySound** is called again with its first parameter set to **NULL**.

What happens if you specify **SND_LOOP** and **SND_SYNC**? You'd expect one of two possibilities: an infinite loop requiring you to reboot your machine, or no loop at all. Fortunately, the designers of **sndPlaySound** thought this one through: you need to combine **SND_LOOP** and **SND_ASYNC** if you really want looping.

One final flag is **SND_NOSTOP**, which says that you don't want to interrupt anyone else. If you specify **SND_NOSTOP** and a sound is currently playing, the function will immediately return **FALSE** without doing anything; if no other sound is currently playing, the function will play the requested sound.

The two major limits of **sndPlaySound** are that the sound must fit in available physical memory and be playable by an installed waveform audio device driver. To play a sound that does not fit in available physical memory you need to use MCI, which we've already discussed. Just for reference, the full specification of **sndPlay-Sound** is:[9]

```
BOOL sndPlaySound(lpszSoundName, fuOptions)

LPCTSTR lpszSoundName; /* name of sound to play  */
UINT fuOptions;  /* options flags  */
```

[9] This and the succeeding specifications are largely as supplied by Microsoft in the manuals referenced at the end of the chapter. They are somewhat more current than the manuals, though, as they are taken from Microsoft's latest online documention. I have edited them very slightly for clarity.

The sndPlaySound function plays a waveform sound specified by a filename or by an entry in the [sounds] section of the registry. If the sound can not be found, the function plays the default sound specified by the SystemDefault entry in the [sounds] section of the registry. If there is no SystemDefault entry or if the default sound can't be found, the function makes no sound and returns FALSE.

Parameter Description

lpszSoundName Specifies the name of the sound to play. The function searches the [sounds] section of the registry for an entry with this name and plays the associated waveform file. If no entry by this name exists, the function assumes the name is the name of a waveform file. If this parameter is NULL, any currently playing sound is stopped.
fuOptions Specifies options for playing the sound. This value can be one or more of the following flags:

Value	Meaning
SND_SYNC	The sound is played synchronously, and the function does not return until the sound ends.
SND_ASYNC	The sound is played asynchronously, and the function returns immediately after beginning the sound. To terminate an asynchronously played sound, call SndPlaySound with the lpszSoundName parameter set to NULL.
SND_NODEFAULT	If the sound can not be found, the function returns silently without playing the default sound.
SND_MEMORY	The parameter specified by lpszSoundName points to an in-memory image of a waveform sound.
SND_LOOP	The sound continues to play repeatedly until sndPlaySound is called again with the lpszSoundName parameter set to NULL. You must also specify the SND_ASYNC flag to loop sounds.
SND_NOSTOP	If a sound is currently playing, the function immediately returns FALSE without playing the requested sound.

Returns

If the sound is played, the return value is TRUE; otherwise it is FALSE.

Comments

The sound must fit in available physical memory and be playable by an installed waveform audio device driver. The directories searched for sound files are, in order, the current directory, the Windows directory, the Windows system directory, the directories listed in the PATH environment variable, and the directories mapped in a network. See the Win32 OpenFile function for more information about the directory search order.

> If you specify the SND_MEMORY flag, the lpszSoundName parameter must point to an in-memory image of a waveform sound. If the sound is stored as a resource, use the LoadResource and LockResource functions to load and lock the resource and get a pointer to it. If the sound is not a resource, use the GlobalAlloc function with the MEM_MOVEABLE flag set to allocate memory for the sound, and the GlobalLock function to lock the memory.

In Win32, **sndPlaySound** has a slightly extended brother, **PlaySound**. The major difference between the two is that **PlaySound** can load a resource from a module by itself: you don't have to use **LoadResource** and **LockResource** ahead of time. **PlaySound** has the calling convention:

```
BOOL PlaySound(lpszName, hModule, fdwSound)

LPCTSTR lpszName;    /* sound string  */
HANDLE hModule;      /* sound resource*/
DWORD fdwSound;      /* sound type */
```

If the **PlaySound** function succeeds, it returns TRUE; otherwise, it returns FALSE. To get extended error information, as with all native Win32 functions, use the **GetLastError** function. The **fdwSound** parameter of **PlaySound** corresponds exactly to the **fuOptions** parameter of **sndPlaySound**.

Suppose you really want to get down to the nuts and bolts level to play audio? You don't have to go directly to the hardware: you can use device-independent low-level audio functions. The low-level audio functions also give you an alternative to using MCI strings or commands for recording.

Using Low-Level Audio

Table 7-3 summarizes the Windows and Win32 low-level wave audio input and output functions. As you can see, the names are fairly self-explanatory. Except for the limited REVERSE example in the Windows SDK, Microsoft provides no examples of using low-level audio calls, so we'll have to wing it.

We might want to consider how to write the equivalent of **sndPlaySound** using low-level functions—perhaps how to write an extended version that can play files that won't fit in memory. Let's start by looking at **waveOutOpen**:

```
MMRESULT waveOutOpen(lphWaveOut, IDDevice, lpwf, dwCallback,
                     dwCallbackInstance, fdwOpen)

LPHWAVEOUT lphWaveOut;  /* handle of output device      (returned) */
UINT IDDevice;          /* identifier of device */
LPWAVEFORMAT lpwf;      /* address of structure with device format */
DWORD dwCallback;       /* address of callback or window handle */
```

Table 7-3   Low-level Waveform Audio Functions

Name	Function
waveInAddBuffer	Send buffer to waveform input device.
waveInClose	Close waveform input device.
waveInGetDevCaps	Get waveform input device capabilities.
waveInGetErrorText	Get text description for waveform error.
waveInGetID	Get waveform input device ID handle.
waveInGetNumDevs	Return number of waveform input devices.
waveInGetPosition	Get current waveform input device position.
waveInMessage	Send message to waveform input device.
waveInOpen	Open waveform input device for recording.
waveInPrepareHeader	Prepare buffer for waveform input.
waveInReset	Stop waveform input device.
waveInStart	Start waveform input device.
waveInStop	Stop waveform input.
waveInUnprepareHeader	Clean up prepared waveform header.
waveOutBreakLoop	Break waveform output loop.
waveOutClose	Close waveform output device.
waveOutGetDevCaps	Get waveform output device capabilities.
waveOutGetErrorText	Get text description for waveform error.

```
DWORD dwCallbackInstance;  /* instance data    */
DWORD fdwOpen;             /* open option   */
```

The waveOutOpen function opens a specified waveform output device for playback.

Parameter Description

lphWaveOut   Points to a variable that will receive a handle that identifies the opened waveform output device. Use this handle of identify the device when calling other waveform output functions. This parameter may be NULL if the WAVE_FORMAT_QUERY flag is specified for fdwOpen.

IDDevice Identifies the waveform output device to open. Use a valid device identifier or the WAVE_MAPPER flag. If WAVE_MAPPER is specified, the function selects a waveform output device capable of playing the given format.

Table 7-3 continued

Name	Function
waveOutGetID	Get waveform output device ID for handle.
waveOutGetNumDevs	Get number of waveform output devices.
waveOutGetPitch	Get current waveform output pitch.
waveOutGetPlaybackRate	Get current waveform playback rate.
waveOutGetPosition	Get current waveform playback position.
waveOutGetVolume	Get current waveform volume.
waveOutMessage	Send message to waveform output drivers.
waveOutOpen	Open waveform output device.
waveOutPause	Pause waveform playback.
waveOutPrepareHeader	Prepare waveform playback data block.
waveOutReset	Stop waveform playback.
waveOutRestart	Restart paused waveform playback.
waveOutSetPitch	Set waveform output pitch.
waveOutSetPlaybackRate	Set waveform playback rate.
waveOutSetVolume	Set waveform output volume.
waveOutUnprepareHeader	Clean up prepared waveform data block.
waveOutWrite	Write to waveform output device.
waveProc	Waveform device callback function.

```
lpwf   Points to a WAVEFORMAT structure that identifies the desired
format for recording waveform data.

dwCallback   Specifies the address of a callback function or a
handle of a window called during waveform playback to process mes-
sages related to the progress of playback. For more information
about the callback function, see the description of the WaveProc
function. Specify NULL for this parameter if no callback mechanism
is to be used.

dwCallbackInstance   Specifies user instance data passed to the
callback function. This parameter is not used with window callbacks.

fdwOpen   Specifies flags for opening the device, as follows.

Value Meaning

WAVE_FORMAT_QUERY   If this flag is specified, the device is queried
to determine if it supports the given format but is not actually
opened.
```

WAVE_ALLOWSYNC   If this flag is not specified, the device will fail to open if it is a synchronous device.
CALLBACK_WINDOW If this flag is specified, dwCallback is assumed to be a window handle.
CALLBACK_FUNCTION   If this flag is specified, dwCallback is assumed to be a callback procedure address.

Returns

If the function succeeds, the return value is zero; otherwise, it is an error code, which can be one of the following:

Value Meaning

MMSYSERR_BADDEVICEID   The specified device ID is out of range.
MMSYSERR_ALLOCATED The specified resource is already allocated.
MMSYSERR_NOMEM   The system is unable to allocate or lock memory.
WAVERR_BADFORMAT The system attempted to open with an unsupported wave format.

Comments

Use waveOutGetNumDevs to determine the number of waveform output devices present in the system. The device identifier specified by IDDevice varies from zero to one less than the number of devices present. The WAVE_MAPPER constant may also be used as a device identifier.

The WAVEFORMAT structure pointed to by lpwf may be extended to include type-specific information for certain data formats. For example, for pulse code modulated (PCM) data, an extra word is added to specify the number of bits per sample. Use the PCMWAVEFORMAT structure in this case.

If a window is chosen to receive callback information, the following messages are sent to the window procedure function to indicate the progress of waveform output: MM_WOM_OPEN, MM_WOM_CLOSE, and MM_WOM_DONE.

If a function is chosen to receive callback information, the following messages are sent to the function to indicate the progress of waveform output: WOM_OPEN, WOM_CLOSE, and WOM_DONE. The callback function must reside in a dynamic-link library (DLL).

Oh, joy. Well, let's try to write some simple code that will open a waveform device for output:

```
#include <windows.h>
#include <mmsystem.h>
//...
MMRESULT mmr;
HWAVEOUT hWave;
```

```
PCMWAVEFORMAT pwf;

pwf.wf.wFormatTag=WAVE_FORMAT_PCM;
pwf.wf.nChannels=2; //stereo
pwf.wf.nSamplesPerSec=11025;   //11 KHz
pwf.wBitsPerSample=8;
pwf.wf.nAvgBytesPerSec=2*11025;
pwf.wf.nBlockAlign=4;

mmr=waveOutOpen(&hWave, WAVE_MAPPER, &pwf, NULL,
                  NULL, WAVE_ALLOW_SYNC);
if(mmr) {
   GoHandleTheError(mmr,"waveOutOpen");
   return FALSE;
   }
```

That should do it for us—although we won't get progress messages since we haven't specified either a callback function or a callback window. Now we have to play something on the device. We can't just play a waveform—first we have to prepare a waveform header:

```
UINT waveOutPrepareHeader(hWaveOut, lpWaveOutHdr, wSize)

HWAVEOUT  hWaveOut
Specifies a handle to the waveform output device.

LPWAVEHDR  lpWaveOutHdr
Specifies a pointer to a WAVEHDR structure that identifies the data
block to be prepared.

UINT  wSize
Specifies the size of the WAVEHDR structure.
```

Isn't this fun? MCI is looking better all the time. Now we have to look at a **WAVEHDR** structure:

```
typedef struct wavehdr_tag {
    LPSTR lpData;
    DWORD dwBufferLength;
    DWORD dwBytesRecorded;
    DWORD dwUser;
    DWORD dwFlags;
    DWORD dwLoops;
    struct wavehdr_tag far * lpNext;
    DWORD reserved;
} WAVEHDR;

lpData          Specifies a far pointer to the waveform data buffer.
```

dwBufferLength	Specifies the length of the data buffer.
dwBytesRecorded	When the header is used in input, this specifies how much data is in the buffer.
dwUser	Specifies 32 bits of user data.
dwFlags	Specifies flags giving information about the data buffer.

Flags:

WHDR_DONE	Set by the device driver to indicate that it is finished with the data buffer and is returning it to the application.
WHDR_BEGINLOOP	Specifies that this buffer is the first buffer in a loop. This flag is only used with output data buffers.
WHDR_ENDLOOP	Specifies that this buffer is the last buffer in a loop. This flag is only used with output data buffers.
WHDR_PREPARED	Set by Windows to indicate that the data buffer has been prepared with waveInPrepareHeader or waveOutPrepareHeader.
dwLoops	Specifies the number of times to play the loop. This parameter is used only with output data buffers.
lpNext	Is reserved and should not be used.
reserved	Is reserved and should not be used.

Comments

Use the WHDR_BEGINLOOP and WHDR_ENDLOOP flags in the dwFlagsfield to specify the beginning and ending data blocks for looping. To loop on a single block, specify both flags for the same block. Use the dwLoops field in the WAVEHDR structure for the first block in the loop to specify the number of times to play the loop.

Deeper and deeper. Well, somewhere we have to have some actual data in a buffer. Let's assume it's a chunk of data we've read from a WAV file with the **mmioRead** function, and that it has a global handle, **hWaveData,** which has been locked down, with the global pointer saved in **lpWaveData**:

```
WAVEHDR wh;
UINT ui;

wh.lpData=lpWaveData;
wh.dwBufferLength=GlobalSize(hWaveData);
```

```
wh.dwBytesRecorded=0;
wh.dwUser=0;
wh.dwFlags=0;
wh.dwLoops=0;
ui=waveOutPrepareHeader(hWave, &wh, sizeof(wh));
if(ui) {
   GoHandleTheError(ui,"waveOutPrepareHeader");
   return FALSE;
   }
```

Well, now we have a waveform ready to roll, so we can play it:

```
ui=waveOutWrite(hWave, &wh, sizeof(wh))
if(ui) {
   GoHandleTheError(ui,"waveOutWrite");
   return FALSE;
   }
```

We're not done, though. We have to clean up after ourselves. First we have to wait for the driver to finish playing our sound. That is accomplished by waiting for the correct messages to come in, or by busy-waiting on the waveform header:

```
while(!(wh.dwFlags & WHDR_DONE))
   SpinTheMessageLoop();
waveOutUnprepareHeader(hWave, &wh, sizeof(wh));
GlobalUnlock(hWaveData);
GlobalFree(hWaveData);
waveOutClose(hWave);
```

Isn't that fun? It certainly makes me appreciate MCI strings all the more.

Wave input is pretty much the same story all over again. We start with **waveInOpen**. Then we allocate a global memory buffer and a wave header and use **wave-InPrepareHeader** to get it ready. **waveInAddBuffer** sends the prepared buffer to the device to be recorded, and **waveInUnprepareHeader** asks the driver to clean it up when we have saved the recording. Finally we free the buffer and call **waveInClose**.

Working with multiple buffers is obviously possible for both recording and playback—and obviously takes a bit of work. It's clear why **sndPlaySound** is limited to sounds that will fit in memory, and it's also clear that a *lot* of work went into MCI to make it handle long sounds smoothly.

Programming MIDI

While waveform sound is the digital equivalent of tape recording, and can handle any sounds that can be recorded through a microphone or played through a speaker, it uses an incredible amount of disk space, especially if you record with decent fidelity. Consider the average bytes per second for a 44.1 KHz, 16-bit stereo waveform recording (the highest standard recording quality):

```
pwf.wf.nAvgBytesPerSec=2*2*44100L;  //176,400 bytes/second
```

That is roughly 10 megabytes/minute. So if you want to record a three-minute song, you'll need 30 MB of disk space. If you want to record a 20-minute symphony, you'll need 200 MB of disk space—assuming no compression. Naturally, you can forget keeping all of that in memory at once so that **sndPlaySound** can play it. Even with compression (and compression standards for Windows WAVE files have yet to be adopted), you'll still need a lot of disk space (and RAM) to do any serious work with waveform audio.

MIDI sound is the digital equivalent of a player piano roll. A MIDI *sequencer* stores and plays a compact sequence of instructions representing the basic operations of an instrument: turn a note on at a given pitch and loudness, turn a note off, and so on. A MIDI *synthesizer* can play notes when sent those instructions. A MIDI keyboard or other *controller* can generate those instructions.

MIDI (Musical Instrument Digital Interface) itself is a protocol or language that allows musical instruments (for instance, synthesizers, samplers, drum machines, and electric pianos) to talk to controllers (for instance, keyboards, wind controllers, sequencers, and guitar controllers) and personal computers. It might seem like a small thing, but in fact MIDI has revolutionized the way composers and musicians work.

How is that? Let me offer myself as an example. I was trained as a classical musician and composer. To compose music I would imagine it, write it down on music staff paper, then attempt to play what I'd written. I'm a decent violinist, so I can play violin and other melodic parts accurately: but I'm only a so-so pianist, so my chord playing leaves something to be desired. I don't play too many other instruments, so if I was writing for, say, a woodwind quartet, I'd have to wait (sometimes for years) until the piece was performed to hear how I'd done.

When I write music now, I either notate it or play it directly into the computer: I can play back the result immediately and hear exactly what I've written—accurate even to the sound of the correct instruments. That instant feedback makes all the difference in the world—I really don't know how I was able to compose before I had MIDI.

I used MIDI sequencers from DOS before Windows supported multimedia; now I use MIDI sequencers and MIDI notation programs from Windows. I have half a dozen MIDI programs for Windows, but the two I use most are *Cakewalk*, a sequencer, and *Encore*, a notation program. The difference between them is that the sequencer is better for working directly with the music—recording it from MIDI instruments, editing it, and playing it back—while the notation program allows me to print scores that live musicians can read, complete with expression markings and lyrics.

I haven't written my own sequencer: that would be a multiple man-year effort. I have written programs that play stored MIDI sequences: that is trivial, since the MCI MIDI sequencer does all the work. (See, for example, the `playMCI` function discussed earlier in the chapter.) But the MCI sequencer does playback only—it doesn't let you record or edit MIDI music, and it doesn't even let you play back selected tracks.

People who write MIDI programs for Windows that do more than the MCI sequencer pretty much have to use the low-level MIDI functions. Older programs that went around Windows to the MIDI hardware don't work properly in enhanced mode Windows, and don't work at all in Windows NT.

The low-level MIDI functions are given in Table 7-4. As you can see, some of the low-level MIDI functions correspond to wave audio functions, and some have no wave equivalents.

How would you use the low-level MIDI functions? You'd probably start off by enumerating the available MIDI devices. You can find out how many physical devices are available with `midiInGetNumDevs` and `midiOutGetNumDevs`. You should always add to the physical devices the MIDI mapper, which is the device used by the Microsoft Media Player applet. The MIDI mapper is represented by the constant MIDI_MAPPER in the device ID field of a `midiInOpen` or `midiOutOpen` call.

What is the MIDI mapper? It's a piece of Windows and Windows NT system software that hides some of the differences between synthesizers from your application. Until recently, there was no standard arrangement for MIDI *patches* or instrument sounds in a synthesizer, nor any standard arrangement of MIDI channels, nor any standard mapping from notes to drum sounds in a drum channel.

There is a standard now—the General MIDI Mode specification—and the MIDI mapper trieds to make any synthesizer look to a Windows application like a GM-standard synthesizer. Even if you don't have a synthesizer, you can get a good feel for what the MIDI mapper does by opening the MIDI Mapper applet from the Windows or Windows NT control panel and examining the setup, patch map, and key map settings using the Edit button.

Unfortunately, the problem of making all synthesizers sound the same is not completely solved by the MIDI mapper. For one thing, synthesizers range from the cheap two-operation FM synthesizers built into game cards to professional synthesizers with CD-quality sampled voices.

Cheap FM synthesizers not only sound tinny, they handle only a small number of voices. If you have a thickly textured MIDI file, it will probably sound terrific on a Turtle Beach MultiSound card or a Roland Sound Canvas, and be unrecognizable on an AdLib card. The AdLib just won't be able to handle all those voices.

By Microsoft's definition, the AdLib is a *base-level* synthesizer, capable of playing three simultaneous melodic instruments in six-note polyphony plus three percussive instruments in three-note polyphony. *Extended* synthesizers must be capable

Table 7-4   Low-level MIDI Audio Functions

Name	Function
midiInAddBuffer	Send input buffer to MIDI device.
midiInClose	Close MIDI input device.
midiInGetDevCaps	Determine MIDI device capabilities.
midiInGetErrorText	Retrieve text description for MIDI error code.
midiInGetID	Retrieve device ID for MIDI device handle.
midiInGetNumDevs	Return number of MIDI devices.
midiInMessage	Send message to MIDI device driver.
midiInOpen	Open MIDI device.
midiInPrepareHeader	Prepare MIDI input buffer.
midiInReset	Stop MIDI input and mark input buffers as done.
midiInStart	Start MIDI input device.
midiInStop	Stop MIDI input.
midiInUnprepareHeader	Clean up prepared header.
midiOutCacheDrumPatches	Preload MIDI percussion patches.
midiOutCachePatches	Preload MIDI patches.
midiOutClose	Close MIDI output device.
midiOutGetDevCaps	Retrieve MIDI output device capabilities.
midiOutGetErrorText	Retrieve text for MIDI output error.
midiOutGetID	Retrieve MIDI output device ID for handle.
midiOutGetNumDevs	Get number of MIDI output devices.
midiOutGetVolume	Retrieve MIDI output device volume.
midiOutLongMsg	Send system-exclusive MIDI message.
midiOutMessage	Send message to MIDI device driver.
midiOutOpen	Open MIDI output device.
midiOutPrepareHeader	Prepare MIDI output data block.
midiOutReset	Stop MIDI output and mark buffers as done.
midiOutSetVolume	Set MIDI output device volume.
midiOutShortMsg	Send short message to MIDI output device.
midiOutUnprepareHeader	Clean up prepared MIDI output header.
MidiProc	Process MIDI device messages.

of handling nine melodic instruments in sixteen-voice polyphony, and eight percussive instruments in sixteen-note polyphony.

Microsoft's convention for Multimedia Windows MIDI files uses channels 1–9 for the melodic instruments of an extended synthesizer, channel 10 for the extended synthesizer percussion, channels 13–15 for base-level melodic instruments, and channel 16 for base-level percussion. Channels 11 and 12 are unused. What you have is essentially two realizations of a piece in a single file—and yes, I know what a royal pain in the neck it is to prepare one MIDI realization, much less two. Few MIDI files come prepared like this: two that do are CANYON.MID and PASSPORT.MID, both of which have been supplied by Microsoft with various versions of Windows.

That said, let's return to our discussion of low-level MIDI functions. Once you've found out what MIDI devices exist on the system, you can open one or more for input and/or output. For playback, you use **midiOutOpen**:

```
UINT midiOutOpen(lphMidiOut, wDeviceID, dwCallback,
                 dwCallbackInstance, dwFlags)

LPHMIDIOUT   lphMidiOut

Specifies a far pointer to an HMIDIOUT handle. This location is
filled with a handle identifying the opened MIDI output device. Use
the handle to identify the device when calling other MIDI output
functions.

UINT   wDeviceID

Identifies the MIDI output device that is to be opened. Specify a
valid MIDI output device ID or the constant MIDI_MAPPER.

DWORD   dwCallback

Specifies the address of a fixed callback function or a handle to a
window called during MIDI playback to process messages related to
the progress of the playback. Specify NULL for this parameter if no
callback is desired.

DWORD   dwCallbackInstance

Specifies user instance data passed to the callback. This parameter
not used with window callbacks.

DWORD   dwFlags

Specifies a callback flag for opening the device.

CALLBACK_WINDOW

If this flag is specified, dwCallback is assumed to be a window
handle.

CALLBACK_FUNCTION

If this flag is specified, dwCallback is assumed to be a callback
procedure address.
```

```
Return Value

Returns zero if the function was successful. Otherwise, it returns
an error number.
```

Once you've successfully opened a MIDI device for output, you can send it ordinary MIDI messages with **midiOutShortMsg**. Or, you can get a block of MIDI data ready with **midiOutPrepareHeader**, then send the block with **midiOutLongMsg**, and finally clean up the block with **midiOutUnprepareHeader**.

Why the distinction between long and short MIDI messages? Short messages are limited to a single **DWORD**, with the first byte of the message in the low-order byte of the **DWORD**. Many MIDI messages—note on, note off, and so on—can be handled in this format. System exclusive messages, however, can include a block of binary data, which requires a buffer-passing mechanism such as is implemented by **midiOutPrepareHeader** and **midiOutLongMsg**.

When you're done performing MIDI playback, you can turn off all MIDI notes and cancel any pending long message buffers with **midiOutReset**, then close the playback device with **midiOutClose**.

When you open a MIDI device for input with **midiInOpen**, you declare a callback function or window to receive incoming MIDI messages:

```
UINT midiInOpen(lphMidiIn, wDeviceID, dwCallback, dwCallbackInstance,
                dwFlags)

LPHMIDIIN  lphMidiIn

Specifies a far pointer to an HMIDIIN handle. This location is
filled with a handle identifying the opened MIDI input device. Use
the handle to identify the device when calling other MIDI input
functions.

UINT  wDeviceID

Identifies the MIDI input device to be opened. Specify a valid MIDI
input device ID or the constant MIDI_MAPPER.

DWORD  dwCallback

Specifies the address of a fixed callback function or a handle to a
window called with information about incoming MIDI messages.

DWORD  dwCallbackInstance

Specifies user instance data passed to the callback function. This
parameter is not used with window callbacks.

DWORD  dwFlags
```

Specifies a callback flag for opening the device.

CALLBACK_WINDOW

If this flag is specified, dwCallback is assumed to be a window handle.

CALLBACK_FUNCTION

If this flag is specified, dwCallback is assumed to be a callback procedure address.

Return Value

Returns zero if the function was successful. Otherwise, it returns an error number.

Callback

```
void CALLBACK MidiInFunc(hMidiIn, wMsg, dwInstance, dwParam1,
                         dwParam2)
```

MidiInFunc is a placeholder for the application-supplied function name. The actual name must be exported by including it in an EXPORTS statement in the DLL's module definition file.

HMIDIIN   hMidiIn

Specifies a handle to the MIDI input device.

UINT   wMsg

Specifies a MIDI input message.

DWORD   dwInstance

Specifies the instance data supplied with midiInOpen.

DWORD   dwParam1

Specifies a parameter for the message.

DWORD   dwParam2

Specifies a parameter for the message.

If a window is chosen to receive callback information, the following messages are sent to the window procedure function to indicate the progress of MIDI input:

* MM_MIM_OPEN
* MM_MIM_CLOSE
* MM_MIM_DATA
* MM_MIM_LONGDATA
* MM_MIM_ERROR

```
*  MM_MIM_LONGERROR

If a function is chosen to receive callback information, the following
messages are sent to the function to indicate the progress of MIDI
input:

*  MIM_OPEN
*  MIM_CLOSE
*  MIM_DATA
*  MIM_LONGDATA
*  MIM_ERROR
*  MIM_LONGERROR

The callback function must reside in a DLL. You do not have to use
MakeProcInstance to get a procedure-instance address for the call-
back function. Because the callback is accessed at interrupt time,
it must reside in a DLL, and its code segment must be specified as
FIXED in the module-definition file for the DLL. Any data that the
callback accesses must be in a FIXED data segment as well. The
callback may not make any system calls except for PostMessage, time-
GetSystemTime, timeGetTime, timeSetEvent, timeKillEvent, midiOut-
ShortMsg, midiOutLongMsg, and OutputDebugStr.
```

Your MIDI input message handler or callback function basically responds to keystrokes on your MIDI keyboard or other controller. Most of the content will be contained in **MIM_DATA** messages—note on messages, note off messages, pitch bend messages, volume change messages, velocity change messages, pan pot messages, and program change messages.

You announce that you're ready to receive MIDI messages with **midiInStart** and that you don't want to recieve messages with **midiInStop**. The current MIDI status is maintained across these calls. When you're completely through listening to MIDI input, stop all input and discard all pending buffers with **midiInReset** and close the port with **midiInClose**.

If you need to accept system-exclusive messages—for instance, patch banks to be reloaded at a later time—you can supply the MIDI device with buffers in much the same way as you handle waveform audio input. The relevant functions are **midiIn-PrepareHeader**, **midiInAddBuffer**, and **midiInUnprepareHeader**.

A few MIDI synthesizer cards are not capable of storing all their own melodic voice and drum sound patches. To support these poor brain-damaged devices you can use the **midiOutCachePatches** and **midiOutCacheDrumPatches** calls. You can find out if a device needs this support with **midiOutDevCaps**. Don't be fooled into asking the MIDI mapper whether it needs patch caching, though—it will say yes whether or not it is attached to a device that does.

Finally, some MIDI cards have a master volume level (as opposed to individual track and note volumes) that you can control via software. **midiOutGetVolume** finds out the current volume level, and **midiOutSetVolume** changes the current volume level.

Table 7-5 Auxiliary Audio Control Functions

Name	Function
auxGetDevCaps	Retrieve auxiliary device capabilities.
auxGetNumDevs	Return number of auxiliary devices.
auxGetVolume	Retrieve current volume setting.
auxOutMessage	Send message to output device.
auxSetVolume	Set auxiliary device volume.

Using the Auxiliary Audio Device

An auxiliary audio device is an audio device whose output is mixed with the output of waveform and MIDI synthesizer devices. Exactly what it represents depends on how the user has wired his system: often the auxiliary audio input is connected to the audio output from the CD-ROM, but it could just as easily be the audio output of an external tape deck, tuner, or audio CD player.

All you can really do with auxiliary audio devices under normal circumstances is to set their volume, but the full set of **aux** functions is given in Table 7-5.

Using Multimedia Timers

Multimedia programs often have more stringent real-time requirements than do ordinary Windows programs. For instance, a MIDI sequencer program might have to record and play back events with an accuracy of a few milliseconds, where an ordinary program would want to get timer ticks a few times a second.

The multimedia timer functions, shown in Table 7-6, provide an application-level interface to Windows enhanced mode virtual timer services, to the millisecond clock in standard mode, and to the clock services in Windows NT.

Table 7-6 Multimedia Timer Functions

Name	Function
timeBeginPeriod	Set minimum timer resolution.
timeEndPeriod	Clear minimum timer resolution.
timeGetDevCaps	Retrieve timer device capabilities.
timeGetSystemTime	Retrieve elapsed time since Windows started.
timeGetTime	Return elapsed time since Windows started.
timeKillEvent	Destroy specified timer callback event.
TimeProc	Timer event callback function.
timeSetEvent	Set up timed callback event.

You'd start by retrieving the minimum and maximum clock resolutions with **timeGetDevCaps**. Then you'd set your desired resolution (within the device limits) with **timeBeginPeriod**. You could then get a high-resolution time reading using **timeGetTime** (which returns milliseconds in a **DWORD**) or **timeGetSystemTime** (which fills an **MMTIME** structure).

You can set up one-shot or periodic timer callback events with **timeSetEvent**, and cancel pending events with **timeKillEvent**. When you're done with the high-resolution timer, signal that fact with **timeEndPeriod** to safely reduce the overhead of all those extra timer interrupts.

Under Windows, a timer callback function is called directly from the timer interrupt. That means the timer callback function under Windows has to be in a FIXED segment in a DLL and has to be exported. The callback function's data must also be in a FIXED segment.

Under Windows, a timer callback may not make any system calls except for **PostMessage**, **timeGetSystemTime**, **timeGetTime**, **timeSetEvent**, **time-KillEvent**, **midiOutShortMsg**, **midiOutLongMsg**, and **OutputDebugStr**. In other words, the timer callback is there primarily for MIDI sequencing, and if you use it for any other purpose, you'll have to settle for whatever delays are incurred by a **PostMessage**.

On the other hand, the call to a **TimeProc** function occurs on a separate thread under Windows NT, so the timer can be in an EXE and it doesn't have to be exported. While Windows NT doesn't have the same restrictions on what a timer callback can do as Windows, Microsoft still recommends that you limit your system calls to the above list plus **EnterCriticalSection**, **PostThreadMessage**, **LeaveCritical-Section** and **SetEvent**.

Performing Multimedia File I/O

The Windows multimedia file I/O (mmio) services provide buffered and unbuffered file I/O and support for a "standard" multimedia file format, Resource Interchange File Format (RIFF). You can extend the mmio services with custom I/O procedures, and those procedures can be shared among applications. The mmio functions are listed in Table 7-7.

The basic mmio services—**mmioOpen**, **mmioClose**, **mmioRead**, **mmioWrite**, **mmioSeek**, and **mmioRename**—do pretty much what you might expect. If you enable buffering when you call **mmioOpen**, you can use the additional functions **mmioAdvance**, **mmioFlush**, **mmioGetInfo**, **mmioSetBuffer**, and **mmioSetInfo** to control the buffering. If you are working with a RIFF file, you can take advantage of the extra support for RIFF *chunks* with **mmioDescend**, **mmioAscend**, and **mmioCreateChunk**.

A RIFF chunk is just a tagged binary segment: each chunk has a four-character code (FOURCC) tag and a DWORD size followed by the actual data in a byte stream.

Table 7-7   Multimedia File I/O Functions

Name	Function
mmioAdvance	Advance direct I/O buffer.
mmioAscend	Ascend out of RIFF chunk.
mmioClose	Close MM file.
mmioCreateChunk	Create RIFF file chunk.
mmioDescend	Descend into RIFF chunk.
mmioFlush	Flush MM I/O buffer to disk.
mmioFOURCC	Convert four characters to FOURC.
mmioGetInfo	Retrieve MM file info.
mmioInstallOProc	Install or remove custom I/O procedure.
mmioOpen	Open a multimedia file.
MMIOProc	MMIO callback procedure.
mmioRead	Read from a file.
mmioRename	Rename a multimedia file.
mmioSeek	Change current file position.
mmioSendMessage	Send message to I/O procedure.
mmioSetBuffer	Control I/O buffering.
mmioSetInfo	Set file information.
mmioStringToFOURCC	Convert string to four-character code.
mmioWrite	Write to a file.

You can convert four individual characters into a FOURCC code with **mmioFOURCC**, and convert a string into a FOURCC with **mmioStringToFOURCC**.

The **mmioOpen** function has a rather interesting specification:

```
HMMIO mmioOpen(szFilename, lpmmioinfo, dwOpenFlags)

LPSTR  szFilename

Specifies a far pointer to a string containing the filename of the
file to open. If no I/O procedure is specified to open the file,
then the filename determines how the file is opened, as follows:

•  If the filename does not contain "+", then it is assumed to be
   the name of a MS-DOS file.
•  If the filename is of the form "FNAME.EXT+boo", then the exten-
   sion "EXT " is assumed to identify an installed I/O procedure
   which is called to perform I/O on the file.
```

- If the filename is NULL and no I/O procedure is given, then adwInfo[0] is assumed to be the MS-DOS file handle of a currently open file.

The MS-DOS filename should not be longer than 128 bytes, including the terminating NULL. When opening a memory file, set szFilename to NULL.

LPMMIOINFO lpmmioinfo

Specifies a far pointer to an MMIOINFO structure containing extra parameters used by mmioOpen. Unless you are opening a memory file, specifying the size of a buffer for buffered I/O, or specifying an uninstalled I/O procedure to open a file, this parameter should be NULL.

If lpmmioinfo is not NULL, all unused fields of the MMIOINFO structure it references must be set to zero, including the reserved fields.

DWORD dwOpenFlags

Specifies option flags for the open operation. The MMIO_READ, MMIO_WRITE, and MMIO_READWRITE flags are mutually exclusive—only one should be specified. The MMIO_COMPAT, MMIO_EXCLUSIVE, MMIO_DENYWRITE, MMIO_DENYREAD, and MMIO_DENYNONE flags are MS-DOS file-sharing flags, and can only be used if file-sharing support is present.

MMIO_READ

Opens the file for reading only. This is the default, if MMIO_WRITE and MMIO_READWRITE are not specified.

MMIO_WRITE

Opens the file for writing. You should not read from a file opened in this mode.

MMIO_READWRITE

Opens the file for both reading and writing.

MMIO_CREATE

Creates a new file. If the file already exists, it is truncated to zero length. For memory files, MMIO_CREATE indicates the end of the file is initially at the start of the buffer.

MMIO_DELETE

Deletes a file. If this flag is specified, szFilename should not be NULL. The return value will be TRUE (cast to HMMIO) if the file was deleted successfully, FALSE otherwise. Do not call mmioClose for a

file that has been deleted. If this flag is specified, all other
flags are ignored.

MMIO_PARSE

Creates a fully qualified filename from the path specified in
szFileName. The fully qualified filename is placed back into
szFileName. The return value will be TRUE (cast to HMMIO) if the
qualification was successful, FALSE otherwise. The file is not
opened, and the function does not return a valid MMIO file handle,
so do not attempt to close the file. If this flag is specified, all
other file opening flags are ignored.

MMIO_EXIST

Determines whether the specified file exists and creates a fully
qualified filename from the path specified in szFileName. The fully
qualified filename is placed back into szFileName. The return value
will be TRUE (cast to HMMIO) if the qualification was successful and
the file exists, FALSE otherwise. The file is not opened, and the
function does not return a valid MMIO file handle, so do not attempt
to close the file.

MMIO_ALLOCBUF

Opens a file for buffered I/O. To allocate a buffer larger or
smaller than the default buffer size (8K), set the cchBuffer field
of the MMIOINFO structure to the desired buffer size. If cchBuffer
is zero, then the default buffer size is used. If you are providing
your own I/O buffer, then the MMIO_ALLOCBUF flag should not be used.

MMIO_COMPAT

Opens the file with compatibility mode, allowing any process on a
given machine to open the file any number of times. mmioOpen fails
if the file has been opened with any of the other sharing modes.

MMIO_EXCLUSIVE

Opens the file with exclusive mode, denying other processes both
read and write access to the file. mmioOpen fails if the file has
been opened in any other mode for read or write access, even by the
current process.

MMIO_DENYWRITE

Opens the file and denies other processes write access to the file.
mmioOpen fails if the file has been opened in compatibility or for
write access by any other process.

MMIO_DENYREAD

Opens the file and denies other processes read access to the file.
mmioOpen fails if the file has been opened in compatibility mode or

for read access by any other process.

MMIO_DENYNONE

Opens the file without denying other processes read or write access to the file. mmioOpen fails if the file has been opened in compatibility mode by any other process.

MMIO_GETTEMP

Creates a temporary filename, optionally using the parameters passed in szFileName to determine the temporary name. For example, you can specify "C:F" to create a filename for a temporary file residing on drive C, with the filename starting with letter F. The resulting filename is placed in the buffer pointed to by szFileName. The return value will be TRUE (cast to HMMIO) if the temporary filename was created successfully, FALSE otherwise. The file is not opened, and the function does not return a valid MMIO file handle, so do not attempt to close the file. This flag overrides all other flags.

Return Value

The return value is a handle to the opened file. This handle is not a MS-DOS file handle—do not use it with any file I/O functions other than MMIO functions.

If the file cannot be opened, the return value is NULL. If lpmmioinfo is not NULL, then its wErrorRet field will contain extended error information returned by the I/O procedure.

Comments

If lpmmioinfo references an MMIOINFO structure, set up the fields as described below. All unused fields must be set to zero, including reserved fields.

- To request that a file be opened with an installed I/O procedure, set the fccIOProc field to the four-character code of the I/O procedure, and set the pIOProc field to NULL.
- To request that a file be opened with an uninstalled I/O procedure, set the pIOProc field to point to the I/O procedure, and set fccIOProc to NULL.
- To request that mmioOpen determine which I/O procedure to use to open the file based on the filename contained in szFilename, set both fccIOProc and pIOProc to NULL. This is the default behavior if no MMIOINFO structure is specified.
- To open a memory file using an internally allocated and managed buffer, set the pchBuffer field to NULL, fccIOProc to FOURCC_MEM, cchBuffer to the initial size of the buffer, and adwInfo[0] to the incremental expansion size of the buffer. This memory file will automatically be expanded in increments of adwInfo[0] bytes when necessary. Specify the MMIO_CREATE flag for the dwOpenFlags parameter to initially set the end of the file to be the beginning of the buffer.

- To open a memory file using a caller-supplied buffer, set the chBuffer field to point to the memory buffer, fccIOProc to FOURCC_MEM, cchBuffer to the size of the buffer, and adwInfo[0] to the incremental expansion size of the buffer. The expansion size in adwInfo[0] should only be non-zero if pchBuffer is a pointer obtained by calling GlobalAlloc and GlobalLock, since GlobalReAlloc will be called to expand the buffer. In particular, if pchBuffer points to a local or global array, a block of memory in the local heap, or a block of memory allocated by GlobalDosAlloc, adwInfo[0] must be zero.
- Specify the MMIO_CREATE flag for the dwOpenFlags parameter to initially set the end of the file to be the beginning of the buffer;otherwise, the entire block of memory will be considered readable.
- To use a currently open MS-DOS file handle with MMIO, set the fccIOProc field to FOURCC_DOS, pchBuffer to NULL, and adwInfo[0] to the MS-DOS file handle. Note that offsets within the file will be relative to the beginning of the file, and will not depend on the MS-DOS file position at the time mmioOpen is called; the initial MMIO offset will be the same as the MS-DOS offset when mmioOpen is called. Later, to close the MMIO file handle without closing the MS-DOS file handle, pass the MMIO_FHOPEN flag to mmioClose.

You must call mmioClose to close a file opened with mmioOpen. Open files are not automatically closed when an application exits.

Did you catch the stuff about memory files? automatic and user-supplied buffers? How about the custom I/O procedures? They're documented separately:

```
LPMMIOPROC mmioInstallIOProc(fccIOProc, pIOProc, dwFlags)

FOURCC  fccIOProc

Specifies a four-character code identifying the I/O procedure to
install, remove, or locate. All characters in this four-character
code should be uppercase characters.

LPMMIOPROC  pIOProc

Specifies the address of the I/O procedure to install. To remove or
locate an I/O procedure, set this parameter to NULL.

DWORD  dwFlags

Specifies one of the following flags indicating whether the I/O
procedure is being installed, removed, or located:

MMIO_INSTALLPROC

Installs the specified I/O procedure. To allow other procedures to
```

use the specified I/O procedure, also specify the MMIO_GLOBALPROC flag.

MMIO_REMOVEPROC

Removes the specified I/O procedure. When removing a global I/O procedure, only the task that registers a global I/O procedure can unregister that procedure.

MMIO_FINDPROC

Searches local, then global procedures for the specified I/O procedure.

MMIO_GLOBALPROC

Identifies the I/O procedure being installed as a global procedure.

Return Value

The return value is the address of the I/O procedure installed, removed, or located. If there is an error, the return value is NULL.

Callback

LRESULT FAR PASCAL IOProc(lpmmioinfo, wMsg, lParam1, lParam2)

IOProc is a placeholder for the application-supplied function name. The actual name must be exported by including it in a EXPORTS statement in the application's module-definitions file.

Callback Parameters

LPSTR   lpmmioinfo

Specifies a far pointer to an MMIOINFO structure containing information about the open file. The I/O procedure must maintain the lDiskOffsetfield in this structure to indicate the file offset to the next read or write location. The I/O procedure can use the adwInfo[] field to store state information. The I/O procedure should not modify any other fields of the MMIOINFO structure.

UINT   wMsg

Specifies a message indicating the requested I/O operation. Messages that can be received include MMIOM_OPEN, MMIOM_CLOSE, MMIOM_READ, MMIOM_WRITE, and MMIOM_SEEK.

LPARAM   lParam1

Specifies a parameter for the message.

LPARAM   lParam2

Specifies a parameter for the message.

Callback Return Value

The return value depends on the message specified by wMsg. If the
I/O procedure does not recognize a message, it should return zero.

Comments

If the I/O procedure resides in the application, use MakeProc-
Instance to get a procedure-instance address and specify this
address for pIOProc. You don't need to get a procedure-instance
address if the I/O procedure resides in a DLL (or under Win32).

The four-character code specified by the fccIOProc field in the
MMIOINFO structure associated with a file identifies a filename
extension for a custom storage system. When an application calls
mmioOpen with a filename such as "FNAME.XYZ!boo", the I/O procedure
associated with the four-character code "XYZ "is called to open
the "boo" element of the file FNAME.XYZ.

The mmioInstallIOProc function maintains a separate list of
installed I/O procedures for each Windows application. Therefore,
different applications can use the same I/O procedure identifier
for different I/O procedures without conflict. To share an I/O
procedure among applications, each application can install and use
local copies of the I/O procedure or one application can install
a blobal copy of the I/O procedure for one or more applications to
use. To use multiple, local copies of an I/O procedure among several
applications, the I/O procedure must reside in a DLL called by each
application using it. Each application using the shared I/O procedure must call mmioInstallIOProc to install the procedure (or call
the DLL to install the procedure on behalf of the application).Each
application must call mmioInstallIOProc to remove the I/O procedure
before terminating.

If an application calls mmioInstallIOProc more than once to register
the same I/O procedure, then it must call mmioInstallIOProc to
remove the procedure once for each time it installed the procedure.
mmioInstallIOProc will not prevent an application from installing
two different I/O procedures with the same identifier, or installing
an I/O procedure with one of the predefined identifiers ("DOS ",
"MEM ", or "BND "). The most recently installed procedure takes
precedence, and the most recently installed procedure is the first
one to get removed.

To use a single copy of an I/O procedure among several applications,
one application must install the I/O procedure as a global procedure. The other applications locate the global procedure before they
use it. An application that installs a global I/O procedure can,
without regard to other applications using the procedure, unregister
that procedure at any time.An application installs a global copy of
an I/O procedure by calling mmioInstallIOProc with the flags
MMIO_INSTALLPROC and MMIO_GLOBALPROC. Once an application globally

installs a procedure, that application can use the global procedure.
To unregister a procedure, the application that installed the procedure must call mmioInstallIOProc.

Other applications must locate an installed, global I/O procedure
before using it. To locate a global procedure, an application calls
mmioInstallIOProc with the flag MMIO_FINDPROC. Once an application
locates the global procedure, it can call the procedure as needed.
Applications that use, but do not install, a global I/O procedure,
are exempt from actions to unregister that procedure.

So, what's a custom I/O procedure good for? For one thing, it doesn't have to operate on a file—it could read and write chunks from a database or a compressed archive. For another thing, it lets you add totally new and different file formats without changing any existing code.

Let's reconsider our infamous image-processing program. If we'd done the file-reading code with mmio functions, we could have opened any sort of image file format with **mmioOpen** and read it with **mmioRead**. Each file format we supported—GIF, PCX, TIFF, VICAR, and so on—would have its own custom I/O procedure registered that would automatically be used when appropriate. You'll remember that we were struggling somewhat to find an architecture that would do this for us back in Chapter 4: well, here it is. We don't need C++, we don't need object-oriented programming: there's already an API that does what we want. And yes, it is supported in Win32 as well as 16-bit Windows: in fact, the Win32 version supports Unicode as well as Windows ANSI strings for filenames.

We should also at least mention the subject of memory files. When you're working with media like waveform audio, a chunk of information can potentially be quite large. You have to trade off between speed and capacity at every step of the way: a waveform editor that works with its data entirely in memory will be faster than one that works on disk files, but have much smaller capacity. A memory file gives you a way to use the same logic in memory as you would on disk: if the data will fit in memory, go ahead and put it in a memory file, but if it won't, write it to a temporary disk file. In either case, the mmio file handle you pass around will be valid, and all the logic for reading and writing the file will be the same.

If you've been paying attention, you might wonder how multimedia memory files relate to Windows NT memory-mapped files. If you're writing solely for Windows NT, you might find the Win32 functions more efficient; if you want to write code that can work in either a Win16 or Win32 program, the mmio functions might be a better choice.

I don't have space to do full justice to all the ins and outs of mmio, but this introduction should get you started. Now let's consider generating files: specifically our favorite kind of file, the DIB.

Drawing in a DIB Device Context

I've had quite a bit of e-mail from readers of *Advanced Windows Programming* who were stimulated by some of my "road not taken" comments and want to know what Windows API lets you write directly into a DIB (device-independent bitmap). That's actually a wrong question, which is why it's so hard for them to find the answer. There is no function for this: it's a device driver.

The Windows MultiMedia Extensions and Windows 3.1 include DIB.DRV, which turns a memory DIB into a DIB device context. To use it, create a DIB in memory and lock it down. Then use the pointer to the DIB memory in a CreateDC call for the "DIB" device:

```
hdcMyDIB = CreateDC( "DIB", NULL, NULL, (LPSTR)lpbiMyDIB);
```

Once the DIB device context has been created, you can use its handle to draw in it with any GDI function. When you're done, delete the device context and display or save the underlying memory DIB. This procedure is quite useful—it lets you, for instance, create 24-bit color images even if you only have an 8-bit display adapter. It can also make quick work of jobs like adding titles to an image, or creating bitmaps of very complex geometric shapes.

For example, I used the DIB device context in *Room Planner* to allow the user to save the current drawing as a DIB:

```
//Save the current room layout to a file as a bitmapped image
#include "rpdefs.h"
#include "declare.h"
#include "rpobject.h"
#include <commdlg.h>
#include "showdib.h"
#include <string.h>
#include <stdio.h>

extern int  dxFile, dyFile;
extern BOOL bPainting;
HANDLE CreateDib(HANDLE hdib,int dx, int dy,int ncolors);
RGBTRIPLE DefaultPalette[16]={
    { 0,      0,      0 },
    { 0,      0,      255 },
    { 0,      255,    0 },
    { 0,      255,    255 },
    { 255,    0,      0 },
    { 255,    0,      255 },
    { 255,    255,    0 },
    { 255,    255,    255 },
    { 85, 85, 255 },
    { 85, 85, 85 },
```

```
    { 0,       170,    0 },
    { 170,     0,      0 },
    { 85, 255,      255 },
    { 255,     85, 255 },
    { 255,     255,    85 },
    { 255,     255,    255 }
    };
#define ALIGNULONG(i)   ((i+3)/4*4)
#define WIDTHBYTES(i)   ((i+31)/32*4)

void SaveImage(HANDLE hInst,HWND hWnd,char *current_function_name,
            char *current_room_name)
{
OPENFILENAME ofn;
char szDirName[256];
char szFile[256], szFileTitle[256];
UINT  i=0, cbString=0;
char  chReplace;      /* string separator for szFilter */
char  szFilter[256];
HFILE hf=NULL;
HANDLE hDib=NULL;
LPBITMAPINFOHEADER lpbi=NULL;
HDC hdcNew = NULL;
RGBQUAD FAR *prgb = NULL;

  //Get file name for save
  memset(&ofn, 0, sizeof(OPENFILENAME));
  szDirName[0] = szFileTitle[0] = szFile[0] = '\0';
  ofn.lStructSize = sizeof(OPENFILENAME);
  ofn.hwndOwner = hWnd;
  ofn.lpstrFilter = "Bitmaps\0*.bmp\0PCX Files\0*.pcx\0";
  ofn.lpstrFile= szFile;
  ofn.nMaxFile = sizeof(szFile);
  ofn.lpstrFileTitle = szFileTitle;
  ofn.nMaxFileTitle = sizeof(szFileTitle);
  ofn.lpstrInitialDir = szDirName;
  ofn.Flags = OFN_OVERWRITEPROMPT;
  if (!GetSaveFileName(&ofn))
      return;
#ifdef DEBUG
  MessageBox(hWnd,szFile,"File to save",MB_OK);
#endif

  //create memory DIB
  SetCursorHourglass();
  dxFile = 640;
  dyFile = 480;
  hDib = CreateDib(NULL,dxFile,dyFile,16);
  if(!hDib) {
      MessageBeep(0);
      MessageBox(hWnd,"Could not create memory DIB",
          "Save Image",MB_OK);
```

```
                goto cleanup;
            }
      lpbi = (LPBITMAPINFOHEADER)GlobalLock(hDib);
    if(!lpbi) {
        MessageBeep(0);
        MessageBox(hWnd,"Could not lock memory DIB",
            "Save Image",MB_OK);
        goto cleanup;
        }

    //set standard palette into DIB
    prgb = (RGBQUAD FAR *)((LPBYTE)lpbi + lpbi->biSize);
    for(i=0;i<lpbi->biClrUsed;i++) {
        prgb[i].rgbRed = DefaultPalette[i].rgbtRed;
        prgb[i].rgbGreen = DefaultPalette[i].rgbtGreen;
        prgb[i].rgbBlue = DefaultPalette[i].rgbtBlue;
        prgb[i].rgbReserved = 0;
        }

    //Open DIB DC

    hdcNew = CreateDC("DIB", NULL, NULL, (LPSTR)lpbi);
      if(hdcNew == NULL) {
        MessageBeep(0);
        if((lpbi->biBitCount == 24) ||
           (lpbi->biCompression != BI_RGB)) {
            MessageBox(hWnd,"Could not create DIB DC\n"
                "DIB format not supported","Save Image",MB_OK);
          }
        else {
            MessageBox(hWnd,"Could not create DIB DC\n"
                "Can't load DIB driver","Save Image",MB_OK);
          }
        goto cleanup;
      }

    //Paint room layout into DIB DC, unlock DIB

    PatBlt(hdcNew,0,0,dxFile,dyFile,WHITENESS);//clear DIB to white
    UnsetCursorHourglass();
    do SpinTheMessageLoop();//allow pending repaints to finish
        while (bPainting);
    RP_Paint(hWnd, hdcNew, TRUE);   //paint into DIB
    SetCursorHourglass();
    if(lpbi) {
        GlobalUnlock(hDib);
        lpbi = NULL;
        }

    //Write memory DIB to file

    if(strstr(szFile,".DIB")||strstr(szFile,".dib")
    || strstr(szFile,".BMP")||strstr(szFile,".bmp"))
```

```
        WriteDIB(szFile,hDib);
    else if(strstr(szFile,".PCX")||strstr(szFile,".pcx"))
        WritePCX(szFile,hDib);    //note: not included in this listing
    else {
        MessageBeep(0);
        OkMsgBox("Save Image",
            "Unrecognized file type in file:\n%s",szFile);
        }
cleanup:
    if(hdcNew)
        DeleteDC(hdcNew);
    if(lpbi)
        GlobalUnlock(hDib);
    if(hDib)
        GlobalFree(hDib);
    UnsetCursorHourglass();
}

/* CreateDib(hdib, dx, dy, ncolors)
 * NOTE EXTRA ncolors parameter — mh
 *
 * Creates a DIB with the same header and color table as the
 * original DIB, with sufficient space to hold the indicated
 * region.
 *
 * If the <hdib> is NULL, creates a DIB header and uninitialized
 * color table.
 */

HANDLE CreateDib(
    HANDLE hdib,      // DIB to copy or NULL
    int dx, int dy,   // Size of new DIB or -1 to use originals
    int ncolors)      // Number of colors or -1 for default
{
    HANDLE              hdibN;
    BITMAPINFOHEADER    bi;
    LPBITMAPINFOHEADER  lpbi1;
    LPBITMAPINFOHEADER  lpbi2;
    RGBQUAD FAR *       pRgb1;
    RGBQUAD FAR *       pRgb2;

    if (hdib)                      // Copy DIB header or create a new one
    {
        DibInfo(hdib,&bi);
    }
    else
    {
        bi.biSize        = sizeof(BITMAPINFOHEADER);
        bi.biPlanes      = 1;
        bi.biBitCount    = 8;
        bi.biWidth       = 0;
        bi.biHeight      = 0;
```

```
        bi.biCompression   = BI_RGB;
        bi.biSizeImage     = 0;
        bi.biXPelsPerMeter = 0;
        bi.biYPelsPerMeter = 0;
        bi.biClrUsed       = 256;
        bi.biClrImportant  = 0;
    }


    if (dx != -1) // Use specified measurements or original extents
        bi.biWidth = dx;

    if (dy != -1)
        bi.biHeight = dy;

    if (ncolors != -1) {              //mh modification
      bi.biClrUsed = ncolors;
      if (ncolors <= 1)
     bi.biBitCount = 1;
       else if (ncolors <= 16)
          bi.biBitCount = 4;
       else if (ncolors <= 256)
          bi.biBitCount = 8;
       else
          bi.biBitCount = 24;
      }
    bi.biSizeImage = WIDTHBYTES(bi.biWidth*bi.biBitCount)
                         * (long)dy;

    hdibN = GlobalAlloc(GHND,sizeof(BITMAPINFOHEADER) +
                (long)bi.biClrUsed * sizeof(RGBQUAD) +
                 bi.biSizeImage);

    /*  Copy the color table across if valid */

    if (hdibN && hdib)
    {
        lpbi1 = (VOID FAR*)GlobalLock(hdibN);
        lpbi2 = (VOID FAR*)GlobalLock(hdib);

        *lpbi1 = bi;

        pRgb1 = (VOID FAR *)((LPSTR)lpbi1 + lpbi1->biSize);
        pRgb2 = (VOID FAR *)((LPSTR)lpbi2 + lpbi2->biSize);

        while (bi.biClrUsed- > 0)
            *pRgb1++ = *pRgb2++;

        GlobalUnlock(hdib);
        GlobalUnlock(hdibN);
    }
    else if (hdibN)      //otherwise just initialize header
    {
```

```
        lpbi1 = (VOID FAR*)GlobalLock(hdibN);
        *lpbi1 = bi;
        GlobalUnlock(hdibN);
    }
    return hdibN;
}
```

Using Enhanced Metafiles

We've just seen how a device-independent bitmap can be a memory object, a file, and a device context. Another Windows object, the metafile, has the same characteristics. A metafile is a collection of structures that store a picture in a scalable, device-independent format. Paint programs manipulate bitmaps; drawing programs manipulate metafiles—or some equivalent.

Win32 supports two metafile formats: a basic format that is compatible with Windows 3 metafiles, and an enhanced metafile format. The difference between the two is that the enhanced metafile contains enough information to provide true device independence—and the Windows metafile does not.

Table 7-8   Enhanced Metafile Functions

Name	Function
CloseEnhMetaFile	Closes an enhanced metafile DC.
CopyEnhMetaFile	Copies an enhanced metafile.
CreateEnhMetaFile	Creates an enhanced metafile DC.
DeleteEnhMetaFile	Invalidates enhanced metafile handle.
EnhMetaFileProc	Processes enhanced metafile data.
EnumEnhMetaFile	Returns GDI calls within an enhanced metafile.
GdiComment	Adds a comment to an enhanced metafile.
GetEnhMetaFile	Creates an enhanced metafile.
GetEnhMetaFileBits	Copies enhanced metafile bits to a buffer.
GetEnhMetaFileDescription	Returns creator and title for enhanced metafile.
GetEnhMetaFileHeader	Returns enhanced metafile header.
GetEnhMetaFilePaletteEntries	Returns enhanced metafile palette entries.
GetWinMetaFileBits	Retrieves metafile contents in Windows format.
PlayEnhMetaFile	Plays an enhanced metafile to a DC.
PlayEnhMetaFileRecord	Plays an enhanced metafile record.
SetEnhMetaFileBits	Creates a memory-based enhanced metafile from data.
SetWinMetaFileBits	Creates enhanced metafile from Windows metafile data.

You can always convert a Windows metafile to an enhanced metafile, using **Set-WinMetaFileBits**. You can also perform a limited conversion of enhanced metafiles to Windows metafiles from Win32, generally by walking the enhanced metafiles and converting each GDI call. Enhanced metafiles cannot be read by Windows 3.1 programs—but they're actually good enough to use for their intended purpose, which more than makes up for the incompatibility.

The enhanced metafile format consists of a header, a table of handles to GDI objects, a private palette, and an array of metafile records. The Windows metafile format consists of a header and an array of metafile records. You manipulate enhanced metafiles using the functions given in Table 7-8, and Windows metafiles using the functions listed in Table 7-9. We won't say any more about Windows metafiles: they were never very useful.

To create an enhanced metafile, first get a reference device context—typically the screen device context, obtained by calling **GetDC**. Use the reference DC to determine the characteristics of the metafile. Then call **CreateEnhMetaFile** to create the metafile device context, and release the reference device context. The syntax of **CreateEnhMetaFile** is:

```
HDC CreateEnhMetaFile(hdcRef, lpFilename, lpRect, lpDesc)

HDC hdcRef;          /* handle of a reference device context   */
LPTSTR lpFilename;   /* address of a filename string           */
```

Table 7-9   Windows Metafile Functions

Name	Function
CloseMetaFile	Closes a Windows metafile DC.
CopyMetaFile	Copies a Windows metafile.
CreateMetaFile	Creates a Windows metafile DC.
DeleteMetaFile	Invalidates Windows metafile handle.
EnumMetaFile	Returns GDI calls within a Windows metafile.
EnumMetaFileProc	Processes metafile data.
GetMetaFile	Creates a Windows metafile.
GetMetaFileBitsEx	Copies Windows metafile bits to a buffer.
PlayMetaFile	Plays a Windows metafile to a DC.
PlayMetaFileRecord	Plays a Windows metafile record.
SetMetaFileBitsEx	Creates a memory-based Windows metafile from data.
GetMetaFileBits	Obsolete; use GetMetaFileBitsEx.
SetMetaFileBits	Obsolete; use SetMetaFileBitsEx.

```
LPRECT lpRect;       /* address of a bounding rectangle */
LPTSTR lpDesc;       /* address of an optional description string  */
```

The CreateEnhMetaFile function creates a device context (DC) for an enhanced-format metafile. This DC can be used to store a device-independent picture.

Parameter Description

hdcRef

Identifies a reference device for the enhanced metafile.

lpFilename

Points to the filename for the enhanced metafile to be created. If this parameter is NULL, the enhanced metafile is memory based and its contents are lost when it is deleted by using the DeleteEnh-MetaFile function.

lpRect
Points to a RECT structure that specifies the dimensions (in .01-millimeter units) of the picture to be stored in the enhanced metafile.

lpDescription

Points to a string that specifies the name of the application that created the picture, as well as the picture's title.

Returns

If the function succeeds, the return value is a handle of the device context for the enhanced metafile; otherwise, it is NULL.

Comments

Where text arguments must use Unicode characters, use this function as a wide-character function. Where text arguments must use characters from the Windows 3.x character set, use this function as an ANSI function.

Windows uses the reference device identified by the hdcRef parameter to record the resolution and units of the device on which a picture originally appeared. If the hdcRef parameter is NULL, it uses the current display device for reference.

The left and top members of the RECT structure pointed to by the lpRect parameter must be less than the right and bottom members, respectively. Points along the edges of the rectangle are included in the picture. If lpRect is NULL, the graphics device interface (GDI) computes the dimensions of the smallest rectangle that surrounds the picture drawn by the application. The lpRect parameter should be provided where possible.

The string pointed to by the lpDescription parameter must contain a null character between the application name and the picture name and must terminate with two null characters—for example, "XYZ Graphics Editor\0Bald Eagle\0\0", where \0 represents the null character. If lpDescription is NULL, there is no corresponding entry in the enhanced-metafile header.

Applications use the DC created by this function to store a graphics picture in an enhanced metafile. The handle identifying this DC can be passed to any GDI function. After an application stores a picture in an enhanced metafile, it can display the picture on any output device by calling the PlayEnhMetaFile function. When displaying the picture, Windows uses the rectangle pointed to by the lpRect parameter and the resolution data from the reference device to position and scale the picture.

The device context returned by this function contains the same default attributes associated with any new DC.

Applications must use the GetWinMetaFileBits function to convert an enhanced metafile to the older Windows metafile format.

The filename for the enhanced metafile should use the .EMF extension.

Once you've created the empty enhanced metafile, you need to draw your picture in the metafile device context (DC), which will automatically store it in the metafile. The difference between drawing in a metafile DC and a DIB or screen DC is that in the metafile DC each GDI call just causes a record to be added to the metafile—nothing is actually rendered. Rendering comes later, when you play back the metafile.

When you're done drawing in the metafile DC, you need to close the DC with **CloseEnhMetaFile**. The enhanced metafile handle returned by **CloseEnhMeta-File** can be used to render the metafile's picture on a screen or printer DC, copy the enhanced metafile, edit the enhanced metafile, and so on.

You can get a metafile handle for an existing enhanced metafile on disk using **GetEnhMetaFile**; this metafile handle is the same kind as is returned by **Close-EnhMetaFile**. You can render an enhanced metafile using **PlayEnhMetaFile**, as in the following Microsoft-supplied example:

```
LoadString(hInst, IDS_FILTERSTRING,
     (LPSTR)szFilter, sizeof(szFilter));

/*
 * Replace occurrences of '%' string separator
 * with '\0'.
 */

for (i=0; szFilter[i]!='\0'; i++)
```

```
      if (szFilter[i] == '%')
            szFilter[i] = '\0';

LoadString(hInst, IDS_DEFEXTSTRING,
      (LPSTR)szDefExt, sizeof(szFilter));


/*
 * Use the OpenFilename common dialog box
 * to obtain the desired filename.
 */

 szFile[0] = '\0';
 Ofn.lStructSize = sizeof(OPENFILENAME);

 Ofn.hwndOwner = hWnd;
 Ofn.lpstrFilter = szFilter;
 Ofn.lpstrCustomFilter = (LPSTR)NULL;
 Ofn.nMaxCustFilter = 0L;
 Ofn.nFilterIndex = 1L;
 Ofn.lpstrFile = szFile;
 Ofn.nMaxFile = sizeof(szFile);
 Ofn.lpstrFileTitle = szFileTitle;
 Ofn.nMaxFileTitle = sizeof(szFileTitle);
 Ofn.lpstrInitialDir = (LPSTR) NULL;
 Ofn.lpstrTitle = (LPSTR)NULL;
 Ofn.Flags = OFN_SHOWHELP | OFN_PATHMUSTEXIST | OFN_FILEMUSTEXIST;

 Ofn.nFileOffset = 0;
 Ofn.nFileExtension = 0;
 Ofn.lpstrDefExt = szDefExt;

 GetOpenFileName(&Ofn);

/* Open the metafile. */

hemf = GetEnhMetaFile(Ofn.lpstrFile);

/* Retrieve a handle to a window DC. */

hDC = GetDC(hWnd);

/* Retrieve the client rectangle dimensions. */

GetClientRect(hWnd, &rct);

/* Draw the picture. */

PlayEnhMetaFile(hDC, hemf, &rct);

/* Release the metafile handle. */

DeleteEnhMetaFile(hemf);

/* Release the window DC. */

ReleaseDC(hWnd, hDC);
```

As you can surmise from the example, when you're done with the enhanced metafile handle, you release it with **DeleteEnhMetaFile**. Don't be scared by the name: the file is deleted from memory, *not* from disk.

Editing an enhanced metafile requires heavy use of **EnumEnhMetaFile** and a callback function to operate on the enumerated metafile records. The **EnhMetaFile-Proc** callback can play back, copy, or ignore each record, but cannot change the records it receives. It *can* change the copies it makes, however. The actual mechanics of editing the metafile are pretty complex—it's hit-testing and bounding-box calculation out the ears.

Onward and Upward with the Arts

In this chapter we've gone from *Ren and Stimpy* and *Star Trek* to the Media Control Interface, and thence to the heights and depths of waveform audio. We've explored MIDI and Aux, learned to use timers, mapped the tracts of RIFF files and multimedia file I/O, and learned to draw in DIB and enhanced metafile device contexts.

An interesting trip, even though we haven't explored half of the interesting areas. But we must move ever onward. Now, comrades, we're off to the wilds of Pen Windows.

8

In which we learn to support Pens, Ink, and Tablets.

The Pen Is Mightier

· ·

Windows for Pen Computing was introduced with great hoopla at a breakfast during Windows World in Chicago in the spring of 1992. Hundreds of press people watched as Bill Gates "appeared" on Wayne and Garth's cable TV show with Pen computers of all shapes and sizes, from portable tablets with wireless LAN connections to giant whiteboards. It was the most relaxed I'd seen Bill in a long time—and despite the corny format, it was a fairly compelling demonstration of what can be done with handwritten input. In addition to showing us the variety of hardware and software coming to fruition in the Pen world, the skit brought out the importance of gestures— symbols drawn to execute commands, which add an amazing directness to the Pen user interface.

Since then Windows for Pen Computing has had only a limited niche in the bigger world of Windows. Part of the problem has been that handwriting recognition needs a lot of computing power, which has been difficult to package in a lightweight, battery-operated tablet form factor.

Perhaps because Pens have not taken the world by storm, there are no Pen extensions to Win32—at least not yet. On the other hand, I think that there will eventually be 32-bit versions of the Pen APIs.

I think this has to happen because Pen input generates a lot of data and requires a lot of processing power. As we discussed near the beginning of this book, applications that are CPU-bound and deal with big chunks of data get boosts to the range of twice to five times their 16-bit speed when you move them to 32-bit code. Doubling the recognition speed in a Pen computer without increasing the power consumption would go a long way toward boosting the acceptance of the whole technology.

So, I'm going to write about the current 16-bit version of Windows for Pen Computing in the full expectation that a 32-bit version will come along soon. With any luck, the 32-bit version will look identical to the programmer and look faster to the user.

Setting up a Pen Environment

First, though, I should tell you how to fake a Windows for Pens environment on your standard Windows installation, on the assumption that you won't necessarily want to run out right away and buy a pen computer for testing. But understand, this fakery doesn't give you the real feel of Pen computers.

The key design element of Pen computers is that the visual feedback you get is just like writing on paper. You hold a stylus that feels like a pen and looks like a pen, you write on a tablet that has the shape of a piece of paper, and you see what you are writing right underneath where you place the stylus.

This is important because it uses the eye-hand coordination for writing that most people develop in school. By contrast, writing with a stylus on an opaque tablet (of the sort used in CAD work) requires you to do something with your hand in one place while looking at the screen for feedback. That uses your writing muscles, but requires you to learn a new and more difficult kind of eye-hand coordination.

Writing with a mouse, which is what you'll have to do if you don't want to invest in a pen computer or tablet, is like writing with a bar of soap. The hand printing skills you learned in grade school won't help much: even if you're already good at pointing with a mouse, you'll find writing with it a challenge. Writing with a trackball is even worse, by the way.

Not only will writing be difficult with a mouse, the screen will have to be VGA. Sorry about that 24-bit color adapter or that high-speed, high-resolution accelerator: the SDK components for Pens include only a Pen-aware VGA driver. Other screen drivers and additional runtime software components are available only if you buy a Pen computer or a tablet with a Pen upgrade kit.

Understanding that what we'll get is a bad compromise, let's go over the steps needed to set up a minimal Windows for Pens environment on a standard Windows machine. Before you do anything else, please make backups of your SYSTEM.INI and WIN.INI files. It might not be a bad idea to back up *all* your INI and GRP files.

I'll assume that you have Windows installed and that you have a modern, professional 16-bit C compiler that includes Pen components for development purposes. In Microsoft Visual C++, these components are found in the MSVC\PEN directory. The principal component, PENWIN.DLL, is also to be found in the MSVC\-

REDIST directory, and possibly in your WINDOWS\SYSTEM directory as well. In other compilers that include Pen components—Borland C++ 3.1, Zortech C++ 3.1, and Watcom C/C++ 9.5—the arrangement of the files is a little different. You should be able to find the file PEN\README.TXT or README\PENWIN.TXT, and the file PENAPI-WH.HLP, by poking around a bit—if you actually installed the pen components when you installed your compiler. If not, you can install them now.

The README file should tell you how to set up two Pen configurations: a minimal configuration that only adds PENWIN.DLL to SYSTEM.INI, and a more complete configuration that adds PENWIN.DLL, VGAP.DRV (the Pen-enabled VGA driver), and YESMOUSE.DRV, a dummy driver that lets you use your mouse for writing. Read this file. Make sure you read the section about editing PENWIN.INI, and absolutely do edit PENWIN.INI so that it contains the correct paths to MARS.DLL and MARS.MOB, which you should verify as being present on your machine on the stated path, and definitely copy the edited PENWIN.INI to your WINDOWS directory. When you've got everything set up as described, restart Windows to get PENWIN.DLL to load. If you run into trouble, check your SYSTEM.INI and PENWIN.INI files, and double-check the location of each component referenced.

The Windows for Pens Architecture

You might well be wondering whether all this pen stuff is from Mars. Not quite: MARS.DLL is the Microsoft Alphanumeric Recognizer: it identifies hand-printed shapes as characters or gestures. The Windows for Pens architecture allows for multiple recognizers and multiple dictionaries. Dictionaries are used to help a recognizer identify handwritten characters in context.

In addition to the recognizer and dictionaries, the Pen system uses pen and display drivers, pen interface applets, and a central manager for all of the above, namely PENWIN.DLL. And by the way, PENWIN.DLL is the place most of the Pen API lives. PENWIN.LIB can be used to statically link to PENWIN.DLL, or you can dynamically link to PENWIN.DLL in a special way we'll describe shortly.

PENWIN.DLL is not an ordinary DLL, by the way: it is an installable driver, which means that it has to be loaded when Windows starts. If you try to link to it like a normal DLL, you'll get an error.

The basic data that flows from a pen is called ink. In fact, ink has two meanings in Windows for Pens. Inking refers to the process of drawing lines on the tablet display to the current pen location to give the illusion that the user is actually drawing on the screen. Ink proper refers to the data from the digitizing device—the stream of spatial coordinates, and possibly pressure and angle data, which describes where the pen has been. As you move the pen, the pen driver collects ink. As each ink point is collected, the pen driver passes it to the RC Manager (which we'll explain shortly), which in turn gives it to the display driver to be drawn.

Once a character, gesture, or word (depending on the current application settings) has been completed, the ink is passed to the recognizer for analysis. The recognizer compares the current ink to the character-drawing database for the current user and returns the recognized data to the application. The Microsoft recognizer, MARS, is a vector-based recognizer for handwritten characters in the ANSI character set, standard Pen Extensions gestures, and circled letters of the alphabet. MARS is trainable: Windows for Pens comes with the capability to recognize characters drawn in standard ways, but each user can train or customize the system to his or her handwriting.

Windows for Pens adds two new standard control classes that can replace the normal **edit** control: **hedit** and **bedit**. **Hedit** is a handwriting-enabled edit control; **bedit** is a boxed handwriting-enabled edit control. An application can add pen support by using these controls, by calling the high-level function **Process-Writing**, or by calling the lower-level function **Recognize**. Recognition is controlled by the **RC** data structure, and recognition results are returned in the **RCRESULT** data structure.

Basic Pen Application Design Considerations

If you build an application specifically for use with Pens, you will probably want to allow for some special design considerations that differ from the usual Windows design guidelines. To begin with, it is much harder to recognize handwriting than it is to accept typed input. That means you should offer selection options rather than text input when at all possible—combo boxes, list boxes, radio buttons, and action buttons are all preferable to having the user scribble something that your program then has to try to read.

Another consideration is that handwritten input takes more room than typed input. The typical 10- to 12-point type size for an edit control doesn't leave the user enough room to hand-print letters. You'll get better character recognition if you leave the user more room, and use a comb or boxed guide (a **bedit** control).

You'll also have to understand the platform. If the application is running on a tablet without a keyboard, you should avoid any user interface that *requires* a keyboard— remember, pen input is not 100 percent reliable. That same tablet probably has only 16 shades of gray for display, so don't rely on color in your interface. And the tablet probably has a limited battery life and system-level power management with idle detection: use the normal **GetMessage** or **WaitMessage**, not a **PeekMessage** loop, so that the system can tell you are idle and waiting for input.

Finally, allow for the difference between a stylus and a mouse. It is harder to double-click with a stylus than with a mouse: an interface that allows everything to be done with single clicks, even if that means adding extra buttons, will be easier to use. And it is harder to use menus with a stylus than it is to use buttons: extra buttons or toolbars are very helpful in pen applications.

If you're building more advanced, "Pencentric" applications, there are additional design considerations. You'll want to support things like dedicated areas for pen input, annotation layers that preserve the raw ink data, special recognizers for industry- or application-specific symbols, and application behavior that is sensitive to where and when the user writes on the tablet.

Something for Nothing

One interesting fact about Pen support is that you can get it for free, by doing exactly nothing to your Windows program. Any place your application currently has an "I-bar" cursor, such as in edit controls, will automatically accept input from the recognizer when Windows for Pens is present.

While you don't *have* to do anything special to get an ordinary Windows application to take advantage of Windows for Pens, you can, if you're willing to put in a little work, make it a much better Pen application without impairing it as a Windows application. Obviously, an unmodified Windows application won't allow for the special Pen design considerations we just discussed; a modified application can, and might even be a better Windows application. The balance of this chapter is devoted to explaining the various steps you can take toward "pen-enabling" your Windows application.

Activate the HEDIT and BEDIT Controls

I see the path from a Windows application to a totally Pen-aware application as having several discrete steps. The first of these is to detect the Pen environment and to use **hedit** and **bedit** controls where appropriate. The second is to control the recognition process. The third step is to use and store ink. There are more steps on the path, but they won't make a lot of sense until you've gotten to the third step.

If you're running on Windows 3.1 or above, you can find out if the Pen environment is present and retrieve a handle for PENWIN.DLL using the **SM_PENWINDOWS** system metric:

```
HANDLE hPenLib = NULL;
DWORD dwVersion = GetVersion();
BOOL fVersionOK= (LOBYTE(LOWORD(dwVersion)) == 3
   && HIBYTE(LOWORD(dwVersion)) >= 10)
   || LOBYTE(LOWORD(dwVersion)) > 3;
if(fVersionOK)
   hPenLib = GetSystemMetrics(SM_PENWINDOWS));
```

Note that we do *not* use the standard way of dynamically linking to a DLL (**LoadLibrary**). Why not? Think about it. PENWIN.DLL can be on a system whether or not it has a Pen. **LoadLibrary** would attempt to bring PENWIN.DLL into the system whether or not it was installed—big mistake.

If **hPenLib** is **NULL**, the pen environment is not available. Otherwise, you can get the addresses of the pen functions you'll need from the library, for instance:

```
(FARPROC)RegisterPenApp =
   GetProcAddress(hPenLib,"RegisterPenApp"));
(FARPROC)ProcessWriting =
   GetProcAddress(hPenLib,"ProcessWriting"));
```

Once you have the procedure addresses, you can call the procedures indirectly. Why not just link with PENWIN.LIB? Because you want to stay compatible with Penless Windows 3.1 systems. If you call PEN APIs directly, users without Pen systems will get a "Cannot find PENWIN.DLL" message when they try to run your program. That isn't what you want to happen.

Of course, you *could* ship PENWIN.DLL with your application. You'd have to install it with your setup program, and document the "Cannot find PENWIN.DLL" as meaning that the installation has been fouled up. You'd also have to be careful with your setup version detection, so that you didn't overwrite a later version of PENWIN.DLL or mess up an existing Windows for Pens installation. If you did all this, you *could* link with PENWIN.LIB, and skip all the dynamic linking we just discussed.

Whether you link to PENWIN.DLL statically or dynamically, the first Pen function to call is **RegisterPenApp**, which tells the Pen library to automatically convert all **edit** controls in the application to **hedit** controls. Calling it through a pointer looks like this:

```
(*RegisterPenApp)(RPA_DEFAULT, TRUE);
```

If you like, you can dispense with the indirect function notation and rely on the compiler to recognize the function name as a pointer, which makes the call look the same whether you linked to PENWIN.DLL dynamically or statically:

```
RegisterPenApp(RPA_DEFAULT, TRUE);
```

No matter how you call it on initialization, you'll have to call **RegisterPenApp** again with the second parameter set to **FALSE** before your application terminates, in order to unregister the application.

The **hedit** control does everything that an ordinary edit control can, and in addition automatically recognizes handwritten text and gestures. The **bedit** control is a lot like the **hedit** control, but it has boxes or a comb to give the user more space to write and help the recognizer separate individual characters and distinguish similar upper- and lowercase letter pairs, such as S/s, C/c, U/u, O/o, W/w, and K/k. You'll want to use **bedit** controls for improved recognition, whenever screen space and application considerations permit—**bedit** controls are larger than **hedit** controls, so they're most appropriate for relatively short, fixed-length fields.

One additional consideration: you should avoid automatic horizontal scrolling in edit fields that will be used with Pens. While automatic scrolling is useful for saving screen space in an edit field when the user has a keyboard, it turns out to be nearly impossible to scroll this sort of field with a pen.

You can dynamically change an **hedit** control to a **bedit** control by the simple expedient of destroying the **hedit** control window and creating a **bedit** control window with the same location, dimensions and control ID. However, the **bedit** control wants to have more room for writing, so you might have to tune your dialogs a bit. In addition, the **bedit** control comb might not be positioned correctly with respect to the text if the dialog font is not the default—which requires your application to do some calculations to fix up the **bedit** control's comb size and position using the **GUIDE** structure.

The **WM_INITDIALOG** section of the following code illustrates this process. It comes from the Microsoft DYNBEDIT sample program, which can be found on the MSDN CD-ROM and at Microsoft's archives on CompuServe and at **ftp.uu.net**, as well as on this book's companion diskette.

```
BOOL FAR PASCAL PenDlg (HWND hDlg,
                        unsigned message,
                        WORD wParam,
                        LONG lParam)
{
   switch (message)
   {
      case WM_INITDIALOG:
         {
         HWND  hEdit, hBEdit;
         char  szBuffer[32];
         RECT  DlgRect, EditRect;
         RECT  rect;
         RC    rc;
         int   NewcyBox;

         // Check to see if Pen Windows is running
         if (!bPenWin)
            return (TRUE);

         // Query the handle to the edit control, the text in the
         // edit control, and the dimensions.

         hEdit = GetDlgItem (hDlg, IDD_BEDIT);
         GetDlgItemText (hDlg, IDD_BEDIT,(LPSTR) szBuffer,
                 sizeof (szBuffer));
         GetWindowRect (hDlg, &DlgRect);
```

```
GetWindowRect (hEdit,&EditRect);
GetClientRect (hEdit, &rect);

// Destroy the original edit control
DestroyWindow (hEdit);

// Create the new bedit control
hBEdit = CreateWindow ((LPSTR)"bedit",
                        (LPSTR) szBuffer,
                        ES_AUTOHSCROLL | WS_TABSTOP |
                       WS_BORDER | WS_CHILD | WS_VISIBLE,
                        (EditRect.left - DlgRect.left),
                        (EditRect.top - DlgRect.top),
                        (rect.right - rect.left),
                        (rect.bottom - rect.top),
                         hDlg,
                         IDD_BEDIT,
                         ghInst,
                         NULL);
if (hBEdit == NULL)
    return (FALSE);

// Get the RC structure for the GUIDE structure.
SendMessage (hBEdit, WM_HEDITCTL, HE_GETRC,
            (long)(LPRC) &rc);
rc.guide.xOrigin = EditRect.left;
rc.guide.yOrigin = EditRect.top;

// New cyBox value  (height of one box)
NewcyBox = (rect.bottom - rect.top);

// Calc new cxBox value by changing window ratio
rc.guide.cxBox    = NewcyBox * rc.guide.cxBox /
                rc.guide.cyBox;

// Calc the new cyBase (distance from top of box to
// baseline)
rc.guide.cyBase   = NewcyBox * rc.guide.cyBase /
                rc.guide.cyBox;

// Set new cyBox value
rc.guide.cyBox    = NewcyBox;

// Calculate the number of cells that can fit in the bedit
rc.guide.cHorzBox = (rect.right - rect.left) /
                rc.guide.cxBox;

// replace the RC structure.
SendMessage (hBEdit, WM_HEDITCTL, HE_SETRC,
            (long)(LPRC) &rc);
}
return (TRUE);

case WM_COMMAND:
```

```
        if ((wParam == IDOK) ||      // "OK" box selected?
            (wParam == IDCANCEL))     // System menu close command?
        {
            EndDialog(hDlg, TRUE);    // Exits the dialog box
            return (TRUE);
        }
        break;
    }

    return (FALSE); // Didn't process a message
}
```

To completely understand the above example, we should probably know the contents of the **RC** and **GUIDE** structures, which are found in PENWIN.H:

```
/****** RC Definition *************/
#define CL_NULL            0
#define CL_MINIMUM         1
#define CL_MAXIMUM         100
#define INKWIDTH_MINIMUM   0
#define INKWIDTH_MAXIMUM   15
#define ENUM_MINIMUM       1
#define ENUM_MAXIMUM       4096
#define MAXDICTIONARIES    16

typedef struct tagGUIDE
    {
    int xOrigin;
    int yOrigin;
    int cxBox;
    int cyBox;
    int cxBase;
    int cyBase;
    int cHorzBox;
    int cVertBox;
    int cyMid;
    }
    GUIDE, FAR *LPGUIDE;

typedef BOOL (CALLBACK * RCYIELDPROC)(VOID);

#define cbRcLanguageMax    44
#define cbRcUserMax        32
#define cbRcrgbfAlcMax     32
#define cwRcReservedMax    8

typedef struct tagRC
    {
    HREC hrec;
    HWND hwnd;
    UINT wEventRef;
```

```
    UINT wRcPreferences;
    LONG lRcOptions;
    RCYIELDPROC lpfnYield;
    BYTE lpUser[cbRcUserMax];
    UINT wCountry;
    UINT wIntlPreferences;
    char lpLanguage[cbRcLanguageMax];
    LPDF rglpdf[MAXDICTIONARIES];
    UINT wTryDictionary;
    CL clErrorLevel;
    ALC alc;
    ALC alcPriority;
    BYTE rgbfAlc[cbRcrgbfAlcMax];
    UINT wResultMode;
    UINT wTimeOut;
    LONG lPcm;
    RECT rectBound;
    RECT rectExclude;
    GUIDE guide;
    UINT wRcOrient;
    UINT wRcDirect;
    int nInkWidth;
    COLORREF rgbInk;
    DWORD dwAppParam;
    DWORD dwDictParam;
    DWORD dwRecognizer;
    UINT rgwReserved[cwRcReservedMax];
    }
    RC, FAR *LPRC;
```

For complete explanation of the RC structure, given its complexity and the number of other structures it contains, I'll defer to the *Microsoft Windows for Pen Computing Programmer's Reference*. The same comment applies to the **RCRESULT** structure, which gives you access to the ink and the completed recognition:

```
typedef HANDLE HPENDATA;

typedef struct tagSYC
    {
    UINT wStrokeFirst;
    UINT wPntFirst;
    UINT wStrokeLast;
    UINT wPntLast;
    BOOL fLastSyc;
    }
    SYC, FAR *LPSYC;

#define wPntAll              (UINT)0xFFFF
#define iSycNull             (-1)
```

```
typedef struct tagSYE
    {
    SYV syv;
    LONG lRecogVal;
    CL cl;
    int iSyc;
    }
    SYE, FAR *LPSYE;

#define MAXHOTSPOT              8

typedef struct tagSYG
    {
    POINT rgpntHotSpots[MAXHOTSPOT];
    int cHotSpot;
    int nFirstBox;
    LONG lRecogVal;
    LPSYE lpsye;
    int cSye;
    LPSYC lpsyc;
    int cSyc;
    }
    SYG, FAR *LPSYG;

typedef int (CALLBACK *ENUMPROC)(LPSYV, int, VOID FAR *);

typedef struct tagRCRESULT
    {
    SYG syg;
    UINT wResultsType;
    int cSyv;
    LPSYV lpsyv;
    HANDLE hSyv;
    int nBaseLine;
    int nMidLine;
    HPENDATA hpendata;
    RECT rectBoundInk;
    POINT pntEnd;
    LPRC lprc;
    }
    RCRESULT, FAR *LPRCRESULT;
```

Control the Recognition Process

The **hedit** and **bedit** controls invoke a recognizer for hand-printed text automagically: your application simply puts up the controls and gets the results. There are cases, though, where you can improve recognition with context clues.

For instance, take a U.S. zip code field. You know, I know, and the user knows that this field should start with five digits. But without help, the recognizer will have trouble distinguishing the number "0" (zero) from the letter "O".

To fix this, you'll have to modify the Recognition Context (**RC**) for the zip code field. The **RC**—which is the principal data structure for the recognition process—includes parameters for recognition control, termination, and hints. In this case, we want to restrict the character set to numeric.

There are a number of APIs used to set the recognition context: the one used for **hedit** and **bedit** controls is the message **WM_HEDITCTL**. The **RC** field we need to set is **alc** (**alc**=alphabet code), and the bit value we need to set is **ALC_NUMERIC**. We'll also want to allow gestures (for editing), set in the **ALC_GESTURE** bit. In order to keep from inadvertently changing parts of the **RC** other than the alphabet code, we'll first get the current **RC**, then change the alphabet code, and finally set the **RC**. The code here assumes that the control is in a dialog box; if it were not, you'd use **SendMessage** rather than **SendDlgItemMessage** and you'd run the code in the context of a **WM_CREATE** message.

```
case WM_INITDIALOG:
{ RC rc;

  SendDlgItemMessage(hWndDialog, IDD_ZIPCODE, WM_HEDITCTL,
        HE_GETRC, (LPRC)&rc);
  rc.alc = ALC_NUMERIC | ALC_GESTURE;
  SendDlgItemMessage(hWndDialog, IDD_ZIPCODE, WM_HEDITCTL,
        HE_SETRC, (LPRC)&rc);
}
```

One other method for accomplishing the same end relies on a "magic" value: if you set the **hedit** or **bedit** title to "ALC<#>", where # is replaced by a valid integer representing the **ALC_*** combination required, the control will automatically use that alphabet code value in its recognition context.

There's a lot more that we can do to control recognition: we can control the character recognition priority, configure recognizers, call custom recognizers, and use custom dictionaries. In fact, we can change any field in the RC structure to get special behavior, including the color of the ink. We can even retain the ink if we wish.

Use Ink

Why would we want to save ink? For one thing, it isn't always necessary for the computer to recognize characters—sometimes writing is only intended for the writer, and sometimes writing has content that would be lost if it were converted to text.

For instance, think about the class notes you used to take. If you're like me, the pages were filled with key words and phrases, often underlined, often with arrows and circles showing relationships and sketches illustrating concepts. That sort of content doesn't easily translate to plain text—while it might be useful to convert the words to text for indexing, it is probably more important to preserve the squiggles and arrows faithfully.

There are a number of strategies you can use to retain ink. If you're working with an **hedit** or **bedit** control, you might want to send the control a **WM_HEDITCTL** / **HE_SETINKMODE** message initially, to delay recognition, and a **WM_HEDITCTL** / **HE_GETINKHANDLE** message when you want to capture the ink (for instance, when OK is pressed). Then you can send a **WM_HEDITCTL** / **HE_STOPINKMODE** message with the **LOWORD** set to **HEP_RECOG** to perform recognition and to display text, or with the **LOWORD** set to **HEP_NORECOG** to remove the ink without performing recognition.

If you're not working with an **hedit** or **bedit** control, you can use **Process-Writing** (a high-level function) or **Recognize** (a lower-level function) to accept ink and convert it to symbols. You should call either function only in response to a **WM_LBUTTONDOWN** message; the recognizer will return the results in a **WM_RCRESULT** message. The ink can be accessed using the **hpendata** field of the **RCRESULT** structure returned by the **WM_RCRESULT** message. Make sure you duplicate the pen data, since the handle returned will become invalid after the **WM_RCRESULT** message; your other alternative is to set the **RCO_SAVEHPENDATA** option in the recognition context before starting to collect ink.

Once you have an **HPENDATA** handle, you might want to compress the pen data using the **CompactPenData** function, and write it out like any other block of binary data. Later you can redraw the ink using **RedisplayPenData** (on a display only) or **DrawPenData** (on any device). And you can convert the saved data to symbols at any time using **RecognizeData**.

Achieving Pen Enlightenment

There's more you can do with ink, and much more you can do with pens. But this is not the place to discuss it.

This has been but the merest introduction to programming Pens. If it has whetted your appetite for further information, I commend you to Microsoft's programmer's reference and Pen samples. I also strongly suggest getting access to a real pen computer: you'll be surprised at what's easy on a pen system, and what's impossible.

9

In which we learn to use Unicode
and do internationalization.

Lingua Franca

· ·

The pioneers who opened up America spoke many languages: English, French, Spanish, Portuguese, Chinese, Japanese, German, Swedish, Norwegian, Russian, Polish, Yiddish, Swahili . . . . Can our computers do as well?

The ANSI character set used by the standard version of 16-bit Windows has eight bits per character. Those 256 characters generally suffice for English, the Germanic and Scandinavian languages, the Romance languages, and most other languages written with the Roman character set. It doesn't work for Russian and other languages written in Cyrillic characters: Greek, Hebrew, Arabic, Turkish, Chinese, Japanese, Hangul . . . .

There have been multiple solutions to this deficiency over the years. For languages with limited numbers of characters, alternative 8-bit character sets called *code pages* have been used. In addition, Windows has supported OEM character sets. The combination has led to a confusing variety of ANSI and OEM code pages. Code page 437 is the OEM code page normally used in the United States.

Other languages, particularly the Asian languages, which use thousands of pictographic characters, use a completely different solution: multibyte character sets, particularly the double-byte character set (DBCS). Unfortunately, programming with a multibyte character set is awkward, since one byte might or might not represent a whole character; worse, there have been multiple standards for multibyte character sets, even within single countries.

With all these different language coding schemes, the best most people can do to adapt to foreign markets is to produce multiple localized versions for their software. To produce true international multilingual software well-nigh demands a single character set that encompasses all known languages.

The new international standard for encoding characters, a 16-bit character set called Unicode, addresses the problems inherent in code pages and multibyte character sets. Every character in the Unicode set is represented by two bytes: the standard accommodates 65,536 total characters. That is more than enough to handle all ancient and modern languages. The Unicode standard supports Roman, Greek, Cyrillic, Hebrew, Arabic, Han, Hiragana, and Katakana scripts, among others. It supports special character sets for mathematics, phonetics, and publishing. Unicode specifies conversions to and from other character-mapping standards, and specifies a standard algorithm for bidirectional text (required for mixing Hebrew or Arabic with English, for instance).

Win32 Unicode Support

Win32 includes a fairly complete implementation of the Unicode standard, and uses Unicode internally. Windows NT files—at least in the NTFS file system—can use Unicode filenames, Windows NT string resources are stored in Unicode, and many Windows NT functions support Unicode as well as ANSI strings. Applications can use Unicode or ANSI or both, and individual windows can choose to get their messages in ANSI or Unicode.

In Win32, an ANSI string has type **char**, while a Unicode string has type **wchar_t**. A standard macro defines the generic type **TCHAR** to be ANSI or Unicode depending on the state of the **UNICODE** switch:

```
#ifdef UNICODE
   typedef wchar_t TCHAR;
#else
   typedef unsigned char TCHAR;
#endif
typedef TCHAR * LPTSTR, *LPTCH;
```

Another macro, **TEXT**, takes care of making string constants Unicode or ANSI depending on the UNICODE switch:

```
#ifdef UNICODE
   #define TEXT(quote) L##quote
#else
   #define TEXT(quote) quote
#endif
```

Additional standard macros define specific 8-bit and Unicode character types:

```
/* 8-bit character specific */
typedef unsigned char CHAR;
typedef CHAR *LPSTR, *LPCH;

/* Unicode specific (wide characters) */
typedef unsigned wchar_t WCHAR;
typedef WCHAR *LPWSTR, *LPWCH;
```

The convention here is that the letter **T** preceding a type definition designates a generic type that can be compiled for either ANSI or Unicode, and the letter **W** preceding a type definition designates a wide-character (Unicode) type. These macros live in WINNT.H.

As is obvious from the definition, you can define an application using generic data types and compile it for Unicode by defining **UNICODE** before the include statements for the header files. To compile the code for ANSI, omit the **UNICODE** definition.

Win32 provides a number of function prototypes in generic, ANSI, and Unicode forms. The generic function prototype implements the standard function name as a macro, which expands into either the ANSI or Unicode form depending on whether **UNICODE** is defined. The letters A (ANSI) and W (wide) are added at the end of the function names in the specific function prototypes, and the parameters are typed appropriately. For example, the generic prototype for **SetWindowText** uses the generic type **LPTSTR** for the **lpText** parameter, but the **A** and **W** prototypes use **LPCSTR** and **LPCWSTR** character types, respectively:

```
SetWindowText(HWND hwnd, LPTSTR lpText);
SetWindowTextA(HWND hwnd, LPCSTR lpText);
SetWindowTextW(HWND hwnd, LPCWSTR lpText);
```

The full set of Win32 functions for manipulating and converting Unicode strings directly is given in Table 9-1. However, many more Win32 functions *support* Unicode, following the **A** and **W** convention as shown above.

If you have existing code that you want to enable for Unicode or ANSI with generic functions, you will need to make a few changes. First of all, you'll need to update your types.

Any existing **char** and **CHAR** types need to become **TCHAR** types. Existing **unsigned char** or **UCHAR** types become **TBYTE** types. True string pointers become **LPTSTR**, or **LPTCH**. Nontext pointers should use the **LPBYTE** type and *not* the **LPTSTR** or **LPTCH** type. Pointers of indeterminate type should be **LPVOID**.

You'll also have to make your pointer arithmetic type independent. Consider the expression:

```
cCount = lpEnd - lpStart;
```

Table 9-1 Win32 Unicode Functions

Function	Action
CharLower	Converts a character or string to lowercase.
CharLowerBuff	Converts a character string to lowercase.
CharNext	Moves to the next character in a string.
CharPrev	Moves to the previous character in a string.
CharToOem	Translates a string to OEM characters.
CharToOemBuff	Translates a string to OEM characters.
CharUpper	Converts a character or string to uppercase.
CharUpperBuff	Converts a string to uppercase.
CompareStringW	Compare two wide character strings.
FoldStringW	Translate one wide character string to another.
FormatMessage	Formats a message string.
GetACP	Get ANSI system codepage.
GetCPInfo	Get code page information.
GetDateFormatW	Get locale-formatted date string.
GetLocaleInfoW	Get locale information from registry.
GetOEMCP	Get OEM system codepage.
GetStringTypeW	Get Unicode string type.
GetSystemDefaultLangID	Get system default language ID.
GetSystemDefaultLCID	Get system default locale ID.
GetThreadLocale	Get locale information for a thread.
GetTimeFormatW	Get locale-formatted time string.
GetUserDefaultLangID	Get user default language ID.
GetUserDefaultLCID	Get user default locale ID.
IsCharAlpha	Determines if a character is alphabetical.
IsCharAlphaNumeric	Determines is a character is alphanumeric.
IsCharLower	Determines if a character is lowercase.
IsCharUpper	Determines if a character is uppercase.

What are the units of **cCount**? Bytes. If you want to count characters, you'll need to correct the units:

```
cCount = (lpEnd - lpStart) / sizeof(TCHAR);
```

Table 9-1 continued

Function	Action
IsDBCSLeadByte	Determines if a character is a DBCS lead byte.
IsValidCodePage	Determines if a code page is valid.
LCMapStringW	Map character string by locale.
LoadString	Loads a string resource.
lstrcat	Appends one string to another.
lstrcmp	Compares two character strings.
lstrcmpi	Compares two character strings.
lstrcpy	Copies a string to a buffer.
lstrlen	Returns the number of characters in a string.
MultiByteToWideChar	Map multibyte string to wide-character string.
OemToChar	Translates an OEM string.
OemToCharBuff	Translates an OEM string.
SetThreadLocale	Set locale information for a thread.
WideCharToMultiByte	Map wide-character string to multibyte.
wsprintf	Formats a string.
wvsprintf	Formats a string.
AnsiLower	Obsolete.
AnsiLowerBuff	Obsolete.
AnsiNext	Obsolete.
AnsiPrev	Obsolete.
AnsiToOem	Obsolete.
AnsiToOemBuff	Obsolete.
AnsiUpper	Obsolete.
AnsiUpperBuff	Obsolete.
OemToAnsi	Obsolete.
OemToAnsiBuff	Obsolete.

What about string constants? Unicode strings are preceded with the letter **L**. You can use the **TEXT** macro shown above to add the prefix when appropriate, or you can keep your string constants in resources, which Windows NT will automatically convert when it loads them. Note that Unicode strings have to be terminated by a code 0x0000: a single zero byte will not suffice. Use **(TCHAR) 0** as a generic string terminator.

Table 9-2 Data Format Specifications for **wsprintf**

Format Specification	ANSI Version	Unicode Version
c	CHAR	WCHAR
C	WCHAR	CHAR
hc, hC	CHAR	CHAR
hs, hS	LPSTR	LPSTR
lc, lC	WCHAR	WCHAR
ls, lS	LPWSTR	LPWSTR
s	LPSTR	LPWSTR
S	LPWSTR	LPSTR

The Win32 function **wsprintf** supports Unicode by providing new and changed data types in its format specifications, listed in Table 9-2. These format specifications control the way **wsprintf** interprets the corresponding passed-in parameter.

The data type for **wsprintf**'s output text depends on the version of the function, ANSI or Unicode. If the data type of the passed-in parameter and of the output text do not agree, **wsprintf** will perform a conversion from Unicode to ANSI, or vice versa, as required. The Unicode version of **wsprintf** uses a Unicode format string as well as generating a Unicode output string.

Using Unicode and the C Library

You can work with strings using the Win32 functions, or with the C library functions. For instance, if you copy a string with the Win32 generic function **lstrcpy**, you will automatically get **lstrcpyA** or **lstrcpyW** depending on whether you're compiling for ANSI or Unicode. These definitions can be found in WINBASE.H. If you want to use a C library function for copying a string, you can explicitly call **strcpy** if you are compiling for ANSI or **wstrcpy** if you are compiling for Unicode—or, if you like, you can use the C library generic function macro **_tcscpy**.

Table 9-3 lists the C library functions used for internationalization. Most of these functions have Win32 equivalents: the only reason to use the C library functions would be to gain compatibility with other platforms, such as MS-DOS.

Table 9-4 lists the C library string functions for ANSI and Unicode. Some of these functions have Win32 equivalents, and some don't. Where there are equivalents, I prefer the Win32 functions: again, use the C library functions only when it is more important to maintain compatibility with other platforms.

The Microsoft C library headers do in fact have a predefined set of macros for generic international functions: they rely on **_UNICODE** being defined, rather than **UNICODE**. The C library generic international macros can be found in TCHAR.H:

Table 9-3 C Library Functions for Internationalization

Function(s)	Action
localeconv	Set a structure with appropriate values for formatting numeric quantities.
mblen	Get the length and determine the validity of a multibyte character.
_mbslen	Get the number of multibyte characters in a multibyte wide-character string.
mbstowcs	Convert a sequence of multibyte characters to a corresponding sequence of wide characters.
mbtowc	Convert a multibyte character to the corresponding wide character.
setlocale	Select the appropriate locale for the program.
strcoll, wcscoll	Compare strings using locale-specific information.
_stricoll, _wcsicoll	Compare strings using locale-specific information (case-insensitive).
strftime, wcsftime	Format a date and time string.
strxfrm, wcsxfrm	Transform a string based on locale-specific information.
wcstombs	Convert a sequence of wide characters to a corresponding sequence of multibyte characters.
wctomb	Convert a wide character to the corresponding multibyte character.

```
#ifndef _INC_TCHAR
#ifdef __cplusplus
extern "C" {
#endif

#ifdef_UNICODE

#ifndef _TCHAR_DEFINED
typedef wchar_t      TCHAR;
#define _TCHAR_DEFINED
#endif

#define __T(x)        L ## x

#define _TEOF     WEOF

#define _tprintf wprintf
#define _ftprintf    fwprintf
#define _stprintf    swprintf
#define _sntprintf   _snwprintf
#define _vtprintf    vwprintf
#define _vftprintf   vfwprintf
#define _vstprintf   vswprintf
#define _vsntprintf _vsnwprintf
```

Table 9-4   C Library String Functions for ANSI and Unicode

ANSI, Unicode Function	Action
strcat, wcscat	Append one string to another.
strchr, wcsrchr	Find first occurrence of a given character in a string.
strcmp, wcscmp	Compare two strings.
strcpy, wcscpy	Copy one string to another.
strcspn, wcscspn	Find first occurrence of a character from a given character set in a string.
_strdup, _wcsdup	Duplicate a string.
strerror	Map an error number to a message string.
_strerror	Map a user-defined error message to a string.
_stricmp, _wcsicmp	Compare two strings without regard to case.
strlen, wcslen	Find length of string.
_strlwr, wcslwr	Convert string to lowercase.
strncat, wcsncat	Append characters of a string.
strncmp, wcsncmp	Compare characters of two strings.
strncpy, wcsncpy	Copy characters of one string to another.
_strnicmp, _wcsnicmp	Compare characters of two strings without regard to case.
_strnset, _wcsnset	Set characters of a string to a given character.
strpbrk, wcspbrk	Find first occurrence of a character from one string in another.
strrchr, wcsrchr	Find last occurrence of a given character in string.
_strrev, _wcsrev	Reverse a string.
_strset, wcsset	Set all characters of a string to a given character.
strspn, wcsspn	Find first substring from a given character set in a string.
strstr, wcsstr	Find first occurrence of a given string in another string.
strtok, wcstok	Find next token in a string.
_strupr, _wcsupr	Convert a string to uppercase.

```
#define _tscanf     wscanf
#define _ftscanf    fwscanf
#define _stscanf    swscanf

#define _fgettc     fgetwc
#define _fgettchar  fgetwchar
#define _fgetts     fgetws
#define _fputtc     fputwc
#define _fputtchar  fputwchar
```

```
#define _fputts      fputws
#define _gettc       getwc
#define _getts       getws
#define _puttc       putwc
#define _putts       putws
#define _ungettc     ungetwc

#define _tcstod      wcstod
#define _tcstol      wcstol
#define _tcstoul     wcstoul

#define _tcscat      wcscat
#define _tcschr      wcschr
#define _tcscmp      wcscmp
#define _tcscpy      wcscpy
#define _tcscspn     wcscspn
#define _tcslen      wcslen
#define _tcsncat     wcsncat
#define _tcsncmp     wcsncmp
#define _tcsncpy     wcsncpy
#define _tcspbrk     wcspbrk
#define _tcsrchr     wcsrchr
#define _tcsspn      wcsspn
#define _tcsstr      wcsstr
#define _tcstok      wcstok

#define _tcsdup      _wcsdup
#define _tcsicmp     _wcsicmp
#define _tcsnicmp    _wcsnicmp
#define _tcsnset     _wcsnset
#define _tcsrev      _wcsrev
#define _tcsset      _wcsset

#define _tcslwr      _wcslwr
#define _tcsupr      _wcsupr
#define _tcsxfrm     wcsxfrm
#define _tcscoll     wcscoll
#define _tcsicoll    _wcsicoll

#define _istalpha    iswalpha
#define _istupper    iswupper
#define _istlower    iswlower
#define _istdigit    iswdigit
#define _istxdigit   iswxdigit
#define _istspace    iswspace
#define _istpunct    iswpunct
#define _istalnum    iswalnum
#define _istprint    iswprint
#define _istgraph    iswgraph
#define _istcntrl    iswcntrl
#define _istascii    iswascii
```

```
#define _totupper    towupper
#define _totlower    towlower

#else /* _UNICODE   */

#ifndef _TCHAR       _DEFINED
typedef char         TCHAR;
#define _TCHAR       _DEFINED
#endif

#define __T(x)       x

#define _TEOF        EOF

#define _tprintf     printf
#define _ftprintf    fprintf
#define _stprintf    sprintf
#define _sntprintf   _snprintf
#define _vtprintf    vprintf
#define _vftprintf   vfprintf
#define _vstprintf   vsprintf
#define _vsntprintf  _vsnprintf
#define _tscanf      scanf
#define _ftscanf     fscanf
#define _stscanf     sscanf

#define _fgettc      fgetc
#define _fgettchar   fgetchar
#define _fgetts      fgets
#define _fputtc      fputc
#define _fputtchar   fputchar
#define _fputts      fputs
#define _gettc       getc
#define _getts       gets
#define _puttc       putc
#define _putts       puts
#define _ungettc     ungetc

#define _tcstod      strtod
#define _tcstol      strtol
#define _tcstoul     strtoul

#define _tcscat      strcat
#define _tcschr      strchr
#define _tcscmp      strcmp
#define _tcscpy      strcpy
#define _tcscspn     strcspn
#define _tcslen      strlen
#define _tcsncat     strncat
#define _tcsncmp     strncmp
#define _tcsncpy     strncpy
#define _tcspbrk     strpbrk
#define _tcsrchr     strrchr
```

```
#define _tcsspn     strspn
#define _tcsstr     strstr
#define _tcstok     strtok

#define _tcsdup     _strdup
#define _tcsicmp    _stricmp
#define _tcsnicmp   _strnicmp
#define _tcsnset    _strnset
#define _tcsrev     _strrev
#define _tcsset     _strset

#define _tcslwr     _strlwr
#define _tcsupr     _strupr
#define _tcsxfrm    strxfrm
#define _tcscoll    strcoll
#define _tcsicoll   _stricoll

#define _istalpha   isalpha
#define _istupper   isupper
#define _istlower   islower
#define _istdigit   isdigit
#define _istxdigit  isxdigit
#define _istspace   isspace
#define _istpunct   ispunct
#define _istalnum   isalnum
#define _istprint   isprint
#define _istgraph   isgraph
#define _istcntrl   iscntrl
#define _istascii   isascii

#define _totupper   toupper
#define _totlower   tolower

#endif /* _UNICODE   */

#define _T(x)       __T(x)
#define _TEXT(x)    __T(x)

#ifdef __cplusplus
}
#endif

#define _INC_TCHAR
#endif /* _INC_TCHAR */
```

You'll note that a lot of this functionality duplicates what is found in Win32. One difference in implementation is that Win32 uses the standard function names as generics, which is easy to remember; TCHAR.H introduces some fairly ugly new names, like **_tcscpy**, for the generic functions, while retaining the standard names for the ANSI functions. I don't think Microsoft had a choice here: they were constrained by the ANSI C standard.

Working with Unicode Fonts

Unicode fonts are very much like ordinary Windows fonts—they just allow a lot more characters. To specify a Unicode font for use by your program, you'll need to use the constant **UNICODE_CHARSET** in the **LOGFONT** structure:

```
LOGFONT logfont = {
    UCFONTHEIGHT ,      //application-defined
    UCFONTWIDTH ,       //application-defined
     0 ,
     0 ,
   400 ,                //normal weight
     0 ,
     0 ,
     0 ,
    UNICODE_CHARSET ,//system constant
     0 ,
     0 ,
     2 ,               //proof quality
     2 ,               //variable pitch
    TEXT("Lucida Sans Unicode")}; //font supplied with NT
```

In this example, **UNICODE** is defined, so that the **TEXT** macro makes the constant that follows it a Unicode string rather than an ANSI string. The Lucida Sans Unicode font is supplied with Windows NT. An older version of the font file was called UCLUCIDA.-TTF; the version supplied with the retail version of NT is called L_10646.TTF. This font includes about 1,000 glyphs from a number of Western character sets, but no Asian character sets (Figure 9-1). Windows NT/J, the localized Japanese version of Windows NT, ships with a font that contains about 7,000 characters, covering all the Hiragana and Katakana characters used for phonetic Japanese, plus most of the common Kanji characters, which are ideograms used both in Chinese and Japanese. Unicode fonts for Hangul (Korean), Thai, Sanskrit, and Arabic are available elsewhere.

The Windows NT SDK includes sample code for working with Unicode fonts, UNIPUT. This MDI application, illustrated in Figure 9-2, allows you to display all the characters in a Unicode font, as shipped. If you add a menu item for the **IDM_NEW-FILE** command, you can also use the UNIPUT sample to add Unicode characters to a file. However, it is more convenient to use national language keyboard mappings to input most European languages: you can change keyboard mappings from the International control panel applet in Windows NT.

One point that is illustrated in the **IDM_NEWFILE** code in UNIPUT is the need for a Unicode byte-order mark at the beginning of any Unicode text file. This mark is defined as 0xFEFF. If you read a Unicode file and find the mark 0xFFEF rather than 0xFEFF, you've opened a file with the byte order reversed. The code to write the byte-order mark is simply:

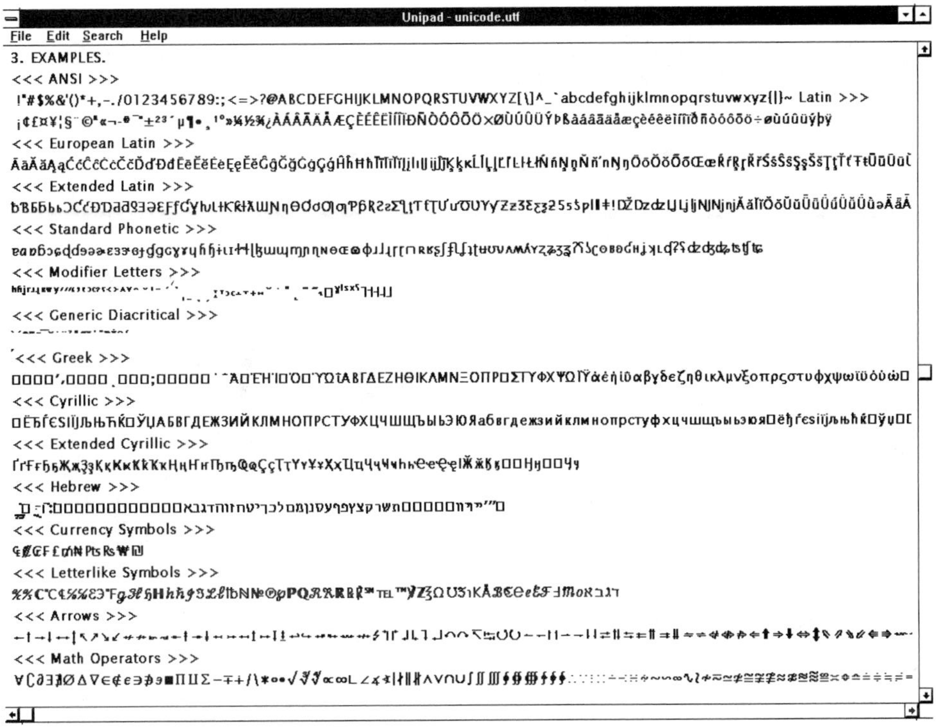

Figure 9-1 Windows NT SDK Unipad application displaying Lucida Sans Unicode.

```
/* Write the unicode byte order mark */
WriteFile (hFile, "\xFE\xFF", 2, &nBytes, NULL);
```

If you prefer C++, another Microsoft sample, GRIDFONT, is also available. GRID-FONT appears to be the work of Asmus Freytag, Microsoft's representative to the Unicode standards committee. You might find this code a little more reusable than the code in UNIPUT, even though the GRIDFONT application is not as sophisticated as the UNIPUT application. If you build the version of GRIDFONT supplied with Visual C++ for Windows NT, you'll have to define UNICODE from the Options/Project/Compiler/Preprocessor dialog before the application will build for Unicode. Otherwise, it will build for ANSI. The version of GRIDFONT supplied with the Windows NT SDK has UNICODE defined in the source code, so it will build for Unicode by default.

Internationalization Issues

Unicode is a big help when you wish to write a single application that supports many national languages. On the other hand, it is not a panacea. There are a number of issues that you must address yourself.

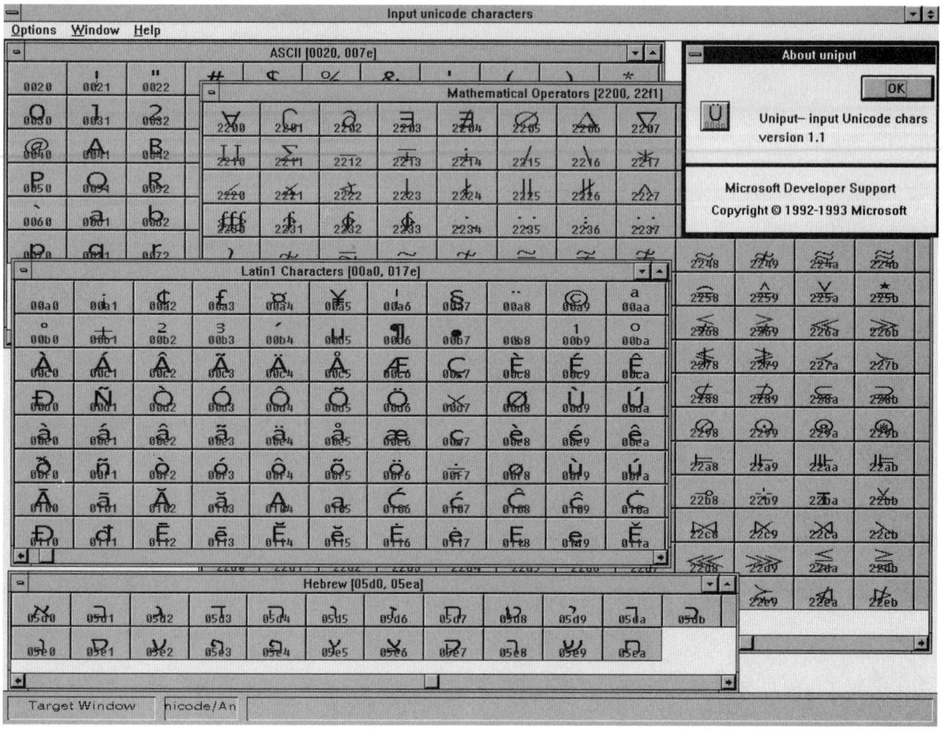

Figure 9-2   Windows NT SDK Uniput sample.

One issue is multiple-language versions of dialogs. You could, of course, try to create a single universal version of each dialog and load different strings depending on the current language. That's fine for message boxes, which size themselves to the string passed. You'd find, however, that a dialog that looks right in English doesn't allow enough horizontal room for wordy languages like German, or enough character height for languages with ideograms like Chinese and Japanese. Another issue is writing direction: Hebrew and Arabic are written right to left, and Chinese is often written top to bottom, although left to right is also used. Correcting the control alignments and positions on the fly for any possible language would be a nightmare.

A more aesthetically pleasing solution is to tune the dialogs for each supported language. But that raises the issue of being able to retrieve the correct dialog for the current language. Actually, there is a convention you should follow: the dialog box identifiers should be identical for each language instance, and each language instance needs to be identified with a different **LANGUAGE** resource:

```
#define DialogID        100

DialogID DIALOG  0, 0, 210, 10
LANGUAGE LANG_ENGLISH,SUBLANG_ENGLISH_US
```

```
          .
          .
          .
DialogID DIALOG  0, 0, 210, 10
LANGUAGE LANG_FRENCH,SUBLANG_FRENCH
```

When you do this, the Win32 version of **FindResource** gets the locale information for the process, then attempts to fetch the resource with that language identifier using **FindResourceEx**, which is language specific. If **FindResourceEx** fails to load the language-specific dialog box, **FindResource** then attempts to load the language-neutral dialog box.

The **LANGUAGE** identifiers in the dialogs should match the **VERSIONINFO** language identifiers. The code page for resources is always Unicode: the system will translate from Unicode to the required national language code page, if the current window is not Unicode.

While maintaining multiple-language versions of dialog is something of a headache, interpreting the results of dialogs in different languages is not the problem in Windows that it is in character-oriented systems, as long as you use your controls properly. What do I mean by that? Suppose you put up an English dialog that says "Overwrite this file? Y/N" and make the user type Y or N into an edit control. Then you retrieve and interpret the character typed into the edit control.

That will work for your first language: you wire in some logic that converts the character to uppercase and tests for Y or N. For your second language, you have a problem. The German mnemonics for *Ja* and *Nein* are J and N, not Y and N. The Japanese equivalent words are *Hai* and *Iie*, which would be H and I. You quickly wind up with a giant switch statement based on the current language.

Obviously, this is the wrong track to follow. If the user is making only one decision, your Yes and No choices can go on buttons, as in a standard message box: you'd get back one of two or three possible language-independent return codes from the dialog (perhaps ID_OK, ID_NO, and ID_CANCEL). Or, you could use a checkbox for the option, if it were one of many choices to be made. Again, you'd get back a language-independent control state—the box is checked or unchecked—not a language-dependent character or string.

When coding for multiple nationalities, you also need to respect the conventions of each country for time display, money display, and so on. Win32 provides **GetDateFormatW** for converting system date structures to localized date strings, and **GetTimeFormatW** for converting system time structures to localized time strings. Both functions use the **SYSTEMTIME** structure.

Other national preferences are kept in the registry and can be retrieved using **GetProfileInt** and **GetProfileString** (for compatibility with Windows) with the section set to **[Intl]**, or by retrieving the **HKEY_CURRENT_USER\Control Panel\International** settings directly from the registry. Mappings between

Windows INI file settings and Windows NT registry entries are kept in the registry under HKEY_LOCAL_MACHINE\SOFTWARE\MICROSOFT\Windows NT\Current Version\IniFileMapping. Accessing the registry directly is less convenient, however, than using the Win32 or C library locale functions.

A Win32 locale identifier is a language/sublanguage identifier and a reserved word combined into a doubleword value. There are two predefined locale identifiers: **LOCALE_SYSTEM_DEFAULT**, which identifies the system default locale, and **LOCALE_USER_DEFAULT**, which identifies the locale of the current user. An application can call **GetSystemDefaultLCID** and **GetUserDefaultLCID** to retrieve the current locale identifiers, or **GetThreadLocale** to determine the locale of the current thread if it might have been changed (with **SetThreadLocale**) since it was created. To retrieve the current language identifiers, call **GetSystemDefaultLangID** and **GetUserDefaultLangID**.

Once you have a locale, you can use **GetLocaleInfoW** to retrieve the locale's language, country, measurement system, decimal separator, monetary symbol, and so on from the registry. If you need to sort strings using the localized collating order, use **CompareStringW** to perform the string comparisons. Use **LCMapStringW** to lowercase, uppercase, byte-reverse, strip nonspacing characters, strip symbols, and/ or normalize a string according to the locale's rules.

The **GetStringTypeW** function retrieves information about a Unicode string on a character-by-character basis. With the **fdwInfoType** option set to **CT_CTYPE1**, **GetStringTypeW** returns classification information on the ANSI and POSIX character types: alphabetic, digits, control characters, and so on. With the **fdwInfoType** option set to **CT_CTYPE2**, **GetStringTypeW** returns information needed for proper layout of Unicode text: right to left, left to right, European and Arabic numbers, separators, terminators, and white space. With the **fdwInfoType** option set to **CT_CTYPE3**, **GetStringTypeW** returns extensions to the POSIX types: nonspacing marks, diacritic and vowel nonspacing marks, and symbols.

If you need compatibility with other platforms and you are using a compiler that supports multiple locales, you can use the C library locale functions defined in LOCALE.H (**setlocale**, **localeconv**, **strcoll**, **strxfrm**, and so on) rather than the Win32 locale functions. Note, however, that the C-language locale is formatted and maintained separately from the Win32 locale of a thread. The Win32 locale is initialized to the system default locale; the C-language locale is initialized to the "C" locale, which assumes that all char data types are one byte, and that their value is always less than 256. Most compilers dated prior to 1993 support only the "C" locale or lack the locale functions entirely.

One more point is in order. Certain national standards are addressed neither by the Win32 or C language locale functions, nor by the Unicode standard. I speak primarily of accounting conventions and tax laws, but there are other issues that arise:

building codes, engineering practices, and so on. Building international software to support these practices correctly is possible—I've participated in several successful examples—but challenging.

Shots Heard 'Round the World

Having done it myself, I'd be the last person to underestimate the time, expense, and pain involved in turning a single-language program into a fully internationalized program. Nevertheless, if you have access to literate native speakers for the languages you wish to target who also read and write passable English, localizing or internationalizing a Win32 program is at least a manageable task: Win32's direct support of Unicode and locales saves you from having to reinvent some rather fancy wheels.

At the same time, it is important to remember that more than half of the sales of many major U.S. software products come from outside the United States. These are products that have been fully localized or internationalized. In many cases, a product considered second-string in its home market turns out to dominate some foreign markets because of superior adaptation to the local language and conventions. Internationalization can turn a successful product into a wildly successful product, and a lackluster product into a successful product.

But one final warning. Not all the countries to which you'd like to sell software respect copyrights and patents—ideas of intellectual property rights tend to vary quite a bit around the world. In much of the Middle and Far East, in particular, there is no enforcement of laws against copying software without paying for it. In these markets, part of the challenge of making software succeed is in finding a workable but effective copy protection mechanism.

10

In which we learn about OLE 2 and
perhaps even OLE 3.

OLÉ Again

· ·

In *Advanced Windows Programming,* I wrote a rather lengthy chapter on DDE, DDE-ML, and OLE 1. In addition to going over DDE fundamentals and walking through the DDEML protocol, I compared OLE with DDEML, went over the basic OLE concepts, explained how OLE interacts with the clipboard, delved into the system registration database, presented the OLE 1 user interface, and went over the structure of OLE 1 client and server applications. Altogether, that chapter takes close to forty pages to present the material at what I consider an introductory level.[1]

Well, I'm not going to reprint all forty pages here. I'm going to assume you already know all that. Don't despair, though: even if you don't already know about OLE 1, you won't have that much more difficult a time with OLE 2 than people who know OLE 1 cold: everything changed for OLE 2. Besides, the Microsoft OLE 2 documentation is well over a thousand pages.

The sound you hear is the author tearing his hair. Don't panic. The author will return momentarily, albeit somewhat the worse for wear.

One wonders, of course, what could possibly take over a thousand pages to explain. One wonders what could make it worthwhile reading over a thousand pages of dense

---

[1] It's funny how advanced books often include introductory-level material. Of course, the introductory treatments are of advanced topics. The current work is no different.

documentation that uses coined terminology, terminology which bears little relationship to anything else in the Windows or Win32 universe.

The promise of OLE 2 is that it will really and truly allow programs and documents to be sharable, reusable, nestable, programmable objects. The cost for programmers, beyond the rather stiff learning curve, is that you'll have to structure your program— maybe your whole architecture—around OLE 2, rather than being able to just add OLE 2 to your program. The good news is that the OLE 2 example programs are a good start: the better news is that you won't have to touch as much of them as you think. The bad news is that, at least as I write, the implementations of OLE 2 for Windows and Windows NT are immature.[2]

OLE 2: The Omen

Let's start simply. OLE's primary purpose is to support *compound documents*— documents in one format that contain or reference documents in another format. The application that manages the compound document is called an OLE *container*; the application or library that provides the functionality of the objects is called an OLE *server*. This container-server scheme is a fairly general mechanism, but some specific examples might help you understand what it's all about.

Start with a memo to your boss. It's all words, to begin with. To support your request for a larger budget for your department, you want to add a spreadsheet that shows your department's revenue growth over the last year. Spreadsheets are a different kind of animal than words, so you use a different program.

OLE 1 enters the picture when you want to combine the words and the spreadsheet in a single memo. OLE 1 offers two containment mechanisms: linking and embedding. In both cases the spreadsheet will be an *object* or *item* inside the word-processing document. In this case *object* refers to an unknown thing inside a wrapper (an embedded object) or an unknown thing referred to by a pointer (a linked object). The embedded object can't be lost (it's right there inside the word file), but won't be automatically updated when the original from which it was copied changes. The linked object will update automatically, but the link might break if you move the original file to which it refers.

Obviously, neither embedding nor linking is a perfect solution in OLE 1. It would be really nice if there were a way to move linked objects that would automatically update the link reference in all containers, or that would leave a forwarding address of some sort in the file system.

When you have an embedded or linked object in a compound document, you can select it and perform actions on it. By convention, double-clicking sends a copy of the object to its native application for editing, and transfers control to that application.

---

[2] Immature is as nice a word I could manage here. Buggy and slow also apply.

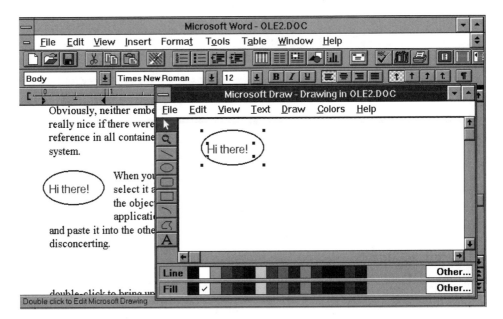

Figure 10-1   Editing an object using OLE 1 can be disconcerting.

That's nicer than having to explicitly put the object on the keyboard and paste it into the other application. Switching from one application to another is, however, somewhat disconcerting (Figure 10-1). There you are innocently double-clicking from your word processor—and suddenly you are running a drawing program! It would be nice if there were a smoother way to switch functions.

Well, not surprisingly, Microsoft (with the cooperation of the usual gang of suspects) has propagated improvements to Object Linking and Embedding: OLE 2.

In-Place Activation

As you might have guessed from my buildup, OLE 2 does in-place activation, which means that a server application can take over the client's menus when you want to edit an object. Figure 10-2 shows a simulation of how Excel might take over Word's menus and toolbar to edit an embedded spreadsheet.

An OLE 2 server could go beyond menu and toolbar replacement. The full interface of Microsoft Paint uses toolboxes and palettes as well as menus: the toolboxes and palettes would be overlaid on the Word frame when you were doing in-place editing of a bitmap, such as the CD cover at the bottom left. That might be disconcerting as well, so OLE 2 allows the user to choose between editing an object in place and opening the object in a new window for editing.

In addition to replaceable global menus, OLE 2 supports context-sensitive pop-up menus of the sort that's become popular in some database and spreadsheet

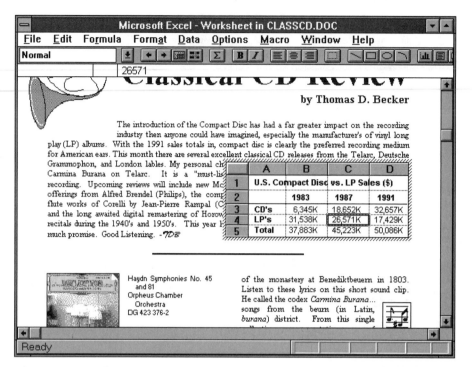

Figure 10-2 In-place activation with OLE 2. Here Excel has taken over Word's menus and toolbars.

applications. The user right-clicks on an object, and up pops a menu of the most-used commands for that kind of object. The pop-up menu for a text selection might include access to a text properties dialog, some transfer commands (Cut, Copy, Paste, and access to a Paste Special dialog), and some contextual commands (for instance, Undo). The pop-up menu for a bitmap selection would have the same transfer commands, but different contextual commands (perhaps Zoom controls) and access to a bitmap properties dialog rather than a text properties dialog.

A Cure for Broken Links?

Earlier, we bemoaned OLE 1's difficulty maintaining links when objects move. OLE 2 has adaptable links, which track links in the two most common scenarios for document movement, although not for all possible document movements. Adaptable links work by using a new referencing mechanism for objects called the *moniker*. In OLE 1 the only way to reference a linked object was by its filename, which included an absolute path. OLE 2's moniker is a much more general way of referencing an object: it allows tracking not only of objects but also of nested objects and storage-independent links (links between objects that are not files).

An OLE 2 linked object's moniker includes the absolute path to the object, as in OLE 1; in addition, it also includes a relative path from the container to the object. When the container wants to reopen the object, the relative path is tried first: if the relative reference fails, the absolute reference is tried.

What this means is that if the container and object are both moved the same way—to a different drive, across the network, or to a different directory tree—the link will hold, because the relative path will still be valid. If the container moves but the object stays in place, the link will still hold, because the absolute path will still be valid. Only if the object moves relative to the container will the link break. This isn't a perfect general solution to broken links, but it sure represents a major improvement.

The general solution will require an object-oriented file system, which should come with "Cairo" (Windows NT 4). The upgrade to an object-oriented file system may well require an upgrade to OLE as well—probably to version 3.

Persistent Storage

The moniker isn't the only fundamental improvement in OLE 2. Another important one is a vastly different—and more flexible—model for persistent storage of objects.

In OLE 1, the client could do things with an OLE object: load it from a stream and save it to a stream. You have perhaps noticed that *any* operation on an OLE 1 object takes a long time and involves a lot of disk activity: the reason for this is that the entire object has to be loaded from disk when it is read, and the entire object has to be saved to disk when it is updated.

OLE 2 expands the persistent storage model to give the object much more control: each object can read from, write to, and append to its own stream or streams, and can load or save as much or as little information as is necessary. So, for instance, if a drawing server has added one rectangle to an embedded picture, it need only append the rectangle to the stream to update the persistent representation of the image.

As far as the object server is concerned, a stream is a stream, and might well be a separate file from the container document's file. However, users don't expect to generate multiple files when they produce compound documents with embedded objects, so OLE 2 multiplexes all the object streams into one underlying file.

Just as DOS has directory and file objects, OLE 2 has **IStorage** and **IStream** objects. An **IStorage** object contains a collection of nested storage objects and streams; an **IStream** object is—logically, at least—very much like a file.

Nested levels of embedded objects (for instance, a chart within a picture within a page layout) are represented by storage objects contained in other storage objects. The actual native and OLE data live in streams within the objects. Nesting is another big improvement from the user's point of view: there's no problem if you want to embed a drawing in your Word document that includes a PowerPoint slide that in turn includes an embedded chart based on data linked from an Excel spreadsheet. As user, you don't have to worry about such things: the burden of tracking all those levels falls on the application program and the OLE 2 libraries.

The OLE 2 persistent storage model is *not* directly tied to files. Therefore it can be *storage-independent*: an OLE server dealing with an **IStream** doesn't care if the **IStream** came from a local disk file, from a database, from an application's in-memory document, from a networked machine with a foreign file system, or from a remote machine linked by a wireless connection.

To allow a user to abandon edits to an embedded object, OLE 2 has a *transaction* mode of access to storage objects as well as a *direct* mode. Just as in a database, sets of changes in transaction mode can be *committed* or *reverted* when editing is complete. In a network situation where multiple processes may be updating a document simultaneously, each user of the storage object gets a *snapshot* copied from the original when he opens it; the snapshot guarantees that the copy one user is reading won't change unexpectedly when another user updates it. A user can open objects for exclusive use to bypass the overhead of snapshot copies, but that will keep other users from being able to read.

If this sounds to you like a description of a database on a network, you're on the right track: in a real sense the OLE 2 persistent storage model is very much like an object-oriented database.

Drag and Drop and the Clipboard

That database-like aspect opens up all sorts of possibilities in OLE 2. Since embedded objects can be accessed efficiently, they can act like first-class rather than second-class citizens. For instance, they can act as drag-and-drop targets—or even as drag-and-drop sources. In fact, OLE 2 offers a whole new set of drag-and-drop functions that are much more general and useful than the drag-and-drop functions of the Windows 3.1 File Manager.

This does not imply that every embedded object in a document will need its own window. OLE 2 container documents are responsible for supporting drag-and-drop on behalf of their embedded objects and passing the dropped object to the appropriate target object.

The new drag-and-drop functions should prove convenient for users and programmers alike. The programming interface provides for functions to give feedback about where an object can be dropped, and for automatic scrolling using a *hot zone* at the edge of the container document's window. From a user's perspective, that means properly written OLE 2 applications will automatically "do the right thing" when you want to drag objects to, from, and within them.

Users can also move OLE 2 objects from document to document using the clipboard. Both embedded and linked objects can be put on the clipboard. Note that

OLE objects can be quite large, and that the clipboard should still be valid even after the source application ends. The OLE 2 libraries take responsibility for maintaining the clipboard without exhausting memory: after the source application ends, they copy the OLE clipboard objects to a temporary file, and when the clipboard is cleared they delete the temporary file.

OLE 2 Programmability

OLE 2 adds three kinds of programmability. The simplest is a new kind of embedded object, which contains commands to be executed by MS-DOS. The second is *property* manipulation; OLE 2 provides a list of standard properties, and properties are actually maintained by the OLE 2 libraries. An application can explicitly change an object's properties, and an object can implicitly inherit properties from its container to blend with the appearance of the rest of the document.

The third kind of programmability is *method* invocation. The standard OLE 1 object model supports calling an object's methods through a table, which corresponds to *early binding*. OLE 2 also supports *late binding* through **IDispatch** calls; information on the parameter types for **IDispatch** calls is provided through the **ItypeInfo** type information interface.

Additional OLE 2 Functionality

One of the limitations of OLE 1 is that an embedded or linked object can occupy only one rectangular region inside its container. That limits the size of an object that can reasonably be embedded, and limits the possibilities for page layout.

OLE 2 allows more flexible object layout. One embedded object can be broken into several rectangular pieces in its container. The container and the object actually negotiate the number of pieces and their size and placement.

Another limitation of OLE 1 is that embedded text can't be searched or edited by the container document. For instance, a page layout program might have a larger dictionary and better hyphenation algorithms than the word processor that created a piece of embedded text. In OLE 2, the container can get and replace text in an embedded object, which allows "tunneling searches."

OLE 2: I Is for Interface

In addition to the new features, OLE 2 introduces some fundamental changes in the OLE programming interface and in the underlying implementation.

A major infrastructure change replaces the DDE communication used by OLE 1 with the new *LRPC* (Lightweight Remote Procedure Call) mechanism, at least on Windows. On Macintosh systems, the transport is instead Apple Events.

The LRPC mechanism is not quite the full, network-aware remote procedure call (RPC) used in Windows NT—rather it is a low-overhead implementation that relies on shared memory, more like Windows NT's *LPC* (Local Procedure Call). LRPC uses a *proxy* function on the sending end, which *marshals* the parameters and sends them to the *stub* function on the receiving end, which *unmarshals* them and calls the server function that does the real work. At some point, OLE will be updated to use full-blown RPCs. See Chapter 11 for more information on RPCs.

As you might expect from all the talk of objects, OLE 2 has been specified using C++ syntax. Microsoft implements a C interface as well—but it uses pointers so heavily that I suspect you'd have to be fairly masochistic to use it.[3] You can find an example of an OLE 2 application in C in OLE2\SAMP\OUTLINE, and an example of an OLE 2 application in C++ in OLE2\SAMP\SPOLY. You can find the OLE 2 directory tree on the Win32 SDK CD-ROM, the OLE 2 SDK CD-ROM, and the MSDN CD-ROM; I don't think it is even available on floppy disks.

The central interface for compound document objects is **IOleObject**, with about twenty-five methods including the familiar **DoVerb** method used to invoke an action on an object, and the new **SetMoniker** and **GetMoniker** functions used instead of ordinary filenames. **IOleObject** inherits from **IUnknown**, the generic OLE 2 object class.

Why **IOleObject** and not just **OleObject**? **I** is for Interface. It makes some sense, I guess. **IOle** as a prefix means that an interface provides services that relate to compound document management; a plain **I** means that an interface provides services that relate to OLE's infrastructure.

As mentioned earlier, OLE 2 continues to support the **vtable** method interface of OLE 1 (early binding) as well as late binding through **IDispatch** calls; information on the parameter types for **IDispatch** calls is provided through the **ItypeInfo** type information interface. **IDispatch** provides a general cross-process way of invoking methods on objects.

The OLE 2 persistent storage model has multiple levels. You open either a **DocFile** or **Storage** or **ILockBytes** to get an **IStorage** instance. The **IStorage** class has a dozen or so methods—among them **CreateStream**, **OpenStream**, **CreateStorage**, **OpenStorage**, **Commit**, and **Revert**. **IStorage** instances can contain both nested streams and nested storage instances; the **IStream** class has its own dozen or so methods, including **Read**, **Write**, **Seek**, **Commit**, and **Revert**.

IPersist is a base interface from which the three persistent storage classes **IPersistStorage**, **IPersistStream**, and **IPersistFile** derive. The **IPersistStorage** class is the one OLE uses for compound-document objects; **IPersistStream** is for nondocument objects like **Monikers**. **IPersistFile** is for opening actual files, as we would to resolve a link.

---

[3] I *told* you learning C++ would come in handy someday.

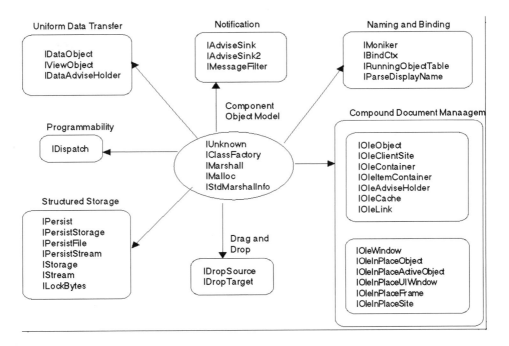

Figure 10-3 OLE interfaces by area.

Perhaps a figure would clarify all this. Figure 10-3, supplied by Microsoft, shows the functional areas of each of the OLE interfaces.

The OLE Interface Classes

Let's look at the middle of Figure 10-3, the bubble labeled "Component Object Model." There are, of course, people who'd say this isn't an object model—that this is just plumbing. Of course, those people are mostly devotees of rival object models, such as IBM's SOM or Apple's OpenDoc. If OLE 2 component object model isn't an object model in the universally accepted sense, it's at least a *big* piece of plumbing that could be used in support of an object model.

The five classes in the OLE 2 component object are **IUnknown**, **IClassFactory**, **IMarshall**, **IMalloc**, and **IStdMarshalInfo**. **IUnknown**, implemented in OLE, provides interface negotiation and interface pointer management services to all objects, and all OLE 2 interfaces are derived from it and inherit its member functions. **IMalloc** provides memory management services: it is implemented in OLE and used by OLE and applications.

IMarshall and **IStdMarshalInfo** provide the "remoting" services that actually transport information from one application to another. And **IClassFactory**, implemented by all OLE link servers and containers, provides the classwide behaviors for objects.

Moving to the top left of Figure 10-3, we come to the data transfer interfaces **IDataObject**, **IViewObject**, and **IDataAdviseHolder**. **IDataObject** is implemented by OLE; OLE and most applications use it to transfer data and register data change notifications. **IViewObject** is also implemented by OLE, and used to display data, print data, and register view change notifications. **IDataAdviseHolder** is also implemented by OLE: applications (mostly server applications) use it to send data change notifications.

You'll note that of the eight OLE classes we've examined so far, only one, **IClassFactory**, needs to be implemented—the rest are services provided by OLE. Let's go on.

Moving to the middle of the top row, we come to the three notification service classes **IAdviseSink**, **IAdviseSink2**, and **IMessageFilter**. **IAdviseSink** handles the receipt of data and view change notifications, and **IAdviseSink2** handles the receipt of link source change notifications. Containers that want to know about these changes need to implement these classes. **IMessageFilter** manages concurrency problems, and needs to be implemented by all servers and containers. Oh well: make that seven provided services, and four interfaces that need to be implemented.

Moving to the top right of Figure 10-3, we encounter the naming and binding service classes. **IMoniker** supports binding monikers to their sources, aided by **IBindCtx**, **IRunningObjectTable** keeps track of running objects for link binding and tracking, and **IParseDisplayName** converts a display name into a moniker.

Jumping back to the left-hand side of Figure 10-3, we find **IDispatch** sitting in lonely splendor under the "Programmability" rubric. **IDispatch** is the class used to expose a set of member functions to allow OLE Automation to get information about your applications objects and to invoke methods and get or set properties. In other words, if you implement **IDispatch** and a few supporting methods in **IUnknown** and **IClassFactory**, languages and other applications can program your application. In some ways, this is better than implementing your own macro language: anybody can program using the exposed objects, methods, and properties of your application from any language or application that supports OLE automation.

We've already introduced the OLE structured storage classes, found at the lower left of Figure 10-3. **IStorage**, **IStream**, and **ILockBytes** are implemented by OLE; **IPersistStorage**, **IPersistStream**, and **IPersistFile** need to be implemented by applications that support structured storage, but derive from **IPersist**, which is implemented by OLE.

The drag-and-drop classes, at the bottom of Figure 10-3, are implemented by applications. Implement an **IDropSource** class if you want to originate drag-and-drop transfers, and an **IDropTarget** class if you want to accept drag-and-drop actions. Note that this means that any application can originate drops, not just File Manager.

Compound document management, found at the bottom right of Figure 10-3, is of course the core of OLE as we know it. `IOleObject`, as we've discussed, provides object management. It is implemented by all servers and used by all containers. `IOleClientSite`, on the other hand, manages the object's site in the container, and is implemented by all containers and used by all servers.

`IOleContainer` and `IOleItemContainer` support binding to item Monikers; they are used by OLE to bind links to embedded objects or to pseudo-objects, which are ranges of items within an object. As you might expect, `IOleContainer` and `IOleItemContainer` are implemented by containers that support linking to embedded objects, and by servers that support linking to pseudo-objects.

`IOleCache` provides control of the data that is cached inside of an embedded object. `IOleLink` manipulates the moniker inside of a link and the link's update options. `IOleAdviseHolder` creates an advise holder object to manage and send object notifications: it is implemented by OLE and used by servers.

`IOleWindow` is implemented and used by both container and servers to support in-place activation of an embedded object. All other in-place activation interfaces are derived from `IOleWindow`, including `IOleInPlaceObject`, `IOleInPlaceActive-Object`, `IOleInPlaceUIWindow`, and `IOleInPlaceFrame`. `IOleInPlaceSite` is implemented by containers and used by servers to obtain the client site for the object that is being activated in place.

Living with OLE 2

I've lost count of the box score, but the conclusion is still easy: OLE 2 provides a lot of functionality, but also requires you to write a fair bit of code to implement your own OLE server or container. The trick is learning how to do it.

One thing you should *not* do is read the entire OLE 2 documentation set. Not to put too fine a point on the matter, the OLE 2 specification and, to a somewhat lesser extent, the OLE 2 programmer's manual represent gross excess in the documentation process. If you try to plow through all that stuff you'll get bogged down and discouraged, and you'll wind up wearing a pin that reads *OLE 2: Just Say No!*

Don't let this happen to you. In the *OLE 2.0 Programmer's Reference*, read Part 1, OLE Concepts and Considerations, which covers the concepts I've introduced above in more detail—about 130 pages, which you can get through in half a day. Then skim Part 2, Getting Started—it's another 130 pages, which you should flip through in two hours. Don't get too bogged down in the tutorial unless it really looks relevant to what you need to accomplish.

Do *not* bother with Part 3 of the *Reference* at this point, and don't even look at the *Specification*. Go directly to the sample code.

I suggest you compile and run all the samples, then browse the sources for a few hours. When you start getting a feel for the samples, copy one of them to a new directory tree and start modifying it to do what you want. Begin slowly and build. Allow several weeks for incremental development before you are likely to have an OLE 2 client or server worth showing to anyone. Start by making the application work like an ordinary OLE 1 program.

Once you have the OLE 2 application working like an OLE 1 application, you can start supporting the advanced features of OLE 2. If it is appropriate, add in-place activation support. Then add drag-and-drop support. And, finally, add programmability through **IDispatch**.

When you are ready to support **IDispatch**, spend half a day working through *Creating Programmable Applications*. Read the first four chapters (about eighty pages) fairly carefully, then skim the rest of the volume, another two hundred pages or so. If you're writing for Windows NT, you can safely skip the chapter on OLE's national language support—the support for Unicode and locales in Windows NT makes OLE's national language functions superfluous. If your application has to support national languages from 16-bit Windows, however, or your application needs to expose programmable objects with meaningful member names in multiple languages, do take the time to learn the OLE national language support functions.

All of this sounds pretty complicated. Well, it is complicated: there is more to learn in OLE 2 than there was in the entire Windows 1.0 API.

I should point out that even Microsoft has suggested that OLE is complicated enough to be a programming specialty in its own right. I think that they are correct: if you have a multiprogrammer shop, one of the more senior people should become the OLE specialist, and everyone else should ignore the subject as much as possible. On the other hand, I think to be an experienced OLE programmer is to be employed for life, especially given the importance of OLE to "Cairo" and "Chicago," so you might want to learn this stuff even if someone else in your shop is responsible for OLE support.

11

Citizen of the Galaxy

· ·

We've forded the rivers, we've crossed the plains, we've gotten over the mountains, we've survived the deserts. The trouble with being a pilgrim is that sometimes you don't recognize the promised land.

We reached the fertile fields of the 32-bit lands a long time ago, but the explorations since have still been worthwhile. Now let's settle down and set up our communications.

The pioneers had the pony express; later they had the telegraph, the telephone, radio, and television. Broadcast television was partially supplanted by cable. Our computer networks are a distant cousin to cable television: at some point, however, they might well merge into a single digital communications technology. For now, it's enough for us to learn to program multiple Win32 processes, both local and over networks.

Windows NT has an astounding range of interprocess and networking mechanisms. Windows has somewhat less of a range, and the choices for Win32s are actually rather restricted. Let's start by looking at the big picture, the road map that relates each networking, interprocess communication and related mechanism: Netbios, Wnet, mailslots, MAPI, pipes, RAS, sockets, RPCs, DDE, NetDDE, OLE, memory-mapped files, security, service control, event logging, and performance monitoring.

Sorting Out NT Interprocess Communications

The Win32 **Netbios** function supports raw IBM NetBIOS, a very low-level protocol controlled by network control blocks (NCBs). According to Microsoft, **Netbios** is in Win32 primarily for compatibility with existing systems written to NetBIOS that need to be ported to Windows and Windows NT. On the other hand, **Netbios** will work whether your Windows NT system is communicating via Netbeui, TCP/IP, or IPX/ SPX. Various **Netbios** commands allow the use of communication sessions with individual partners, as well as datagram broadcasts to specific recipients or entire networks. The Win32 **Netbios** function works in Win32s as well as Windows NT; other implementations of NetBIOS are available for DOS, OS/2, and 16-bit Windows.

The **WNet** functions allow you to enumerate, connect, and disconnect from network resources (shares). One of the **WNet** functions also gives you access to the current network user name. The **WNet** functions work in Win32s as well as Windows NT.

A mailslot is a one-way interprocess communication (IPC) mechanism, amounting to a temporary pseudofile, which works over a network. Mailslot communications are not guaranteed to be reliable, as they use the datagram, but they are convenient for broadcasting messages throughout a domain. Mailslots do *not* work in Win32s.

MAPI is the Messaging Application Program Interface. MAPI gives an application a simple way to send messages and files to network users via the Microsoft Mail application included with every copy of Windows NT and Windows for Workgroups. Don't confuse MAPI with mailslots: MAPI is really the programmatic interface to Microsoft Mail, while mailslots are a system-level interprocess communication mechanism. MAPI is supported in 16-bit Windows and in Windows NT, but not in Win32s.

A pipe is a communication conduit with two ends: a process with a handle to one end can communicate with a process having a handle to the other end. Win32 supports both named pipes and anonymous pipes; only named pipes can work over a network. Named pipes were the preferred IPC mechanism in OS/2, so applications ported from OS/2 to Windows NT often use named pipes. Pipes are inherently reliable—they use a protocol that lets you know that each message has been received—and are therefore preferable to mailslots when reliability is important. Named pipes can be a two-way mechanism, where mailslots are strictly a one-way mechanism. However, pipes cannot broadcast messages to multiple clients: for broadcasting, mailslots are preferable to pipes. Named pipes are not supported in 16-bit Windows or in Win32s.

Remote Access Services (RAS) allow one Windows NT machine to connect to another over a serial line, modem, X.25 connection, or ISDN connection. While the Windows NT RAS applets probably will allow most people to use RAS well enough, it is possible to use the RAS API functions to control the process from within another program—which might make sense for applications involving remote reporting and wide-area networking. RAS services are not supported in Win32s.

Sockets are a standard networking mechanism that originated in Berkeley Unix; more recently, the Windows Socket (WinSock) specification codified extensions to Berkeley Sockets for the Windows environment. Windows NT implements a 32- bit version of Windows Sockets. Sockets allow for a wide variety of network addressing schemes and protocols, although they were historically associated with TCP/IP. Sockets are supported in Win32s as well as in Windows NT and most Unix implementations. Implementations of 16-bit Windows Sockets are available from several vendors.

The Windows NT Remote Procedure Call (RPC), a partial implementation of the OSF DCE (Open Software Foundation Distributed Computing Environment) specification, is conceptually a simple mechanism for distributed computing, but is by its nature complex to program and debug. The NT implementation of RPC includes a Microsoft implementation of the Interface Description Language (IDL) compiler, used for specifying the interface to remote procedures and generating the required local stub functions; RPC runtime libraries, which let the local stubs call the remote procedures; and the actual network transport used by the client and server run-time libraries.

RPC can use a variety of transports, network address formats, and protocols. Windows NT RPC 1.0 supports TCP/IP, named pipe, Netbios, and Local Procedure Call transports. Network addresses can be in IP, DECNet, or OSI formats as needed. The RPC protocol can be NCA connections or NCA datagrams. The exact combination of protocol, address format, and transport used by a given connection is specified by an ASCII *protocol sequence*, which is combined with the actual endpoints to form a *binding*. RPC *naming services* allow a client to find a server on the network.

NT RPCs are supposed to work with DOS and Windows clients and Unix servers as well as other NT RPC clients and servers. The DOS/Windows client software ships with the NT SDK, although it needs to be installed separately from the native Windows NT tools. It is not clear whether NT RPC servers will work with all Unix clients, as the Unix clients might rely on DCE services not present in the NT RPC implementation. RPC is not supported in Win32s.

Dynamic Data Exchange (DDE) is an old local Windows interprocess communication protocol that is supported in Windows NT in both 16-bit and 32-bit form. Net-DDE is an enhancement to DDE that allows it to work over networks. Object Linking and Embedding (OLE) is a different enhancement to DDE to support compound documents and application programmability. OLE is not completely network-enabled as I write, but should be in the near future. DDE works in Win32s and 16-bit Windows as well as in Windows NT. OLE does not seem to be supported in Win32s 1.1.

Memory-mapped files are Windows NT's answer to 16-bit Windows' shared memory, which is not supported since each process in Windows NT has its own address space. While not useful as a network connection, memory-mapped files are useful as a high-bandwidth interprocess communications method on a single machine, which might well provide a network service. For instance, memory-mapped files could be used to implement the high-bandwidth part of a database server involving several processes; one of these processes could then accept queries and send results over the network using named pipes or another network transport. Memory-mapped files are supported in Win32s as well as in Windows NT.

Windows NT has built-in security designed to be certifiable at the US C2 level. While security functions are not specifically interprocess or networking functions, it is often in networking applications that the programmer must pay attention to security issues. Similarly, the Windows NT Service Control Manager, Event Logging, and Performance Monitoring services are not specifically for networks, but are often used when programming for networks.

Windows NT also includes the full Lan Manager API, although this is not considered part of the Win32 API. Existing Lan Manager code can be ported to Windows NT with little more than some code tweaks and a recompile. More information on the LAN Manager API under Windows NT can be found in DOC\SDK\MISC\LMAPI.HLP on the Windows NT SDK CD-ROM.

In the balance of this chapter, we will briefly introduce the functions provided by each of the service groups mentioned above. When appropriate, we will go over fairly brief examples of their use.

Netbios

There is one and only one function to support NetBIOS in Win32, **Netbios**. It takes one parameter: a pointer to a network-control block (NCB) structure, which holds all the semantic content for the service. The NCB contains a command, a return code, information about the network environment, and a pointer to a buffer that is used for messages or for further data about the network:[1]

```
typedef struct _NCB { /* ncb */
    UCHAR   ncb_command;  /* command code                */
    UCHAR   ncb_retcode;  /* return code                 */
    UCHAR   ncb_lsn;      /* local session number        */
    UCHAR   ncb_num;      /* number of network name      */
    PUCHAR  ncb_buffer;   /* address of message buffer   */
```

---

[1] This and succeeding reference materials are based on information supplied by Microsoft in their Win32 documentation.

```
    WORD     ncb_length;    /* size of message buffer      */
    UCHAR    ncb_callname[NCBNAMSZ];
                            /* blank-padded name of remote */
    UCHAR    ncb_name[NCBNAMSZ];
                            /* blank-padded name of local  */
    UCHAR    ncb_rto;       /* receive timeout/retry count */
    UCHAR    ncb_sto;       /* send timeout/system timeout */
    void (*ncb_post) (struct _NCB *);
                            /* POST routine address        */
    UCHAR    ncb_lana_num; /* lana (adapter) number        */
    UCHAR    ncb_cmd_cplt; /* 0xff => command pending      */
    UCHAR    ncb_reserve[10]; /* reserved, used by BIOS       */
    HANDLE   ncb_event;    /* signaled when ASYNCH completes */
} NCB, *PNCB;
```

The Win32 implementation of the Netbios function includes some enhancements that are not part of the IBM NetBIOS 3.0 specification, and a few differences in implementation from IBM NetBIOS 3.0. The enhancements allow POST routines to be called from C, and allow for completion notification using a Win32 event object. The differences are minor.

The **ncb_command** member of the **NCB** structure specifies the command code and a flag in the most significant bit (the ASYNCH constant) that indicates whether the NCB is processed asynchronously. The command codes have the actions given in Table 11-1. Note that the symbolic NCB command names used here, which match those in the NB30.H file supplied with the Win32 SDK, might be somewhat different from the symbolic names defined for DOS NetBIOS programming environments.

The **ncb_retcode** member of **NCB** specifies the return code. This value is set to **NRC_PENDING** while an asynchronous operation is in progress. Once the operation is completed, the return code is set to one of the values listed in Table 11-2.

The **ncb_lsn** member of **NCB** specifies the local session number, **ncb_buffer** points to the message buffer, and **ncb_length** specifies the size, in bytes, of the message buffer. **ncb_callname** specifies the string that contains the remote name, and **ncb_name** specifies the string that contains the local name. Trailing space characters should be supplied in both names to pad the length of the strings out to the length specified by the **NCBNAMSZ** command.

ncb_rto sets the receive timeout period, in 500-millisecond units, for the session, and is used only for **NCBRECV** commands. Likewise, **ncb_sto** sets the send timeout period, in 500-millisecond units, for the session, and is used only for **NCBSEND** and **NCBCHAINSEND** commands. A value of 0 implies no timeout.

ncb_post specifies the address of the routine to call when an asynchronous NCB finishes. The completion routine is passed a pointer to the completed network-control block.

ncb_lana_num specifies the LAN adapter number. This zero-based number

Table 11-1 Netbios Commands

NCB Command Code	Action
NCBACTION	Enable extensions to the transport interface. NCBACTION commands are mapped to TdiAction. When this value is specified, the ncb_buffer member points to a buffer to be filled with an ACTION_-HEADER structure, which is optionally followed by data. NCBACTION commands cannot be canceled by using NCBCANCEL.
NCBADDGRNAME	Add a group name to the local name table.
NCBADDNAME	Add a unique name to the local name table.
NCBASTAT	Retrieve the status of the adapter. When this value is specified, the ncb_buffer member points to a buffer to be filled with an ADAPTER_STATUS structure, followed by an array of NAME_BUFFER structures.
NCBCALL	Open a session with another name.
NCBCANCEL	Cancel a previous command.
NCBCHAINSEND	Send the contents of two data buffers to the specified session partner. For Windows NT, this is equivalent to the NCBCHAINSENDNA command.
NCBCHAINSENDNA	Send the contents of two data buffers to the specified session partner and do not wait for acknowledgment. For Windows NT, this is equivalent to the NCBCHAINSEND command.
NCBDELNAME	Delete a name from the local name table.
NCBDGRECV	Receive a datagram from any name.
NCBDGRECVBC	Receive broadcast datagram from any host.
NCBDGSEND	Send datagram to a specified name.
NCBDGSENDBC	Send a broadcast datagram to every host on the local area network (LAN).
NCBENUM	Enumerate LAN adapter (LANA) numbers. When this value is specified, the ncb_buffer member points to a buffer to be filled with a LANA_ENUM structure.
NCBFINDNAME	Determine the location of a name on the network. When this value is specified, the ncb_buffer member points to a buffer to be filled with a FIND_NAME_HEADER structure followed by one or more FIND_NAME_BUFFER structures.

corresponds to a particular transport provider using a particular LAN adapter board. **ncb_cmd_cplt** specifies the command-complete flag, which has the same value as the **ncb_retcode** member. **ncb_reserve** is reserved, and must be set to zero.

Table 11-1   continued

NCB Command Code	Action
NCBHANGUP	Close a specified session.
NCBLANSTALERT	Notify the user of LAN failures that last for more than one minute.
NCBLISTEN	Enable a session to be opened with another name.
NCBRECV	Receive data from the specified session partner.
NCBRECVANY	Receive data from any session corresponding to a specified name.
NCBRESET	Reset a LAN adapter. An adapter must be reset before any other NCB command that specifies the same number in the ncb_lana_num member will be accepted. The IBM Netbios 3.0 specification documents several NCB_RESET NCB's. Win32 implements the "NCB.RESET Using the Dynamic Link Routine Interface". Particular values can be passed in specific bytes of the NCB. More specifically: If ncb_lsn is not 0x00, all resources associated with ncb_lana_num are to be freed. If ncb_lsn is 0x00, all resources associated with ncb_lana_num are to be freed, and new resources are to be allocated. The byte ncb_callname[0] specifies the maximum number of sessions, and the byte ncb_callname[2] specifies the maximum number of names. A nonzero value for the byte ncb_callname[3] requests that the application use NAME_NUMBER_1.
NCBSEND	Send data to the specified session partner. For Windows NT, this is equivalent to the NCBSENDNA command.
NCBSENDNA	Send data to specified session partner and do not wait for an acknowledgment. For Windows NT, this is equivalent to the NCBSEND command.
NCBSSTAT	Retrieve the status of the session. When this value is specified, the ncb_buffer member points to a buffer to be filled with a SESSION_-HEADER structure, followed by one or more SESSION_BUFFER structures.
NCBTRACE	Activate or deactivate NCB tracing. Support for this command in the system is optional and system specific.
NCBUNLINK	Unlink the adapter.

ncb_event specifies a handle to a Windows NT event to be set to the signaled state when an asynchronous network-control block finishes. The event is signaled if the **Netbios** function returns a nonzero value. The **ncb_event** member of **NCB** must be zero if the **ncb_command** member does not have the **ASYNCH** value set or if **ncb_post** is nonzero. Otherwise, **NRC_ILLCMD** is returned. In other words, you can't ask for more than one notification that a NCB request has completed: it is either synchronous, signals an event, or calls a completion routine.

Table 11-2 NCB Return Codes

Return Code	Meaning
NRC_GOODRET	The operation succeeded.
NRC_BUFLEN	An illegal buffer length was supplied.
NRC_ILLCMD	An illegal command was supplied.
NRC_CMDTMO	The command was timed out.
NRC_INCOMP	The message was incomplete. The application is to issue another command.
NRC_BADDR	The buffer address was illegal.
NRC_SNUMOUT	The session number was out of range.
NRC_NORES	No resource was available.
NRC_SCLOSED	The session was closed.
NRC_CMDCAN	The command was canceled.
NRC_DUPNAME	A duplicate name existed in the local name table.
NRC_NAMTFUL	The name table was full.
NRC_ACTSES	The command finished; the name has active sessions and is no longer registered.
NRC_LOCTFUL	The local session table was full.
NRC_REMTFUL	The remote session table was full. The request to open a session was rejected.
NRC_ILLNN	An illegal name number was specified.
NRC_NOCALL	The system did not find the name that was called.
NRC_NOWILD	Wildcards are not permitted in the ncb_name member.
NRC_INUSE	The name was already in use on the remote adapter.
NRC_NAMERR	The name was deleted.
NRC_SABORT	The session ended abnormally.

The event specified by **ncb_event** is set to the nonsignaled state by the system when an asynchronous NetBIOS command is accepted, and is set to the signaled state when the asynchronous NetBIOS command finishes. Using ncb_event to submit asynchronous requests requires fewer system resources than using **ncb_post**. Also, when **ncb_event** is nonzero, the pending request is canceled if the thread terminates before the request is processed. This is not true for requests sent by using **ncb_post**.

Only manual reset events should be used with Netbios. A given event should not be associated with more than one active asynchronous NetBIOS command.

Table 11-2 continued

Return Code	Meaning
NRC_NAMCONF	A name conflict was detected.
NRC_IFBUSY	The interface was busy.
NRC_TOOMANY	Too many commands were outstanding; the application can retry the command later.
NRC_BRIDGE	The ncb_lana_num member did not specify a valid network number.
NRC_CANOCCR	The command finished while a cancel operation was occurring.
NRC_CANCEL	The NCBCANCEL command was not valid; the command was not canceled.
NRC_DUPENV	The name was defined by another local process.
NRC_ENVNOTDEF	The environment was not defined. A reset command must be issued.
NRC_OSRESNOTAV	Operating system resources were exhausted. The application can retry the command later.
NRC_MAXAPPS	The maximum number of applications was exceeded.
NRC_NOSAPS	No SAPs available for netbios.
NRC_NORESOURCES	The requested resources were not available.
NRC_INVADDRESS	The NCB address was not valid. This return code is not part of the IBM NetBIOS 3.0 specification. This return code is not returned in the NCB; instead, it is returned by the Netbios function
NRC_INVDDID	The NCB DDID was invalid.
NRC_LOCKFAIL	The attempt to lock the user area failed.
NRC_OPENERR	An error occurred during an open operation being performed by the device driver. This return code is not part of the IBM NetBIOS 3.0 specification.
NRC_SYSTEM	A system error occurred.
NRC_PENDING	An asynchronous operation is not yet finished.

How can we use NetBIOS? Let's go through a *very* simple example, one that doesn't actually do anything, but does illustrate working successfully with NetBIOS from Win32. We'll start by initializing the session and adding a name. This is normally done from the server:

```
#define WIN32
#include <windows.h>
#include <nb30.h>
#include <stdlib.h>
```

```
#include <stdio.h>
#include <memory.h>

#define NSESSIONS   1
#define NNAMES      1
//...

char chNameBuffer [ NCBNAMSZ ];
unsigned char ucRc;
int i;
NCB ncb;
//...

// Code to initialize chNameBuffer should come here (not shown)

//....

/* reset Netbios session */

memset(&ncb,0,sizeof(ncb));
ncb.ncb_command = NCBRESET;
ncb.ncb_callname[0] = NSESSIONS;
ncb.ncb_callname[1] = NNAMES;
ucRc = Netbios (&ncb);

/* Add a Name */

memset(&ncb,0,sizeof(ncb));
ncb.ncb_command = NCBADDNAME;
memcpy (ncb.ncb_name, chNameBuffer, NCBNAMSZ);
ucRc = Netbios (&ncb);
if (ucRc )
   return (1);
```

The server would normally start a session and post a receive at this point, assuming it uses connections and not datagrams. Basically the server now has to wait for the client. The client first has to find the server by name:

```
struct {
   FIND_NAME_HEADER fnh;
   FIND_NAME_BUFFER fnb;
   } fn;

/* Find the Name  */

memset(&ncb,0,sizeof(ncb));
memset(&fn.fnh,0,sizeof(fn.fnh));
memset(&fn.fnb,0,sizeof(fn.fnb));
fn.fnh.node_count = 1;
fn.fnb.length = sizeof(fn.fnb);
ncb.ncb_command = NCBFINDNAME;
memcpy (ncb.ncb_callname, chNameBuffer, NCBNAMSZ);
ncb.ncb_buffer = (PUCHAR)&fn.fnh;
```

```
ncb.ncb_length =  sizeof(fn);
ucRc = Netbios (&ncb);
```

Now we can send a datagram, or establish a session and send messages. When the server is all done, it needs to delete the name:

```
/* Delete the Name */

memset(&ncb,0,sizeof(ncb));
ncb.ncb_command = NCBDELNAME;
memcpy (ncb.ncb_name, chNameBuffer,   NCBNAMSZ);
ucRc = Netbios (&ncb);
```

If you're already familiar with NetBIOS programming from DOS, Windows, or OS/2, you probably now understand the Win32 **Netbios** function well enough to use it. If you aren't familiar with NetBIOS programming and need to use it from Windows NT, you'll want to consult a good NetBIOS programming book—but expect to have to mentally translate between systems.

The Win32 **Netbios** function, unlike DOS, doesn't require you to issue interrupts. Unlike Windows, it doesn't require you to call it from assembly language, from a DLL, or with locked NCBs. Unlike OS/2, it doesn't require you to call additional functions. Like all of those, however, it requires NetBIOS names to be padded with blanks, so you'll want to use a function like **CopyToBuffer** to work with them:

```
void CopyToBuffer ( char *pchDest , char *pchSrc)
{
    register count;

    /* Check for null pointer */
    if ((!pchDest) || ( ! pchSrc))
        return ;

    /* set the name field with nulls */
    memset ( pchDest, 0x20, NCBNAMSZ);

    /* copy from source to destination */
    count =  NCBNAMSZ;
    while ((*pchSrc) && ( count))
    {
        *pchDest++ = *pchSrc++;
        count—;
    }
    return;
}
```

As you are probably aware, you can build entire client-server systems using only NetBIOS—although no one would call that a convenient way to develop new programs. Fortunately, Win32 supports a number of other network mechanisms.

Table 11-3 WNet Functions

Function Name	Action
WNetAddConnection	Redirects a local device to a network resource.
WNetAddConnection2	Redirects a local device to a network resource.
WNetCancelConnection	Breaks an existing network connection.
WNetCancelConnection2	Breaks an existing network connection.
WNetCloseEnum	Ends a network resource list.
WNetConnectionDialog	Starts a network connection dialog box.
WNetDisconnectDialog	Starts a network disconnection dialog box.
WNetEnumResource	Continues listing network resources.
WNetGetConnection	Gets name of network resource.
WNetGetLastError	Returns last error for network functions.
WNetGetUser	Gets the current network user name.
WNetOpenEnum	Starts listing network resources.

WNet

The WNet group of functions allows you to explicitly manipulate network disk and printer connections and other network resources from your applications. As such, they allow you to add some of the functionality of File Manager, Print Manager, **net use**, and **net view** to your own programs. The WNet functions are listed in Table 11-3. To use any of these functions, you need to link to MPR.LIB, the multiple-provider router library.

Note that **WNetAddConnection** and **WNetCancelConnection** are already obsolete: they are present in Win32 for compatibility with Windows for Workgroups programs, and have been replaced with **WNetAddConnection2** and **WNet-CancelConnection2**, respectively, which are considerably more flexible. **WNet-AddConnection2** and the resource enumeration functions **WNetOpenEnum**, **WNetEnumResource**, and **WNetCloseEnum** use the **NETRESOURCE** structure to describe network resources:

```
typedef struct _NETRESOURCE {  /* nr */
    DWORD   dwScope;            //connected, global, or persistent
    DWORD   dwType;             //any, disk, or print
    DWORD   dwDisplayType;      //domain, generic, server, or share
    DWORD   dwUsage;            //connectable or container
    LPTSTR lpLocalName; //i.e. H: or LPT3:
    LPTSTR lpRemoteName;        //remote network name
    LPTSTR lpComment;           //provider-supplied comment
```

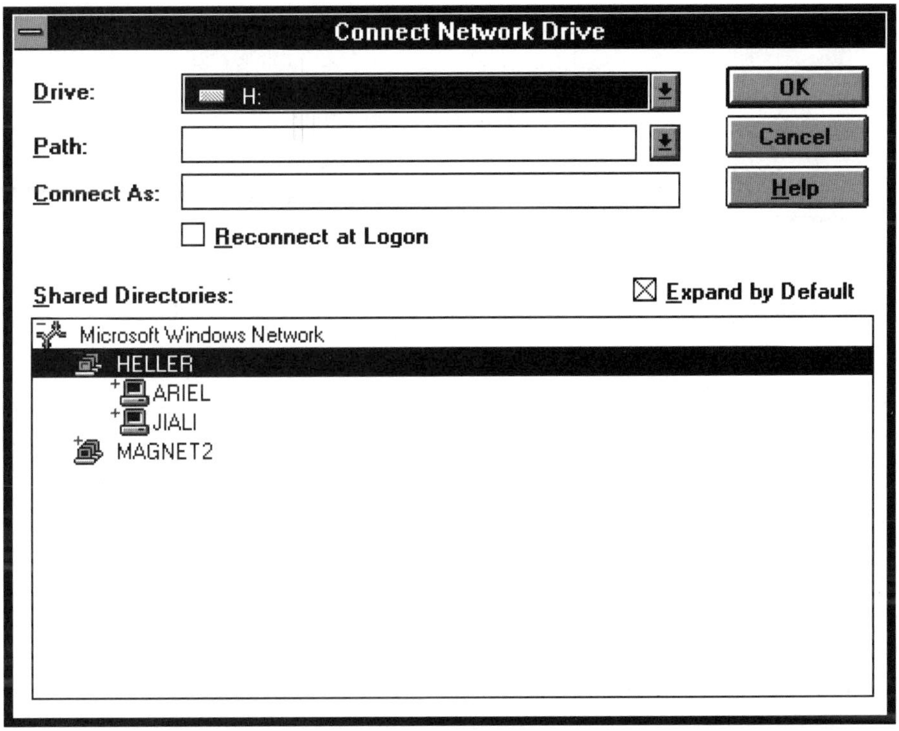

Figure 11-1 `WNetConnectionDialog` invokes the Connect Network Drive dialog.

```
    LPTSTR lpProvider;        //provider name
} NETRESOURCE;
```

If you want to give control of network connections to the user, use the
WNetConnectionDialog function to put up a dialog box, enumerate the network
resources and display them, and allow the user to connect to resources:

```
DWORD dwResult;
dwResult = WNetConnectionDialog(hWnd, RESOURCETYPE_DISK);
if(dwResult != NO_ERROR) {
    MyErrorHandler(hWnd, dwResult, (LPSTR)"WNetConnectionDialog");
    return FALSE;
    }
```

In general, the alternatives to **RESOURCETYPE_DISK** are **RESOURCETYPE_-
PRINT** and **RESOURCETYPE_ANY**. **WNetConnectionDialog**, however, works
only with **RESOURCETYPE_DISK**—it brings up the standard "Connect Network
Drive" dialog (Figure 11-1). One wonders whether some future version of the function
will implement printer browsing as well.

One more function in this group bears comment. **WNetGetUser** does more than meets the eye: it not only can find the current default user name, but it can also find the user name used to establish any given network connection:

```
DWORD WNetGetUser(lpszLocalName, lpszUserName, lpcchBuffer)

LPTSTR lpszLocalName;   /* address of local name to get user name
                              for */
LPTSTR lpszUserName;    /* address of buffer for user name    */
LPDWORD lpcchBuffer;    /* address of buffer-size variable    */
```

If you use **NULL** for the local name, you get the current user name for the process. If you specify a share name, you will get the user name used to connect to the share. If there are multiple connections with multiple names, you'll get one of the user names—but there's no telling which one.

Mailslots

As we mentioned earlier, mailslots are convenient for broadcasting messages and other one-way communications tasks. Only three API functions are needed to support mailslots, as shown in Table 11-4; the rest of the mailslot functionality is performed with standard file functions, since mailslots act as pseudofiles.

Note that, unlike real files, mailslots are temporary. When every handle of a mailslot is closed or the process owning the last handle exits, the mailslot and all the data it contains are deleted. The data in a mailslot message can be in any form, within the length limit set when the mailslot was created.

A server process creates a mailslot with the **CreateMailslot** function, which returns a handle to the mailslot:

```
HANDLE CreateMailslot(lpszName, cbMaxMsg, dwReadTimeout, lpsa)

LPCTSTR lpszName;       /* address of string for mailslot name   */
DWORD cbMaxMsg;         /* maximum message size */
DWORD dwReadTimeout;    /* milliseconds before read time-out   */
LPSECURITY_ATTRIBUTES lpsa;   /* address of security structure   */
```

Table 11-4 Mailslot API Server Functions

Function	Action
CreateMailslot	Creates a mailslot.
GetMailslotInfo	Retrieves mailslot information.
SetMailslotInfo	Sets mailslot read timeout.

The **lpszName** parameter to **CreateMailslot** is required to be of the form **\\.\mailslot\[path]name**, and must be unique. The name may include multiple levels of pseudodirectories separated by backslashes. For example, both **\\.\mailslot\example_mailslot_name** and **\\.\mailslot\abc\def\ghi** are valid names. The **cbMaxMsg** parameter specifies the maximum message size that can be written to the mailslot, in bytes; zero means that the size is unlimited.

dwReadTimeout specifies the amount of time, in milliseconds, a read operation can wait for a message to be written to the mailslot before a timeout occurs. A value of zero means that reads return immediately if no message is present. A value of **MAILSLOT_WAIT_FOREVER**, defined as –1, means that reads to the mailslot never time out.

lpsa is a security descriptor for the mailbox; we'll discuss security descriptors a little later on. Most of the time you can safely use **NULL** for the security descriptor, which causes the object to get default security attributes. You'll need a real security descriptor if you want to pass the mailbox handle to child processes or you actually want to restrict access to the mailbox to authorized processes.

To open a mailslot from a client process, use **CreateFile** on the mailslot name, with **FILE_SHARE_READ** and **OPEN_EXISTING** specified as flags. If the mailslot is local to the client, its name is the same one used when it was created, for example, **\\.\mailslot\name**. If the mailslot is remote, you can specify **\\computername\mailslot\name**, **\\domainname\mailslot\name**, or ***\mailslot\name**. The last two forms are used for domainwide broadcasts: the ***** form broadcasts in the local system's primary domain, and the **\\domainname** form broadcasts in the specified domain. If you use either domainwide broadcast form, you cannot write more than 400 bytes at a time to the mailslot.

Note that opening a mailslot from the client side can return a valid handle even if the mailslot doesn't exist. And remember that mailslot communications use datagrams, which are not inherently reliable. Don't use a mailslot for a message that absolutely, positively has to get through.

Once you've opened the mailslot, you can write messages to it using **WriteFile** and the handle returned from **CreateFile**. The server reads messages with **ReadFile**. When you are done with the mailslot, release it with **CloseHandle**. The only other functions that can be used with mailslots are **GetMailSlotInfo**, **SetMailSlotInfo**, **GetFileTime**, **SetFileTime**, and **DuplicateHandle**. Mailslot clients should restrict themselves to **CreateFile**, **DuplicateHandle**, **WriteFile**, and **CloseHandle**.

MAPI

While mailslots are good for sending transient one-way interprocess messages and message broadcasts, they are inappropriate for persistent messages, reliable messages,

Table 11-5 Simple MAPI Functions

Function	Description
MAPIAddress	Addresses a Mail message.
MAPIDeleteMail	Deletes a Mail message.
MAPIDetails	Displays a recipient details dialog box.
MAPIFindNext	Returns the ID of the next (or first) Mail message of a specified type.
MAPIFreeBuffer	Frees memory allocated by the messaging system.
MAPILogoff	Ends a session with the messaging system.
MAPILogon	Begins a session with the messaging system.
MAPIReadMail	Reads a Mail message.
MAPIResolveName	Displays a dialog box to resolve an ambiguous recipient name.
MAPISaveMail	Saves a Mail message.
MAPISendDocuments	Sends a standard Mail message using a dialog box.
MAPISendMail	Sends a Mail message, allowing greater flexibility in message generation.

and applications that require two-way communication. For persistent, reliable one-way messages, it might be better to use MAPI, the Messaging Application Program Interface. For transient, reliable two-way interprocess communications, named pipes might be a better choice. Let's address MAPI first.

MAPI is a set of high-level functions that applications use to create, manipulate, transfer, and store messages. MAPI provides a common interface that application developers use to create mail-enabled and mail-aware applications independent of the underlying messaging system. In addition to a message store interface used to create and manage collections of messages, MAPI also includes an address book interface for access to mail recipients and distribution lists.

MAPI comes in two flavors, Simple MAPI and Extended MAPI. Simple MAPI is built into Windows NT and Windows for Workgroups, as Microsoft Mail comes with both systems. You can add Simple MAPI capabilities to a Windows 3.1 system by adding Microsoft Mail to the system. Extended MAPI will require a *Windows Messaging Subsystem*, expected in future releases of Windows, probably both "Chicago" and "Cairo."

Extended MAPI augments Simple MAPI with functions for advanced addressing, and folder and message management. Applications will be able to use Extended MAPI to create and deal with large and/or complex messages, to access portions of a directory service, and to organize and search a large store of messages.

The Simple MAPI functions are listed in Table 11-5. To use these functions, you will need to include MAPI.H and dynamically link to MAPI32.DLL (from a 32-bit application) or MAPI.DLL (from a 16-bit application).

The following code will allow you to dynamically link to the MAPI service DLL and get the address of the single function needed to mail-enable an application, **MAPISendDocuments**:

```
#ifdef WIN32
#define MAPIDLL "MAPI32.DLL"
#else
#define MAPIDLL "MAPI.DLL"
#define SZ_MAPISENDDOC "MAPISendDocuments"
extern ULONG (FAR PASCAL *lpfnMAPISendDocuments)(ULONG, LPSTR,
                                        LPSTR, LPSTR, ULONG);

extern HANDLE hLibrary;

int FAR PASCAL InitMAPI() {
  if ((hLibrary = LoadLibrary(MAPIDLL)) < 32)
    return(ERR_LOAD_LIB);
  if ((lpfnMAPISendDocuments= GetProcAddress(hLibrary,
        SZ_MAPISENDDOC)) == NULL)
    return(ERR_LOAD_FUNC);
  return(0);
}
```

Once you've successfully linked to MAPI32.DLL or MAPI.DLL and retrieved a pointer to **MAPISendDocuments**, you should add a **Send** menu item to the File menu of your application. Enable the menu item when there is a current document in the application, and disable it when there is no current document.

When the menu item is picked, you'll need to process it. If yours is an MDI application, you might want to offer a choice between "Send current document" or "Send all documents." Whether you are sending a single document or multiple documents, the logic for each document is the same: save the current file as a temporary, call **MAPISendDocuments** for the temporary file, and finally delete the temporary file. The following code snippet calls **MAPISendDocuments**:

```
ulResult = (*lpfnMAPISendDocuments)(hWnd, ";",
  lpszFullPathToTemporaryFile, lpszTemporaryFileName, 0L);
```

Amazingly, that's all there is to mail-enabling an application. The user will see a login dialog if not already logged into Mail, and then will see a mail dialog with the file already listed, like the one shown in Figure 11-2. Where in the world did all *that* user interface come from? From MS-Mail. You're actually using MAPI to tap into MS-Mail, which is acting as the mail service provider.

That's quite a bit of application to get from one function call. If you want to send documents or mail messages without involving the user—or you simply want more control over the message—you can use an alternate function, **MAPISendMail**:

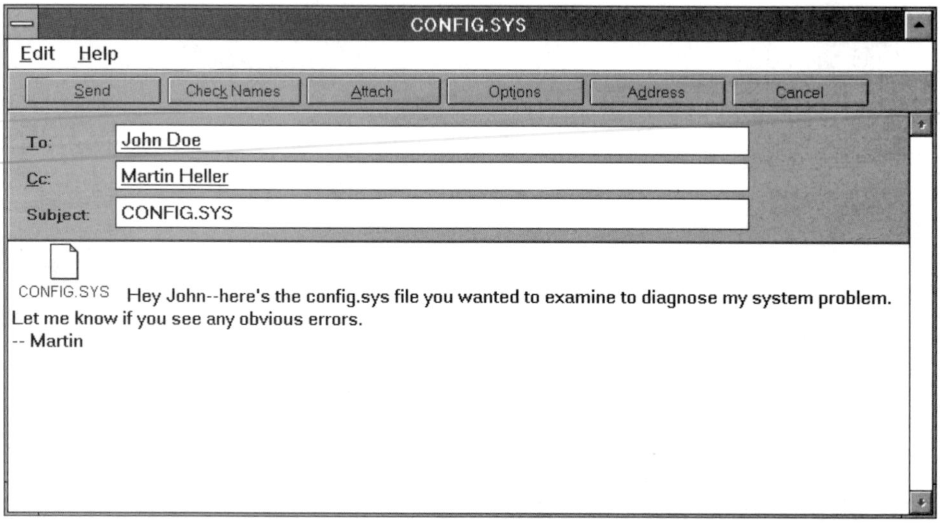

Figure 11-2 This dialog appears when you call **MAPISendDocuments**.

```
ULONG MAPISendMail(lhSession, ulUIParam, lpMessage, flFlags,
                   ulReserved)
LHANDLE   lhSession; //session handle, 0 or as returned by MAPILogon
ULONG  ulUIParam;    //parent window handle, or 0
lpMapiMessage  lpMessage; //pointer to MapiMessage structure
ULONG   flFlags;  //specify whether or not to display login and send
                  //message dialogs, and whether to use a default
                  //MAPI session if it exists
ULONG   ulReserved;  //must be 0
```

You can use **MAPISendMail** to accomplish much the same end as **MAPISend-Documents**, if you wish:

```
long err;
MapiFileDesc file = {0, 0, "c:\tmp\tmp.wk3", "budget17.wk3", NULL};
MapiMessage note =
{0,NULL,NULL,NULL,NULL,NULL,0,NULL,0,NULL,1,&file};

err = MAPISendMail (0L,0L,&note,MAPI_DIALOG,0L);
if (err != SUCCESS_SUCCESS )
  printf("Unable to send the message.\n");
```

Or, you can use **MAPISendMail** to send a completely automated message:

```
MapiRecipDesc recip[2];
MapiFileDesc file = {0, 0, "c:\budget17.wk3", "budget17.wk3",
                     NULL};
```

```
MapiMessage note = {0,NULL,
   "Attached is the budget proposal.\r\nSee you Monday.\r\n",
   NULL,NULL,NULL,0,NULL,2,NULL,1,&file};

recip[0].ulReserved = 0;
recip[0].nRecipClass = MAPI_TO;
recip[0].lpszName = "Sally Jones";
recip[0].lpszAddress = NULL;
recip[0].ulEIDSize = 0;
recip[0].lpEntryID = NULL;

recip[1].ulReserved = 0;
recip[1].nRecipClass = MAPI_CC;
recip[1].lpszName = "Marketing";
recip[1].lpszAddress = NULL;
recip[1].ulEIDSize = 0;
recip[1].lpEntryID = NULL;

note.lpRecips = &recip;

err = MAPISendMail (0L,0L,&note,0L,0L);
if (err != SUCCESS_SUCCESS )
   printf("Unable to send the message.\n");
```

None of the other Simple MAPI functions are any trickier than this. You would use **MAPILogon** and **MAPILogoff** to control sessions; **MAPIFindNext, MAPI-ReadMail, MAPISaveMail,** and **MAPIDeleteMail** to read and dispose of incoming mail; and **MAPIAddress, MAPIDetails,** and **MAPIResolveName** to assist the user in addressing outgoing mail. **MAPIFreeBuffer** is needed to release memory allocated by **MAPIAddress, MAPIReadMail,** and **MAPIResolveName**.

Pipes

A pipe is a communication conduit with two ends: a process with a handle to one end can communicate with a process having a handle to the other end. Pipes can be one-way—where one end is read-only and the other end is write-only; or two-way—where both ends of the pipe can read or write. Pipes are similar to mailslots in that they are written to and read from like files. Win32 supports both anonymous (unnamed) pipes and named pipes. The pipe functions are listed in Table 11-6.

Anonymous Pipes

Anonymous pipes are unnamed, one-way pipes intended to transfer data between a parent process and a child process, or between two child processes of the same parent process. Anonymous pipes are always local: they cannot be used over a network. The **CreatePipe** function creates an anonymous pipe and returns two handles: one to the read end and one to the write end of the pipe. The read handle has only read

Table 11-6 Pipe Functions

Function	Action
CallNamedPipe	Multiple pipe operations.
ConnectNamedPipe	Waits for a client to connect.
CreateNamedPipe	Creates an instance of a named pipe.
CreatePipe	Creates an anonymous pipe.
DisconnectNamedPipe	Disconnects server end of a named pipe.
GetNamedPipeHandleState	Returns named-pipe handle information.
GetNamedPipeInfo	Returns named-pipe handle information.
PeekNamedPipe	Previews pipe-queue data.
SetNamedPipeHandleState	Sets pipe read and blocking mode and controls local buffering.
TransactNamedPipe	Reads and writes a named pipe.
WaitNamedPipe	Waits for a named pipe.

access to the pipe, and the write handle has only write access to the pipe. To communicate through the pipe, a handle to one of the ends must be passed to another process. Usually, this is done through inheritance, where a child process inherits a handle from its parent process.

To read from the pipe, a process uses the read handle in a call to the **ReadFile** function. To write to the pipe, a process uses the write handle in a call to the **WriteFile** function. Neither **ReadFile** nor **WriteFile** returns until the specified number of bytes has been read or written or an error occurs. Asynchronous I/O is not supported for pipes. An anonymous pipe exists until all handles to both read and write ends of the pipe are closed by the **CloseHandle** function.

Named Pipes

Named pipes are considerably more flexible than anonymous pipes. Named pipes can be one-way or two-way, they can work over a network, and a server process can use a named pipe to communicate with one or more client processes.

The server process uses **CreateNamedPipe** to create one or more instances of a named pipe. All instances of a named pipe share the same pipe name, but each instance has its own buffers and handles and provides a separate conduit for client server communication. When a client process specifies a pipe name in the **CreateFile** or **CallNamedPipe** functions, it connects to an instance of the pipe. This enables multiple client processes to use the same named pipe simultaneously. It is entirely possible for a single process to act as both a named pipe client and server.

The **CreateNamedPipe** function offers a number of options:

```
HANDLE CreateNamedPipe(lpName, dwOpenMode, dwPipeMode,
   nMaxInstances, nOutBufferSize, nInBufferSize, nDefaultTimeOut,
   lpSecurityAttributes)

LPCTSTR lpName;                      /* address of pipe name  */
DWORD dwOpenMode;                    /* pipe open mode  */
DWORD dwPipeMode;                    /* pipe-specific modes  */
DWORD nMaxInstances;                 /* maximum number of instances  */
DWORD nOutBufferSize;                /* out buffer size in bytes  */
DWORD nInBufferSize;                 /* in buffer size in bytes  */
DWORD nDefaultTimeOut;               /* time-out time in milliseconds */
LPSECURITY_ATTRIBUTES lpSecurityAttributes;/* security attributes */
```

The pipe name at creation has the form: **\\.\pipe\pipename**. The pipename part of the name can include any character other than a backslash, including numbers and special characters. The entire pipe name string can be up to 256 characters long. Pipe names are not case sensitive. When a client connects to a named pipe over a network, it uses the name form **\\servername\pipe\pipename**. If the pipe is local, the **\\.\pipe\pipename** can be used by the client.

The pipe's open mode can be **PIPE_ACCESS_DUPLEX**, **PIPE_ACCESS_IN-BOUND**, or **PIPE_ACCESS_OUTBOUND**, corresponding to bidirectional data flow, flow from client to server, and flow from server to client, respectively. A pipe can optionally use write-through and/or overlapped mode, which can vary for different instances of the same pipe.

FILE_FLAG_WRITE_THROUGH, which enables write-through mode, only affects write operations on byte-type pipes, which we'll explain shortly. Write-through mode keeps the system from buffering data written into the pipe: in write-through mode, any function that writes to the pipe returns only when the data is actually transmitted across the network to the remote computer. Write-through mode improves reliability at the expense of efficiency.

FILE_FLAG_OVERLAPPED, which enables overlapped mode, allows functions that perform read, write, and connect operations to return immediately. Overlapped mode allows one thread to service multiple instances of a pipe or perform simultaneous read and write operations on the same pipe handle. The alternative to overlapped mode, assuming that you want your named pipe server to handle multiple clients, is to spawn a thread per client.

In addition to directionality, write-through, and overlap, a named pipe's open mode can include any combination of security access flags, which can be different for different instances of the same pipe. The three possible security access flags are **WRITE_DAC**, which gives the caller write access to the named pipe's discretionary ACL, **WRITE_OWNER**, which gives the caller write access to the named pipe's owner, and **ACCESS_SYSTEM_SECURITY**, which gives the caller write access to the named pipe's system ACL. An ACL is an access control list, the basic security control structure in

Windows NT. A discretionary ACL is controlled by the owner of the object; a system ACL is controlled by the system administrator.

All of the above options apply to the named pipe's *open* mode, specified in the second parameter to `CreateNamedPipe`. A named pipe's *pipe* mode, specified in the third parameter to `CreateNamedPipe`, determines the pipe's type, read mode, and wait mode.

We mentioned earlier that a pipe must be in byte mode for write-through mode to be effective. `PIPE_TYPE_BYTE` means that data is written to the pipe as a stream of bytes. The alternative, `PIPE_TYPE_MESSAGE`, means that data is written to the pipe as a stream of messages. A pipe's write mode has to be the same for all instances.

In addition to a type or write mode, a named pipe has a read mode and a wait mode, which can differ among instances. `PIPE_READMODE_BYTE` is valid no matter what write mode was specified for the pipe. `PIPE_READMODE_MESSAGE` works only for a message-type pipe: the pipe data has to be written as messages to be read as messages, but messages can always be broken down into bytes.

`PIPE_WAIT` enables blocking mode, which means that actions on the pipe do not complete until there is data to read, all data is written, or a client is connected. Blocking pipes can in fact wait indefinitely. For nonblocking pipes, enabled by `PIPE_NOWAIT`, `ReadFile`, `WriteFile`, and `ConnectNamedPipe` always return immediately. Nonblocking mode is basically there for compatibility with LAN Manager: if you want to enable asynchronous pipe I/O, use `FILE_FLAG_OVERLAPPED` in the open mode.

The fourth parameter to `CreateNamedPipe` specifies the maximum number of instances that can be created for the pipe, in the range of 1 through `PIPE_-UNLIMITED_INSTANCES`. The fifth and sixth parameter size the pipe's output and input buffers, in bytes: the system will actually round the suggested sizes to allocation boundaries and limit them to some range.

The sixth parameter assigns the pipe a default timeout value, in milliseconds. The final parameter points to a `SECURITY_ATTRIBUTES` structure; it can be `NULL` if you want the pipe to have a default security descriptor.

The server calls `CreateNamedPipe` the first time specifying the pipe's maximum number of simultaneous instances. To create additional instances, the server calls `CreateNamedPipe` again.

Once a pipe instance is created, a client process can connect to it by calling either `CreateFile` or `CallNamedPipe`. If a pipe instance is available, it returns a handle to the client end of the pipe instance. If no instances of the pipe are available, a client process can use `WaitNamedPipe` to wait for one to become available, then try `CreateFile` again.

`CallNamedPipe` is a client function that combines connecting to a pipe instance (and waiting for one to be available, if necessary), writing a message, reading a message, and closing the pipe handle. `CallNamedPipe` can be used only with a message-type pipe.

The server process uses **ConnectNamedPipe** to determine when a client process is connected to a pipe handle. If the pipe handle is in blocking mode, **Connect-NamedPipe** does not return until a client is connected.

Both clients and servers can use **ReadFile** and **WriteFile** with pipes. Alternatively, **ReadFileEx** and **WriteFileEx** functions can be used if the pipe handle was opened for overlapped operations.

PeekNamedPipe performs a nondestructive read on a pipe, and also reports information about the pipe instance. **TransactNamedPipe**, which works only with message-type pipes in message-read mode, writes a request message and reads a reply message in a single operation.

DisconnectNamedPipe is a server function to close the connection to the client process: it makes the client's handle invalid (if it has not already been closed), and discards any unread data in the pipe. The server can avoid closing the connection before the client has read all the data by calling **FlushFileBuffers** prior to calling **DisconnectNamedPipe**. Once the client is disconnected, the server can either call **CloseHandle** to destroy the pipe instance, or call **ConnectNamedPipe** to let a new client connect to this instance.

GetNamedPipeInfo returns the type of the pipe, the size of the input and output buffers, and the maximum number of pipe instances that can be created. **Get-NamedPipeHandleState** reports on the read and wait modes of a pipe handle, the current number of pipe instances, and so on. **SetNamedPipeHandleState** function sets the read mode and wait modes of a pipe handle, maximum number of bytes to collect (for a client), and/or the maximum time to wait before transmitting a message.

Let's recap the high points of named pipes. Named pipes are reliable network pseudofiles of the form **\\servername\pipe\pipename**. They can be unidirectional or bidirectional, buffered or unbuffered, overlapped or synchronous, and contain byte or message streams. For compatibility with LAN Manager, pipes can be nonblocking, but normally you should use blocking pipes and enable overlapping if you want asynchronous I/O. Servers can create multiple instances of a pipe, and vary some of the pipe's parameters on an instance-by-instance basis; they can spawn a thread-per-synchronous-pipe instance, or use a single thread to service multiple asynchronous pipe instances. Clients connect to a single instance of a pipe at a time.

Named pipes are reliable and have good performance for communications across a network. Because a single named pipe server can optionally connect to multiple clients, named pipes can be the basis of any client-server application requiring 1-to-1 or 1-to-N connections in which it is reasonable for each client to establish its own connection. Named pipes would be a reasonable choice of transport for a database server, a transaction-processing system, a multi-user chat application, or a multiplayer game. Named pipes would not be a reasonable way to implement a message broadcast facility—that would be better implemented with mailslots, which don't require each receiver to explictly connect to the sender.

The following listing is a Microsoft-supplied example of a multithreaded server process. It has a main thread that loops continuously, creating a pipe instance and waiting for a client process to connect. When a client process connects, the server process creates a thread to service that client and the loop starts over.

The thread created to service each pipe instance reads requests from the pipe and writes replies to the pipe until the client process closes its handle. When this happens, the thread flushes the pipe, disconnects, closes its pipe handle, and terminates.

```c
#include <stdio.h>
#include <stdlib.h>
#include <string.h>
#include <windows.h>

VOID InstanceThread(LPVOID);
VOID GetAnswerToRequest(LPTSTR, LPTSTR, LPDWORD);

int xx = 0;

DWORD main(VOID) {
  BOOL fConnected;
  DWORD dwThreadId;
  HANDLE hPipe, hThread;
  LPTSTR lpszPipename = "\\\\.\\pipe\\mynamedpipe";


  /*
   * Main loop creates an instance of the named pipe, and
   * then waits for a client to connect to it. When the client
   * connects, a thread is created to handle communications
   * with that client, and the loop is repeated.
   */

  for (;;) {
     hPipe = CreateNamedPipe(
         lpszPipename,              /* pipe name          */
         PIPE_ACCESS_DUPLEX,        /* read/write access  */
         PIPE_TYPE_MESSAGE |        /* message type pipe  */
         PIPE_READMODE_MESSAGE |    /* message-read mode  */

         PIPE_WAIT,                 /* blocking mode       */
         PIPE_UNLIMITED_INSTANCES, /* max. instances      */
         BUFSIZE,                   /* output buffer size */
         BUFSIZE,                   /* input buffer size  */
         PIPE_TIMEOUT,              /* client time-out     */
         NULL);                     /* no security attr.  */
     if (hPipe == INVALID_HANDLE_VALUE)
         MyErrExit("CreatePipe");

     /*
      * Wait for the client to connect; if it succeeds
      * the function returns TRUE. If the function returns FALSE,
```

```
                * GetLastError returns ERROR_PIPE_CONNECTED.
                */

           fConnected = ConnectNamedPipe(hPipe, NULL) ?
                       TRUE :
                       (GetLastError() == ERROR_PIPE_CONNECTED);

           if (fConnected) {

               /* Create a thread for this client. */

               hThread = CreateThread(
                   NULL,               /* no security attr. */
                   0,                  /* default stack size    */
                   (LPTHREAD_START_ROUTINE) InstanceThread,

                   (LPVOID) hPipe, /* thread parameter     */
                   0,                  /* not suspended        */
                   &dwThreadId);   /* returns thread ID    */
               if (hThread == INVALID_HANDLE_VALUE)
                   MyErrExit("CreateThread");

           } else

               /* The client could not connect, so close the pipe. */

               CloseHandle(hPipe);
   }
   return 1;
}

VOID InstanceThread(LPVOID lpvParam) {
   CHAR chRequest[BUFSIZE];

   CHAR chReply[BUFSIZE];
   DWORD cbBytesRead, cbReplyBytes, cbWritten;
   BOOL fSuccess;
   HANDLE hPipe;

   /* The thread's parameter is a handle to a pipe instance. */

   hPipe = (HANDLE) lpvParam;

   while (1) {

       /* Read client requests from the pipe. */

       fSuccess = ReadFile(
           hPipe,          /* handle to pipe            */
           chRequest,      /* buffer to receive data */
           BUFSIZE,        /* size of buffer           */
           &cbBytesRead,   /* number of bytes read     */
           NULL);          /* not overlapped I/O       */
       if (! fSuccess || cbBytesRead == 0)
           break;
```

```
        GetAnswerToRequest(chRequest, chReply, &cbReplyBytes);

        /* Write the reply to the pipe. */

        fSuccess = WriteFile(
            hPipe,          /* handle to pipe          */
            chReply,        /* buffer to write from    */
            cbReplyBytes,   /* number of bytes to write */
            &cbWritten,     /* number of bytes written  */
            NULL);          /* not overlapped I/O       */
        if (! fSuccess || cbReplyBytes != cbWritten) break;

    }

/* Flush the pipe to allow the client to read the pipe's contents
before disconnecting, then disconnect the pipe and close the handle
to this pipe instance. */

    FlushFileBuffers(hPipe);
    DisconnectNamedPipe(hPipe);
    CloseHandle(hPipe);
}
```

Alternatively, a server can use overlapped I/O to service multiple pipes:

```
#include <windows.h>
#define CONNECTING_STATE 0
#define READING_STATE 1
#define WRITING_STATE 2
#define INSTANCES 4

typedef struct {
  OVERLAPPED oOverlap;
  HANDLE hPipeInst;
  CHAR chBuf[BUFSIZE];
  DWORD cbToWrite;
  DWORD dwState;
  BOOL fPendingIO;
} PIPEINST, *LPPIPEINST;

VOID DisconnectAndReconnect(DWORD);
BOOL ConnectToNewClient(HANDLE, LPOVERLAPPED);
VOID GetDataToWriteToClient(LPPIPEINST);

PIPEINST Pipe[INSTANCES];
HANDLE hEvents[INSTANCES];

DWORD main(VOID) {
  DWORD i, dwWait, cbBytes, dwErr;
  BOOL fSuccess;
  LPTSTR lpszPipename = "\\\\.\\pipe\\mynamedpipe";
```

```
/*
 * The initial loop creates several instances of a named pipe,
 * along with an event object for each instance. An
 * overlapped ConnectNamedPipe operation is started for
 * each instance.
 */

for (i = 0; i < INSTANCES; i++) {

    /* Create an event object for this instance. */

    hEvents[i] = CreateEvent(
        NULL,     /* no security attr. */
        TRUE,     /* manual reset event      */
        TRUE,     /* initial state = signaled */
        NULL);    /* unnamed event object    */
    if (hEvents[i] == NULL)
        MyErrExit("CreateEvent");

    Pipe[i].oOverlap.hEvent = hEvents[i];

    Pipe[i].hPipeInst = CreateNamedPipe(
        lpszPipename,            /* pipe name          */
        PIPE_ACCESS_DUPLEX |     /* read/write access  */

        FILE_FLAG_OVERLAPPED,    /* overlapped mode    */
        PIPE_TYPE_MESSAGE |      /* message-type pipe  */
        PIPE_READMODE_MESSAGE |  /* message-read mode  */
        PIPE_WAIT,               /* blocking mode      */
        INSTANCES,               /* number of instances */
        BUFSIZE,                 /* output buffer size */
        BUFSIZE,                 /* input buffer size  */
        PIPE_TIMEOUT,            /* client time-out    */
        NULL);                   /* no security attr   */

    if (Pipe[i].hPipeInst == INVALID_HANDLE_VALUE)
        MyErrExit("CreatePipe");

    /* Call the subroutine to connect to the new client. */

    Pipe[i].fPendingIO = ConnectToNewClient(
        Pipe[i].hPipeInst,
        &Pipe[i].oOverlap);

    Pipe[i].dwState = Pipe[i].fPendingIO ?
        CONNECTING_STATE : /* still connecting   */
        READING_STATE;     /* ready to read      */
}

while (1) {

    /*
     * Wait for the event object to be signaled, indicating
```

```
 * completion of an overlapped read, write, or
 * connect operation.
 */

dwWait = WaitForMultipleObjects(
   INSTANCES,     /* number of event objects */
   hEvents,       /* array of event objects  */
   FALSE,         /* does not wait for all   */
   INFINITE);     /* waits indefinitely      */

/* dwWait shows which pipe had completed operation. */

i = dwWait - WAIT_OBJECT_0; /* determines which pipe */
if (i < 0 || i > (INSTANCES - 1))
   MyErrExit("index out of range");

/* Get the result if the operation was pending. */

if (Pipe[i].fPendingIO) {
   fSuccess = GetOverlappedResult(
         Pipe[i].hPipeInst, /* handle to pipe       */
         &Pipe[i].oOverlap, /* OVERLAPPED structure */
         &cbBytes,          /* bytes transferred    */
         FALSE);            /* do not wait          */

   switch (Pipe[i].dwState) {

       /* Pending connect operation */

       case CONNECTING_STATE:
           if (! fSuccess)
               MyErrExit("ConnectNamedPipe");

           Pipe[i].dwState = READING_STATE;
           break;

       /* Pending read operation */

       case READING_STATE:
           if (! fSuccess || cbBytes == 0) {
               DisconnectAndReconnect(i);
               continue;
           }
           Pipe[i].dwState = WRITING_STATE;
           break;

       /* Pending write operation */

       case WRITING_STATE:
           if (! fSuccess ||
                   cbBytes != Pipe[i].cbToWrite) {

               DisconnectAndReconnect(i);
               continue;
           }
```

```
                    Pipe[i].dwState = READING_STATE;
                    break;

            default:
                MyErrExit("invalid pipe state");

    }

}

/* The pipe state determines which operation to do next. */

switch (Pipe[i].dwState) {

    /*
     * READING_STATE:
     * The pipe instance is connected to the client
     * and ready to read a request from the client.
     */

    case READING_STATE:

            fSuccess = ReadFile(
            Pipe[i].hPipeInst,
            Pipe[i].chBuf,
            BUFSIZE,
            &cbBytes,
            &Pipe[i].oOverlap);

        /* The read operation was successfully completed. */

        if (fSuccess && cbBytes != 0) {
            Pipe[i].fPendingIO = FALSE;
            Pipe[i].dwState = WRITING_STATE;
            continue;
        }

        /* The read operation is still pending */

        dwErr = GetLastError();
        if (! fSuccess &&
             (dwErr == ERROR_IO_PENDING)) {
          Pipe[i].fPendingIO = TRUE;
          continue;
        }

        /* An error occurred; disconnect from the client. */

        DisconnectAndReconnect(i);
        break;

    /*
     * WRITING_STATE:
     * The request was successfully read from the client.
     * Get the reply data and write it to the client.
     */
```

```
            case WRITING_STATE:

                GetDataToWriteToClient(&Pipe[i]);

                fSuccess = WriteFile(
                    Pipe[i].hPipeInst,
                    Pipe[i].chBuf,
                    Pipe[i].cbToWrite,
                    &cbBytes,
                    &Pipe[i].oOverlap);

                /* Write operation completed successfully */

                if (fSuccess &&
                        cbBytes == Pipe[i].cbToWrite) {
                    Pipe[i].fPendingIO = FALSE;
                    Pipe[i].dwState = READING_STATE;

                    continue;
                }

                /* The write operation is still pending. */

                dwErr = GetLastError();
                if (! fSuccess &&
                        (dwErr == ERROR_IO_PENDING)) {
                    Pipe[i].fPendingIO = TRUE;
                    continue;
                }

                /* An error occurred; disconnect from the client. */

                DisconnectAndReconnect(i);
                break;

            default:
                MyErrExit("invalid pipe state");

        }
    }

    return 0;
}


/*
 * DisconnectAndReconnect(DWORD)
 * This function is called when an error occurs or when the client
 * closes its handle to the pipe. Disconnect from this client, and
 * then call ConnectNamedPipe to wait for another client to
 * connect.
 */

VOID DisconnectAndReconnect(DWORD i) {

    /* Disconnect the pipe instance. */
```

```
   if (! DisconnectNamedPipe(Pipe[i].hPipeInst) )
       MyErrExit("DisconnectNamedPipe");

   /* Call a subroutine to connect to the new client. */

   Pipe[i].fPendingIO = ConnectToNewClient(
       Pipe[i].hPipeInst,
       &Pipe[i].oOverlap);

   Pipe[i].dwState = Pipe[i].fPendingIO ?
       CONNECTING_STATE : /* still connecting   */
       READING_STATE;     /* ready to read      */

}

/*
 * ConnectToNewClient(HANDLE, LPOVERLAPPED)
 * This function is called to start an overlapped connect
 * operation. It returns TRUE if an operation is pending or FALSE
 * if the connection has been completed.
 */

BOOL ConnectToNewClient(HANDLE hPipe, LPOVERLAPPED lpo) {

   BOOL fConnected, fPendingIO = FALSE;

   /* Start an overlapped connection for this pipe instance. */

   fConnected = ConnectNamedPipe(hPipe, lpo);

   /* Overlapped ConnectNamedPipe should return FALSE */

   if (fConnected)
       MyErrExit("ConnectNamedPipe");

   switch (GetLastError()) {

       /* Overlapped connection in progress */

       case ERROR_IO_PENDING:
           fPendingIO = TRUE;
           break;

       /* Client already connected, so signal an event. */

       case ERROR_PIPE_CONNECTED:

           if (SetEvent(lpo->hEvent))
               break;

       /* If an error occurs during the connection operation... */

       default:
           MyErrExit("ConnectNamedPipe");
   }
   return fPendingIO;
}
```

You could also implement a server using **ReadFileEx** and **WriteFileEx**, which call completion routines instead of signaling an event. You'll find an example of this in the Windows NT SDK manuals and help file, near the examples you've just seen.

A named pipe client has to worry about servicing only one pipe, which makes it a bit simpler than a named pipe server:

```c
#include <windows.h>
 DWORD main(int argc, char *argv[]) {
 HANDLE hPipe;
 LPVOID lpvMessage;
 CHAR chBuf[512];
 BOOL fSuccess;
 DWORD cbRead, cbWritten, dwMode;
 LPTSTR lpszPipename = "\\\\.\\pipe\\mynamedpipe";

 /* Try to open a named pipe; wait for it, if necessary. */

 while (1) {
     hPipe = CreateFile(
         lpszPipename,    /* pipe name           */
         GENERIC_READ |   /* read/write access   */
         GENERIC_WRITE,
         0,               /* no sharing          */
         NULL,            /* no security attr. */
         OPEN_EXISTING,   /* opens existing pipe */
         0,               /* default attributes  */
         NULL);           /* no template file    */

     /* Break if the pipe handle is valid. */

     if (hPipe != INVALID_HANDLE_VALUE)
         break;

     /* Exit if an error other than ERROR_PIPE_BUSY occurs */

     if (GetLastError() != ERROR_PIPE_BUSY)

         MyErrExit("Could not open pipe");

     /* All pipe instances are busy, so wait for 20 seconds. */

     if (! WaitNamedPipe(lpszPipename, 20000) )
         MyErrExit("Could not open pipe");
 }

 /* The pipe connected; change to message read mode. */

 dwMode = PIPE_READMODE_MESSAGE;
 fSuccess = SetNamedPipeHandleState(
     hPipe,    /* pipe handle       */
     &dwMode,  /* new pipe mode     */
     NULL,     /* don't set max. bytes */
     NULL);    /* don't set max. time  */
```

```
if (! fSuccess)
    MyErrExit("SetNamedPipeHandleState");

/* Send a message to the pipe server. */

lpvMessage = (argc > 1) ? argv[1] : "default message";

fSuccess = WriteFile(
    hPipe,                   /* pipe handle     */
    lpvMessage,              /* message         */
    strlen(lpvMessage) + 1,  /* message length  */
    &cbWritten,              /* bytes written   */
    NULL);                   /* not overlapped  */
if (! fSuccess)
    MyErrExit("WriteFile");

do {

    /* Read from the pipe. */

    fSuccess = ReadFile(
        hPipe,      /* pipe handle            */
        chBuf,      /* buffer to receive reply */
        512,        /* size of buffer         */
        &cbRead,    /* number of bytes read   */
        NULL);      /* not overlapped         */

    if (! fSuccess && GetLastError() != ERROR_MORE_DATA)
        break;

    /* Reply from pipe written to stdout. */

    if (! WriteFile(GetStdHandle(STD_OUTPUT_HANDLE),
            chBuf, cbRead, &cbWritten, NULL))
        break;

} while (! fSuccess); /* repeat loop if ERROR_MORE_DATA */

CloseHandle(hPipe);
return 0;
}
```

That should get you rolling with named pipes. You might also want to examine the SDK example programs NPSERVER and NPCLIENT, which together implement a primitive multi-user chat system. In the Windows NT SDK, you'll find them under the \MSTOOLS\SAMPLES\NAMEPIPE directory; in Visual C++ for NT, you'll find them under \MSVCNT\SAMPLES.

Remote Access

The Remote Access Services, or RAS, functions offer the opportunity to develop applications that log into physically distant networks over modems and phone lines,

Table 11-7   Remote Access Functions

Function	Action
RasDial	Establishes a RAS connection.
RasDialFunc	Callback function called by RasDial on state changes.
RasEnumConnections	Lists active RAS connections.
RasEnumEntries	Lists entries in a RAS phone book.
RasGetConnectStatus	Reports current status of a RAS connection.
RasGetErrorString	Converts RAS error code to error string.
RasHangUp	Terminates a RAS connection.

or over better connections like X.25, ISDN, or T1 links. The RAS functions are listed in Table 11-7. RAS is an attractive alternative to developing your own remote access protocols or setting up bulletin board systems for remote reporting.

As you can see, the RAS API exposes the high-level functions used by the Windows NT RAS applets: functions to dial to and hang up from remote networks, functions to list the active connections and the entries in a RAS phone book, and a function to report the status of a connection. This set of functions is so simple we won't even show you a code sample: you won't have any trouble figuring out how to use them yourself. Once you have a connection established, you can use the WNet services to connect to remote hard disks, and then use ordinary file services to transfer information to the remote server.

Sockets

Aside from being the standard network programming mechanism in Berkeley Unix, sockets are quite flexible and simple to use. The Windows and Windows NT implementation of sockets includes some extensions to make sockets more efficient, but you only really have to use the initialization and termination routines (**WSAStartup** and **WSACleanup**) from the Windows extensions.

The basic Berkeley-style socket routines included in Windows Sockets are listed in Table 11-8; the so-called "database" or "getXbyY" functions are listed in Table 11-9; and the Windows extensions are listed in Table 11-10.

You initialize Windows Sockets by calling **WSAStartup**. You'll find the appropriate logic in the **WM_CREATE** section of **MainWndProc** in WSOCK.C, the Microsoft-supplied sample that follows. A client can connect to a server by calling **socket** with the required socket type and the desired protocol, as shown in the **WM_COMMAND** / **IDM_CONNECT** case of **MainWndProc**; identifying the server, which is done in **FillAddr** in the example; and calling **connect**, shown in the **IDM_CONNECT** case.

Table 11-8 Berkeley-Style Socket Routines

Function	Action
accept()	An incoming connection is acknowledged and associated with an immediately created socket. The original socket is returned to the listening state.
bind()	Assign a local name to an unnamed socket.
closesocket()	Remove a socket descriptor from the per-process object reference table. Only blocks if SO_LINGER is set.
connect()	Initiate a connection on the specified socket.
getpeername()	Retrieve the name of the peer connected to the specified socket descriptor.
getsockname()	Retrieve the current name for the specified socket.
getsockopt()	Retrieve options associated with the specified socket descriptor.
htonl()	Convert a 32-bit quantity from host byte order to network byte order.
htons()	Convert a 16-bit quantity from host byte order to network byte order.
inet_addr()	Convert a character string representing a number in the Internet standard "." notation to an Internet address value.
inet_ntoa()	Convert an Internet address value to an ASCII string in "." notation i.e. "a.b.c.d".
ioctlsocket()	Provide control for descriptors.
listen()	Listen for incoming connections on a specified socket.
ntohl()	Convert a 32-bit quantity from network byte order to host byte order.
ntohs()	Convert a 16-bit quantity from network byte order to host byte order.
recv()*	Receive data from a connected socket.
recvfrom()*	Receive data from either a connected or unconnected socket.
select()*	Perform synchronous I/O multiplexing.
send()*	Send data to a connected socket.
sendto()*	Send data to either a connected or unconnected socket.
setsockopt()	Store options associated with the specified socket descriptor.
shutdown()	Shut down part of a full-duplex connection.
socket()	Create an endpoint for communication and return a socket descriptor.

* The routine can block if acting on a blocking socket.

A server waits for a connection with **socket**, **bind**, and **listen**, as shown in the **IDM_LISTEN** case. When a client connects, the server calls **accept**. The **WSAAsync-Select** function causes window messages to be sent when socket events, like incoming data, need to be handled. Alternatively—most appropriately in a threaded application—the server can use **select** to determine when a socket needs to be read,

Table 11-9 Socket "Database" Functions

Function	Action
gethostbyaddr()*	Retrieve the name(s) and address corresponding to a network address.
gethostname()	Retrieve the name of the local host.
gethostbyname()*	Retrieve the name(s) and address corresponding to a host name.
getprotobyname()*	Retrieve the protocol name and number corresponding to a protocol name.
getprotobynumber()*	Retrieve the protocol name and number corresponding to a protocol number.
getservbyname()*	Retrieve the service name and port corresponding to a service name.
getservbyport()*	Retrieve the service name and port corresponding to a port.

* The routine can block under some circumstances.

or simply use **recv** or **recvfrom** to read the next data packet. This is demonstrated in **AcceptThreadProc**. To send data, use **send** or **sendto**, as shown in case **IDM_SENDTCP**.

The functions **recv** and **send** work only with connected stream sockets—the rough equivalent of NetBIOS sessions or named pipes. The functions **recvfrom** and **sendto** can also work with datagrams—the unreliable protocol that also allows broadcasting. You can use datagram sockets in the same sort of applications as you would use NetBIOS datagrams or mailslots.

With the above summary in mind, you'll find WSOCK.C enlightening:

```
/*******************************************************************\
 *  wsock.c — sample program demonstrating Windows Sockets APIs.
 *
 *  Demonstrates basic sockets programming with the Windows Sockets
 *    API. Allows two occurances of the application to connect. Also,
 *    displays information about a host computer.
 *
 *******************************************************************/

#include <windows.h>    /* required for all Windows applications */
#include <winsock.h>
#include <stdio.h>      /* for sprintf                           */
#include <string.h>     /* for strlen                            */
#include <memory.h>
#include <process.h>    /* for _beginthread                      */
#include "wsock.h"      /* specific to this program              */

HANDLE hInst;           /* current instance                      */

SOCKET sock;
```

Table 11-10 Windows Asynchronous Socket Functions

Function	Action
WSAAsyncGetHostByAddr() WSAAsyncGetHostByName() WSAAsyncGetProtoByName() WSAAsyncGetProtoByNumber() WSAAsyncGetServByName() WSAAsyncGetServByPort()	A set of functions that provide asynchronous versions of the standard Berkeley getXbyY() functions. For example, the WSAAsyncGetHostByName() function provides an asynchronous message-based implementation of the standard Berkeley gethostbyname() function.
WSAAsyncSelect()	Perform asynchronous version of select().
WSACancelAsyncRequest()	Cancel an outstanding instance of a WSAAsyncGetXByY() function.
WSACancelBlockingCall()	Cancel an outstanding "blocking" API call.
WSACleanup()	Sign off from the underlying Windows Sockets DLL.
WSAGetLastError()	Obtain details of last Windows Sockets API error.
WSAIsBlocking()	Determine if the underlying Windows Sockets DLL is already blocking an existing call for this thread.
WSASetBlockingHook()	"Hook" the blocking method used by the underlying Windows Sockets implementation.
WSASetLastError()	Set the error to be returned by a subsequent WSAGetLastError().
WSAStartup()	Initialize the underlying Windows Sockets DLL.
WSAUnhookBlockingHook()	Restore the original blocking function.

```
u_short portno;        /* Which tcp port are we going to use?   */

char szBuff[ 80 ];     /* Temp buffer - used to pass strings    */
                       /* to and from dialog boxes, etc         */

#define MAX_PENDING_CONNECTS 4 /* The backlog allowed for listen*/
#define NO_FLAGS_SET         0 /* Used with recv()/send()       */
#define MY_MSG_LENGTH       80 /* msg buffer sent back and forth*/

/**************************************************************
 *
 *    FUNCTION: WinMain(HANDLE, HANDLE, LPSTR, int)
 *
 *    PURPOSE: calls initialization function, processes message loop
 *
 \**************************************************************/

WINAPI WinMain(
    HANDLE hInstance,
```

```
    HANDLE hPrevInstance,
    LPSTR lpCmdLine,
    int nCmdShow
    )
{
    MSG msg;
    UNREFERENCED_PARAMETER( lpCmdLine );

    if (!hPrevInstance)        /* Other instances of app running? */
        if (!InitApplication(hInstance))
            return (FALSE);   /* Exits if unable to initialize   */
    /*
     *   Perform initializations that apply to a specific instance
     */
    if (!InitInstance(hInstance, nCmdShow))
        return (FALSE);

    while (GetMessage(&msg,/* message structure              */
            NULL, /* handle of window receiving the message */
            0,    /* lowest message to examine              */
            0))   /* highest message to examine             */
        {
        TranslateMessage(&msg); /* Translates virtual key codes */
        DispatchMessage(&msg);  /* Dispatches message to window */
    }
    return (msg.wParam);/*Returns the value from PostQuitMessage*/
}


/************************************************************
 *
 *    FUNCTION: InitApplication(HANDLE)
 *
 *    PURPOSE: Initializes window data and registers window class
 *
 \************************************************************/

BOOL InitApplication(HANDLE hInstance)
{
    WNDCLASS  wc;
    wc.style =  0;        /* Class style(s).                   */
    wc.lpfnWndProc = (WNDPROC)MainWndProc;
    wc.cbClsExtra = 0;  /* No per-class extra data.          */
    wc.cbWndExtra = 0;  /* No per-window extra data.         */
    wc.hIcon = LoadIcon (hInstance, "wsockicon");
    wc.hInstance = hInstance;/* Application that owns the class.*/
    wc.hCursor = LoadCursor(NULL, IDC_ARROW);
    wc.hbrBackground = GetStockObject(WHITE_BRUSH);
    wc.lpszMenuName =   "WSockMenu";
    wc.lpszClassName = "WSockWClass";
 /* Register the window class and return success/failure code. */
    return (RegisterClass(&wc));
}
```

```
/*********************************************************\
*
*     FUNCTION:   InitInstance(HANDLE, int)
*
*     PURPOSE:   Saves instance handle and creates main window
*
\*********************************************************/

BOOL InitInstance(
    HANDLE          hInstance,/* Current instance identifier.*/
    int             nCmdShow) /* Param for first ShowWindow call.*/
{
    HWND            hWnd;       /* Main window handle.*/

    hInst = hInstance;

    /* Create a main window for this application instance.  */

    hWnd = CreateWindow(
        "WSockWClass", /* See RegisterClass() call.*/
        "Windows Sockets Sample Application",
        WS_OVERLAPPEDWINDOW,/* Window style.*/
        CW_USEDEFAULT,        /* Default horizontal position. */
        CW_USEDEFAULT,        /* Default vertical position.   */
        CW_USEDEFAULT,        /* Default width.               */
        CW_USEDEFAULT,        /* Default height.              */
        NULL,                 /* Overlapped windows have no parent.*/
        NULL,                 /* Use the window class menu. */
        hInstance,            /* This instance owns this window.*/
        NULL                  /* Pointer not needed. */
    );

    /* If window could not be created, return "failure" */

    if (!hWnd)
        return (FALSE);

/* Make the window visible; update its client area; and return
"success" */

    ShowWindow(hWnd, nCmdShow);   /* Show the window*/
    UpdateWindow(hWnd);           /* Sends WM_PAINT message */
    return (TRUE);

}

/*********************************************************\
*
*     FUNCTION: AcceptThreadProc(PTHREADPACK tp)
*
*     PURPOSE:  Use blocking accept() calls and display a message
*               box when a connection is made.
*
\*********************************************************/
```

```
void AcceptThreadProc( PTHREADPACK ptp )
{
    SOCKADDR_IN acc_sin;/* Accept socket address - internet style */
    int acc_sin_len;    /* Accept socket address length */
    int status;
    char szMsg[ MY_MSG_LENGTH ];

    acc_sin_len = sizeof(acc_sin);
    wsprintf( szBuff, "thread #%d created.", ptp->nThread);
    MessageBox(ptp->hWnd, szBuff, "FYI", MB_OK);

    sock = accept( sock,(struct sockaddr FAR *) &acc_sin,
            (int FAR *) &acc_sin_len );

    if (sock < 0) {
        sprintf(szBuff, "%d is the error", WSAGetLastError());
        MessageBox(ptp->hWnd, szBuff, "accept(sock) failed", MB_OK);
        }

    wsprintf( szBuff, "Thread #%d accepted something\n\n"
    "Check for incoming messages?", ptp->nThread);

    /*
    *    Now have a connection —
    *    SetConnectMenus() grays/enables proper menu items
    */
    SetConnectMenus( ptp->hWnd );

    while (1) {
        /*
        *    By default sockets are created in blocking mode.
        *    Just keep reading until process destroyed.
        */
        status = recv( sock, szMsg, MY_MSG_LENGTH, NO_FLAGS_SET );

        if (status == SOCKET_ERROR) {
            wsprintf( szMsg, "Error %d", WSAGetLastError() );
            MessageBox( ptp->hWnd, szMsg, "Error with recv()", MB_OK);
            _endthread();
            }
        szMsg[status] = '\0';  /* NULL-terminate the string */

        if (status)
            MessageBox( ptp->hWnd, szMsg, "From thread", MB_OK);
        else  {
            MessageBox( ptp->hWnd, "Connection broken", "Error",
                    MB_OK);
            _endthread();
            }
    }    /* while (forever) */
}
```

```
/*******************************************************************\
*
*    FUNCTION:  FillAddr(HWND, PSOCKADDR_IN, BOOL)
*
*    PURPOSE:  Retrieves the IP address and port number.
*
*    COMMENTS:
*        This function is called in two conditions.
*            1.) When a client is preparing to call connect(), or
*            2.) When a server host is going to call bind(),
*                listen() and accept().
*        In both situations, a SOCKADDR_IN structure is filled.
*        However, different fields are filled depending on the
*           condition.
*
*   ASSUMPTION:
*        szBuff is a global variable that contains the remote host
*        name or NULL if local.
*        bConnect determines if the socket address is being set up
*        for a listen() (bConnect == TRUE) or a connect()
*        (bConnect == FALSE)
*
*
\*******************************************************************/

BOOL FillAddr(
        HWND hWnd,
        PSOCKADDR_IN psin,
        BOOL bConnect)
{
    DWORD dwSize;
    PHOSTENT phe;
    PSERVENT pse;
    char szTemp[200];
    int status;

    psin->sin_family = AF_INET;
    /*
    *   If we are setting up for a listen() call (bConnect = FALSE),
    *   fill servent with our address.
    */
    if (!bConnect) {
        /*
        *   Retrieve my ip address.  Assuming the hosts file in
        *   in %systemroot%/system/drivers/etc/hosts contains my
        *   computer name.
        */

        dwSize = sizeof(szBuff);
        gethostname(szBuff, dwSize);
        }
```

```
   phe = gethostbyname(szBuff);
   if (phe == NULL) {
      sprintf(szTemp, "%d is the error. Make sure '%s' is listed"
      " in the hosts file.", WSAGetLastError(), szBuff);
      MessageBox(hWnd, szTemp, "gethostbyname() failed.", MB_OK);
      return FALSE;
   }
   memcpy((char FAR *)&(psin->sin_addr), phe->h_addr,
      phe->h_length);
   /*
    *   Retrieve the Port number
    */
   status = DialogBox(hInst,   /* current instance          */
      "TCPPORTNUM",            /* resource to use           */
      hWnd,                    /* parent handle             */
      GetTcpPort);            /* instance address          */

   switch(status) {
      case 0:                 /* User cancelled */
         return FALSE;

      case 1:                 /* actual port number entered */
         /* Convert to network ordering */
         psin->sin_port = htons(portno);
         break;

      case 2:                 /* service name entereted */
         /*
          *   Find the service name, szBuff, which is a type tcp
          *   protocol in the "services" file.
          */
         pse = getservbyname(szBuff, "tcp");
         if (pse == NULL)  {
            sprintf(szBuff, "%d is the error. Make sure this is"
            " a valid TCP service.", WSAGetLastError());
            MessageBox(hWnd, szBuff, "getservbyname(sock) failed",
            MB_OK);
            return FALSE;
         }
         psin->sin_port = pse->s_port;
         break;

      default:
         return FALSE;
   }
   return TRUE;
}

/************************************************************
 *
 *    FUNCTION: SetConnectMenus( HWND )
 *
```

```
 *    PURPOSE: Gray/Enable the proper menu items after a connection
 *             has been established.
 *
\******************************************************************/

void SetConnectMenus( HWND hWnd )
{
   /*
    *    Disable/enable proper menu items.
    */
   EnableMenuItem(GetMenu( hWnd ), IDM_HOSTNAME, MF_ENABLED );
   EnableMenuItem(GetMenu( hWnd ), IDM_LISTEN, MF_GRAYED );
   EnableMenuItem(GetMenu( hWnd ), IDM_CONNECT, MF_GRAYED );
   EnableMenuItem(GetMenu( hWnd ), IDM_ALISTEN, MF_GRAYED );
   EnableMenuItem(GetMenu( hWnd ), IDM_TLISTEN, MF_GRAYED );
   EnableMenuItem(GetMenu( hWnd ), IDM_CANCEL, MF_GRAYED );
   EnableMenuItem(GetMenu( hWnd ), IDM_SENDTCP, MF_ENABLED );

   /*
    *    Reflect socket connection in title bar.
    */
   SetWindowText( hWnd, "Connected");
}

/******************************************************************\
 *
 *    FUNCTION: MainWndProc(HWND, unsigned, WORD, LONG)
 *
 *    PURPOSE:  Processes main window messages
 *
 * MESSAGES:
 *  WM_CREATE   - call WSAStartUp() and display description message
 *  WSA_ACCEPT  - User-defined message used with WSAAsyncSelect().
 *                Sent by the Windows Sockets DLL when a socket
 *                connection is pending.
 *
 *  WM_COMMAND
 *  IDM_CONNECT - Connect to a remote host.
 *  IDM_LISTEN  - Use the BSD-Style accept().
 *  IDM_ALISTEN - Use the Windows Sockets Asynchronous APIs to
 *                detect when a connection is made.
 *  IDM_CANCEL  - Cancel the Asynchronous call above.
 *  IDM_TLISTEN - Uses two threads to accept network connections
 *                (using the BSD-Style accept().
 *  IDM_HOSTNAME- Display information about a host.
 *  IDM_ABOUT   - About box.
 *
 *  WM_DESTROY  - destroy window and call the WSACleanUp()
 *
\******************************************************************/

LONG APIENTRY MainWndProc(
```

```
      HWND hWnd,      /* window handle                    */
      UINT message, /* type of message                    */
      UINT wParam,  /* additional information             */
      LONG lParam)  /* additional information             */
{
   int status;            /* Status Code */
   SOCKADDR_IN local_sin;/* Local socket - internet style */
   SOCKADDR_IN acc_sin;/* Accept socket address - internet style */
   int acc_sin_len;    /* Accept socket address length */

   switch (message) {
   case WM_CREATE:
   {
      WSADATA WSAData;
      char szTemp[80];

      if ((status = WSAStartup(MAKEWORD(1,1), &WSAData)) == 0) {
         MessageBox( hWnd, WSAData.szDescription,
                 WSAData.szSystemStatus, MB_OK);
      }
      else {
         sprintf(szTemp, "%d is the err", status);
         MessageBox( hWnd, szTemp, "Error", MB_OK);
      }
   }
   break;   /* WM_CREATE */

   /*
    *    Notification if data is waiting on a socket.  This comes
    *    from Windows Sockets (via WSAAsyncSelect()).
    */
   case WSA_READ:
   {
      char szTemp[ MY_MSG_LENGTH ];

      if (WSAGETSELECTEVENT(lParam) == FD_READ) {
         status = recv((SOCKET)wParam, szTemp, MY_MSG_LENGTH,
                 NO_FLAGS_SET );
         if (status) {
            szTemp[ status ] = '\0';
            MessageBox( hWnd, szTemp, "WSA_READ", MB_OK);
         }
         else
            MessageBox( hWnd, "Connection broken", "Error", MB_OK);
      }
      else {    /* FD_CLOSE — connection dropped */
         MessageBox( hWnd, "Connection lost", "WSA_READ", MB_OK);
         EnableMenuItem(GetMenu( hWnd ), IDM_HOSTNAME, MF_ENABLED);
         EnableMenuItem(GetMenu( hWnd ), IDM_LISTEN, MF_ENABLED);
         EnableMenuItem(GetMenu( hWnd ), IDM_CONNECT, MF_ENABLED);
         EnableMenuItem(GetMenu( hWnd ), IDM_ALISTEN, MF_ENABLED);
         EnableMenuItem(GetMenu( hWnd ), IDM_TLISTEN, MF_ENABLED);
```

```
         EnableMenuItem(GetMenu( hWnd ), IDM_CANCEL, MF_GRAYED);
         EnableMenuItem(GetMenu( hWnd ), IDM_SENDTCP, MF_GRAYED);
     }
}
break;        /* WSA_READ*/

case WSA_ACCEPT: /* Notification if a socket connection is
                    pending. */
    /*
     *   Disable/enable proper menu items.
     */
    EnableMenuItem(GetMenu( hWnd ), IDM_HOSTNAME, MF_ENABLED);
    EnableMenuItem(GetMenu( hWnd ), IDM_LISTEN, MF_ENABLED);
    EnableMenuItem(GetMenu( hWnd ), IDM_CONNECT, MF_ENABLED);
    EnableMenuItem(GetMenu( hWnd ), IDM_ALISTEN, MF_ENABLED);
    EnableMenuItem(GetMenu( hWnd ), IDM_TLISTEN, MF_ENABLED);
    EnableMenuItem(GetMenu( hWnd ), IDM_CANCEL, MF_GRAYED);

    if (WSAGETSELECTERROR( lParam ) == 0) {    /* Success */

        /*
         *   Accept the incoming connection.
         */
        acc_sin_len = sizeof( acc_sin );
        sock = accept( sock,(struct sockaddr FAR *) &acc_sin,
            (int FAR *) &acc_sin_len );

        if (sock < 0) {
            sprintf(szBuff, "%d is the error", WSAGetLastError());
            MessageBox(hWnd, szBuff, "accept(sock) failed", MB_OK);
            break;
        }

        MessageBox(hWnd, "accept()", "Accepted a connection!",
                  MB_OK);
        /*
         *   Now have a connection —
         *   SetConnectMenus() grays/enables proper menu items
         */
        SetConnectMenus( hWnd );

        /*
         *   Send main window a WSA_READ when either data is
         *   pending on the socket (FD_READ) or the connection is
         *   closed (FD_CLOSE)
         */
        if ((status = WSAAsyncSelect( sock, hWnd, WSA_READ,
                FD_READ | FD_CLOSE )) > 0) {
            wsprintf(szBuff, "%d (0x%x)", status, status);
            MessageBox( hWnd, "Error on WSAAsyncSelect()", szBuff,
                    MB_OK);
            closesocket( sock );
        }
```

```
      }
      else {
        MessageBox(hWnd, "accept()", "Error occured!", MB_OK);
        /*
        *    Cancel any further notifications.
        */
        WSAAsyncSelect( sock, hWnd, 0, 0);
        SetWindowText( hWnd, "Async Listen call canceled");
      }
      break;    /* WSA_ACCEPT */

  case WM_COMMAND: /* message: command from application menu */
    switch(LOWORD(wParam)) {
    case IDM_CONNECT: /* Client - connect to remote host */
    {
        /*

        When a network client wants to connect to a server,
        it must have:
          1.) a TCP port number (gotten via getservbyname())
        and
          2.) an IP address of the remote host (gotten via
          gethostbyname()).

        The following summarizes the steps used to connect.
        Make a dialog box (HostName)
        Get the name of the remote host computer in which to
        connect from the user (store string in "szBuff" global var)
        * Check to see if the hosts file knows the computer
          (gethostbyname)
        * Get the host information (hostent structure filled)
        * Fill in the address of the remote host into the servent
          structure (memcpy)
        * Make a dialog box (TCPPORTNUM)
        * Get the NAME of the port to connect to on the remote host
          from the user.
        * Get the port number (getservbyname)
        * Fill in the port number of the servent structure
        Establish a connection (connect)

        The * prefixed steps are done in the FillAddr() procedure.
        */
        SOCKADDR_IN dest_sin;   /* DESTination Socket INternet */

/* Get the name of the remote host. Store the string in szBuff. */

        status = DialogBox(hInst,
            "HOSTNAME",
          hWnd,
          GetHostName);
        if (!status)    /* User cancelled */
          break;
```

```
      sock = socket( AF_INET, SOCK_STREAM, 0);
      if (sock == INVALID_SOCKET) {
         MessageBox(hWnd, "socket() failed", "Error", MB_OK);
         break;
      }

      /*
       *    Retrieve the IP address and TCP Port number
       *    Global variable szBuff contains the remote host name.
       */
      if (!FillAddr( hWnd, &dest_sin, TRUE)) {
         closesocket( sock );
         break;
      }

      if (connect( sock, (PSOCKADDR) &dest_sin,
         sizeof( dest_sin)) < 0) {
         closesocket( sock );
         MessageBox(hWnd, "connect() failed", "Error", MB_OK);
         break;
      }
      MessageBox(hWnd, "connect() worked!", "Success!", MB_OK);

      /*
       *   Now have a connection —
       *   SetConnectMenus() grays/enables proper menu items
       */
      SetConnectMenus( hWnd );

      /*
       *   Send main window a WSA_READ when either data is
       *   pending on the socket (FD_READ) or the connection is
       *   closed (FD_CLOSE)
       */
      if ((status = WSAAsyncSelect( sock, hWnd, WSA_READ,
         FD_READ | FD_CLOSE )) > 0) {
         wsprintf(szBuff, "%d (0x%x)");
         MessageBox( hWnd, "Error on WSAAsyncSelect()", szBuff,
             MB_OK);
         closesocket( sock );
      }
   }
   break;   /* IDM_CONNECT */

   case IDM_LISTEN:
   {
      sock = socket( AF_INET, SOCK_STREAM, 0);
      if (sock == INVALID_SOCKET) {
         MessageBox(hWnd, "socket() failed", "Error", MB_OK);
         closesocket(sock);
         break;
      }
```

```
/*
 *    Retrieve the IP address and TCP Port number
 */

if (!FillAddr(hWnd, &local_sin, FALSE ))
   break;

/*
 *    Disable/enable proper menu items.
 */
EnableMenuItem(GetMenu( hWnd ), IDM_HOSTNAME, MF_GRAYED);
EnableMenuItem(GetMenu( hWnd ), IDM_LISTEN, MF_GRAYED);
EnableMenuItem(GetMenu( hWnd ), IDM_ALISTEN, MF_GRAYED);
EnableMenuItem(GetMenu( hWnd ), IDM_TLISTEN, MF_GRAYED);
EnableMenuItem(GetMenu( hWnd ), IDM_CONNECT, MF_GRAYED);
SetWindowText( hWnd, "Waiting for connection..");
/*
 *    Associate an address with a socket. (bind)
 */
if (bind( sock, (struct sockaddr FAR *) &local_sin,
     sizeof(local_sin)) == SOCKET_ERROR) {
   sprintf(szBuff, "%d is the error", WSAGetLastError());
   MessageBox(hWnd, szBuff, "bind(sock) failed", MB_OK);
   break;
}

if (listen( sock, MAX_PENDING_CONNECTS ) < 0) {
   sprintf(szBuff, "%d is the error", WSAGetLastError());
   MessageBox(hWnd, szBuff, "listen(sock) failed", MB_OK);
   break;
}

acc_sin_len = sizeof(acc_sin);
sock = accept( sock,(struct sockaddr FAR *) &acc_sin,
   (int FAR *) &acc_sin_len );
if (sock < 0) {
   sprintf(szBuff, "%d is the error", WSAGetLastError());
   MessageBox(hWnd, szBuff, "accept(sock) failed", MB_OK);
   break;
}

MessageBox(hWnd, "accept()", "Accepted a connection!",
 MB_OK);

 /*
  *    Now have a connection —
  *    SetConnectMenus() grays/enables proper menu items
  */
SetConnectMenus( hWnd );

 /*
  *    Send main window a WSA_READ when either data is
  *    pending on the socket (FD_READ) or the connection is
```

```
 *     closed (FD_CLOSE)
 */
 if ((status = WSAAsyncSelect( sock, hWnd, WSA_READ,
     FD_READ | FD_CLOSE )) > 0) {
    wsprintf(szBuff, "%d (0x%x)");
    MessageBox( hWnd, "Error on WSAAsyncSelect()", szBuff,
     MB_OK);
    closesocket( sock );
 }
}
break;   /* IDM_LISTEN */

/*
 *   Asynchronous Listen - Using WSA extensions.
 */
case IDM_ALISTEN:
{
   sock = socket( AF_INET, SOCK_STREAM, 0);
   if (sock == INVALID_SOCKET) {
      MessageBox(hWnd, "socket() failed", "Error", MB_OK);
      break;
   }
   /*
    *   Retrieve the IP address and TCP Port number
    */

   if (!FillAddr( hWnd, &local_sin, FALSE)) {
      closesocket( sock );
      break;
   }

   /*
    *   Disable/enable proper menu items.
    */
   EnableMenuItem(GetMenu( hWnd ), IDM_HOSTNAME, MF_GRAYED);
   EnableMenuItem(GetMenu( hWnd ), IDM_LISTEN, MF_GRAYED);
   EnableMenuItem(GetMenu( hWnd ), IDM_CONNECT, MF_GRAYED);
   EnableMenuItem(GetMenu( hWnd ), IDM_ALISTEN, MF_GRAYED);
   EnableMenuItem(GetMenu( hWnd ), IDM_TLISTEN, MF_GRAYED);
   EnableMenuItem(GetMenu( hWnd ), IDM_CANCEL, MF_ENABLED);
   SetWindowText( hWnd, "Waiting for connection.. (Async)");
   /*
    *   Associate an address with a socket. (bind)
    */
   if (bind( sock, (struct sockaddr FAR *) &local_sin,
       sizeof(local_sin)) == SOCKET_ERROR) {
      sprintf(szBuff, "%d is the error", WSAGetLastError());
      MessageBox(hWnd, szBuff, "bind(sock) failed", MB_OK);
      closesocket( sock );
      break;
   }

   if (listen( sock, MAX_PENDING_CONNECTS ) < 0) {
```

```
                  sprintf(szBuff, "%d is the error", WSAGetLastError());
                  MessageBox(hWnd, szBuff, "listen(sock) failed", MB_OK);
                  break;
               }

               /*
                *    Send window a WSA_ACCEPT when something is trying to
                *    connect.
                */
               if ((status = WSAAsyncSelect( sock, hWnd, WSA_ACCEPT,
                  FD_ACCEPT)) > 0) {
                  wsprintf( szBuff, "%d (0x%x)");
                  MessageBox( hWnd, "Error on WSAAsyncSelect()", szBuff,
                   MB_OK);
                  SetWindowText( hWnd, "Async listen cancelled");
                  closesocket( sock );
               }
            }
            break;   /* IDM_ALISTEN */
            /*
             *   Cancel an asynchronous call.
             */
            case IDM_CANCEL:
               WSAAsyncSelect( sock, hWnd, 0, 0);
               SetWindowText( hWnd, "Async Listen cancelled..");
               /*
                *    Disable/enable proper menu items.
                */
               EnableMenuItem(GetMenu( hWnd ), IDM_HOSTNAME, MF_ENABLED);
               EnableMenuItem(GetMenu( hWnd ), IDM_LISTEN, MF_ENABLED);
               EnableMenuItem(GetMenu( hWnd ), IDM_CONNECT, MF_ENABLED);
               EnableMenuItem(GetMenu( hWnd ), IDM_ALISTEN, MF_ENABLED);
               EnableMenuItem(GetMenu( hWnd ), IDM_TLISTEN, MF_ENABLED);
               EnableMenuItem(GetMenu( hWnd ), IDM_CANCEL, MF_GRAYED);
               EnableMenuItem(GetMenu( hWnd ), IDM_SENDTCP, MF_GRAYED);
               break;    /* IDM_CANCEL */

            /*
             * Listen in the main thread — spawn and accept two network
             * connections inside two threads.
             */
            case IDM_TLISTEN:
            {
               static THREADPACK tp;

               sock = socket( AF_INET, SOCK_STREAM, 0);
               if (sock == INVALID_SOCKET) {
                  MessageBox(hWnd, "socket() failed", "Error", MB_OK);
                  closesocket(sock);
                  break;
               }
```

```
        /*
        *   Retrieve the IP address and TCP Port number
        */

        if (!FillAddr(hWnd, &local_sin, FALSE ))
          break;

        /*
        *   Disable/enable proper menu items.
        */
        EnableMenuItem(GetMenu( hWnd ), IDM_HOSTNAME, MF_GRAYED);
        EnableMenuItem(GetMenu( hWnd ), IDM_LISTEN, MF_GRAYED);
        EnableMenuItem(GetMenu( hWnd ), IDM_ALISTEN, MF_GRAYED);
        EnableMenuItem(GetMenu( hWnd ), IDM_TLISTEN, MF_GRAYED);
        EnableMenuItem(GetMenu( hWnd ), IDM_CONNECT, MF_GRAYED);
        EnableMenuItem(GetMenu( hWnd ), IDM_SENDTCP, MF_GRAYED);
        SetWindowText( hWnd, "Waiting for connection..");
        /*
        *   Associate an address with a socket. (bind)
        */
        if (bind( sock, (struct sockaddr FAR *) &local_sin,
            sizeof(local_sin)) == SOCKET_ERROR) {
          sprintf(szBuff, "%d is the error", WSAGetLastError());
          MessageBox(hWnd, szBuff, "bind(sock) failed", MB_OK);
          break;
        }
        if (listen( sock, MAX_PENDING_CONNECTS ) < 0) {
          sprintf(szBuff, "%d is the error", WSAGetLastError());
          MessageBox(hWnd, szBuff, "listen(sock) failed", MB_OK);
          break;
        }

        tp.nThread = 0;
        tp.hWnd = hWnd;

        _beginthread(AcceptThreadProc, 0, &tp);


      }
      break;    /* IDM_TLISTEN */

  /*
  *   Display host information.
  */
  case IDM_HOSTNAME:
      /*
      *   Prompt the user and retrieve the text name of the host.
      */
      status = DialogBox(hInst,
          "HOSTNAME",
          hWnd,
          GetHostName);
```

```
    if (status == TRUE) {    /* If user hit "OK" .. */
    /*
    *   Get the host information
    */
    if ((phe = gethostbyname( szBuff )) == NULL) {
        MessageBox(hWnd, "gethostbyname() failed", "Error",
        MB_OK);
        break;
    }
    else {

    /*
    *   Display the host information ..
    */
        DialogBox(hInst,
            "DISPLAYHOST",
            hWnd,
            DisplayHostEnt);
    }
}
break;    /* IDM_HOSTNAME */
/*
*   Send a message to (via TCP connection) to remote host.
*/
case IDM_SENDTCP:
    DialogBox(hInst,  /* current instance        */
        "GetString",   /* resource to use         */
        hWnd,          /* parent handle           */
        GetSendString);/* instance address        */

    /*
    *   Assumption — The GetString dialog box proc fills the
    *   global string buffer, szBuff, with the desired string to
    *   send.
    */
    send(sock, szBuff, strlen(szBuff), NO_FLAGS_SET );

    break;    /* IDM_SENDTCP */


case IDM_ABOUT:
    DialogBox(hInst, /* current instance         */
        "AboutBox",   /* resource to use          */
        hWnd,         /* parent handle            */
        About);       /* About() instance address */

    break;    /* IDM_ABOUT */

default:
    /* Lets Windows process it              */
    return (DefWindowProc(hWnd, message, wParam, lParam));
    break;
```

```
        }
    break;

    /*
    *   Clean up.  Takes care of any open socket descriptors.
    */
    case WM_DESTROY:
        WSACleanup();
        PostQuitMessage(0);
        break;

    default:       /* Passes it on if unproccessed     */
        return (DefWindowProc(hWnd, message, wParam, lParam));
    }
    return (0);
}
```

Remote Procedure Calls

Remote Procedure Calls, or RPCs, are simultaneously the simplest and most compli-cated network programming mechanism supported by Windows NT. They are the simplest in concept: a program on one machine asks another program possibly running on another machine to perform some function on its behalf, in a way that looks a lot like an ordinary function call. But they are the most complicated in practice: defining the interface to a remote procedure requires a whole separate specification language, the Interface Definition Language (IDL), and implementing the call requires several layers of services.

The *RPC Programmer's Guide and Reference* is completely separate from the five-volume *Win32 Programmer's Reference*. The RPC manual and the MIDL compiler come with the Windows NT SDK; they do not come with Visual C++ for Windows NT. Obviously, I'm not going to give you the contents of a 650-page manual here: all I want to do is give you a good feel for what RPCs can do and how to go about learning more. Table 11-11 lists the RPC API functions, but the API functions don't give you the whole picture.

In addition to the RPC API functions, you need to understand the IDL, bindings, attributes, and transports. You can get all of this from the Microsoft RPC documentation, but you'll find it hard going unless you're already familiar with another implementa-tion of RPCs, such as the Open System Foundation's Distributed Computing Environ-ment (OSF DCE) standard for Unix. What I'd like to do is walk you through "Hello, World" done with RPCs at the most basic level (as basic as Chapter 2 of the RPC manual, but more concise), so that you'll be ready to attack the Microsoft RPC materials on your own.

I won't bore you with the standard code for "Hello, World." The example we'll use first takes the small step of using a **HelloProc** function to write the string (I won't bore you with that, either); then it makes **HelloProc** a remote procedure.

Table 11-11   RPC API Functions (1.0)

RpcAbnormalTermination	RpcMgmtWaitServerListen	RpcNsProfileEltInqBegin
RpcBindingCopy	RpcNetworkInqProtseqs	RpcNsProfileEltInqDone
RpcBindingFree	RpcNetworkIsProtseqValid	RpcNsProfileEltInqNext
RpcBindingFromStringBinding	RpcNsBindingExport	RpcNsProfileEltRemove
RpcBindingInqAuthClient	RpcNsBindingImportBegin	RpcObjectInqType
RpcBindingInqAuthInfo	RpcNsBindingImportDone	RpcObjectSetInqFn
RpcBindingInqObject	RpcNsBindingImportNext	RpcObjectSetType
RpcBindingReset	RpcNsBindingInqEntryName	RpcProtseqVectorFree
RpcBindingSetAuthInfo	RpcNsBindingLookupBegin	RpcRaiseException
RpcBindingSetObject	RpcNsBindingLookupDone	RpcRevertToSelf
RpcBindingToStringBinding	RpcNsBindingLookupNext	RpcServerInqBindings
RpcBindingVectorFree	RpcNsBindingSelect	RpcServerInqIf
RpcEndExcept	RpcNsBindingUnexport	RpcServerListen
RpcEndFinally	RpcNsEntryExpandName	RpcServerRegisterAuthInfo
RpcEpRegister	RpcNsEntryObjectInqBegin	RpcServerRegisterIf
RpcEpRegisterNoReplace	RpcNsEntryObjectInqDone	RpcServerUnregisterIf
RpcEpResolveBinding	RpcNsEntryObjectInqNext	RpcServerUseAllProtseqs
RpcEpUnregister	RpcNsGroupDelete	RpcServerUseAllProtseqsIf
RpcExcept	RpcNsGroupMbrAdd	RpcServerUseProtseq
RpcExceptionCode	RpcNsGroupMbrInqBegin	RpcServerUseProtseqEp
RpcFinally	RpcNsGroupMbrInqDone	RpcServerUseProtseqIf
RpcIfIdVectorFree	RpcNsGroupMbrInqNext	RpcStringBindingCompose
RpcIfInqId	RpcNsGroupMbrRemove	RpcStringBindingParse
RpcImpersonateClient	RpcNsMgmtBindingUnexport	RpcStringFree
RpcMgmtEnableIdleCleanup	RpcNsMgmtEntryCreate	RpcTryExcept
RpcMgmtInqComTimeout	RpcNsMgmtEntryDelete	RpcTryFinally
RpcMgmtInqStats	RpcNsMgmtEntryInqIfIds	RpcWinSetYieldInfo
RpcMgmtIsServerListening	RpcNsMgmtHandleSetExpAge	YieldFunctionName
RpcMgmtSetComTimeout	RpcNsMgmtInqExpAge	UuidCreate
RpcMgmtSetServerStackSize	RpcNsMgmtSetExpAge	UuidFromString
RpcMgmtStatsVectorFree	RpcNsProfileDelete	UuidToString
RpcMgmtStopServerListening	RpcNsProfileEltAdd	

The first step in setting up a remote procedure is to define the interface in IDL. An IDL file also needs a unique identification string, which you generate by running UUIDGEN, a tool that comes with the NT SDK. A minimal IDL file for HELLO might look like this:

```
[ uuid (6B29FC40-CA47-1067-B31D-00DD010662DA), version(1.0) ]
interface hello
{
void HelloProc([in, string] unsigned char * pszString);
}
```

The top line of the file, the IDL header, contains the unique ID and the version number in square brackets. The last three lines of the file—the curly brackets and the declaration—constitute the IDL body. The non-C stuff in square brackets in the declaration gives additional information about the interface—in this case, **pszString** is an input string variable.

In addition to an IDL file, you need an ACF (Application Configuration File). A minimal ACF file for HELLO might look like the following:

```
[implicit_handle(handle_t hello_IfHandle)]
interface hello
{
}
```

While the IDL file contains the interface definition, the ACF contains RPC data and attributes that don't relate to the transmitted data. In this case, a binding handle is defined, which the RPC client uses to connect to the server. The interface name has to match the interface name given in the ACF file; the interface body is empty.

Compiling the IDL and ACF files with MIDL generates client and server C stub files and an include file. The stub files generated are actually pretty complicated—they're C programs to handle the client-server interaction over the network with RPC function calls. For instance, the client and server stubs for **HelloProc** look like this:

Hello_C.C (HelloProc client stub generated by MIDL)

```
#include <string.h>
#include "hello.h"
handle_t hello_IfHandle;
extern RPC_DISPATCH_TABLE hello_DispatchTable;
static RPC_CLIENT_INTERFACE ___RpcClientInterface = {
  sizeof(RPC_CLIENT_INTERFACE),
  {{0x906B0CE0,0xC70B,0x1067,{0xB3,0x17,0x00,0xDD,0x01,0x06,0x62,
  0xDA}},   {1,0}},
  {{0x8A885D04L,0x1CEB,0x11C9,{0x9F,0xE8,0x08,0x00,0x2B,0x10,0x48,
```

```
    0x60}},   {2,0}}, 0,0,0,0 };
RPC_IF_HANDLE hello_ClientIfHandle =
   (RPC_IF_HANDLE) &___RpcClientInterface;
void HelloProc(unsigned char *pszString)
   {
  unsigned char * _packet;
  unsigned int    _length;
  RPC_STATUS _status;
  RPC_MESSAGE _message;
  PRPC_MESSAGE _prpcmsg = & _message;

  ((void)( _packet ));
  ((void)( _length ));
  _message.Handle = hello_IfHandle;
  _message.RpcInterfaceInformation =
       (void __RPC_FAR *) &___RpcClientInterface;
  _prpcmsg->BufferLength = 0;
  if (pszString == (void *)0)
   RpcRaiseException(RPC_X_NULL_REF_POINTER);
  tree_size_ndr(&(pszString), _prpcmsg, "s1", 1);
  _message.ProcNum = 0;
  _status = I_RpcGetBuffer(&_message);
  if (_status) RpcRaiseException(_status);
  _packet = _message.Buffer;
  _length = _message.BufferLength;
  _message.BufferLength = 0;
  tree_into_ndr(&(pszString), _prpcmsg, "s1", 1);
  _message.Buffer = _packet;
  _message.BufferLength = _length;
  _status = I_RpcSendReceive(&_message);
  if (_status) RpcRaiseException(_status);
  _status = I_RpcFreeBuffer(&_message);
  if (_status) RpcRaiseException(_status);
  }
```

Hello_S.C (HelloProc server stub generated by MIDL)

```
#include <string.h>
#include "hello.h"
extern RPC_DISPATCH_TABLE hello_DispatchTable;
static RPC_SERVER_INTERFACE ___RpcServerInterface = {
  sizeof(RPC_SERVER_INTERFACE),
  {{0x906B0CE0,0xC70B,0x1067,{0xB3,0x17,0x00,0xDD,0x01,0x06,
   0x62,0xDA}}, {1,0}},
  {{0x8A885D04L,0x1CEB,0x11C9,{0x9F,0xE8,0x08,0x00,0x2B,0x10,
   0x48,0x60}}, {2,0}}, &hello_DispatchTable,0,0,0 };
RPC_IF_HANDLE hello_ServerIfHandle =
   (RPC_IF_HANDLE) &___RpcServerInterface;
void __RPC_STUB hello_HelloProc(PRPC_MESSAGE _prpcmsg)
   {
  unsigned char *pszString = (void *)0;
```

```
unsigned long _alloc_total;
unsigned long _valid_lower;
unsigned long _valid_total;
unsigned char * _packet;
unsigned char * _tempbuf;
unsigned char * _savebuf;
RPC_STATUS _status;
_packet = _prpcmsg->Buffer;
((void)( _alloc_total ));
((void)( _valid_total ));
((void)( _valid_lower ));
((void)( _packet ));
((void)( _tempbuf ));
((void)( _savebuf ));
RpcTryExcept
  {
  _tempbuf = _prpcmsg->Buffer;
  // recv total number of elements
  long_from_ndr(_prpcmsg, &_alloc_total);
  if (pszString == (void *)0)
    {
    pszString = MIDL_user_allocate ((size_t)
    (_alloc_total * sizeof(char)));
    }
  data_from_ndr(_prpcmsg, (void __RPC_FAR *) (pszString),
    "s1", 1);
  }
RpcExcept(1)
  {
      RpcRaiseException(RpcExceptionCode());
  }
RpcEndExcept
if (((unsigned int)(((unsigned char *)_prpcmsg->Buffer)
  - _packet)) > _prpcmsg->BufferLength)
  RpcRaiseException(RPC_X_BAD_STUB_DATA);
RpcTryFinally
  {
  if (_prpcmsg->ManagerEpv)
    {
    ((hello_SERVER_EPV *)(_prpcmsg->ManagerEpv))
        ->HelloProc(pszString);
    }
  else
    {
    HelloProc(pszString);
    }
  _prpcmsg->BufferLength = 0;
  _prpcmsg->Buffer = _packet;
  _status = I_RpcGetBuffer(_prpcmsg);
  if (_status) RpcRaiseException(_status);
  }
```

```
RpcFinally
  {
  MIDL_user_free ((void __RPC_FAR *)pszString);
  }
RpcEndFinally
  }
```

You aren't, however, saved from writing all the RPC code. In this application, the client is responsible for connecting to the server. You'll notice that the default protocol sequence used is for a named pipe, **\pipe\hello**:

from HELLOC.C (hand-written client code)

```
RPC_STATUS status;
unsigned char * pszUuid              = NULL;
unsigned char * pszProtocolSequence  = "ncacn_np";
unsigned char * pszNetworkAddress    = NULL;
unsigned char * pszEndpoint          = "\\pipe\\hello";
unsigned char * pszOptions           = NULL;
unsigned char * pszStringBinding     = NULL;
unsigned char * pszString            = "hello, world";
unsigned long ulCode;
int i;
//...
  status = RpcStringBindingCompose(pszUuid,
                                   pszProtocolSequence,
                                   pszNetworkAddress,
                                   pszEndpoint,
                                   pszOptions,
                                   &pszStringBinding);
printf("RpcStringBindingCompose returned 0x%x\n", status);
printf("pszStringBinding = %s\n", pszStringBinding);
if (status) {
    exit(status);
  }
status = RpcBindingFromStringBinding(pszStringBinding,
                                     &hello_IfHandle);
printf("RpcBindingFromStringBinding returned 0x%x\n", status);
if (status) {
    exit(status);
  }
printf("Calling the remote procedure 'HelloProc'\n");
printf("Print the string '%s' on the server\n", pszString);

RpcTryExcept {
    HelloProc(pszString);   // make call with user message
  }
RpcExcept(1) {
    ulCode = RpcExceptionCode();
    printf("Runtime reported exception 0x%lx = %ld\n", ulCode,
```

```
                  ulCode);
    }
RpcEndExcept

status = RpcStringFree(&pszStringBinding);
printf("RpcStringFree returned 0x%x\n", status);
if (status) {
    exit(status);
  }

status = RpcBindingFree(&hello_IfHandle);
printf("RpcBindingFree returned 0x%x\n", status);
if (status) {
    exit(status);
    }
```

Boiled down to its essentials, the above code amounts to composing the binding string, establishing the binding, calling the remote procedure through its stub, freeing the binding string, and freeing the binding.

In addition to establishing its own binding prior to calling the remote procedure, the client has to provide callback routines so that the RPC libraries can allocate and free memory. In this case, they are trivial:

```
void    __RPC_FAR *  __RPC_API midl_user_allocate(size_t len)
{
    return(malloc(len));
}

void __RPC_API midl_user_free(void __RPC_FAR * ptr)
{
    free(ptr);
}
```

On the server side, you need to write code to set the protocol sequence, register the interface, and listen for a client. The protocol used has to match on client and server:

```
RPC_STATUS status;
unsigned char * pszProtocolSequence = "ncacn_np";
unsigned char * pszSecurity         = NULL;
unsigned char * pszEndpoint         = "\\pipe\\hello";
unsigned int    cMinCalls           = 1;
unsigned int    cMaxCalls           = 20;
unsigned int    fDontWait           = FALSE;
int i;
//...

  status = RpcServerUseProtseqEp(pszProtocolSequence,
                      cMaxCalls,
```

```
                                pszEndpoint,
                                pszSecurity);   // Security descriptor
printf("RpcServerUseProtseqEp returned 0x%x\n", status);
if (status) {
    exit(status);
    }

status = RpcServerRegisterIf(hello_ServerIfHandle, //interface
                             NULL,    // MgrTypeUuid
                             NULL);   // MgrEpv
printf("RpcServerRegisterIf returned 0x%x\n", status);
if (status) {
    exit(status);
    }

printf("Calling RpcServerListen\n");
status = RpcServerListen(cMinCalls,
                         cMaxCalls,
                         fDontWait);
printf("RpcServerListen returned: 0x%x\n", status);
if (status) {
    exit(status);
    }

if (fDontWait) {
    printf("Calling RpcMgmtWaitServerListen\n");
    status = RpcMgmtWaitServerListen(); // wait operation
    printf("RpcMgmtWaitServerListen returned: 0x%x\n", status);
    if (status) {
        exit(status);
        }
    }
```

You'll need to provide **midl_user_allocate** and **midl_user_free** call-backs on the server side: they're the same as on the client side. And finally, you'll need a way to tell the server to shut down, which we've omitted here for brevity. (You'll find it in the Microsoft MSTOOLS\SAMPLES\RPC\HELLO sample.)

If we build the client and server and run the server we'll see:

```
RpcServerUseProtseqEp returned 0x0
RpcServerRegisterIf returned 0x0
Calling RpcServerListen
```

Then the server will stop. If we run the client on another machine or in another CMD session on the same machine, the server will continue and display:

```
hello, world

Calling RpcMgmtStopServerListening
RpcMgmtStopServerListening returned: 0x0
```

```
Calling RpcServerUnregisterIf
RpcServerUnregisterIf returned 0x0
RpcServerListen returned: 0x0
```

What the client will display in its CMD session is:

```
RpcStringBindingCompose returned 0x0
pszStringBinding = ncacn_np:[\\pipe\\hello]
RpcBindingFromStringBinding returned 0x0
Calling the remote procedure 'HelloProc'
Print the string 'hello, world' on the server
Calling the remote procedure 'Shutdown'
RpcStringFree returned 0x0
RpcBindingFree returned 0x0
```

Obviously, that was an awful lot of work to make "Hello, World" display. On the other hand, a great deal of the work was done with a few lines of IDL and ACF code, and the resulting client-server application works not only on a single Windows NT machine, but between two NT machines linked by a network, and between a DOS or Windows client and a Windows NT server. In addition, it works on a variety of network transports: in addition to named pipes, the NT implementation of RPC supports NetBIOS and TCP/IP transports. The Windows implementation supports all three of these plus DECnet, and the DOS implementation supports all the aforementioned plus SPX. There is no Win32s implementation of RPCs, however, at least in version 1.1 of Win32s.

I have the sense that RPCs are, at least in the long term, *the* strategic way to write distributed applications. Learning the IDL and ACF languages shouldn't be much of a challenge for a C or C++ programmer: make the effort, and you won't regret it.

DDE and NetDDE

DDE is the principal mechanism for interprocess communication in 16-bit Windows. The Microsoft Windows Dynamic Data Exchange (DDE) protocol defines a method for communicating among applications that takes place as applications send messages to each other to initiate conversations, to request and share data, and to terminate conversations.

In the *hot link* form of DDE transfer, the *server* application sends data to the *client* application whenever the data changes; this guarantees that the derived form of the data (perhaps a table in a word processing document) will always reflect the current state of the original data (perhaps a spreadsheet). A variation of this, the *warm link*, notifies the client when the data has changed, but sends the data only if the client wants it; this enables the client to control the rate at which it receives data. A simpler mechanism, the *request*, is equivalent to a single copy operation from the server and

Table 11-12 New DDE Functions in Win32

Function	Action
DdeImpersonateClient	Impersonates a DDE client window.
DdeSetQualityOfService	Specifies DDE quality of service.
FreeDDElParam	Frees a DDE message lParam.
ImpersonateDdeClientWindow	Impersonates a DDE client window.
PackDDElParam	Packs data into a DDE message lParam.
ReuseDDElParam	Reuses a DDE message lParam.
UnpackDDElParam	Unpacks data from a DDE message lParam.

a single paste operation to the client, without the need for the intermediate step of putting the data on the clipboard.

DDE also supports a back channel transfer, the *poke*. And *execute*, perhaps the most intriguing DDE mechanism of all, allows one application to control another.

DDE supports a *client-server* architecture in which both client and server programs carry on multiple *conversations* with other applications. Each conversation has a *topic* and may include multiple *advisories*, each of which refers to an *item*. The application is responsible for keeping track of ongoing conversations and advisories; conversations are uniquely identified by the window handles of the client and server.

Windows NT and Windows for Workgroups continue to support DDE as an inter-process communication protocol, and additionally support NetDDE, a special form of DDE that allows it to work across the network. Because of NT's security requirements and change from 16-bit handles to 32-bit handles, a few new DDE functions have been added in Win32. They are listed in Table 11-12.

The functions **PackDDElParam** and **UnpackDDElParam** allow the 32-bit program to pack and unpack parameters in the DDE message's **lParam**: use them instead of **MAKELONG**, **LOWORD**, and **HIWORD**. **ReuseDDElParam** and **FreeDDEl-Param** allow you to manage the dynamic memory used for packing parameters. The two impersonation functions allow a DDE server to take on the security attributes of its client: this is useful when a server has more privilege than the client and needs to maintain security.

While you can still program DDE by sending messages, the preferred method for programming DDE is to use the Dynamic Data Exchange Management Library (DDEML). Both methods are explained in Chapter 5 of my book *Advanced Windows Programming*. For your convenience, the DDEML functions are listed in Table 11-13.

NetDDE is a minor variation on DDE that can be used by all DDE-aware applications. Normally, you establish a DDE conversation with an application on a topic and specify items within the topic. With NetDDE, the true application and topic are

Table 11-13 DDEML Functions

Function	Action
DdeAbandonTransaction	Abandons an asynchronous transaction.
DdeAccessData	Accesses a DDE data object.
DdeAddData	Adds data to a DDE data object.
DdeCallback	Processes DDEML transactions.
DdeClientTransaction	Begins a DDE data transaction.
DdeCmpStringHandles	Compares two DDE string handles.
DdeConnect	Establishes a conversation with a server.
DdeConnectList	Establishes multiple DDE conversations.
DdeCreateDataHandle	Creates a DDE data handle.
DdeCreateStringHandle	Creates a DDE string handle.
DdeDisconnect	Terminates a DDE conversation.
DdeDisconnectList	Destroys a DDE conversation list.
DdeEnableCallback	Enables or disables one or more DDE conversations.
DdeFreeDataHandle	Frees a DDE data object.
DdeFreeStringHandle	Frees a DDE string handle.
DdeGetData	Copies data from a DDE data object to a buffer.
DdeGetLastError	Returns an error code set by a DDEML function.
DdeInitialize	Registers an application with the DDEML.
DdeKeepStringHandle	Increments the usage count for a string handle.
DdeNameService	Registers or unregisters a service name.
DdePostAdvise	Prompts a server to send advise data to a client.
DdeQueryConvInfo	Retrieves information about a DDE conversation.
DdeQueryNextServer	Obtains the next handle in a conversation list.
DdeQueryString	Copies string-handle text to a buffer.
DdeReconnect	Reestablishes a DDE conversation.
DdeSetUserHandle	Associates a user-defined handle with a transaction.
DdeUnaccessData	Frees a DDE data object.
DdeUninitialize	Frees an application's DDEML resources.

maintained in a DDE share, which is kept in a database. You establish a DDE conversation indirectly, by connecting to the special application NDDE$ on the remote machine, using the share name as the topic. This is the way the ClipBook applet works: it establishes a DDE share for each ClipBook page on each machine.

Table 11-14 Win32 Network DDE Functions

Function	Action
NDdeGetErrorString	Converts net DDE error code to error string.
NDdeGetShareSecurity	Obtains net DDE share's security descriptor.
NDdeGetTrustedShare	Retrieves net DDE trusted share options.
NDdeIsValidAppTopicList	Validates net DDE app and topic string syntax.
NDdeIsValidShareName	Validates net DDE share name syntax.
NDdeSetShareSecurity	Sets a net DDE share's security information.
NDdeSetTrustedShare	Applies trust options to a net DDE share.
NDdeShareAdd	Adds a net DDE share.
NDdeShareDel	Deletes a net DDE share.
NDdeShareEnum	Lists net DDE shares.
NDdeShareGetInfo	Obtains information about a net DDE sharer.
NDdeShareSetInfo	Modifies an existing net DDE share's info.
NDdeTrustedShareEnum	Lists trusted shares in calling process's context.

NetDDE acts as a redirector for DDE, and communicates over the network using NetBIOS. In Windows NT, NetBIOS can work on any transport protocol. When NetDDE establishes the conversation, it retrieves the DDE share and connects to the real application and topic locally. Then the applications can exchange data on the actual items, and neither application needs to be explicitly aware of NetDDE.

On the other hand, a network application that is aware of NetDDE can browse for shares, establish its own shares, and delete its own shares. The Network DDE Functions are listed in Table 11-14.

With the exception of the functions that deal with trusted shares and security, the Win32 NetDDE functions are also supported in Windows for Workgroups. They are not, however, included in Win32s. Accessing them in Windows for Workgroups programs requires you to have a copy of NDDEAPI.H and NDDEAPI.LIB, or dynamically link to the functions in NDDEAPI.DLL.

Should you build networked applications with NetDDE? If you want them to work on Windows for Workgroups and Windows NT machines, or they already support DDE, certainly. If you need to access other environments, no. And if you have a high-volume communications application and care about transfer rate, consider another mechanism.

If you're only interested in networked communications, you can skip the rest of this chapter. On the other hand, there's more to network programming than the core communications functions, so you might want to read on.

Table 11-15 Win32 File Mapping Functions

Function	Action
CreateFileMapping	Returns handle to a new file mapping object.
FlushViewOfFile	Flushes a byte range within a mapped view.
MapViewOfFile	Maps a view into an address space.
MapViewOfFileEx	Maps a view into an address space.
OpenFileMapping	Opens a named-file mapping object.
UnmapViewOfFile	Unmaps a file view.

File Mapping (Memory-Mapped Files)

File mapping does not work over a network, but it is often used for interprocess communications—partly because it allows high-rate local communications, and partly because it is very similar to a Unix mechanism often used to implement databases. 16-bit Windows allows you to pass pieces of global shared memory among processes: file mapping is as close as Windows NT comes. The Win32 file mapping functions are listed in Table 11-15.

File mapping actually has two uses. The first is to let you treat a file like memory: mapping is the copying of a file's contents to a process's virtual address space. The copy of the file's contents is called the file view, and the internal structure the operating system uses to maintain the copy is called the file-mapping object.

The second use is data sharing. Another process can create an identical file view in its own virtual address space by using the first process's file-mapping object to create the view. Any process that has the name or a handle of a file-mapping object can create a file view. Note that you can map named files, or simply ask for shared memory backed by the system paging file. The signal that you want shared memory backed by the page file is a file handle of **(HANDLE)FFFFFFFF**.

The following example demonstrates data sharing using file mapping. As you can see, the process creating the shared memory uses **CreateFileMapping** and **MapViewOfFile**, while the process sharing the memory uses **OpenFileMapping** and **MapViewOfFile**.

```
//————————————————————
// In creating process
//————————————————————
hFileMapping = CreateFileMapping(
        hFile,          //file handle to map
        NULL,           //security
        PAGE_READWRITE, //protection
```

428 Citizen of the Galaxy

```
                dwSizeHigh,        //high 32 bits of size
                dwSizeLow,         //low 32 bits of size
                "NameOfFileMappingObject");
assert(hFileMapping);
base = MapViewOfFile(
                hFileMapping,
                FILE_MAP_WRITE,    //access mode
                dwOffsetHigh,      //high 32 bits of file offset
                dwOffsetLow,       //low 32 bits of file offset
                dwSizeToMap);      //size to map, 0 means whole file
// base points to mapped view of file
assert(base);
//...

//------------------------------
// In sharing process
//------------------------------
hFileMapping = OpenFileMapping(
                FILE_MAP_READ,     //access mode
                FALSE,             //inherit handle?
                "NameOfFileMappingObject");
assert(hFileMapping);
base = MapViewOfFile(
                hFileMapping,
                FILE_MAP_READ,     //access mode
                dwOffsetHigh,      //high 32 bits of file offset
                dwOffsetLow,       //low 32 bits of file offset
                dwSizeToMap);      //size to map, 0 means whole file
//
// base points to mapped view of file.
// Note that the value of base
// is not necessarily the same in both
// processes sharing the file
// mapping object.
//
assert(base);
```

When the processes are done with the mapped file, they should call **Unmap-ViewofFile** to remove the map from their address space and flush any dirty pages to the disk image of the file. Processes that need to commit portions of the shared file map to disk without unmapping the file can use **FlushViewOfFile** as needed.

Security

Windows NT has a centralized security facility in which all named objects, and some unnamed objects, have security descriptors (SDs), and all users and processes have access tokens and security identifiers (SIDs). Security descriptors include information about the owner of the object and an access-control list (ACL), which contain access-control entries (ACEs) that identify the users and groups allowed or denied access to the object.

When you program Windows NT, you access objects by getting handles to them, then using the handles. The security process applies when you try to get the handle: the system compares your access token with the object's access-control entries, and grants you a handle only if at least one ACE exists that allows your token access, and additionally no ACE exists that denies your token access.

There can be two kinds of access control lists in a security descriptor. A system ACL is controlled by the system administrator. A discretionary ACL is controlled by the owner of the object.

With sufficient privilege, you can manipulate access programmatically, often by adding a discretionary ACL to an object's security descriptor. The functions to manipulate SDs, ACLs, ACEs, tokens, SIDs, and related objects like audit alarms are listed in Table 11-16.

We won't give any security example programs here: you can find them readily in the Win32 SDK help files and in the CHECK_SD, EXITWIN, REGISTRY, SIDCLN, and TAKEOWN samples. We will summarize the key points, though.

If you want to deny all access to an object, you can add an *empty* discretionary ACL to its security descriptor. If you want to allow all access to an object, you can give it a **NULL** discretionary ACL. Note the difference between empty and NULL here: empty means there is an ACL, but it has no entries; NULL means there is no ACL.

Table 11-16 Win32 Security Functions

Function	Action
AccessCheck	Validates a client's access rights.
AccessCheckAndAuditAlarm	Validates access, generates audit and alarm.
AddAccessAllowedAce	Adds ACCESS_ALLOWED_ACE to ACL.
AddAccessDeniedAce	Adds ACCESS_DENIED_ACE to ACL.
AddAce	Adds an ACE to an existing ACL.
AddAuditAccessAce	Adds SYSTEM_AUDIT_ACE to ACL.
AdjustTokenGroups	Enables/disables groups in a token.
AdjustTokenPrivileges	Enables/disables token privileges.
AllocateAndInitializeSid	Allocates and initializes SID with subauthorities.
AllocateLocallyUniqueId	Allocates an LUID.
AreAllAccessesGranted	Checks for all desired access.
AreAnyAccessesGranted	Checks for any desired access.
CopySid	Copies an SID to a buffer.
CreatePrivateObjectSecurity	Allocates and initializes a protected SD.
DdeImpersonateClient	DDE server impersonates client.
DeleteAce	Deletes an ACE from an existing ACL.

Table 11-16 continued

Function	Action
DestroyPrivateObjectSecurity	Deletes a protected server object's SD.
DuplicateToken	Duplicates an access token.
EqualPrefixSid	Tests two SID prefixes for equality.
EqualSid	Tests two SID security IDs for equality.
FindFirstFreeAce	Retrieves a pointer to first free ACL byte.
FreeSid	Frees an allocated SID.
GetAce	Retrieves a pointer to an ACE in an ACL.
GetAclInformation	Retrieves access-control list information.
GetFileSecurity	Gets file or directory security information.
GetKernelObjectSecurity	Retrieves kernel object SD.
GetLengthSid	Returns length of an SID.
GetPrivateObjectSecurity	Retrieves protected server object SD.
GetProcessWindowStation	Returns process window-station handle.
GetSecurityDescriptorControl	Retrieves SD revision and control info.
GetSecurityDescriptorDacl	Retrieves SD discretionary ACL.
GetSecurityDescriptorGroup	Retrieves SD primary group information.
GetSecurityDescriptorLength	Returns SD length.
GetSecurityDescriptorOwner	Retrieves SD owner.
GetSecurityDescriptorSacl	Retrieves SD system ACL.
GetSidIdentifierAuthority	Returns ID authority field address.
GetSidLengthRequired	Returns required length of SID.
GetSidSubAuthority	Returns subauthority array address.
GetSidSubAuthorityCount	Returns subauthority field address.
GetThreadDesktop	Returns thread desktop handle.
GetTokenInformation	Retrieves specified token information.
GetUserObjectSecurity	Retrieves server object SD information.
ImpersonateNamedPipeClient	Pipe server acts as client.
ImpersonateSelf	Gets impersonation token for calling process.
InitializeAcl	Creates a new access-control list.
InitializeSecurityDescriptor	Initializes a security descriptor.

Table 11-16 continued

Function	Action
InitializeSid	Initializes an SID.
IsValidAcl	Validates an access-control list.
IsValidSecurityDescriptor	Validates security descriptor.
IsValidSid	Validates an SID.
LookupAccountName	Translates account name to SID.
LookupAccountSid	Translates SID to account name.
LookupPrivilegeDisplayName	Retrieves a displayable privilege name.
LookupPrivilegeName	Retrieves a programmatic privilege name.
LookupPrivilegeValue	Retrieves LUID for privilege name.
MakeAbsoluteSD	Creates absolute SD from self-relative.
MakeSelfRelativeSD	Creates self-relative SD from absolute.
MapGenericMask	Maps generic access to specific/standard.
ObjectCloseAuditAlarm	Generates audit/alarm when object is deleted.
ObjectOpenAuditAlarm	Generates audit/alarm when object is accessed.
ObjectPrivilegeAuditAlarm	Generates audit/alarm on privileged operation.
OpenProcessToken	Opens process token object.
OpenThreadToken	Opens thread token object.
PrivilegeCheck	Tests client security context for privileges.
PrivilegedServiceAuditAlarm	Audit/alarm on privileged system service.
RevertToSelf	Stops impersonation.
SetAclInformation	Sets information in an ACL
SetFileSecurity	Sets file or directory security.
SetKernelObjectSecurity	Sets kernel object security.
SetPrivateObjectSecurity	Modifies existing SD.
SetSecurityDescriptorDacl	Sets DACL information.
SetSecurityDescriptorGroup	Sets SD primary group information.
SetSecurityDescriptorOwner	Sets SD owner.
SetSecurityDescriptorSacl	Sets SACL information.
SetTokenInformation	Sets various token information.
SetUserObjectSecurity	Sets security-descriptor values.

Both File Manager and REGEDT32 include security editors that use the above functions extensively. These security editors follow certain conventions about combining ACEs: for instance, they don't allow you to mix access-denied ACEs and access-allowed ACEs in the same list. If you want the security editors to work on an object whose security you've set programmatically, follow the editors' conventions.

Service Control Manager

A service is an executable object that is installed in a registry database maintained by the service control manager. The services database determines whether each installed service is started on demand or is started automatically when the system starts up; it can also contain logon and security information for a service so that a service can run even though no user is logged on.

Win32 services conform to the interface rules of the service control manager. Driver services conform to the device driver protocols for Windows NT. The service control manager functions are listed in Table 11-17. Device drivers are beyond the scope of this work.

The service control manager is actually an RPC server, so you can control services on remote machines. You can write three kinds of programs that would use service control functions: a Win32 service process, which provides executable code for services and provides status information to the service control manager; a service configuration program, which manipulates the service control database; and a service control program, which starts a service and controls a running service.

The SDK SERVICE sample demonstrates a simple service process, a client for it, and a program to install and remove service processes. SIMPLE.C is a service process that echoes and mangles input it receives on a named pipe. CLIENT.C sends a string on the named pipe and displays the resulting echo. And INSTSRV.C demonstrates using **CreateService** and **DeleteService**.

A Win32 service process has to include a main function that immediately calls the **StartServiceCtrlDispatcher** function to connect the main thread of the process to the Service Control Manager. It also needs an entry point function, **ServiceMain** in Table 11-17, for each service that can run in the process, and a control handler function, **Handler** in Table 11-17, for each service that can run in the process. The actual names for the service entry points are determined by the dispatch table passed to **StartServiceCtrlDispatcher**:

```
VOID main() {
    SERVICE_TABLE_ENTRY dispatchTable[] = {
        { TEXT("SimpleService"), //first service in list
          (LPSERVICE_MAIN_FUNCTION)service_main },
```

Table 11-17 Win32 Service Control Manager Functions

Function	Action
ChangeServiceConfig	Change service configuration parameters.
CloseServiceHandle	Close Service Control Manager object.
ControlService	Send a control to a service.
CreateService	Create a service object.
DeleteService	Remove service from SC Manager database.
EnumDependentServices	Enumerate services dependent on device.
EnumServicesStatus	Enumerate services in SC manager database.
Handler	Control handler function of a service.
LockServiceDatabase	Lock specified SC Manager database.
NotifyBootConfigStatus	Notify/respond to acceptability of boot configuration.
OpenService	Open an existing service.
OpenSCManager	Connect to service control manager.
QueryServiceConfig	Get service configuration parameters.
QueryServiceLockStatus	Get service database lock status.
QueryServiceObjectSecurity	Get service object security descriptor.
QueryServiceStatus	Get service status.
RegisterServiceCtrlHandler	Register service control request handler.
ServiceMain	Main function of a service.
SetServiceStatus	Update service status to SC Manager.
SetServiceObjectSecurity	Modify service object security descriptor.
StartService	Start running a service.
StartServiceCtrlDispatcher	Connect thread as dispatch thread.
UnlockServiceDatabase	Unlock specified database.

```
        { NULL, NULL }  //NULLs terminate list of services
   };

   if (!StartServiceCtrlDispatcher(dispatchTable)) {
       StopSimpleService("StartServiceCtrlDispatcher failed.");
   }
}
```

The actual name for the handler is determined by the main service entry point, and registered with the service control manager using the **RegisterServiceCtrl-Handler** function:

```
VOID service_main(DWORD dwArgc, LPTSTR *lpszArgv) {
    DWORD                   dwWait;
    PSECURITY_DESCRIPTOR    pSD;
    SECURITY_ATTRIBUTES     sa;

    // register our service control handler:
    //
    sshStatusHandle = RegisterServiceCtrlHandler(
                          TEXT("SimpleService"),
                          service_ctrl);
    if (!sshStatusHandle)
        goto cleanup;
```

A simple service process might include all the code it needed to do its job in its own executable. A more complicated service process might well spawn additional daemon processes. For instance, you could write a service process that accepted an SQL query on a named pipe, submitted the query to a separate database process through named shared memory, signaled the database that a query was pending using an event, and returned the query result to the originator via the named pipes.

It might also be possible to write a generic service process that did nothing but start and stop other processes. For instance, you might have a character-mode OS/2 server process that you want to run on your Windows NT system. You could make it look and act like a real NT server process, even though it runs in the OS/2 subsystem, by writing a small NT service process to start and control it. The OS/2 process would handle its own interprocess communications.

It's really fairly easy to turn an service application of any kind into a true Win32 service process. Consider doing this for any server application that should run independent of the current user—which applies to most network services.

You should also consider making your service configuration program a Control Panel applet. A Control Panel applet resides in a DLL, typically given the CPL extension, and includes a standard callback entry-point function named **CPlApplet**, which must be exported. The application needs to include the CPL.H header file for the definition of the meessages that Control Panel sends to the applet.

You can find all the information you need to write your own Control Panel applets in the Win32 SDK help by searching for "Control Panel Applications Overview." From there, you can browse through the successive help topics, or investigate the cross-references. There is a fairly complete example included in one of the help topics, as well, although it won't make much sense until you've read the preceeding topics. In any case, doing a control panel applet isn't difficult—once you have the information.

Event Logging

One issue many server applications face is how to display error conditions. Often, the server process has no user interface, and can't even be sure it is running on a

Table 11-18 Win32 Event Logging Functions

Function	Action
BackupEventLog	Saves an event log in a backup file.
ClearEventLog	Clears the event log.
CloseEventLog	Closes an event-log handle.
DeregisterEventSource	Closes a registered event handle.
GetNumberOfEventLogRecords	Gets number of records in event log.
GetOldestEventLogRecord	Retrieves number of oldest record.
OpenBackupEventLog	Opens a handle to a backup event log
OpenEventLog	Opens an event-log handle.
ReadEventLog	Reads entries from an event log.
RegisterEventSource	Returns a registered event-log handle.
ReportEvent	Writes an event-log entry.

machine with an active screen: even a standard message box might pop up on a screen that is powered down, or hidden in a closet.

Event logging provides a standard, centralized way for applications (and Windows NT) to record important software and hardware events—not only error conditions, but events that ought to leave an audit trail. The Windows NT Event Viewer offers a standard user interface for viewing the logs, and the event logging functions provide ways to examine and back up the logs as well as to report events. The Win32 event logging functions are listed in Table 11-18.

Events are classified as information, warnings, and errors. All event classifications have well-defined common data and can optionally include event-specific data. For example, information can assert that a service has started or is stopping, that a process connected or disconnected, or that some specific action was performed.

To give a moderately silly example, we might have a process that is controlling a soda machine. Information might record that the machine was filled, or that a column of cans was changed to a different kind of soda. Information might also record each transaction on the machine—what kind of soda was dispensed, what coins were tendered, and what coins were given in change. A viewing process for the soda machine's event log would be able to deduce the machine's exact status, plot historical usage, and predict future usage for ordering purposes.

Warnings are used for recoverable problems. For our soda machine, we might want to log a warning when any column drops below three cans, or when the machine got low on change. Errors are used for nonrecoverable conditions that might cause an application to fail. For the soda machine, this might be running out of soda in any column, running out of change, or being unable to keep the soda cold.

Table 11-19 Win32 Performance Monitoring Functions

Function	Action
RegConnectRegistry	Connects to registry on a remote system.
RegQueryValueEx	Retrieves the type and data for a specified value name associated with an open registry key.
QueryPerformanceCounter	Obtains performance counter value.
QueryPerformanceFrequency	Returns performance counter frequency.

Of course, you can use event logs for more serious purposes as well. Windows NT itself uses the event log for conditions like drivers failing to load, disk drive timeouts, and network errors. It also uses the event log to keep an audit trail (if the administrator enables it) of users logging in and out, security policy changes, system restarts, and so on.

Performance Monitoring

Network administrators often need to monitor network and disk server performance in order to maintain and tune their facilities. Windows NT has a useful Performance Monitor program in the Administrative Tools group. True to the open spirit of Win32, the key functions used by the Performance Monitor are exposed in the API and available for anyone to use. They are listed in Table 11-19.

Why would anyone want to reinvent the Performance Monitor? You might, for instance, want to write more of a statistics-gathering program, or an alarm panel. The statistics-gathering program might collect selected performance numbers from a list of machines on the network at predetermined intervals and save them in a database: a companion program would process the saved data on demand, computing means and standard deviations, displaying time series graphs, histograms, and scatter plots, and otherwise making sense of the network's behavior over time. The alarm panel would scan the network at intervals and send a message to the designated administrator when hard disks were full or performance figures fell outside their normal range.

NT's high-resolution performance counter functions allow you to access the system's high-speed timer. **QueryPerformanceFrequency** tells you the number of counts per second for the timer, and **QueryPerformanceCounter** tells you the current reading of the timer. These functions are similar to the C library function **clock** and the associated constant **CLOCKS_PER_SEC**, but might give you better time resolution.

NT's *system* performance numbers are accessed through the registry, although they are not actually stored in the registry. You can get system performance information by calling **RegQueryValueEx** with the key **HKEY_PERFORMANCE_DATA**. If you wish, use **RegOpenKey** to open the **HKEY_PERFORMANCE_DATA** handle, but remember to use **RegCloseKey** to close the handle when you're done with it.

Using **RegQueryValueEx** with **HKEY_PERFORMANCE_DATA** causes the system to collect the data from the appropriate system object managers. To collect data from a remote system, use **RegConnectRegistry** with the name of the remote system and the **HKEY_PERFORMANCE_DATA** key to retrieve a key usable with **RegQuery-ValueEx** to actually retrieve performance data from the remote system.

RegQueryValueEx returns a **PERF_DATA_BLOCK** structure followed by one **PERF_OBJECT_TYPE** structure and accompanying data for each type of object being monitored. The system being observed defines objects that can be monitored, typically processors, disks, and memory.

The performance data block describes the performance data returned by **RegQueryValueEx**:

```
typedef struct _PERF_DATA_BLOCK { /* pdb */
    WCHAR           Signature[4];
    DWORD           LittleEndian;
    DWORD           Version;
    DWORD           Revision;
    DWORD           TotalByteLength;
    DWORD           HeaderLength;
    DWORD           NumObjectTypes;
    DWORD           DefaultObject;
    SYSTEMTIME      SystemTime;      //time of measurement in UTC format
    LARGE_INTEGER PerfTime;          //actual data value counts
    LARGE_INTEGER PerfFreq;          //timer counts per second
    LARGE_INTEGER PerfTime100nSec;   //data value in 100 ns units
    DWORD           SystemNameLength;
    DWORD           SystemNameOffset;
} PERF_DATA_BLOCK;
```

The **PERF_OBJECT_TYPE** structure describes the object-specific performance information:

```
typedef struct _PERF_OBJECT_TYPE {  /* pot */
    DWORD  TotalByteLength;
    DWORD  DefinitionLength;
    DWORD  HeaderLength;
    DWORD  ObjectNameTitleIndex;
    LPWSTR ObjectNameTitle;
    DWORD  ObjectHelpTitleIndex;
    LPWSTR ObjectHelpTitle;
    DWORD  DetailLevel;
    DWORD  NumCounters;
    DWORD  DefaultCounter;
    DWORD  NumInstances;
```

```
    DWORD   CodePage;
    LARGE_INTEGER PerfTime;
    LARGE_INTEGER PerfFreq;
} PERF_OBJECT_TYPE;
```

The **PERF_OBJECT_TYPE** structure for an object is followed by a list of **PERF_COUNTER_DEFINITION** structures:

```
typedef struct _PERF_COUNTER_DEFINITION { /* pcd */
    DWORD   ByteLength;
    DWORD   CounterNameTitleIndex;
    LPWSTR  CounterNameTitle;
    DWORD   CounterHelpTitleIndex;
    LPWSTR  CounterHelpTitle;
    DWORD   DefaultScale;
    DWORD   DetailLevel;
    DWORD   CounterType;
    DWORD   CounterSize;
    DWORD   CounterOffset;
} PERF_COUNTER_DEFINITION;
```

The **PERF_INSTANCE_DEFINITION** is used to define each instance of a block of object-specific performance data. Not all counters have instances. Memory objects don't have instances, since the system has only one memory. Disk objects do have instances, because the system can have more than one disk.

```
typedef struct _PERF_INSTANCE_DEFINITION { /* pid */
    DWORD ByteLength;
    DWORD ParentObjectTitleIndex;
    DWORD ParentObjectInstance;
    DWORD UniqueID;
    DWORD NameOffset;
    DWORD NameLength;
} PERF_INSTANCE_DEFINITION;
```

Finally, the object-specific data is held in a **PERF_COUNTER_BLOCK** structure:

```
typedef struct _PERF_COUNTER_BLOCK { /* pcd */
    DWORD ByteLength;
} PERF_COUNTER_BLOCK;
```

The names of the objects and counters, as well as the text that explains their meaning, are kept in the registry. To access them, open the registry node:

```
\SOFTWARE\Microsoft\Windows NT\CurrentVersion\Perflib\<langid>
```

The language node (langid) is the ASCII representation of the three-digit hexa-decimal language identifier. For example, the U.S. English node is "009". This node, once opened, can be queried for values of either 'Counters' or 'Help'. The names of object types are included in the 'Counters' data. The 'Help' data supplies the Explain text. The 'Counters' and 'Help' data are stored in **MULTI_SZ** strings, listed in index-name pairs, for example:

```
2         System
4         Memory
6         % Processor Time
10        Read Operations/sec
12        Write Operations/sec
```

Navigating the performance registry tree is somewhat complicated. You can find some working code samples, however, in the Win32 help file: search for "Performance Monitoring Overview," then select the item "Using Performance Monitoring." The next two sections of the help file give examples that display counters and their titles.

Summary

We've introduced a lot of material here. We started with a road map to the different NT interprocess communication mechanisms, then went over the details of programming the individual mechanisms. In addition, we looked briefly at Windows NT security, services, event logging, and performance monitoring.

In a few cases, we've given enough information for you to actually write programs. In the rest of the cases, we only got you started. You'll find more information in the Win32 SDK help files, and in the Recommended Readings section at the end of this book.

CHAPTER

12

In which we look into the future.

The Far Horizon

. . . .

It's been quite a trip. Here we are in the promised land of 32-bit programming, revelling in Windows NT and Win32s. It's a shame that we have to keep returning to the old world of 16-bit programming to visit our relatives who still live in plain Windows.

A Tale of Two Cities

In my crystal ball, I see two cities: Cairo and Chicago. And they're both right here in the 32-bit lands.

Chicago is a little closer, and more interesting for now. Close your eyes, and think about a cross between Windows for Workgroups and Windows NT, with a user interface that is far closer to the original Xerox icon-folder model than to Windows 3.1. Let this system have built-in preemptive multitasking support and a file system that supports long filenames. Let it have support for most of Win32—excluding the security API and a few other areas, but including support for processes, and threads. Let it also support Pens, "Plug and Play" peripherals, and OLE 2.0.

This is Chicago as I see it shaping up. It'll probably ship as Windows 4.0 but the version number could easily change. The important thing is that you already know 98 percent of what you need to know about programming for Chicago: you've learned it right here in *Advanced Win32 Programming*, and in its predecessor *Advanced*

441

Windows Programming. Very little of the Chicago API, Win32c, is likely to be new, even though the Chicago user interface looks different: Win32c will mostly be a larger subset of Win32 than is supported by Win32s. I do think that Win32c will include a 32-bit Pen API—but I showed you how to work with Pens in Chapter 8, and I strongly doubt that the 32-bit Pen API will differ from the 16-bit Pen API in any significant way.

I should point out that the Chicago user interface will be implemented using OLE 2. As you probably remember from Chapter 10, OLE 2 has drag-and-drop and automation capabilities as well-embedded document support: it's a natural way to implement hierarchical file folders with a drag-and-drop interface. Microsoft made a big deal about this at the OLE 2 conference: to program for the Chicago and Cairo interface, program for OLE 2. If you were put off by the complexity and immaturity of OLE 2 as implemented for Windows 3.1 and Windows NT 3.1, think again as Chicago and Cairo start to become real.

I wonder how much of the Win32 networking API will make it into Chicago: I expect that a lot of it will. NetBIOS will certainly be there: I expect RPCs, sockets, pipes, and mailslots as well. I think that the implementation of OLE built into Chicago will be based on true RPCs so that it will work transparently over a network.

It's not clear to me how much server functionality will go into Chicago, but I expect Chicago to be a great network client, and at least a decent peer server. I also expect Chicago to ship with extended MAPI and an improved version of Microsoft Mail. Something called EMS that extends Mail to work with multiple post offices external mail systems should be available for Chicago, although it will probably be a rather expensive add-on that you put on one station to upgrade a workgroup, or maybe to upgrade the whole network.

Right now Chicago is expected to ship in mid-1994. Knowing Microsoft's record for slipping ship dates, that could be as late as 1996—but mid-to-late 1994 is more likely. Cairo will come after Chicago: optimistically, in late 1994, or pessimistically sometime in 1997.

What will be the difference? Chicago is the next version of Windows and DOS; Cairo is the next version of Windows NT. I expect Cairo to include pretty much everything now in Windows NT, plus everything in Chicago. It'll have the new interface and an object-oriented file system; it'll also have NTFS and security. I expect the network client and server support in Cairo to be even better than what you can find in Windows NT today.

Win32 Ubiquitous

Meanwhile, Windows NT will move to more and more platforms. Right now, you can run Windows NT on Intel 80386, 80486, and Pentium-based machines with single or multiple processors; on MIPS R4000 and R4400-based machines; and on DEC Alpha

AXP-based machines. I eventually expect to see versions of Windows NT for Inter-graph Clipper boxes, Hewlett-Packard Precision Architecture (HP-PA) machines, for Sparc systems, for PowerPC-based machines—in fact, for pretty much any new workstation-class chip set.

There will still be sites that don't run Windows NT because they already use an operating system they like better: Macintosh System 7.x, or perhaps some version of Unix or Mach. Microsoft doesn't want to lose those markets for Win32 applications, so it's building Wings to take them there.

Wings—which was once called Alar—is a cross-development system from Micro-soft that runs Win32 (or a subset of Win32) on top of other operating systems, with the help of a thunking layer much like Win32s. I expect Wings for Macintosh System 7 early in 1994, and Wings for Unix systems—perhaps requiring X-Windows or Motif underneath the Wings layer—sometime after that.

Alternative Tools

Of course, there are other vendors working on multiplatform development solutions: for one, Symantec is hard at work on Bedrock. As I understand it, to use Wings you write to the Win32 API, optionally using any application framework that supports Win32; to use Bedrock, you write to a new Bedrock application framework. Bedrock 1.0 will target Windows (which I think means 16-bit Windows 3.1) and the Macintosh; I expect that later versions of Bedrock will target Windows NT, OS/2, and perhaps some Unix systems.

Bedrock 1.0 is limited to single-tasking, single-threaded applications; its major benefits are that it lets you build Windows and Macintosh applications from the same source code, and that it provides a default application that handles most of the GUI functionality you need. To be as useful as Wings for sophisticated systems, a future version of Bedrock would have to support multitasking, multithreaded applications, and other advanced features of Win32. On the other hand, the Bedrock application framework appears to be written at a somewhat higher level than other class librar-ies: the additional leverage and productivity you gain by working at this level might well be an overriding consideration for applications that don't need threads.

There are other alternatives to Microsoft's APIs in the works, as well. In the area of object-oriented systems, there is a significant alternative to OLE 2 brewing: OpenDoc comes from a consortium of Microsoft's competitors, including Apple, Borland, IBM and WordPerfect. The claim is that OpenDoc will do more than OLE 2 and run on more systems, but be completely compatible with OLE 2 and support everything that OLE 2 supports. The implementation projected by this consortium at OpenDoc's announcement in June 1993 had beta toolkits becoming available in late 1993 and retail implementations available in mid-1994.

While I am deeply skeptical of anything produced by a committee or consortium, especially until I have it in my hands, OpenDoc has considerable promise. The basic embedding and interprocess communication technology comes from Apple, and they've proved they're good at that sort of thing. The object model is IBM's SOM (System Object Model), which has a lot of appeal. And OpenDoc is supposed to be fully implemented—eventually—on any operating system you'd care to write for, even systems like OS/2 for which Microsoft will never implement OLE.

Interesting Times

All of which leads us to the conclusion that we live in—and will continue, for the foreseeable future, to live in—interesting times, here in the 32-bit lands. Do I have to tell you that "May you live in interesting times" is an ancient Chinese curse? We might have marauders at the walls any minute, or an occupying army could storm us from the south.

There are a number of proven strategies for surviving interesting times. One is to build good walls and avoid getting involved. Another is to pick the winning side and join it. Still another is to support whichever side happens to be in possession of your territory at the moment—but not too vociferously, lest someone remember you the next time power changes hands.

I don't know about you, but I'm already involved: I just spent over a year writing about Win32 programming. I think writing to Win32 is a winning strategy. At the same time, I'm hedging my bets like crazy, and trying not to make too many enemies.

And always, always, I keep my eyes and ears open. . . .

In which we describe some resources
and tools for Win32 development.

Cornucopia

· ·

As I write, there are four major C/C++ compilers available for generating Intel Win32 programs. In addition, one Win32 C/C++ compiler is available for MIPS R4x00 systems, and one for DEC Alpha AXP systems.

I don't want to play favorites here: all the compiler packages have their own strengths. I do want you to understand the tradeoffs, however. Also note that compilers and tools are a volatile area: the information given here is as of September 1993, and could have become obsolete by the time you read it.

Microsoft Win32 Software Development Kit

The Win32 SDK comes in several flavors. The "Final Release Version 3.1" received by developers involved in the Win32 beta program includes Windows NT, the SDK proper, and C/C++ compilers for Intel and MIPS. The retail version of the Win32 SDK includes the SDK proper, the MIPS C/C++ compiler, and the Windows NT Device Driver Kit, but no compiler for Intel. The DEC Alpha AXP version of the Win32 SDK, which includes the Alpha C/C++ compiler, is available as a fulfillment item for a nominal fee.

The SDK is the most complete source of Win32 sample code; it also seems to be the *only* place to find RPC and POSIX tools and samples. You can purchase a CD-only edition of the Win32 SDK, which has all the documentation on the CD-ROM, quite cheaply. An edition with paper documentation is more expensive, but more convenient: while the documentation in WinHelp is easy enough to use, the online manuals are in a sad assortment of formats. The core paper documentation, the five-volume *Win32 Programmer's Reference*, is available separately, if you wish.

Elements of the Win32 SDK that are not found in separate compilers include the following:

- RPC tools and samples
- POSIX libraries and samples
- Microsoft Setup Toolkit
- Microsoft Test
- MASM386
- NWLink samples
- SDK tools—20 of them—with source code
- OLE 2.0 beta toolkit
- Working Set Tuner
- REBASE utility
- MIPS compilers and tools

Microsoft Visual C++ 32-bit Edition

If you are familiar with the 16-bit Windows/DOS edition of Visual C++, the 32-bit edition (a separate product that does not generate 16-bit executables) will hold few surprises. It includes an graphical integrated development environment (IDE) as well as command-line tools, and a subset of the Win32 SDK. The VC++/32 IDE runs only on Windows NT, but the command-line compiler and tools also run from DOS or a DOS box. VC++/32 generates Win32 code for Windows NT and Win32s, and includes a separate Win32s debugger and profiler.

Most of the suprises you'll find in VC++/32 are pleasant: it has a beefed-up editor, a built-in grep facility, and an integrated profiler; it can debug threads and structured exceptions; and it lets you browse memory when you debug. The most unpleasant surprise is that it does not support VBXs: there actually is no such thing as a 32-bit VBX.

As with the 16-bit edition, VC++/32 includes the MFC 2.0 application framework and classes, App Studio, App Wizard (for generating applications quickly), Class Wizard (for maintaining class hierarchies and message maps), and a slick code browser. The debugger integrates very tightly with the editor: you can even edit source code while you debug.

VC++/32 is available with and without printed documentation. The documentation on the CD is available both as WinHelp and "documents online." The latter makes it easy to print documentation on demand, and makes printed and bound documentation less important.

If you are developing only for Intel-based machines and have no need to use RPCs or POSIX, VC++/32 will fill most of your Win32 development needs all by itself. Otherwise, you might want to combine it with the Win32 SDK.

The biggest weakness in VC++/32 is its lack of support for ANSI C++ templates and exceptions. It does support structured exception handling, of course, but not the **throw** keyword. And it does have a utility for generating templates, but not built-in ANSI C++ or CFRONT 3.0 templates. But it does support both Unicode and multibyte character sets as well as ANSI characters.

Borland C++ 4.0

Borland's approach to a C/C++ compiler and tools package for Win32 is a little different from Microsoft's. Instead of shipping separate 16-bit and 32-bit products, Borland ships a single unified package that can generate either 16-bit or 32-bit executables. BC++ 4.0 is able to manage multiple projects from one Window, and maintain multiple builds from project sources. In many ways, this is the ideal approach, since a developer can build 16-bit and 32-bit applications from a single environment and a single set of sources.

Borland's Object Windows Library 2.0 (OWL 2) is a major upgrade from previous versions of OWL. It not only has 16-bit and 32-bit versions that shield you from parameter packing and other system details, it has considerably improved coverage of the Windows APIs compared to OWL 1.x. Other welcome additions in BC++ 4.0: App Expert (for generating applications quickly); Class Expert (for creating new classes, browsing classes, and editing your implementations); an integrated debugger; and a vastly improved editor—a cross between the old IDE and Brief, although without Brief's programmability. In addition to the new integrated debugger, BC++ 4.0 retains Turbo Debugger for Windows and adds TD32. For assembly-language work, BC++ retains TASM and adds TASM32.

In addition to retaining CFRONT 3.0-compatible template support, BC++ 4.0 supports ANSI C++ exception handling and structured exception handling; three character types; ANSI C++ operator new[] and operator delete[] semantics; the ANSI C++ string class; ANSI C++ runtime type information (RTTI); and the proposed ANSI C++ new style casts: static_cast, const_cast, and reinterpret_cast. And, it supports VBXs.

On the down side, the BC++ 4.0 IDE is 16-bit only: Borland expects that you will develop with Windows as your primary platfrom. The compilers and tools will work from Windows NT, but you are more likely to be happy with BC++ if you are building 16-bit applications or Win32s applications. Finally, you cannot mix Microsoft and Borland 32-bit object files and libraries: they use incompatible object formats.

Symantec C++ 6.0

Symantec has taken a packaging approach much like Borland's: Symantec C++ 6.0 targets 16-bit Windows and DOS and 32-bit Windows NT, Win32s, and extended DOS applications from 16-bit Windows with an integrated development and debugging environment. A DOS extender is included. Rather than release their own application framework at this point (Bedrock, an ambitious cross-platform framework for Windows and Macintosh applications, is still under development as I write), Symantec has licensed MFC 2.0 from Microsoft. In addition, they've licensed a version of WindowsMaker, one of the most capable application design tools and code generators available, from Blue Sky software. In SC++, WindowsMaker is renamed Visual Programmer.

The compiler in SC++ 6.0 is a new version of Zortech C++: it generates code every bit as good as ZC++ did, but compiles much more quickly. SC++ links much more quickly and generates smaller executables, too, by including SLR's Optlink.

The integrated debugging is basically the next generation of MultiScope, one of the most capable debuggers around. The package also includes MED, MultiScope's useful post-mortem debugging technology. The SC++ integrated development and debugging environment uses an "open desktop" drag-and-drop environment that is a lot like Norton Desktop for Windows.

SC++ supports CFRONT 3.0-compatible templates and structured exception handling; it does not appear to support ANSI C++ exceptions. It supports double-byte character sets, but not Unicode. SC++ *does* support the NCEG numerical extensions and complies fully with the IEEE 754 specification.

Watcom C/C++ [32] Version 9.5

Watcom considers their 16-bit and 32-bit compilers separate products, but supports multiple operating systems with each. The 32-bit version of Watcom C/C++[32] 9.5 supports pretty much all the available DOS extenders (and includes a royalty-free DOS extender). It supports 32-bit Windows programming on Windows 3.1 with its own Windows extender, plus it supports Windows NT programming. This compiler version does not ship with Win32s; the Win32 executables it produces should be compatible with Win32—although this version is compatible only with the March 1993 beta version of Windows NT. I assume Watcom will update their tools to work with the retail build of Windows NT shortly.

In addition to extended Windows, extended DOS, and Windows NT, Watcom C/C++[32] 9.5 supports OS/2 2.x, Novell Netware NLM development, PenPoint development, and AutoCAD ADS applications. Watcom sells 16-bit C/C++, and both 16-bit and 32-bit Fortran-77 compilers, as well as its 32-bit C/C++ compiler, both as separate products and as upgrades. All the products can be combined in a single directory tree as they share tools.

Watcom's code generation and optimization tends to be very good—often so good that other compiler vendors don't want their runtime performance compared with Watcom's. On the other hand, Watcom's tools are designed for power and performance, not ease of use, and Watcom's documentation assumes a certain level of sophistication.

Unlike the other C++ compiler packages discussed here, Watcom C/C++[32] 9.5 does not include an application framework for Windows programming. It does, however, include standard C++ classes as well as a set of container classes implemented using templates.

Rounding the Horn

Let me reiterate: the area of tools for Win32 is a volatile one. If you are a Win32 programmer looking for tools, I strongly encourage you to follow the latest developments by reading magazines and electronic communication services (America Online, BIX, CompuServe, Delphi, Usenet, and local bulletin boards).

If you are a tool vendor, I encourage you to contact me (care of John Wiley & Sons, 605 Third Ave., New York, NY 10158-0012) as soon as possible with information about your product. While I can't promise to include everything I hear about, I firmly intend to update this appendix each time it is reprinted.

Martin Heller
September 1993

Recommended Reading

. . . .

Chapter 1

Microsoft Windows NT Software Development Kit *Programming Techniques.* Redmond, WA: Microsoft Corporation, 1992.

Microsoft Windows NT Software Development Kit *Programmer's Reference: Overviews.* Redmond, WA: Microsoft Corporation, 1992.

Microsoft Windows NT Software Development Kit *Programmer's Reference: Application Programming Interface (Parts 1 and 2).* Redmond, WA: Microsoft Corporation, 1992.

Microsoft Windows NT Software Development Kit *Tools.* Redmond, WA: Microsoft Corporation, 1992.

Chapter 3

C++

Ammeraal, L. *C++ for Programmers.* Chichester, England: John Wiley & Sons, 1991.

Ellis, M., and Stroustrup, B. *The Annotated C++ Reference Manual.* Reading, MA: Addison-Wesley, 1990.

Meyers, S. *Effective C++.* Reading, MA: Addison-Wesley, 1992.

Microsoft *C++ Language Reference.* Redmond, WA: Microsoft Corporation, 1991.

Microsoft *C++ Tutorial.* Redmond, WA: Microsoft Corporation, 1991.

Stroustrup, B. *The C++ Programming Language,* Second Edition. Reading, MA: Addison-Wesley, 1992.

Class Libraries

Gorlen, Orlow, and Plexico. *Data Abstraction and Object-Oriented Programming in C++.* Chichester, England: John Wiley & Sons, 1991.

Microsoft *C/C++ Class Libraries Reference*. Redmond, WA: Microsoft Corporation, 1991.

Microsoft *C/C++ Class Libraries User's Guide*. Redmond, WA: Microsoft Corporation, 1991.

zApp Programmer's Reference. Mountain View, CA: Inmark Development Corporation, 1991.

Object-Oriented Design

Booch, Grady. *Object-Oriented Design with Applications*. Redwood City, CA: Benjamin/Cummings, 1991.

Khoshafian and Abnous. *Object Orientation*. New York: John Wiley & Sons, 1990.

Wirfs-Brock, Wilkerson, and Wiener. *Designing Object-Oriented Software*. Englewood Cliffs, NJ: Prentice-Hall, 1990.

Windows NT

Microsoft Windows NT Software Development Kit *Programming Techniques*. Redmond, WA: Microsoft Corporation, 1992.

Chapter 4

Booch, Grady. *Object-Oriented Design with Applications*. Redwood City, CA: Benjamin/Cummings, 1991.

Gorlen, Orlow, and Plexico. *Data Abstraction and Object-Oriented Programming in C++*, Chichester, England: John Wiley & Sons, 1991.

Microsoft *Visual C++ Tutorial*. Redmond, WA: Microsoft Corporation, 1993.

Microsoft Visual C++ *Class Libraries Reference*. Redmond, WA: Microsoft Corporation, 1993.

Microsoft Visual C++ *Class Libraries User's Guide*. Redmond, WA: Microsoft Corporation, 1993.

Chapter 5

Foley, van Dam, Feiner, and Hughes. *Computer Graphics*, Second Edition. Reading, MA: Addison-Wesley, 1990.

Microsoft Visual C++ *Class Libraries Reference*. Redmond, WA: Microsoft Corporation, 1993.

Microsoft Visual C++ *Class Libraries User's Guide*. Redmond, WA: Microsoft Corporation, 1993.

Microsoft Win32 Software Development Kit for Windows NT *Programmer's Reference (Overviews, Part 1, and Part 2)*. Redmond, WA: Microsoft Corporation, 1993.

Chapter 6

Microsoft Win32 Software Development Kit for Windows NT *Programmer's Reference (Overviews, Part 1, and Part 2)*. Redmond, WA: Microsoft Corporation, 1993.

Microsoft Win32 Software Development Kit for Windows NT *Win32s Programmer's Reference*. Redmond, WA: Microsoft Corporation, 1993.

Shulman, Andrew. "At Last—Write Bona Fide 32-bit Programs that Run on Windows 3.1 Using Win32s." *Microsoft Systems Journal*, April 1993.

Chapter 7

Microsoft Win32 Software Development Kit for Windows NT *Programmer's Reference (Overviews, Part 1, and Part 2)*. Redmond, WA: Microsoft Corporation, 1993.

Microsoft Windows Software Development Kit *Multimedia Programmer's Reference*. Redmond, WA: Microsoft Corporation, 1992.

Microsoft Windows Software Development Kit *Multimedia Programmer's Guide*. Redmond, WA: Microsoft Corporation, 1992.

Microsoft Multimedia Development Kit *Multimedia Authoring Guide*. Redmond, WA: Microsoft Corporation, 1991.

Chapter 8

Microsoft Windows Software Development Kit *Microsoft Windows for Pen Computing: Programmer's Reference*. Redmond, WA: Microsoft Corporation, 1992.

Chapter 9

Microsoft Win32 Software Development Kit for Windows NT *Programmer's Reference (Volumes 1–5)*. Redmond, WA: Microsoft Corporation, 1993.

The Unicode Standard: Worldwide Character Encoding (Volumes 1 and 2). Reading, MA: Addison-Wesley, 1992.

Chapter 10

Microsoft Object Linking and Embedding Version 2.0 *Creating Programmable Applications.* Redmond, WA: Microsoft Corporation, 1993.

Microsoft Object Linking and Embedding Version 2.0 *Programmer's Reference.* Redmond, WA: Microsoft Corporation, 1993.

Microsoft Object Linking and Embedding Version 2.0 *Release Notes.* Redmond, WA: Microsoft Corporation, 1993.

Microsoft Object Linking and Embedding Version 2.0 *Specification.* Redmond, WA: Microsoft Corporation, 1993.

Microsoft Object Linking and Embedding Version 2.0 *Technotes.* Redmond, WA: Microsoft Corporation, 1993.

Chapter 11

Heller, Martin. *Advanced Windows Programming.* New York: John Wiley & Sons, 1992.

Microsoft Windows NT Software Development Kit *Remote Preocedure Call Programmer's Guide and Reference.* Redmond, WA: Microsoft Corporation, 1993.

Microsoft Windows NT Software Development Kit *Programmer's Reference, Vols. 1–5.* Redmond, WA: Microsoft Corporation, 1993.

Nance, Barry. *Network Programming in C.* Carmel, IN: Que Corporation, 1990.

Sinha, Alok and Raymond Patch. "An Introduction to Network Programming Using the NetBIOS Interface." *Microsoft Systems Journal,* March–April 1992.

Sinha, Alok and Raymond Patch. "Developing Network-aware Programs Using Windows 3.1 and NetBIOS." *Microsoft Systems Journal,* July–August 1992.

Index